INDIA'S DEVELOPMENT

Social and Economic Disparities

INDIA'S DEVELOPMENT
Social and Economic Disparities

Edited by

S. MAHENDRA DEV
K.S. BABU

IDPAD

MANOHAR
2008

First published 2008

ISBN 978-81-7304-789-3

Published by
Ajay Kumar Jain *for*
Manohar Publishers & Distributors
4753/23 Ansari Road, Daryaganj
New Delhi 110 002

Typeset by
Kohli Print
Delhi 110 051

Printed at
Lordson Publishers Pvt. Ltd.
New Delhi 110 007

Contents

Preface

The Indo-Dutch Programme on Alternatives in Development (IDPAD), which started twenty-five years ago, came to an end during 2006. On the eve of concluding this programme, two seminars (one at Hyderabad and other at The Hague) were conducted. This volume is based on the selected papers presented during the three-day End Symposium on 'India's Development: Even or Uneven? Reflections on Development Theory and Practice' held from 1 to 3 November 2006 at the Centre for Economic and Social Studies, Hyderabad.

When IDPAD started in the early 1980s, India's Hindu rate of growth and poverty was high. The country has come to be seen as a fast-growing success economy to first is more and more competitive on a global scale and may even threaten Western hegemony in fields like information technology and IT-enabled services. India is witnessing high economic growth and successful development of science and technology, which raises new opportunities and opens up new area of cooperations. Such fast development also harbours new problems and contradictions where existing issues of poverty and inequality meet with new trends in a global context. IDPAD research has brought out the increasing disparities and contrasts that pose enormous challenges to the future development of India. The End Symposia provided an opportunity for academics, policymakers and other stakeholders to critically assess India's development. In the light of the increasing inequalities between rural and urban regions and between the rich and the poor that are resulting in complex socio-political dynamics in India, taking a critical account of the achievements and causes for concern is identified as the goal of the IDPAD End Symposia. This is also appropriate in the context of the Eleventh Five-Year Plan. The approach paper talks about inclusive growth and concentrates on agriculture, employment, the social sector and the disparities between rural-urban, regional and social disparities.

The End Symposia were organized by CESS and ISS, Hague. S. Mahendra Dev and Joop de Wit were the convenors from the Indian and the Dutch sides respectively. Sanchita Dutta, the coordinator from the India and Cora Groves, the coordinator from the Netherlands, and Sailaja from ISS, Hague, worked hard to make the symposia a success. We thank all of them for their help in organizing the symposia. We are also grateful to Andre Beteille, C.H. Hanumantha Rao, T.C. Anant, Jan Breman, Kaushik Basu, Abhijit Sen for their participation in the symposia.

S. MAHENDRA DEV
K.S. BABU

Abbreviations

AAGR	Annual Average Growth Rates
ADBI	Asian Development Bank Institute
AHADS	Attappady Hills Area Development Society
ALM	Advanced Locality Management
AP	Andhra Pradesh
BOA	Board of Approvals
BJP	Bharatiya Janata Party
BPL	Below Poverty Line
CBAA	Coal Bearing Areas Act
CBO	Community-based Organization
CEC	Consumption Expenditure Class
CIL	Coal India Limited
CO	Community Organization
CT	Computerized Tomography
FDI	Foreign Direct Investment
FNGO	Field NGO
FTZ	Free Trade Zone
GOI	Government of India
GRC	Gender Resource Centre
HSR	Health Sector Reform
ICDS	Integrated Child Development Scheme
ICT	Information and Communication Technology
IGG	Income Generation Group
IMR	Infant Mortality Rate
IPP-VIII	India Population Project-8th Phase
ISRO	Indian Space Research Organisation
ITES	IT Enabled Services
KMF	Karnataka Milk Federation
LAA	Land Acquisition Act
LACC	Local Area Citizens Committee
MCA	Master's in Computer Applications
MCD	Municipal Corporation of Delhi
MCGM	Municipal Corporation of Greater Mumbai

MOHFW	Ministry of Health and Family Welfare
MRI	Magnetic Resonance Imaging
MTI	Mother Tongue Influence
NDP	Net Domestic Product
NFP	Not-for-Profit
NGO	Non-Governmental Organization
NPV	Net Present Value
NSS	National Sample Survey
NTPC	National Thermal Power Corporation
OBC	Other Backward Caste
ODC	Overseas Development Centre
OPD	Outpatient Department
PAP	Project-Affected Person
PHC	Public Health Centre
PLA	Project Linkage Approach
PPP	Public-Private Partnership
PRA	Participatory Rural Assessment
PRI	Panchayati Raj Institution
RKS	Rogi Kalyan Samiti
RNTCP	Revised National Tuberculosis Control Programme
SC	Scheduled Caste
ST	Scheduled Tribe
SDP	State Domestic Product
SEZ	Special Economic Zone
SHG	Self-help Group
SMS	Sawai Madho Singh
SSP	Sardar Sarovar Project
TA	Tank Association
TPA	Third Party Administrator
TRPP	Tank Rehabilitation Project Pondicherry
VO	Voluntary Organization
WHO	World Health Organization
WUA	Water Users' Association

Overview

S. MAHENDRA DEV AND K.S. BABU

INTRODUCTION

India celebrated sixty years of Independence on 15 August 2007. There have been several achievements and failures in economic and social development in the last sixty years. On the eve of Independence, Jawaharlal Nehru declared: 'Long years ago we made a tryst with destiny, and now the time comes when we shall redeem our pledge.' He reminded the country that the tasks ahead included 'the ending of poverty and ignorance and disease and inequality of opportunity'.[1] India adopted the institutional framework of a mixed economy where both public and private sectors co-exist. Politically India opted for a democratic form of government. It was also among the first countries to aim at affirmative action in the form of reservations for socially oppressed sections. Dr B.R. Ambedkar concluded his work on the Constitution with a warning: 'On the 26 January 1950, we are going to enter into a life of contradictions. In politics we will have equality and in social and economic life we will have inequality.'

The strategy underlying the first three five-year plans was that if the growth process could be established in a sustained fashion, the institutional changes would ensure percolation of the benefits of growth to the poor. In agriculture and rural development, the emphasis was given to community development, national extension and irrigation financed from public budgets. Nehru also mooted the idea of co-operative farming. Importance was given to the public sector, and import substitution policies were followed in the first three decades after Independence. These policies are laudable. In spite of low growth, there were some achievements such as the creation of institutional capacities, irrigation development, bank nationalization, development of social institutions and legal framework for a market economy, priority of science and technology, establishment of the capital goods sector, etc.[2]

In 1980s, there were attempts at deregulation particularly during the Rajiv Gandhi regime, more or less coinciding with the Seventh Five-Year Plan (1985–90). However, economic reforms in India started in a big way only in 1991. These reforms aimed at a fundamental shift towards greater reliance on the market mechanism to allocate resources and influence decision-making. They amounted to a shift from a model of accumulation based on the domestic market and import substitution to one oriented towards the international market.

India's performance, post-Independence, in terms of economic growth is creditable when compared to the pre-Independence period. India registered a Gross Domestic Product (GDP) growth rate of 3.5 per cent per annum in the first three decades after Independence. It is well known that the country has moved beyond the 'Hindu Rate of Growth' (3.5 per cent per annum) in the last two and half decades. GDP growth was more than 5 per cent per annum in the 1980s. In the post-reform period, the Eighth Plan recorded a growth of 6.8 per cent per annum while it declined to 5.5 per cent during the Ninth Plan period. During the Tenth Plan period (2002–7), India recorded its highest growth rate of 7.6 per cent per annum. In fact, India's GDP growth was nearly 9 per cent per annum in the last four years (8.5 per cent in 2003–4, 7.5 per cent in 2004–5, 9.0 per cent in 2005–6 and 9.8 per cent in 2006–7). The Eleventh Five-Year Plan (2007–12) aims to achieve a growth rate of 9 to 10 per cent per annum. This growth can double per capita income in one decade. The Goldman Sachs report says that Brazil, Russia, India, and China—the Brazil, Russia, India and China's (BRICs) economies—could become a large force in the world economy by 2050.[3]

In the post-reform period there were improvements in some indicators such as growth in services, Information Technology (IT) and communication revolutions, balance of payments, resilience to external stocks, significant accumulation of foreign exchange reserves, a booming stock market, etc. In recent years, the savings of the Indian economy have been more than 30 per cent. The investment rate is expected to be more than 35 per cent in 2006–7. All the sources of savings have improved but the rate of increase was the highest for the private corporate sector. These are important achievements. India now seen as a fast-growing success economy which is more and more competitive on a global scale and may even threaten Western hegemony in fields like information technology and IT-enabled services.

However, there is an increasing feeling that the development strategies have helped only a few sections of the population such as the rich and middle class. The exclusion problems have not been seriously addressed by the government programmes and strategies since Independence. Regional, social and personal inequalities, and rural-urban disparities have increased, particularly in the post-reform period. The approach paper of the Eleventh Five-Year Plan stresses on faster and more inclusive growth to bridge the divides. According to the approach paper, there are many divides. Foremost among these is the divide between the rich and the poor. There is also a divide between those who have access to essential services such as health, education, drinking water, sanitation, etc., and those who do not. Marginalized sections, which have hitherto been excluded from Indian society, such as Scheduled Castes (SC), Scheduled Tribes (ST) and some minorities and Other Backward Classes (OBC), continue to lag behind the rest. Gender disparity is another important divide in Indian society. The large divide between rural and urban areas is well known. Similarly, regional disparities are an important issue in the country. There is a feeling that progress in inclusive sectors like agriculture and the social sector has been slow particularly in the post-reform period.

Also, as shown in this volume, the new forms of governance, decentralization, public-private partnerships, current natural resource management, etc., have not helped to bridge the divides in the society. For example, the IT labour market reproduces existing caste, class and gender inequalities. Within castes, well-off sections (creamy layer) have cornered most of the jobs (through the reservation policy)—those at the bottom have been largely bypassed (especially the OBCs). Similarly, creating new democratic spaces (as in trade unions and user committees) does not necessarily ensure women's participation.

There are concerns regarding the agriculture sector, poverty reduction, employment generation, social sector development, reduction in regional disparities and protection of the environment. The agriculture sector faces many problems. Its growth rate was less than 2 per cent in decade of the 1990s. Yield growth has also declined. Suicides the farmers have either continued or increased in some states. Farming is becoming a non-viable activity.

Regarding poverty reduction, recent research has revealed two unambiguous conclusions. One is that is there is no evidence of a higher rate of decline in poverty in the post-reform period as a whole as compared to the pre-reform period. Secondly, inequality increased significantly in the post-reform period as compared to the earlier decade. Similar to poverty trends, the employment growth in the post-reform period (1.89 per cent during 1993–2005) was not higher than the pre-reform period (2.01 per cent during 1983–4).

The performance in social sector development indicates that there are basically five problems with health and education:

(a) low levels and slow progress of human development indicators such as infant and child mortality, maternal mortality and malnutrition;
(b) significant regional, social and gender disparities;
(c) slow growth in public expenditures in the social sector;
(d) poor quality delivery systems in both health and education; and
(e) privatization of health and education services. The percentage of children suffering from malnutrition has not declined despite of high economic growth.

The growth rate in the State Domestic Product (SDP) across states seems to be more uneven in the post-reform period as compared to the pre-reform period. Disparities have increased in India in poverty, inequality in consumption, underweight children and infant mortality. In the case of enrolment, inter-state variations have declined. Historical factors and initial endowments explain only part of the reasons for regional disparities. The experience of different states shows that some western and southern states have done better than some eastern and northern states because of better infrastructure, fiscal management, investment in the social sector and institutions including governance.

Protecting the environment is another important component of inclusive growth. The degradation of land and water is particularly alarming. The shortage of drinking water has become acute and the quality of the water has declined over time. An integrated approach is needed for water resources management in the country. Pricing policies for water may be needed but institutional factors are more important. A more participatory approach, community management and the involvement of women would lead to the sustainability of land, forestry and water. There are also many urban and industrial pollution-related problems which have to be solved with government intervention and institutional approach rather than only with price reforms. Similarly, climate change can create problems for agriculture and human development and push vulnerable people into deprivation.

We cannot take India's democracy for granted. It is a process which requires constant care and nurturing. The gradual but continuing erosion of standards in key institutions must be checked in order to sustain people's faith in the democratic system. For a better functioning of democracy, there is a need for electoral judicial and administrative reforms and the decentralization of powers to panchayats. There is also a need for more professionals and leaders with a social conscience in politics. Civil society organizations need to be continually energized and empowered.

To conclude, India has been relatively successful in GDP growth in recent years. This higher growth has to be translated into equitable development. There has been slow progress in the last sixty years in important elements of inclusive growth such as agriculture, poverty reduction and generation of employment, human development including basic services to the poor, reduction in regional disparities and protection of the environment. India is a political democracy: one can, however, ask the question that with so much hunger and poverty, has India achieved 'real' or 'substantive' or economic and social democracy? There is a need to focus on pro-poor policies instead of concentrating only on foreign direct investment and the corporate sector. Effective public policy with higher allocations to the 'inclusive sectors' and better delivery of public services to poor are needed. Therefore, the State's role is important in achieving faster growth in all the elements of equitable development. It is increasingly clear that the process of development in India must become more socially and economically inclusive. The governments, markets and civil society should try to achieve this objective of development in the future.

About the Book

In this volume there are eleven chapters organized into six themes: (1) Revisiting the State: New Forms of Governance; (2) Public-Private Partnerships in Basic Service Delivery: Impacts on the Poor; (3) Access to Public and Corporate Sector Employment: Rural and Urban Dynamics; (4) Uneven Economic Growth and Environmental Implications; (5) Gender and Generation as Divisions in India's Development; and (6) Displacement, Conflict and Crises: The Flipside of Globalization.

Cooperation between the local government and citizens was established in the process of the decentralization of administration in Mumbai. The paper by I.S.A. Baud and Navtej Nainan have tried to show which groups are excluded or included in the urban governance of 'negotiated spaces'.

Many governments are now working together with private sector and citizen movements to provide basic services in different parts of the world. In this context, the authors have tried to examine the various interfaces between Mumbai's local government and citizens (citizen groups), and also the potential of such 'invited spaces'. There has been a discussion in India on the decreasing rights of the urban poor (people living in unauthorized slums). These groups of citizens are treated as 'trespassers on public land'. About 54 per cent of Mumbai's population lives in slum areas. These areas are treated as illegal housing areas until they have gone through the process of regularization. The authors have compared two types of invited spaces provided by government. The first is the formation and functioning of the local political representation processes established as envisaged in the 74th Constitutional Amendment (1992) which was aimed at decentralization. In Mumbai its implementation led to the formation of sixteen ward committees including locally elected councillors, ward officers, non-governmental organizations (NGO), community based organizations (CBO), etc. The second type is the Advanced Locality Management (ALM) programme initiated by the Municipal Corporation of Greater Mumbai (MCGM) to improve basic solid waste management services. Elected councillors have a strong mandate from low-income voters in slum areas and naturally they represent the needs of slum residents. The ALMs are formed by housing co-operative societies and street-based residents' organizations. Though ALMs are formed for solid waste management, they address a number of other issues such as garbage clearance, composting, drainage, water supply, beautification, encroachments, road excavation, pothole filling, roads and pavement levelling, surfacing and management of stray animals. There is an overlap between the ward committees (include all eleven to fifteen elected councillors with the ward officer as their member secretary) and the ALMs as both addresses issues of solid waste management. Due to the nature of their backgrounds, their interests also differ. The authors' research shows that the residential ALMs and councillors tried to increase their influence and extended their activities with the same motive to the new areas, which resulted in conflict between these two. Ultimately, the power is shifting slowly in favour of the middle class (widely represented in the ALMs) and this can make slum dwellers and vulnerable groups even more dependent on the political will of their political representatives.

Public–Private Partnerships in Basic Service Delivery: Impacts on the Poor

In the light of states' withdrawal from various public tasks, the public-private partnership (PPP) has occupied an important position. There are two chapters on this one theme, on provision of basic services in Delhi and the other on health care services. Shipra Maitra's chapter highlights the perfect combination of poor women and NGOs with state government in the provision of basic health services. The chapter on public-private partnership in health services by A. Venkat Raman and J.W. Bjorkman is based on sixteen in-depth case studies covering both successful and failed or problematic partnerships.

Globally it is a well-recognized fact that the PPP is an important instrument for resource generation and inclusive governance. Though India is making impressive economic growth, the benefits are not reaching the vulnerable sections of the society (poor women constituting a significant part of it), who also suffer from a poor quality of life. According to Shipra Maitra, PPPs may help in reducing gap in the provision of basic service delivery. The National Health Policy has also noted that women and other underprivileged are handicapped due to their low access to health care; they have to wait for long period to avail themselves of public services whereas private services are expensive.

According to the estimates of the Delhi government, 800,000 poor women (5.71 per cent of total population of Delhi) living in notified slums need health care coverage. With the objective of bringing them under health coverage, the Delhi government has started the Stree Shakti (Women Empowerment) programme involving CBOs and other NGOs. Shipra Maitra's is based on a primary survey of 5,000 households in the slums of Delhi.

The Department of Social Welfare (DSW) of the Delhi goverment runs a number of institutions for beggars, juveniles, handicapped, women, aged persons, etc. It also promotes a partnership (Bhagidari) scheme for providing better implementation and better utilization of resources in partnership with people-centric organizations.

One such programme of the DSW is the Stree Shakti (Gender Empowerment) scheme, which aims at empowering the women of the economically weaker sections through intervention in (1) health; (2) skill development; and (3) income generation. In this programme, various facilities are taken to their doorstep by organizing camps at periodic intervals and establishing Gender Resource Centres (GRC) for dissemination of information and assistance. The programme is run in coordination with a number of NGOs. For the entire programme in Delhi state, there is one mother NGO. In the next level there are a number of field-level (local) NGOs called FNGOs. The mother NGO supervises all camp activities and is also involved in designing of the programme and training all FNGOs. This programme has been operational since 2002. It has clearly brought changes in the lives of deprived women through a decentralized delivery process.

The next chapter is on health services. It is a well documented fact that the public health care system has failed to cater to all the health care needs of the people. As a result, many people, including the poor, have to depend on the private sector for health services. India has the highest levels of out-of-pocket financing. Hospitalization and chronic illnesses often lead the poor into indebtedness or the liquidation of their assets. Some of them even fall below the poverty line due to the heavy expenditure involved. Interestingly, India's public spending has remained stagnant at one per cent of the GDP (0.9 per cent) whereas it is 5.5 per cent at the global level. In India, private health sector is providing a large volume of the health services to the poor (not free). Therefore, it is clear from the successive plan documents since the Eighth Five-Year Plan in 1992 and the 2002 National Health Policy that there is an emphasis on reforms in India's public health sector. The private health sector is providing health services without much regulation by the state. It has emerged as the most potential area that needs to be tapped for wider usage. In this direction, many state governments have undertaken health sector reforms to establish PPPs essentially to take the health services to the poor and under-served sections of the population. This type of partnership is a complex phenomenon with a whole range of issues such as motives of the private sector, scope and objectives of the partnerships, technical and managerial capabilities of both players and the explicit benefits to the poor out of this partnership.

Venkat Raman and Bjorkman have conducted a study under the Indo-Dutch Programme on Alternatives in Development (IDPAD) to explore the above-mentioned issues in PPPs. This chapter is based on sixteen in-depth case studies spread over nine states. Of the sixteen case studies and nineteen partnership agreements, only eight partners are NGOs. Some partnerships deal with simple contracts (diet, laundry, cleaning) whereas others are more complex contracts involving many stakeholders (Yeshasvini is a community-based self-financed health insurance scheme). In almost all partnerships, the principal public partner, either directly or through health facility level committees is the department of health and family welfare. In their study, no uniform pattern emerges to make any concrete suggestions. But when it comes to the operational level of PPP, it is not always an easy task. Public sector managers perceive the new initiative as a burdensome task. On the other hand, private partners who are known for their informal and flexible systems are uncomfortable with the rigid organizational and managerial processes and procedures of the public sector. Venkat Raman and Bjorkman's study concludes that these PPP initiatives cannot be uniform across all the regions and suitable under all kinds of administrative arrangements.

Access to Public and Corporate Sector Employment: Rural and Urban Dynamics

There are three chapters in this section. India's current impressive economic growth is largely due to the contribution of the service sector. More precisely, the performance of IT has been impressive. Carol Upadhya's chapter brings out the caste and class inequalities in the IT labour market. According to Alakh Sharma, even the reservation policy does not work well for the poor among the reserved sections of the population. The well-off sections (creamy layer) are found to be availing themselves of most of the opportunities. Sunanda Sen and Byasdeb Dasgupta found in their study that the growth-centric reform process do not improve the economic status of labourers.

Carol Upadhya's chapter is on the caste and class composition of the IT sector in India. In the process of globalization, India has immensely benefited in the field of IT. IT employ more than a million people and is likely to provide many more jobs in the coming years. India is taking advantage of its cheap manpower. Many Indians are employed in outsourced and off-shored activities (IT and

IT-enabled services [ITES]) of the advanced industrial economies within India. The IT industry in India is often represented as providing employment opportunities to wider sections of the population. However, according to Upadhya's research, the social reality appears to be somewhat different. The majority of software engineers come from the middle class, although some are from lower and lower-middle class backgrounds. In urban-rural break-up, the urban educated are the most preferred and a rural background operates as a major constraint because of poor standards of education. Social category-wise, a majority of the IT professionals are from forward castes followed by the OBCs. Students from higher classes have a clear advantage in getting admission to premier institutes due to the better coaching in private institutes and better education in private/corporate English medium schools. On the other hand, students from lower castes and rural backgrounds are more likely to study in government schools in the vernacular medium. All these factors work together to create a bias in the social composition of potential IT hires. This bias is further attributed to the recruitment process. Each IT company maintains a rating of engineering colleges and visits only certain ranked colleges during campus placements. The large IT companies such as Infosys and TCS usually visit fifty to sixty campuses, while the Multi-National Companies (MNC) may visit about ten select campuses. Thus many engineering or qualified people are naturally left out in this process. In the recruitment process, the candidates have to undergo two types of interviews; technical and human resource. Most of these software jobs are of 'client facing' and good communication skills are needed. Even the technically well qualified may be rejected purely on the basis of poor communication skills. The 'culture capital' of the candidate is an added advantage for entering the IT profession. The students who studied in English-medium schools generally have good English language skills and can also communicate well without mother tongue influence (MTI). Thus the IT industry looks for candidates within certain social types and designs recruitment procedures to filter out those who do not fit. Though the IT industry is against implementing reservations, it wants to take appropriate measures to increase the diversity and inclusiveness of their work-force. Thus the chapter points at the contradiction between the dominant representation of IT and the actual practices of recruitment and employment, as well as the ideological operation of the 'merit' argument against the background of the debate on reservations in the private sector.

During liberalization there is significant growth in trade, capital flows and foreign direct investment. This is also marked by a deceleration in employment growth and rise in open employment. Moreover, there have been growing disparities in wages and incomes between skilled and unskilled workers. The benefits of recent economic growth are not reaching all sections of the population. Therefore the basic aim of the Eleventh Five-Year Plan was to address these issues and make the economic growth more inclusive of all these sections of the Indian population. According to A.N. Sharma, there is a sharp decline in the share of agriculture in the national income and also the proportion of labour employed in it. Regarding the rural-urban divide in employment, during 1970–1, 62 per cent of India's national income was generated in rural areas and only 38 per cent of it came from urban areas. During 1999–2000, the urban share increased to about 50 per cent of the national income. Though the share of rural areas in the national income has reduced to half, a vast majority of workers (71.6 per cent) continue to live in rural areas. Even within the rural income, the share of agriculture has reduced to half. The share of services has risen from 9 per cent to 17 per cent. There is an expansion of income from rural transport, storage and communications.

Though the SDP at the all-India level was higher in the 1990s, the disparities in growth rates across states have increased. The backward states could generate adequate resources for their development; however, the generation of resources on their own is limited. Their plan size was much lower than the rich states. States are competing with each other to attract foreign investors. Ultimately the favourable destination (for Foreign Direct Investment [FDI]) for foreign investment is in the rich states like Maharashtra, Gujarat, Karnataka, Tamil Nadu and Andhra Pradesh.

The incidence of poverty in India (27 per cent in 1999–2000) is much higher. Though there is improvement in the employment rate, the incidence of poverty is higher as most of jobs are of casual nature with low pay. As far as the quality of employment is concerned, regular workers are best placed and casual workers are worst. The Indian market is highly segmented and there exist large differentials among various groups. Upper Hindu, Upper Muslim and 'Others' (Sikhs, Christians, Buddhists, Jains, etc.) are placed well in accessing the better employment opportunities as they are more urbanized. On the other hand, STs, SCs and OBCs are overwhelmingly concentrated in the lowest-paid types of employment. Despite job reservation, the proportion of their workforce employed in the public sector is less than half of the upper-caste Hindus. Compared to the OBCs and Muslims, the reservation policy has helped the SCs and STs in getting employment. Based on the consumption expenditure pattern, among the reserved social category, the richest class cornered the majority of the opportunities than their counterparts in the lowest consumption expenditure class. There is also a regional variation as SCs in the south and west were found to have cornered most of the employment opportunities.

The Indian economic reform process which was started in 1991, was basically aimed at strengthening the markets *vis-à-vis* the state, inflow of foreign capital on a large scale and promoting competition and efficiency in production. Thus there was a shift from long protected 'non-competitive' to competitive markets. With liberalization, higher economic growth is made possible due to the optimal utilization of labour and capital. However, this process is not always smooth as it involves stressful adjustments of occupational dislocations and unemployment in the case of labour. In the case of capital, industrial restructuring is often needed. Consequently, in this process, the disparities between fast-growing and slow-growing industries are increasing. There will be considerable stress on the labour due to occupational dislocation and rising unemployment. FDI inflows have affected the Indian industry adopting productivity augmenting technology and recruiting flexible labour (mostly on contract or casual basis). In fact, the additional flow of FDI did not create much additional employment. Sunanda Sen and Byasdeb Dasgupta have conducted an in-depth inquiry of conditions of labour under globalization through their field survey of organized labour employed in manufacturing industries.

During the study, 615 factory labourers in West Bengal, Delhi, Haryana, Gujarat and Maharashtra (including some labourers from Special Economic Zones [SEZ]) were interviewed. The study results show that the casual labourers are more insecure in terms of their job prospects and have less to do with union membership. Their savings are much lower compared to their permanent counterparts. Even they are mostly deprived of non-wage benefits like provident fund (PF), gratuity and bonus. The labourers in import industries are better placed *vis-à-vis* non-wage benefits compared to their counterparts working in export industries. During the liberalization period, the technological structure of industries is undergoing a lot of changes adopting labour-displacing technologies. Moreover, the appropriation of surplus labour is compensated by adopting labour-displacing technology and increasing average work-time. The study also throw some light on labour conditions in SEZs. In these economic zones, India's labour and taxation laws do not apply. The labour laws are so flexible to hire and fire practices. The variance for mean hours of work is more here indicating flexible time and very long working hours for a few workers. Compared to labourers working in other factories, in the SEZs only some labourers receive retirement benefits in the form of PF and gratuity and a yearly bonus. Moreover, very few of them reported some savings. Sen and Dasgupta advocate the building of a strong social safety network for the labourers in SEZs. According to the study, the growth-centric reform process does not seem to have had a favourable impact on the economic status of labourers.

Uneven Economic Growth and Environmental Implications

The impact of uneven growth on the environment and various natural resources is evident in the chapters by Abey George and Jyothi Krishnan, and Jyothis Sathyapalan and Derek Johnson. George and Krishnan has highlighted the miseries of the tribal people and the failure of decentralized governance in improving the living conditions of the tribals in Kerala. The Sathyapalan and Johnson, in their chapter, have discussed clearly how modern resource management neglected the traditional institutional arrangements at the grass-roots level, which resulted in the cornering of the benefits of natural resources like fisheries by a few, leaving the majority in misery.

The 'Kerala Model of Development' is well known for its significant achievements in social development. During the last decade, Kerala was adjudged as the best performing state as has as democratic decentralization and panchayati raj were amend. Abey George and Jyothi Krishnan argue that the state's achievements have not benefited the marginalized sections of the population. In Kerala there are 38 tribal communities who are distinct from one another in terms of their cultural patterns, diversity of habitats, lifestyles, languages and livelihoods. Tribal literacy is not up to the mark compared to the general population. Even the incidence of poverty among them is three times that of the total population of the state. Land alienation is another problem. The chapter is based on a case study of Attapady Block in Palakkad district of Kerala, and examines the impact of a massive eco-restoration programme. Two forms of decentralization have been underway in the study area since 1992. In tune with the spirit and process of the decentralization campaign in the state, the concept of 'oorkootam' was introduced in the tribal areas. Around the same time, the JBIC-funded Attappady Comprehensive Eco-restoration project was implemented by the Attapady Hill Area Development Society (AHADS) in the area. AHADS has constituted a large number of user associations to promote a participatory mode of implementation. Due to electoral reservations, the representation of women and tribals is quite impressive in various user groups. But their numbers did not help much as they largely fell into the category of 'silent nodders'. In the local body elections of Attappady Block, an Irula tribal woman was elected as president. Over a period of time, it was evident that the newly elected president could do little within the boundaries laid out by the political party she represented. There was no happy ending even where the tribals had organized themselves effectively to take up some activities. For example, road work was undertaken by the people's committee (mostly consisting of tribals) in the Nackupathy hamlet. This action antagonized the contractor lobby and even on the successful completion of the road work, the tribals' bills were kept pending on the grounds of poor quality of work. The poor tribals had completed the work with personal advances of money. The delay in payments precipitated internal conflicts among the poor tribals. In other places, the project works helped them in getting higher real wages. Since a practice of proper saving habits does not exist, the tribals spent their wages on liquor which resulted in domestic violence. Thus these initiatives did not have much impact on the tribal population in accessing critical resources.

The chapter by Sathyapalan and Johnson is on the development of the outward-oriented fisheries in Gujarat and its economic or livelihood security impact on marine fishing communities. They discuss the environmental degradation arising out of high growth-oriented resource extraction using trawler technology for fishing. Due to the predominance of vegetarianism in the state, there is less demand for fish there. Most of the fish catch is exported to other states and also to other countries. Most of the fishing communities earn their livelihood under risky and insecure conditions. In marine fishing, fishermen using advanced productive technologies like trawlers, capture a disproportionate share of the fish depriving those without access to these resources. This situation often leads to inter-sectoral conflicts among the fishing committee. The chapter is based on a study conducted in Junagadh district of Gujarat and the Union Territory of Diu. Junagadh district has the largest fishing population in Gujarat. In this district, the Kolis and Kharvas are the Hindu caste groups involved in fishing. The remaining fishing communities—Bhadelas, Khureshis, Memons and Patnis—are the Muslim. During Sathyapalan and Johnson's study, 1,056 representatives of the fishing households were contacted using the 'random walk method' of data collection. About 90 per cent of them are illiterate. Among them, the Ghogaliya fisher community is better educated with 61 per cent literacy. Even the sex ratio of the fisher population is only 896. The distribution of the fishing asset base shows that 23.8 per cent of fisher households own trawlers, 4.5 per cent own Inbound Motor Boats (IBM), 5.6 per cent own dol netters, 22.4 per cent own Outdoor Motor Boats (OBM) and 1.5 per cent own non-motorized boats. The remaining 42.1 per cent of households do not have any fishing assets. Most of the fisher communities are facing the problem of overexploitation of fish due to the use of trawlers. This kind of technology-induced risk often provokes inter-sectarian conflicts in the fishery sector. Quoting the use of this technology, there is a gradual decline in fish catch. It can also be attributed to the opening up of the sea to foreign vessels for fishing. The Gujarat fisheries Act was passed in 2003 to regulate excessive catch of juvenile fishes to allow the recruitment base to remain sufficient for the next season. The Act also imposes a ban on fishing during the monsoon season since which is the breeding season. As most of the fishing communities depend on marine resources for their livelihood, the authors are of the opinion that there is a need to strengthen the present institutional base for better resource allocation and conservation, particularly protecting product and factor markets from imperfections. They suggest the strengthening of the traditional institutions like caste *samaj* and infrastructure support for all.

Gender and Generation as Divisions in India's Development

Loes Schenk-Sandbergen argues that though democratic space was created for women in water management committees, it has neither helped them nor ensured the participation of women in these committees.

It is evident from the reforms in institutions and organizations that the state is slowly withdrawing from providing the basic services and passing on these responsibilities to civil society organizations, privatizing some of the services, decentralization of these activities, promoting participatory user-management of resources, etc., in the name of efficiency, transparency and accountability. In India, the farmers are now directly involved in Participatory Irrigation Management (PIM) in irrigation sector. Along with these reforms, donors of various development projects stress on 'mainstreaming' women in the core activities of development projects. Though there is high involvement of women in irrigated agriculture and agricultural decision-making, women's participation in Water Users' Associations all over the world is very low. Schenk-Sandbergen's chapter is based on a case study of the Tank Rehabilitation Project in Pondicherry (TRPP). The Pondy project started in 1999 and is still running although the Technical Assistance was closed by the donor (European Commission) in July 2004. Historically, a large part of the land in Pondicherry was irrigated by 84 tanks. All through that period there was a clear mechanism for timely maintenance of tanks. Today, due to the extensive usage of bore wells, only one-third of the 84 tanks are more or less in use, while most of the tanks are not used for irrigation purposes at all. These tanks are in a deplorable condition as a result of heavy weed infestation in the water-spread area, heavy siltation in the tank bed and supply channels. About 20 to 60 per cent of tank beds have been encroached on for housing or for cultivation. The basic aim of the TRPP project is to transfer the management of water resources from the 'state' to the 'community'. Unfortunately, despite initial intense community participation work with pro-poor and pro-women policy formulation by NGOs and Community Organizers (CO), at the end of it all, the large farmers dominate the Water Users' Associations (WUA) and are the beneficiaries. In India, traditionally, 'water user' means 'one who owns the land'. Though the landless women do the transplanting, weeding and harvesting work, they are not perceived as 'water users' and therefore not perceived as being eligible for membership in WUAs. Therefore the landholder is considered as the 'water user' and legally controls the water rights. Due to the patriarchal nature of Indian society, the post-marriage residence pattern cuts women off from house-, land- and water rights. Though some women are members of WUAs, they are much more under time pressure due to their regular heavy household works. The timings of meetings are not convenient for the women.

Even if they speak on some issues during meetings, their views are discounted. Though the WUAs are promoted as non-political institutions, 'elite capture' and political involvement dominate their functioning. The strategy of the project is that the rehabilitation of the tanks will be carried out together with the local 'community', and by handing over the irrigation tanks and their assets to Tank Associations. During the implementation stage many problems cropped up due to the interests and backgrounds of different sections of the population involved in the Tank Associations. Due to their background differentials, tank restorations benefit only the landed and the poor are the worst sufferers. For instance, once the recharging capacity of the tank is successful, the richest and most powerful landowning farmers will bore it wells in the tank command area are the main beneficiaries as they get double benefits. On the other hand, the poor mostly landless, who built settlements on the encroached tank bed land, will have to vacate their encroached land to give way for tank restoration works. Moreover, these people do not get compensation as the land was not a legal holding. As regards the gender issue, Reddiar women are not allowed to do agricultural work to ensure the 'prestige' of the family. Hence they do not participate in Associations though they have land in their names. The Vanniyar women are the farmwomen of small landholdings who do the weeding, harvesting and transplanting of rice in their own land. Mostly they have to buy water from the Reddiars. A few women initially became members of the Executive Committee and they participated very well in the planning and implementation of the technical works. The key point of the 'all-stakeholder' approach in Pondy was that it challenged caste/class, landownership, political, religious and gender relations as it perserved to give a voice and rights to the poor and landless women for whom the tank is often their survival. The rehabilitation of the tanks created immense survival problems for hundreds of poor households and created immense tension and brought unpopularity to the Community Organizers after the WUAs were formed.

Displacement, Conflict and Crises: The Flipside of Globalization

There are two chapters in this section. In the first, Mario Rutten examines the development trends across various countries. He discuss issues of migration from and to India and further argues that the inequalities are not just confined to India or developing countries. Inequalities exist in the developed countries as well. In the second chapter Amita Shah also discuss the conflicts arising out of displacements from various development projects such as the establishment of SEZs.

Mario Rutten's chapter is an anthropological study of the Indian diaspora/social change in Asia. It is based on 313 households in 6 villages in central Gujarat which have relatives in Britain. Of the 313 households, 157 were selected for in-depth case studies. A similar survey was conducted among 159 Patidar households in Greater Britain, of which 80 were selected for in-depth case studies.

In India, people move from their home village to the city, yet they maintain close ties with their place of origin. It is also common for these migrated people to organize get-togethers with their caste members in the new place of residence. To keep these ties, the family members who were left behind in the village occasionally pay visits to their family and caste members in the latters' city. Interestingly, according to the case study results presented, the board meeting of the Vepargam Patidar organization (Rutten's study community) was held in London. His study results give the impression that today the world resembles a village community. The explosive increase in cross-country migratory movements, flows of goods and financial operations have created the image of a 'global village' which encompasses the whole earth. Large portions of the world population seem to have been brought closer by the developments in the fields of transport and communications, like TV, the Internet, etc. In the literature all these are viewed as a kind of Westernization (a process marked by a spread of influences from the Western part of the world to what have become known as non-Western societies in Africa, Latin America and Asia). In other words, these nations follow in the footsteps of Western countries in the modernization process. It is widely believed that homogenization is the dominant trend in this globalization process and this can be evidenced by the spread of the three big Ms, namely McDonald's, Microsoft and MTV. However, these developments are detrimental to local culture, which will slowly erode. The speed of this process varies across different locations in the world. However, Rutten contradicts this view and this can be evidenced from the contributions of Asian immigrants in Europe in their cultural diversity in terms of introducing new types of foods, fashion and music. Though these contributions have benefited the Western societies, they have generated a more negative attitude towards the process of Easternization. In his chapter, Rutten has tried to examine the social linkages between the Patidar immigrants in London and their family members in central Gujarat, and also to show how the Westernization of Asia and the Easternization of Europe are two interconnected aspects of globalization. His findings indicate that the members of this community maintain frequent long-distance family linkages with their home region in India, which has resulted in a two-way flow of people, capital and ideas. Marriage arrangements, kinship networks, frequent visits, property, remittances and religious affiliations ensure that many of the Patidar immigrants in London maintain close links with the villages in Gujarat. The Patidars in London organize meetings to celebrate Indian festivals like Nava Ratri, Diwali, etc., they also organize marriage melas. Rutten also shows how these activities differ among the older and younger generations due to their different upbringing. He also clearly shows the Patidar's contributions in the spread of Hinduism at home and in the West. Thus, with these evidences he argues that the process of Easternization cannot be overlooked.

Amita Shah is of the opinion that in the process of the economic development of India, a large number of the human population is being displaced from its socio-cultural milieu as well as natural resources. Of late there is severe pressure for converting agricultural land to set up projects in sectors like industry, mining and infrastructure. This land diversion for developmental projects such as irrigation, mining and other infrastructure like ports has triggered many controversies. The latest among them is over SEZs. Though data clearly suggests the diversion, it has failed to capture the real picture owing to the limitations in the system of land records and illegal (*benami*) transactions, especially in the peri-urban areas. There is no systematic or comprehensive mechanism to assess the actual magnitude and complexities of the people displaced in various situations. Roughly 11 to 18 million people have been displaced since the 1950s. According the data presented by Shah in her chapter, only 25 per cent of the displaced have been resettled. A large number of the displaced suffered owing to a complex mix of factors—weak policy, inadequate funds as well as administrative set up and, above all, low political commitment. In the case of irrigation projects, the displaced are the inhabitants of the upper reaches. The farmers in the lower reaches (command area) reap all the benefits. Though the Resettlement &

Rehabilitation (R&R) policy in irrigation suggests the provision of land in the command area, in practice it is not feasible—politically as well as administratively. As regards mining, it has a severe negative impact on the land quality and directly contributes to environmental degradation and pollution in the project areas. Some people in the mining areas are even being affected by radioactivity. Moreover, water resources get exhausted or contaminated with time. In the case of land for industrialization, the idea was to create more jobs. In fact, very few benefit from the additional jobs which are low-paid or non-technical such as manual or semi-manual labour.

The recent debate is on the creation of SEZs throughout India. The Board of Approvals has (as of October 2006) granted approvals for 237 formal EZs and 166 in-principle SEZs. Recently, the International Monetary Fund (IMF), in its observations has questioned the validity of setting up a large number of relatively smaller SEZs in India, in contrast to China where the strategy was to promote a few large SEZs. Many experts are critical of these SEZs and alleged that they are instrumental in the abuse of labour as well as environmental laws, and provide land-grabbing opportunities for many. Protected areas like forests, on the other hand, have different problems. The people trapped in the Protected Areas are neither covered by the regular developmental activities nor do they receive adequate compensation for the lost opportunities while cooperating in conservation measures.

NOTES

1. Quoted by Dreze and Sen (2002), *India: Development and Participation*, New Delhi: Oxford University Press.
2. For more on this see Deepak Nayyar (2006), 'Economic Growth in Independent India: Lumbering Elephant or Running Tiger?, *Economic and Political Weeky,* 15 April.
3. D. Wilson, and R. Purushothaman (2003), 'Dreaming with BRICs: The Path to 2050', Global Economics Paper 99, Goldman Sachs.

THEME 1

REVISITING THE STATE: NEW FORMS OF GOVERNANCE

CHAPTER 1

'Negotiated Spaces' for Representation in Mumbai: Ward Committees, Advanced Locality Management and the Politics of Middle-Class Activism

I.S.A. BAUD AND NAVTEJ NAINAN

Introduction

The discussion on the new ways in which governments have moved from providing services directly to working together with the private sector and citizens' movements is well-established in different parts of the world (Pierre and Peters 2000; Kooiman 2003; Baud 2004; World Bank 2003). Such governance processes have provided new opportunities for non-government actors to work together with different levels of government. Local city governments see this as an opportunity to direct policy implementation outwards through the involvement of non-governmental organizations (NGO), the private sector and community-based organizations (CBO). This movement includes not only public-private arrangements as well as the public-community arrangements but also setting up of inter-organizational networks—urban platforms of various types, which are said to provide better opportunities for various citizens' groups to promote their claims (Harris 2003: 2542). These new arenas in which citizens are requested by local governments to work with them in determining local needs and providing basic services to citizens have been termed 'invited spaces' (Cornwall 2004).

In the 1990s, the debate on governance showed a fairly neo-liberal slant; the idea was that the private sector could provide basic urban services in a more efficient and effective manner than could government (cf. World Bank 2003). This view has been partially revised in that it is now recognized that under certain circumstances governments themselves can best provide services (natural monopolies, lack of market demand), and that the variety of arrangements needs to reflect differences in the institutional context (World Bank 2003). However, the interaction between government and citizens also requires wider issues to be raised, namely, who participates, what kind of processes occur within the interface and what kind of outcomes it produces.

The debate is currently centered on such issues, being framed in terms of 'deepening democracy', asking whether institutionalization of invited spaces (through form and process) is sufficient to make them inclusive and substantive, i.e. to lead to 'more just and equitable societies' (Gaventa 2006). The question raised in this chapter is, what happens in such relationships and networks in the urban context of one large Indian city, where there are a variety of interfaces between local government and citizens, and what is the potential for such 'invited spaces'. Three will be addressed here: (1) who is 'invited'; (2) the substance and process of partnering; and (3) the perceived outcomes for both invited and excluded groups of citizens.

The increase in 'invited spaces' is occurring in a period in which decentralization initiatives in many countries have provided local urban governments with mandates for working directly with local citizens. There are several contrasting views about the value of this process: some authors consider it to be a sign of increased democracy that the central state is reduced in favour of local arrangements; others feel it is a hollowing-out of the state (Gaventa 2006). The question decentralization primarily raises regards the shifts in the relationship between central and local scales of government, and the extent to which it provides effective channels for citizens to make their voices heard.

This is not necessarily always the case. Luckham et al. (2000) distinguish four types of 'democratic deficits' (quoted in Gaventa 2006):

(i) hollow citizenship, where different groups of citizens have different rights and obligations;
(ii) no vertical accountability, so that citizens cannot hold their governments and ruling elites to account;
(iii) weak horizontal accountability, particularly of local executive government; and

(iv) lack of international accountability, as multinational corporations and international organizations bypass national governments.

The view put forward in this chapter is that when decentralization is accompanied by new forms of local representation, such 'invited spaces' can become the focus of new forms of collective action and engagement with government. However, it remains to be seen whether these spaces offer only the possibility to citizens of making their views heard as 'consumers of services' or whether they are actually recognized as citizens with rights.

In terms of the issue of which citizens are 'invited', India provides an interesting example, with decentralization and new forms of local representation for citizens as well as strong civic engagement with local authorities. It has put in place decentralization legislation and new forms of local representation for citizens. The 74th Constitutional Amendment in 1992 provided for a policy of urban decentralization, which has been ratified and implemented to different degrees by state governments. In Mumbai its implementation led to the formation of sixteen ward committees consisting of locally elected councillors and ward officers (the administrative side of government). Although the design to include NGOs and CBOs as advisory members in these committees is only partially implemented, the constitutional amendment has strengthened citizenship by allowing residents to elect representatives who can play a role in decision-making at the (electoral and administrative) ward level.

The first question concerns which groups of citizens are 'invited' to participate in public-community arrangements. Are different groups of citizens differentiated by local governments, and accorded different rights according to their status? There has been a discussion in India on the decreasing rights of the urban poor who are living in non-authorized slums. Local and state courts are increasingly treating these groups of citizens as 'trespassers on public land', with no rights to basic housing and services. This is in contrast to the housing policies that have been in place since independence (Ramanathan 2006; Ramanathan and Dupont 2005 on Delhi; Desai 2003 on Mumbai), which have focused on rehabilitation schemes for citizens living in slums.[1] This suggests that very real differences exist in the rights of different groups of urban citizens in reality.

The second question concerns the mandates local government gives to citizens' groups and representatives, what activities citizens carry out and what rights they claim, and what interface citizens themselves prefer to have with local government. What degree of collective action do citizens' groups have, and is there a significant degree of interface with government compared to the mandates elected representatives have?

Finally, the question arises whether 'invited spaces'—through either direct connections or elected representatives—actually lead to a better quality of life in the city. We define quality of life as 'the extent to which basic needs and rights of local citizens are reflected in the activities carried out within the interface between local government and citizens'. This includes both their rights as consumers to receive basic public services as well as their political right as citizens to co-determine and obtain their right to direct and indirect representation (Cornwall 2004; Kabeer 2002; Fung and Wright 2003).

This chapter, contrasts two types of invited spaces provided by government. The first concerns the case of a programme initiated by the Municipal Corporation of Greater Mumbai (MCGM) to improve basic solid-waste management services, called Advanced Locality Management (ALM), since 1996, which has grown into a larger movement of citizen-local government interface. The second concerns the formation and functioning of local political representation processes established in the same period. Since 1992, administrative ward committees have been established, and two elections for councillors have been held. The main issues taken up in this chapter are analysed, contrasting the situation of these two 'invited' spaces.

The Case of Mumbai

Mumbai is the capital of Maharashtra, one of India's most developed states, with a population of some 16.4 million people (Greater Mumbai or Corporation area).[2] The population consists of a variety of groups, with people from the state itself forming only about 40 per cent of the population. Large proportions of the population are migrants from other states and other countries. The growing economy has led to an influx of migrants looking for employment in both the top end of the formal labour market as well as in the lower-end in informal economic activities.

The city is a trading hub, with strong links to international companies, ICT and creative industries and (business) services. Currently, two types of economic activities dominate: first, capital-intensive service sectors like finance and producer services, software development, mass media and entertainment, communications and information technologies, and residential and commercial real estate and property development; and second, labour-intensive production of electronics, garments, plastics and consumer goods in small-scale workshops in informal settlements.

Mumbai started out as a manufacturing city, with the cotton textile industry remaining dominant until the 1940s. Automation then resulted in the reduction of jobs from 200,000 to 60,000 workers from the 1970s–90s (Pacione 2006). The loss of formal employment in cotton mills was accompanied by the development of 'unregistered production units' using downgraded technology to which a large part of manufacturing was contracted out.[3] Displaced textile workers with few opportunities relocated to informal economic activities, in which employment increased from 49 per cent in 1971 to 66 per cent of the total workforce in 1991 (ibid.).

In contrast, finance insurance and real estate services expanded during the 1970s and 1980s, with employment growing by 43 per cent (ibid.). Combined with the entry of international financial groups in Bombay's stock exchange, this stimulated related service industries. Other tertiary sector activities include culture industries, tourism, offshore printing and publishing and data processing for international companies. They also include provision of higher education for south. Asian and Sub-Saharan African countries and labour-intensive medical and nursing facilities. The growth of the urban economy was 8 per cent in 2004 and 2005 (ibid.).

This new private sector is associated with the growth of the middle-class and a concomitant consumer lifestyle. The expansion is noticeable in the growth of middle-class housing and suburban sprawl, as well as in civil society groups which demand better services and accountability from the urban local bodies, putting new energies into the politics of local governance.

Such growth and expansion of lifestyle pose great challenges for urban government in expanding housing, services, and basic infrastructure to all those they recognize as citizens of the city. At the moment, it is estimated by Risbud (2003) that 54 per cent of the population lives in slum areas (according to the Census 2001 definition).[4] The majority of the slums are in the inner western suburbs, where 58 per cent of the slum population is concentrated.[5] Slums are not a homogeneous category, ranging from areas where pavement dwellers live to chawls and zhopadpattis (cf. Risbud 2003). Slum areas are treated as illegal housing areas unless they go through the process of regularization.[6] Until such time, residents receive no rights to proof of residence or basic services from the local administration. This is becoming increasingly an issue, as the middle-class and elite are demanding that slums be removed because of their illegal status (through public interest litigations) (Patel, Cruz and Burra 2002).

The MCGM is responsible for a wide range of services to its residents. These include solid-waste management, water supply, drainage and sewerage systems, and public roads. It runs hospitals, health centres, primary schools and a local bus service. City planning also resides with the MCGM; it implements development plans and sanctions building proposals.[7] The planning function is jointly undertaken with the Mumbai Metropolitan Regional Development Authority (MRDA) and the Maharashtra Housing and Area Development Authority (MHADA). The former has jurisdiction over the agglomeration area and the latter over city-wide infrastructure when foreign funding is obtained.[8]

The largest department in terms of employment is the conservancy department (solid-waste management), whose staff are also the most strongly unionized. This is in keeping with the situation in other large cities in India, which show similar patterns of staffing and organization (Baud et al. 2004). Adding new employees to this department has often been a debated issue as it is seen to increase the strength of an outspoken trade union. To cut down expenditures and reduce deficits a policy of restriction on new staff recruitment has been practised since 1995.

RESEARCH METHODOLOGY

The analysis of the two types of 'invited spaces' was done as follows. The analysis of the political representation at electoral ward level was carried out by N. Nainan in 2001 as part of a postgraduate study on NGO participation in the decentralization process in Mumbai (Nainan 2001). The data collected for analysing the decentralization process to ward committees consisted of strategic discussions with four councillors, two ward officers, and NGOs and CBOs (twenty-four) working in various areas of Mumbai. It was also complemented by interviews with councillors who are party leaders (three) and ward officers (four), and further interviews with fourteen councillors in different wards (see Table 1.2). It was followed up by a study of a large (administrative) ward in the north of Mumbai, where thirteen councillors and three ward officers were interviewed and observed for a three-month period (Vogel 2005).

The analysis of the ALM programme was undertaken within the framework of a larger comparative study of three mega-cities in India on new forms of urban governance.[9] In that research project, a number of smaller studies were carried out which this study drew upon for a background knowledge of the decentralization processes in Mumbai (Nainan 2001), and on the first phase of the ALM programme (Redkar 2004). The bulk of the data on ALMs and their activities was collected by undertaking a sample survey from the complete list of ALMs provided by the MCGM on ten administrative wards (out of twenty-four administrative wards[10]). Almost 30 per cent of the 217 ALMs found in these 10 administrative wards were interviewed using a standard questionnaire developed on the basis of exploratory interviews with active ALMs (see Table 1.1). Interviews were conducted with the leaders of the ALMs who were identified on the basis of their holding the position of either president or secretary in the ALM. Residential ALMs were selected—as the focus of this study is in the extent to which citizens were organizing and the ALMs based at commercial company premises or government offices were not included.[11] These interviews were complemented by interviews with councillors and MCGM officers to get their perspectives on the ALM programme.[12] Secondary data such as lists of ALMs, newspaper articles as well as documents put up on the Karmayog website was also studied.

Producing 'Invited Spaces'

In opening up new 'invited spaces', what mandates did local government in Mumbai give and what groups did it recognize? To what extent did the invited groups claim more or different spaces than those provided?

The MCGM has two sides: the political and the executive (see Figure 1.1). These two wings of the MCGM have simultaneously produced invited spaces in the city of Mumbai. Within the 'deliberative wing', elected representatives became part of ward committees

TABLE 1.1: CENSUS AND SAMPLE OF ALMs IN SELECTED ADMINISTRATIVE WARDS IN MUMBAI[13]

Administrative Wards	Census of ALMs	Contactable ALMs	Sample of ALMs
E-Ward	12	4	–
H-East	14	5	8
H-West	56 (73 in 2005)	24	23
K-East	19	5	–
K-West	63 (23 in 2005)	25	–
M-East	25	16	9
M-West	19	5	18
P-South	12	1	–
P-North	24	2	–
R-North	24	2	–
R-Central	13	3	–
R-South	27	7	–

Source: Karmayog site, April 2006.

TABLE 1.2: COUNCILLORS: CENSUS OF SELECTED WARDS AND COUNCILLORS INTERVIEWED

Administrative Wards	No. of Councillors in Concerned Wards	No. of Councillors Interviewed
E-Ward	9	
H-East	11	--
H-West	7	
K-East	15	2
K-West	13	–
M-East	11	2, 8
M-West	8	3
P-South	6	
P-North	13	13
R-North	15	7
R-Central	9	
R-South	7	3
Total in relevant wards	124	38 (31%)

Source: No. of total Councillors derived from BMC website.
Note: Only wards which have ALMs are covered in this table.

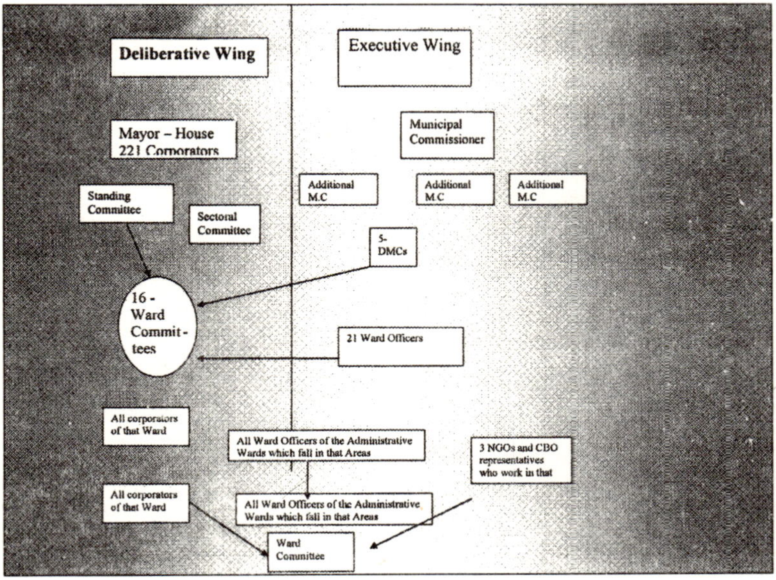

Source: N. Nainan, 2001.

FIGURE 1.1: MUMBAI CORPORATION GOVERNMENT: ADMINISTRATIVE AND POLITICAL WINGS

at the level of the administrative wards (24). Within the executive wing a space was created for Advanced Locality Management (ALM) at neighbourhood levels.[14] This section examines how these two invited spaces differs in their membership and mandate and which groups of citizens it recognizes.

The deliberative wing of the MCGM consists of the 227 municipal councillors directly elected by the city's voting population. Each councillor is allocated an annual budget of Rs. 2 million ($43,478) to undertake developmental work in his or her constituency.[15] The executive wing includes its employees (around 160,000 employees). These two wings of local government come together at the administrative ward level (24), which each have a ward office and a ward committee. There are sixteen ward committees formed, combining between 15 to 20 electoral wards in each committee. The councillors, the ward officer, and possibly co-opted CBOs (to a maximum of three) form the ward committees.

The two arms of the MCGM compete with each other for power and resources. The conflict between these two groups has its roots in the relationship between the Government of Maharashtra and the MCGM. Despite the passing of the 74th Constitutional Amendment, which aimed at strengthening local self-government, power within the MCGM is with senior IAS officers appointed by the state government (Pinto forthcoming; Nainan and Baud forthcoming). Competition becomes fiercer when different parties rule the city and the state—the Shiv Sena has ruled the MCGM since 1985 while the state has been ruled by the Congress.[16] Thus the control of the MCGM by state-appointed IAS officers is much resented by the elected representatives of the city.

The elected councillors have a strong mandate from low-income voters in slum areas. It is estimated that at least 167 wards of the 227 (about 73 per cent of election wards) are slum wards, and the rest are mixed. An analysis of voting patterns of the 1997 corporation elections shows that slum residence is correlated with high levels of voting (Baud, Pfeffer, Sridharan and Nainan 2006). This suggests that councillors will represent the needs of slum residents as they recognize them as their main constituency (see also Vogel 2005).

The two main spaces identified, then, are the ward committee which come under the Deliberative Wing, and the ALMs which come under the Executive Wing, both of which models emerged around 2000–1.

Most ALMs were formed between 2002–5. Since then, the process has slowed down (Table 1.3). ALMs have come up either in housing colonies (Parsi colony, Tata power colony) or in the Christian communities of Bandra (H-West) and Andheri (K-West), building on existing organizations. The large role of the Christian community is probably due to the role played by the basic Christian communities, which are attached to churches and church-based NGOs. ALMs were also being promoted by organizations such as Action Good Governance Network India—AGNI—an advocacy NGO with close ties to Bombay First, a lobby of the new commercial sector.[17]

ALMs are unevenly spread across the city (Figure 1.2). The spatial coverage is much stronger in some administrative wards than in others. A study of ALMs found that only 67 of the 700 ALMs on the MCGM list could be contacted. Useful data could only be gathered from 45, of which 22 were in M-Ward (Palnitkar et al. 2005). This confirms the findings in the present study where the largest numbers of ALMs were found in M-Ward.

TABLE 1.3: YEAR OF ESTABLISHMENT OF ALMs BY ADMINISTRATIVE WARDS IN MUMBAI

Year of Establishment of ALM	H/West	M/East	M/West	R/South	Total
1998–9	2	1	2	0	5
2000–1	0	1	6	1	8
2001–2	2	0	2	0	4
2002–3	6	2	1	2	11
2003–4	7	0	0	0	7
2004–5	2	3	4	4	13
2005–6	0	0	0	3	3
1999–2000	0	0	2	0	2
Not available	4	2	1	0	7
Total	23	9	18	10	60

Source: Sample survey in 4 wards, 2005.

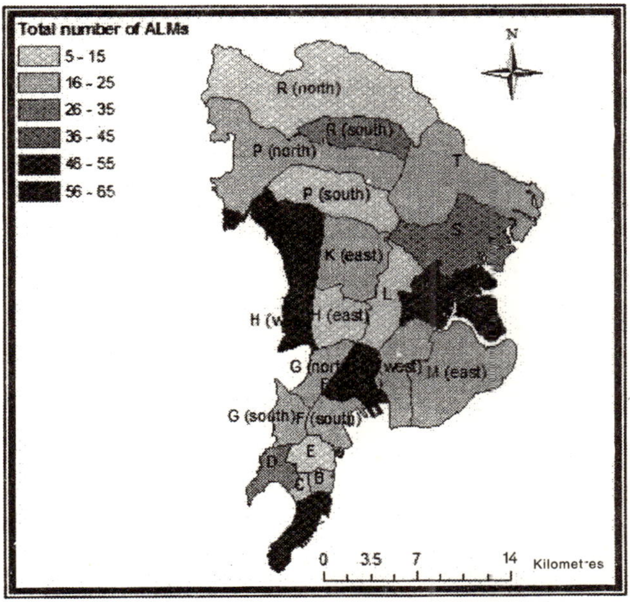

FIGURE 1.2: SPREAD OF ALMs BY ADMINISTRATIVE WARDS IN MUMBAI (KARMAYOG WEBSITE APRIL 2006)[18]

Wards Committees	Number of Councillors	Wards Committees	Number of Councillors
A, B&E	16	P-South	8
C&D	13	P-North	14
F-South and F North	19	R-South	8
G-North	10	R-North	15
G-North	13	M-East and M-West	19
H-East and H-West	18	S & T	20
K-East	15	L	14
K-West	13	N	12

FIGURE 1.3: NUMBER OF COUNCILLORS BY WARD COMMITTEES PER ADMINISTRATIVE WARDS

Membership in 'Invited Spaces'

A ward committee includes all ten to twenty elected councillors with the Ward Officer as the member secretary (Fig. 1.3). There is also a provision for nominating three NGO/CBO members to the ward committee. The advisory membership for NGOs/CBOs to the ward committees is tightly controlled by the councillors, who use this arena to voice the needs and claims of the low-income residents (Vogel 2006; Nainan 2001). Currently, the NGO/CBO seats in the ward committees are largely occupied by political party nominees (Nainan and Baud forthcoming).

The ALMs on the other hand have been formed by housing co-operative societies (or their federations) and street-based residents' organizations. They vary in membership, size and composition. ALMs which mainly include residents have between 100 and 200 people (13 ALMs) or 200 and 300 people as members (14 ALMs). Eight of the ALMs are much larger (more than five hunred residential members each). These members usually reside in housing society complexes (high-rise buildings), which have a mandatory organization for collective measures in and around the housing complex. This makes it relatively easy to build up a further agenda on an existing structure (Table 1.4).

Two-thirds of the ALMs from the sample survey also have commercial establishments as members. The survey found that 34 per cent have up to ten commercial establishments as members, and 20 per cent more than 10 (Table 1.5). There are differences between the wards in the extent to which commercial establishments are

TABLE 1.4: NUMBER OF RESIDENT MEMBERS BY WARD

Number of Resident Members	Name of Ward				Total
	H-West	M-East	M-West	R-South	
Less than 50	6	3	3	1	13
51–100	0	0	2	4	6
101–200	4	1	6	2	13
200–300	7	2	3	2	14
300–400	2	2	1	0	5
400–500	1	0	0	0	1
500–1000	2	0	2	0	4
1000 more	1	1	1	1	4
Total	23	9	18	10	60

TABLE 1.5: NUMBER OF COMMERCIAL MEMBERS BY WARD

Number of Commercial Members	Name of Ward				Total
	H-West	M-East	M-West	R-South	
0	12	4	4	1	21
1–10	10	2	10	5	27
> – 10	1	3	4	4	12
Total	23	9	18	10	60

members. R-South and M-West have the most ALMs with commercial members, whereas in H-West and M-East only half the ALMs have commercial members. The number of political party members is limited: in M-West and R-south 20 per cent of the ALMs have political party members (Table 1.6). ALMs have contrasting views on membership of political party adherents—some consider it a good channel into party support for their issues; others want to avoid party politics because it could undermine their capacity to push through their own agenda.

The membership of the two 'spaces' shows a clear divide based on the citizens they aim to represent. It also shows a different geographic-scale level. While the slum residents and their ward councillors are represented through the ward committee at the administrative ward levels, middle-class communities are represented at the colony or street level through the ALMs.

TABLE 1.6: NUMBER OF POLITICAL PARTY MEMBERS

Number of Political Party Members	Name of Ward				Total
	H-West	M-East	M-West	R-South	
0	22	8	14	8	52
1	1	1	2	1	5
2	0	0	1	1	2
3	0	0	1	0	1
Total	23	9	18	10	60

MANDATES GIVEN BY GOVERNMENT

The mandate of the ward committee is based on the 74th Amendment to the Constitution from which the state government has selected a number of areas which it recommends for implementation. Implementation at the ward level has been diluted to a platform for responding to civic grievances of citizens and giving budgetary recommendation along with a small budget to undertake projects.[19]

The mandate of the ALMs was provided by the executive wing of the MCGM while dealing with solid waste management (SWM).[20] As a ban on new staff recruitment existed within the MCGM, the executive wing evolved new strategies to expand solid waste collection to larger sections of the city by contracting-out such activities. One strategy was to involve housing cooperative societies and their associations in SWM, using the concept of ALM.[21] Thus the mandate for ALMs derives from the attempts by senior officers to solve a problem within given constraints. Therefore, despite a lack of a state-level mandate, the ALMs have good access to various executive departments within the MCGM.

An ALM is to cover a neighbourhood or street with about 1,000 citizens, and to be registered by the municipal ward office. The issues addressed by the ALM are to include garbage clearance, composting, drainage, water supply, beautification, encroachments, road excavation, pothole filling, roads and pavement levelling, surfacing, and management of stray animals.[22] Many residents have taken the responsibility of segregating garbage at source, recycling and composting. At a later stage, street waste pickers were also involved in recycling waste (Redkar 2004). The MCGM supported the initiative by addressing grievances of residents with alacrity (Palnitkar et al. 2005).

There is an overlap between the ward committee and the ALMs in their focus, as both address issues of SWM. However, ALMs are organized user groups, whereas ward committee members are elected representatives voicing the concerns of all citizens living in the ward. The role of both is distinct, as ALMs are engaged in maintenance and operation services, whereas the ward committee has a planning and decision-making role.

CLAIMING 'SPACE'

The second question concerns what 'space' the two types of groups claim for themselves in addition to the mandate provided by government.

Councillors have expanded their mandate formally and informally in several ways. Formal claims were established when the councillors persuaded the state and local governments to implement the ward committee legislation. Informally, councillors in north Mumbai spent a great deal of time responding to individual slum citizens' demands for basic amenities, which could be seen as part of their mandate, but also on counselling women with family problems, which is not (Vogel 2005). Other councillors were also constrained to comply with the demands made by their political party leaders and the real estate development activities in their areas (Nainan 2008).

The original mandate for the ALMs consisted mainly of monitoring and improving one of the most visible basic services at the neighbourhood level—SWM. This was supported by the MCGM by its cleaning of construction waste from roads and more effective collection of waste at neighbourhood level. This is reflected in the number of ALMs that carry out this activity as part of their programme. They are involved in segregation of dry and wet waste and house-to-house collection. Eighty per cent of the ALMs are involved in one or the other of these activities, with 10 per cent working in collection activities (mainly in M-West), and 90 per cent involved in segregation.

However, the ALMs have started branching out into other activities, mainly concentrating on monitoring basic services in their neighbourhood and including other issues which members consider important. Table 1.7 shows the activities of ALMs in the various wards.

TABLE 1.7: ACTIVITIES TAKEN UP BY THE ALMs PER WARD IN ABS. NO. AND PERCENTAGE

	Name of Ward				Total
	H-West	M-East	M-West	R-South	
Activities taken up in water management	4 (17)	3 (33)	1 (16)	4 (40)	12 (20)
Activities taken up in sewerage management	8 (35)	5 (56)	7 (39)	6 (60)	26 (43)
Activities in SWM	20 (87)	6 (66)	15 (83)	8 (80)	49 (82)
Park/street beautification	16 (70)	6 (66)	9 (50)	4 (40)	35(58)
Composting	1 (4)	–	4 (22)	–	5 (8)
Maintenance in the housing society	2 (8)	3 (33)	9 (50)	2 (20)	16 (27)
Total number of ALMs	23	9	18	10	60

Source: Sample survey, 2005.
Notes: None of the ALMs dealt with electricity management.
Percentage are given in parentheses.

Table 1.7 shows that the second most widespread activity concerns 'street beautification' or greening. Many streets still have open concrete drains along the side of the road. The importance given to sewerage management is also shown by the fact that more than 40 per cent of the ALMs have cleaned and closed street drains. ALMs close these drains by constructing and filling planters over them, and planting bushes and trees along the roads. Almost 60 per cent of the ALMs have beautified the streets in their own neighbourhoods. Almost 30 per cent of the ALMs are also more active in maintaining the area around the housing complexes, as well as the complexes themselves, in their neighbourhoods. This seems to be a spin-off of a higher level of group interaction and commitment to collective activities. Finally, some 20 per cent of the ALMs have taken up activities in water management.

This data confirms Zerah's (2006) impressions of ALMs, who distinguished two types of ALMs—the 'civic-minded' ALMs and those based on 'utilitarian mobilization'. The latter includes ALMs concerned mostly with specific issues of their own area. They use their bargaining power, even with political representatives, and exert continuous pressure over a short period of time. Once their objective is achieved, they become much less active. The civic-minded ALMs show a 'civic' type of mobilization, positioning themselves as civic-minded people with broader interests. Such ALMs are usually very active and their members were active before the creation of the ALMs (participation in local newsletters, involvement in beautification schemes).

In conclusion, one can say that in both the 'invited spaces' created by local and state governments, councillors and the ALMs have gone beyond their original mandates and are actively taking up issues which concern their respective constituencies—be it that councillors are found to be focused much more on low-income residents who feel powerless and the ALMs represent middle-class residents who are feeling more powerful in their own neighbourhoods. Although the ALMs started out with the purpose of improving the rights of citizens as 'consumers of services', they have gradually started to realize that they need a role in 'setting the political agenda'.

Interface with the Government

The interface with government at the administrative ward level is embedded in the set-up of the ward committee, where ward officers and councillors have to work together. The situation since the 74th Amendment has changed fairly radically. Before the formation of the ward committees, councillors visited ward officers to get projects sanctioned and implemented, sharing with them a portion of the money involved. Now, the ward officer has to be present at the monthly meetings of the ward committee, and has to get administrative sanctions from the councillors to implement projects.[23]

Relations between councillors and ward officers are usually tense. Elected representatives believe that ward officers block the effective serving of their 'clients', while the officers perceive elected representatives to be lacking the necessary education to make 'engineering' decisions.

Outcomes of discussions with councillors in two wards indicated the following views (Nainan 2001). The majority of the councillors felt that the establishment of ward committees gave them more powers.[24] The councillors listed the positive changes experienced as follows:

— Clearer budgetary provisions for their wards; with monitoring systems in place;
— Better monitoring of project implementation, with officers reporting on project progress;
— Pressurizing non-performing officers by calling them to joint meetings of Ward Committee Members and BMC officials;
— Councillors have to come up with proposals for their wards, so they keep in touch with their constituency's needs and grievances;
— Speedier provision of services;
— Rise in status as a public official.

The newly acquired powers are limited, so some wards committee members are searching for means to expand their powers. Because budget allocations to the wards are now published, transparency between the administrative and elected representatives has increased. The question is whether they will be willing to share it further with NGOs, when these become members of the wards committees. Information on the ward budgets has not percolated down to members of the community or to the NGOs interviewed, none of whom had any information about the ward budgets in 2001.

However, councillors also have a regular interface with the deliberative wing of government through their city-wide council and its committees. This interface has not been systematically analysed by anyone as yet; preliminary interviews indicate that the councillor-party bosses (city-wide) relations are very influential in determining allocations of councillors to committees dominated by the party in power (Vogel 2005).

The ALM programme also provides for direct and regular contact with local government. However, local government consists of a number of different departments providing services all over the corporation area, as well as the area-based ward offices which have a mandate for carrying out particular activities in one administrative ward only. The survey examined several possible interfaces by activity; with the ward office in their area; with different corporation departments; with state government organizations; or with NGOs/ private companies. Finally, ALM relations with local councillors and party politicians were considered.

Two-thirds of the ALMs were aware of the ward office, with no significant differences between the four wards (Table 1.8). Representatives visited the ward office for the following reasons: to raise

TABLE 1.8: AWARENESS OF WARD OFFICE AMONG ALMs BY WARD

	Name of Ward				Total
	H-West	M-East	M-West	R-South	
Yes	17	5	14	5	41
No	1	2	1	3	7
Not applicable	5	2	3	2	12
Total	23	9	18	10	60

Source: Survey of ALMs, 2005.

grievances and complaints (72 per cent), to seek help (63 per cent), and to get expert advice (62 per cent). They also held their ALM meetings with the ward officer and councillors at the ward office. These should be held once a month. However, this varies by ward office, depending on the interest the ward officer takes in the initiative.

The ALMs prefer to work with the executive side of government in their various activities. They work almost twice as often with the ward officer as with the ward councillor in their main activities of SWM, sewerage and water issues (Table 1.9).

ALMs also work with the specific departments of the MCGM at the city-wide level. Almost half the ALMs had contacts with the sewerage department, 70 per cent worked with the SWM department, 34 per cent with the garden department, and 10 per cent with the water department. This reflects the focus of the activities promoted by the ALMs and the interest of the SWM department with which the programme originated.

TABLE 1.9: PERCENTAGE OF ALMs WORKING WITH WARD OFFICERS AND COUNCILLORS IN MAIN ACTIVITIES

	Working with Ward Officers	Working with Councillors	Working with Wards Committee
SWM	55	20	8.3
Composting	50	20	5.0
Sewerage	30	20	1.7

Source: Survey of ALMs, 2005.

ALM leaders indicated that trust between them and the corporation officers had gradually built up, which improved the response they received from officers on their complaints, although that varied from issue to issue. The ALMs also indicated that their experiences with higher officers at the corporation level were more encouraging than at the ward level.

Although the awareness amongst ALMs on wards committees is high, it does not translate into approaching the ward committees or councillors to address their issues (Table 1.9). Two-thirds of the ALM leaders did contact the respective councillors; however, only half of them visited the councillors occasionally on issues in which the councillors have some role to play. The experience of ALMs with politicians within the wider city is not one of cooperation from the latter; 10 per cent of the ALMs felt that politicians were not interested in ALMs, 7 per cent felt that the politicians did not know enough about ALMs, and 7 per cent felt that politicians see ALMs as competitors (Table 1.10). Councillors also feel antagonistic toward ALMs, as indicated in the newspaper quotes (see Box 1.1).

The ALMs were also asked about possible requests for bribes which they had received from government or elected officials. This turned out to be low: 7 per cent had experienced requests for bribes by politicians and 8 per cent by corporation officers. However, in contrast, when asked to identify problems faced by the MCGM, 52 per

TABLE 1.10: EXPERIENCES OF ALM MEMBERS WITH POLITICIANS

	Actual	Percentage
No experience with politicians		
Probable reasons for not supporting ALMs	37	61
Did not know about ALMs	4	7
Politicians did not like ALMs	1	2
They are not interested	6	10
Councillors view ALMs as political competitors	4	7
ALM members do not approach them	2	3
Probable reason for Supporting ALMs		
Selective support for votes	5	8
Cooperative	2	3
Total	61	100

Box 1.1: Councillors' Perception of Relations with ALMs

The councillors complained that they are the elected representatives of the ward, and best suited to tackle civic problems. According to them, citizens' groups cannot think beyond their lanes and are unwilling to listen to reason. They keep on insisting that a particular work be done immediately and this leads to a clash of interests.

In the words of a BJP councillor, 'Elected representatives are better suited to tackle problems like lack of funds and labour for example. We understand them but these citizens' groups are unwilling to listen to reason and insist on a particular work being done immediately' (*TOI*, 17 February 2005).

According to an NCP councillor, 'Citizens will create the impression that councillors are incompetent and NGOs are doing all the work. NGOs are already represented in the ward committees along with the Councillors. So the LACCs are really not required' (*TOI*, 17 February 2005).

A Congress councillor: 'Gang war. That's the only word to describe their working' (*Indian Express*, 1 July 2005).

A Congress Party woman councillor: 'I cannot do any work because of the ALMs. Please get this harassment stopped' (*Indian Express*, 1 July 2005).

cent of those interviewed felt the root of the problem was in the corrupt practices of the corporation. The majority of the ALMs were very positive about the current changes in the MCGM and were optimistic about its future. According to 62 per cent of them, the problems of the MCGM's lack of co-ordination with different agencies; 57 per cent of the interviewed believed it was due to the quality of municipal staff, and half the respondents stated it was to do with the politics of the MCGM.

This implies that the two interfaces for citizens and local government represent different constituencies and do not work together. The ALM-executive government departments work with middle-class citizens and the councillors and ward officers in the ward committee work with low-income groups.

Interface of ALMs with NGOs

The AGNI, an NGO, was established in 1999 and functions as a network and advocacy group on local governance issues in Mumbai. Among its key leaders are ex-bureaucrats and media people. AGNI was assigned an in-formal role in facilitating the formation, networking and capacity-building of ALMs and ALM networks. Thus from their very formation the ALMs came in contact with AGNI and often became members of its network. The network was further strengthened as AGNI took on the role of representing the political voice of middle-class citizens at the city and state level. Among the various campaigns that it took up, AGNI's efforts to scuttle an MCGM workers' strike brought it into the limelight (Box 1.2).

Expanding Spaces, Excluding Others?

Finally, the question is taken up about what changes in citizenship these invited spaces have brought about in the neighbourhoods where ward committees and ALMs are active (for the groups involved, as well as for other groups in the neighbourhood who are excluded).

Ward committees generally see NGOs and CBOs as the representatives of residents with complaints and protests, so that the relationship is generally one of confrontation. They make an exception for a few CBO organizations using service delivery strategies, which partner with government at the local level. This occurs largely in sectors such as education, health and SWM.[26] Generally, NGOs do not work with the deliberative wing of the MCGM at city level, and the relationship with ward councillors is full of conflict and confrontation for all types of NGOs. NGOs perceive councillors as political opportunists, corrupt and sometimes even as criminals. NGOs recognize themselves to be a threat to the councillors' power base, and are perceived by them as competitors.

NGOs work more generally with the executive arm of the MCGM at city level. The majority of the NGOs associate with the administrative departments for services at ward level. Organizations with a good relation with the central departments of the MCGM may have a less close or even conflictive relationship at the ward level. This means that councillors especially, and ward officers to a lesser degree, prefer not to expand the space for middle-class citizens who are organized in NGOs or ALMs. Councillors on wards committees

Box 1.2: AGNI's Actions against Municipal Workers' Union

On the eve of Diwali in October 2000, 140,000 workers of the MCGM went on a two-day strike called by the largest union of municipal workers,[25] after the Mayor of Mumbai refused union demands for higher bonus and ex-gratia payments. This strike hampered the functioning of the city, as taps dried up, garbage piled up on the streets, and municipal hospital staff joined the strike. (*Indian Express*, 26 October 2000)

As a strategy to control the growing disruption of life in the city nearly 200 councillors decided to support strikers' demands by passing a unanimous resolution to pay 65 per cent of the bonus to municipal employees. However, AGNI's vice-chairman (IAS), former municipal commissioner and chief secretary of the Maharashtra government approached the High Court of Bombay asking for urgent interim relief on his petition admitted in 1997, which challenged high salaries and bonus to civic employees.

The Bombay High Court restrained the MCGM administration from giving in to worker demands and struck down the councillor resolution. The Municipal Workers Union leader was reported to have challenged the 'citizen groups and non-governmental organizations to lift garbage from the roads . . . no one will be available as nobody has the stamina to do the kind of work that BMC workers do' (2000, rediff.com/news).

Under similar conditions the following year in October 2001, (Times News Network), AGNI along with various member ALMs, pressurized the state government to put an end to the municipal workers' threat to strike the second time based on the essential services maintenance. The union did not go ahead with the strike and since then it has only issued threats or undertaken one-day-strikes keeping essential services untouched.

see their constituency as being low-income residents who need their political clout to gain access to resources, such as housing and basic and social services. However, they want to keep them dependent on themselves and be the 'brokers' through whom resources are channelled when they are directed towards low-income residents, for example, the SAP programme (see Desai 2006).[27]

ALMs prefer not to deal with the political side of government but have a strong preference for the executive wing at either city or administrative ward level. The survey of 60 ALMs showed that 70 per cent perceived positive results in their quality of life from the ALM work in terms of cleaner roads, regular garbage pick-up, more green spaces and organized groups. This suggests that they have been able to claim more public policy and implementation 'space' as user groups.

However, exclusionary processes are also taking place. In the wards where ALMs are active, people from the slum areas are usually not included. The original idea of the SWM department of the corporation was that both slums and higher-income areas would work together in improving SWM. However, the slum representatives (youth who were interested in taking up cleaning activities) were said to feel intimidated by the ALM meetings. The use of the English language and formalized processes requiring writing and reading written proposals led to the gradual exclusion of slum representatives (Redkar, pers.com. May 2006).[28]

Zerah's survey also indicates that ALMs in other wards have lobbied to exclude groups from their neighbourhoods, particularly hawkers on the streets (Zerah 2006).[29] The present survey also found the exclusion of other groups as well as efforts for the inclusion of marginalized groups. The general direction of PIL at this moment in India suggests that in further studies it will be important to include both sides of the picture—both the increasing inclusion of mainly middle-class citizens in interfaces with the executive side of government as well as the exclusion of vulnerable groups who are not well represented (cf. Ramanathan 2006).

Effects on Service Delivery and Political Rights?

This section deals with the question of what the outcomes of 'invited spaces' have been for the quality of services provided and the political rights of different groups of residents. In the middle-class (and elite) areas where the majority of ALMs were formed, ALM respondents have indicated that service delivery has improved (70 per cent of respondents). Particularly the responsiveness of local MCGM employees has been greater than before. In low-income areas, the lack of ALM action has meant that service delivery presumably has not changed, unless it has done so under the Slum Adoption Programme.

If one looks at citizenship rights, one will see a clear expansion of 'spaces'—beyond the mandate and interface provided in the initial 'invited spaces'. Middle-class citizens, through their collective action in ALMs, are opening up further 'negotiated spaces' in two ways. They are claiming more and better services on a priority basis, and are organizing to exclude groups from their neighbourhoods they feel are 'unwanted' (slums, hawkers, unorganized economic activities). Secondly, they are moving from user groups to chooser groups as citizens, claiming a larger political space at ward and city level, although this is heavily contested.

The political negotiating of space has shown up most clearly in a number of recent developments around ALMs and Local Area Citizens Committees (LACC). Since the success of ALMs in high-income areas (around 2004), the MCGM-executive wing wants to expand the programme of ALMs to all electoral wards, and to include councillors into this set-up. The idea was that a local area committee consisting of the ward officer, residents and councillors would have weekly meetings and have an expanded mandate (beyond SWM) to deal with complaints. The first LACCs (about 30) started pressurizing the councillors in the electoral wards in terms of their effectiveness. When the councillors began to feel threatened, they organized a protest at the city-wide council level, and urged the municipal commissioner of the MCGM to disband all such committees (*TOI*, 19 February 2005). As a result, a proposal is now on the table with the MCGM that LACCs should work at an intermediary level between electoral and administrative wards, so that the contestation between political representatives and CBOs would be reduced. In the meantime, ALMs (and LACCs) have supported and candidates and one set of ALMs has put forward their own candidates for the local elections held in 2007.

CONCLUSION

Coming back to the main question raised in this chapter, namely, whether 'invited spaces' provides effective channels for citizens to make their voices heard, one can draw the following conclusions. There are contrasting 'invited spaces' in Mumbai which each provide effective channels for their particular social constituency. The ALMs provide a channel for the middle-class residents to directly deal with the executive wing of local government; the ward committees provide 'effective' channels for vulnerable groups to address local government on an individual basis to improve their quality of life situation. The opportunity for collective action, which the ALMs have, is not usual in the case of the councillors and ward committees. The role of the political parties at the city level limits the autonomy of the councillors in certain areas, and keeps them as well as their constituencies dependent on higher political authorities.

The widening space of the ALMs is reflected in the negotiating process, which is taking place in the ALM-executive wing of local government. There the mandate provided is being expanded and widened to include other political spaces at higher scale levels (e.g. the Citizen Action Group working at the city and metropolitan level). Its effectiveness can be deduced from the backlash of political representatives, who fear a diminishing of their power.

Finally, this means that we find two models of what we prefer to call 'negotiated spaces'. For low-income vulnerable groups of citizens, the political space remains the one through which they are able—to some extent—negotiate rights. For middle-class citizens, an 'executive space' is opening up which increases their direct negotiating power with local government, and provides a basis for collection organization to expand their rights at the city-wide level. To what extent is there a 'democratic deficit' in these contrasting models? It is clear that different groups of citizens have different rights and obligations in Mumbai—and that power is shifting slowly in favour of the middle-class. This can make slum dwellers and vulnerable groups even more dependent on the political will of representatives working for them. Vertical and horizontal accountability has increased for the middle-class, as citizens can now hold their government to account to some extent.

NOTES

1. Of course, the implementation of such rehabilitation schemes and housing programmes has always been very uneven in the last 40 years (see Desai 2003; de Wit 1997; van Eerd 2003).
2. The Mumbai Metropolitan region has a population of almost 24 million people (Sivaramakrishnan, Kundu and Singh 2005).
3. See, e.g. H. van Wersch (1992). *The Bombay Textile Strike, 1982–3*. Delhi: Oxford University Press.

4. Risbud (2003) bases her discussion on the report prepared by YUVA and Montgomery-Watson (2000–1) for Slum Sanitation within the Mumbai Sewerage Disposal Project.
5. Pavement dwellers and chawls—i.e. premises for rent constructed originally by factory owners—are included in slums.
6. This has to be done under the auspices of the state Slum Development Authority.
7. As per the Development Control Rules.
8. The MCGM has a yearly budget of Rs. 12,000 crore (about US $ 300,000,000) and over 150,000 regular employees. It is probably the largest Municipal Corporation in India (Sivaramakrishnan, Kundu, Singh 2005). Its revenues come from octroi and property taxes in almost equal proportions, and it is one of the few corporations which generate the major part of their revenues internally (Rath 2006).
9. An Indo-Dutch Programme on Alternatives to Development (IDPAD); project during Phase Five 2003–6.
10. The full list of ALMs was compiled only in April 2006, as a result of the discussions held in 2005 on the lack of a complete overview with the MCGM.
11. The University of Amsterdam works with the Centre de Sciences Humaines (CSH) group in clubbing two sets of data on ALMs in Mumbai; Zerah's sample survey was carried out mainly in two wards (H-West and H-East), consisting of 60 interviews. The combined results will be published later.
12. We would like to thank Mrs Nutan Shivtare for interviewing different stakeholders, Harpreet Kaur for developing notes which feed into this article and Seema Redkar for introducing the research team to various ALMs for a set of exploratory interviews.
13. The list of ALMs is a formal list. A second column in the Karmayog site indicates which ALMs were actually active in terms of the researchers being able to contact them (only 26 per cent).
14. Since this initiative, further decentralization is taking place to the electoral ward level, where the initiative has named them Local Area Citizens Committees (LACCs).
15. Each councillor is paid a sitting allowance for attending meetings of the BMC (Rs. 2,700 per month). They also get a free bus pass to travel by the BMC-owned public transport utility BEST within the city during their term of office.
16. With the exception of 1995–2001 when the Shiv Sena also ruled at the state level.
17. The web page of AGNI identifies its role as 'AGNI helps citizens form a body called an ALM', and then goes on to describe the steps involved in forming an ALM, getting linked to the local ward office.

18. The official picture presented here is somewhat nuanced by knowledgeable insiders, who indicate that the majority of the ALMs in a ward are not functioning ones.
19. (a) Redress common grievances of citizens, connected with local municipal services;
    (b) Make recommendations on existing proposals for expenditures in the ward before they are forwarded to the commissioner;
    (c) Grant administrative approval and financial sanction to existing plans for municipal works within the area of the ward committee up to a limit of Rs. 500,000 (US $ 11,500); and
    (d) Move on any other powers the corporation may delegate to a ward committee.
20. SWM is one of the major activities of local governments, which absorbs a major part of their staff and finances.
21. An alternative model developed for low-income areas, called the Slum Adoption Programme (SAP), was also directed towards more effective SWM.
22. Web page of AGNI.
23. Sharing of the money received for getting projects cleared, or cuts from contractors, still remains a part of the process.
24. Four councillors were interviewed for this study, two from each ward. Three of them were from different political parties. The fourth was an independent, and one of the four was a woman. In one ward, the majority of the councillors were from the Shiv Sena, whereas in the other ward, the representation was across the board.
25. Municipal Mazdoor Union, lead by Sharad Rao with George Fernandes as its leader who had by then joined the BJP-lead coalition government and was defence minister in 1998. BJP has an alliance with the Shiv Sena in Maharashtra.
26. Two of the three sectors in which NGOs are in partnership with the BMC—health and SWM—are programmes with international funding, in which there are national guidelines which clearly prescribe NGO participation. Even with the executive wing of the BMC, participation of NGOs is easier said than done. NGOs are included at the implementation level only under severe prescriptive conditions.
27. In the slum areas where the SAP was promoted by the MCGM by contracting out solid-waste collection and slum cleaning to CBOs, its implementation has strengthened the existing patron-client relation–ships between slum residents and local councillors.
28. Such slum areas now generally fall under the SAP established in 1998 as part of a cleanliness drive by the MCGM (Redkar 2004). Within the SAP, CBOs are treated as commercial entities supported by municipal financing for carrying out SWM, collection and segregation activities (Desai 2006).

29. This phenomenon seems to be restricted to the one administrative ward where Zerah did her fieldwork. It was not confirmed for the other wards in a later survey by Baud and Nainan in the other wards.

REFERENCES

Baud, I.S.A. (2004), *Learning from the South: Placing Governance in International Development Studies*. Amsterdam: University of Amsterdam.

Baud, I.S.A., J. Post et al. (2004), *Solid Waste Management and Recycling: Actors, Partnerships and Policies in Hyderabad, India and Nairobi, Kenya*. New York, Kluwer Academic.

Baud, I.S.A. et al. (2006), 'Matching Knowledge to Urban Governance: Mapping Deprivations in Three Indian Mega-cities'. Paper presented at the Conference New Forms of Urban Governance in Indian Mega-cities, 20–21 June, New Delhi, JNU.

Baud, I.S.A. and R. Dhanalakshmi (2007), 'Multi-actor Arrangements in Urban Environmental Services: New Forms of Governance in Indian Mega-cities', *Cities* 42(2): 133–47.

Cornwall, A. (2004), 'Introduction, New Democratic Spaces? The Politics and Dynamics of Institutionalized Participation', *IDS Bulletin*, 35(2): 1–10.

De Wit, J. (1997), *Poverty, Policy, and Politics in Madras Slums: Dynamics of Survival, Gender and Leadership*. Delhi: Sage.

Desai, P. (2003), 'Institutional Dimensions of Program Planning and Implementation: Three Cases of Squatter Upgrading in Mumbai, India'. PhD thesis, Free University, 31 January.

——— (2006), 'Slum Adoption Program: Background Paper'. IDPAD Project Paper New Forms of Urban Governance.

Eerd, van M. (2003). 'Local Initiatives in Relocation: The State and NGOs as Partners'?, PhD thesis, University of Leiden.

Fung, A. and E.O. Wright (eds.), *Deepening Democracy: Institutional Innovation in Empowered Participatory Governance*. London: Verso.

Gaventa, J. (2006), *Triumph, Deficit of Contestation? Deepening the 'Deepening Democracy' Debate*, WP 264, IDS, Brighton.

Harris, N. (2003), 'Globalisation and Management of Cities', *Economic and Political Weekly* 48(25): 2535–43.

Kabeer, N. (2002), 'Citizenship, Affiliation and Exclusion: Perspectives from the South' *IDS Bulletin* 33(2): 12–23.

Karmyog.com, 2006, web pg on ALMs and LACC.

Kaur, Harpreet and Nutan Shivtare (2005), 'ALMs, LACCs—New Institutions for Governance in Mumbai: Old Wine in a New Bottle?' Unpublished paper.

Kooiman, J. (2003), *Governing as Governance*, Sage: Palo Alto.

Luckham, R. et al. (2000). *Democratic Institututions and Politics in a Contexts of Inequality, Poverty, and Conflicts*. IDS Working Paper 104, Brighton, IDS.

Nainan, K.B. (2004), 'Ward Committees of Mumbai: Functions, Finances and Practices', IDPAD Conference, January, Delhi.

Nainan, N. (2001), 'Negotiating for Participation by NGOs in the City of Mumbai'. Masters Thesis, Institute of Housing and Urban Development Studies. Rotterdam: IHS.

Nainan N. and I.S.A. Baud (2008), 'Negotiating for Participation: Decentralization and NGOs in Mumbai, India', in I.S.A. Baud and J. de Wit (eds.), *New Forms of Urban Governance in India: Shifts, Models, Networks and Contestations*. Sage: New Delhi.

Pacione, M. (2006). 'Mumbai', *Cities* 23(3): 229–38.

Palnitkar, S., A.K Jain and Clean Sweep (2005), *Reviewing the Advanced Locality Management (ALM) Concept and Institutionalization of the ALM Movement in Mumbai*. AIISLSG: Mumbai.

Patel S., C. Cruz and S. Burra (2002), 'Beyond Evictions in a Global City: People-managed Resettlement in Mumbai', *Environment and Urbanization*, 14.1, pp. 159–72.

Pierre, J. and G. Peters (2000), *Governance, Politics and the State*. New York: St. Martin's Press.

Pinto, M. (2008), 'Urban Governance in India—Spotlight on Mumbai, in I.S.A. Baud and J. de Wit, (eds.), *New Forms of Urban Governance in India: Shifts, Models, Networks and Contestations*, New Delhi: Sage.

Ramanathan, U. (2006), 'Illegality and the Urban Poor', in *EPW*, 22 July pp. 3193–7.

Ramanathan, U. and V. Dupont (2005), 'The Courts and the Squatter Settlements in Delhi—or the Interventions of the Judiciary in Urban Governance, Paper IDPAD Conference, January, New Delhi.

Rath, A. (2006), 'Fiscal Federalism and Mega City Finances: The Greater Mumbai Case', paper presented at the conference, New Forms of Urban Governance in Indian Mega-cities, 20–21 June, New Delhi, JNU.

Risbud, N. (2003), 'The Case of Mumbai', Report for Understanding Slums: Case Studies for the Global Report on Human Settlements, 2003. Delhi, School of Planning and Architecture.

Redkar, Seema (2004), 'New Management Tools for the Solid Waste of Mumbai: Some Concerns', IDPAD conference, January, New Delhi.

Sivaramakrishnan, A. Kundu and K. Singh (2005). *Urbanization in India*. New Delhi: Sage.

Van Wersch, H. (1992), *The Bombay Textile Strike, 1982–3*. New Delhi: Oxford University Press.

Vogel, T. (2005), Post-74th CA Ward Governance in Mumbai: How and to What Extent Does this Brand of Decentralisation and Affirmative

Action Benefit the Intended?. MSc thesis (International Development Studies), University of Amsterdam.

World Bank (2003), *World Development Report: Delivering Services Effectively for the Poor*. Oxford: Oxford University Press.

Zerah, M.H. (2006), 'Assessing Surfacing Collective Action in Mumbai: A Case Study of Solid Waste Management'. Workshop paper on Actors, Policies, and Urban Governance in Mumbai, 23 February, Mumbai.

THEME 2

PUBLIC-PRIVATE PARTNERSHIPS IN BASIC SERVICE DELIVERY: IMPACTS ON THE POOR

CHAPTER 2

Public-Private Partnership in Basic Service Delivery: Women Empowerment Programme in Delhi

SHIPRA MAITRA

Public-private partnerships (PPP) are recognized globally as an important instrument for resource generation as well as inclusive governance. The demand for basic services is rising with the increase in economic development, which does not automatically ensure balanced distribution of benefits. Income growth generally bypasses the vulnerable section of society, poor women constituting a significant part of it. Along with the income poverty, this section also suffers from a poor quality of life. The public sector alone is incapable of meeting their need and reducing their exclusion from the mainstream development. PPPs offer tremendous scope reducing this gap with an increase in basic service delivery.

In Delhi, the state government has introduced an innovative way to deliver the services at the doorstep of the stakeholders with PPP. India's National Health Policy recognizes that women and other underprivileged groups are significantly handicapped due to disproportionately low access to health care. A significant proportion of these women live in the slums. They do not have time to avail themselves of public health care services as the waiting period is long and private services are expensive. The Delhi government has estimated

*The author is indebted to Dr. A.N. Sharma, Director, Institute for Human Development, New Delhi for providing me the opportunity to conduct the study on Stree Shakti Project of the Delhi Government and permitting me to present the paper in the seminar at CESS, Hyderabad.

that there are more than 800,000 poor women (5.71 per cent of the total population of Delhi) living in notified slums who need health care coverage.

The state government has started the Stree Shakti (Women's Empowerment) Programme with the involvement of community-based organizations (CBO) and other non-governmental organizations (NGO), along with government agencies. These organizations are engaged in generating awareness health care, legal issues and various skill development programmes. This initiative has helped to reduce the waiting time for availing of these services. Poor women cannot take time off from their daily working hours to avail themselves even the basic health services. The NGOs, with continuous government support, have been able to extend these services to the doorstep of the needy. The primary focus being on health, legal issues and skill development programmes have also been included in this initiative for total empowerment of economically weaker women thus reducing the level of exclusion.

This chapter tries to examine the impact of PPPs in extending these services to poor women in Delhi. This analysis is based on a primary survey of 5,000 households in the slums of Delhi. The results of this survey will help in understanding whether PPPs have been able to break the barriers that public agencies could not in order to reach the target group. The chapter is divided into the following sections. Section 1 describes the nature of split development in India and Delhi in particular. Section 2 deals with forms of PPP available in social sectors in India. Section 3 will explain the details of state government initiatives and highlight the innovative elements of PPPs, in carrying out government schemes, and the concluding section, Section 4 will discuss the connectivity through PPPs with the target group and analyse whether this kind of direct intervention can tackle the problem of exclusion towards reducing the dichotomy of development.

1. Macro-Economic Scenario: Split Development at National and State Levels

The Indian economy grew at an average rate of 3.5 per cent per annum since 1951, when the First Five-Year Plan was introduced, to 1981, the beginning of the Sixth Five-Year Plan. The growth rate accentuated during 1981–90 to 5.6 per cent but was accompanied by large macro-economic imbalances reflected in the accumulating fiscal deficit, increasing foreign debt and rising debt service ratio. The growth process also took place in a largely protected environment. The reform measures undertaken since 1991 related to two major components: (a) trade liberalization aiming at outward orientation and integration with the rest of the world and (b) deregulation and privatization of industrial production aimed at reducing the dominance of the public sector. The first component concentrated on the abolition of import quotas and reduction of tariff rates to moderate levels; devaluation of the Indian rupee to correct for bias against exports; introduction of market-determined foreign exchange rates; and introduction of current account convertibility. The second component dealt with the abolition of the industrial licencing system; promotion of foreign investment; interest rate deregulation; and disinvestments by the government of its equity in public sector enterprises. The primary objective of the reform was to put the economy on a sustainable high-growth path through an incentive framework for best possible allocation of factors of production and most efficient input combination within each sector of the economy. It was expected that the high rate of growth of Gross Domestic Product (GDP) would be broad based enough to improve the welfare of the marginalized sector.

The growth rate of last two decades can be traced in Table 2.1. There is macro-economic stability in several aspects compared to the earlier decade. There is low level of inflation for a fairly long-term period, the exchange rate is reasonably stable, foreign exchange reserves are rising, short-term external debt is low and there is ade-

TABLE 2.1: AVERAGE ANNUAL GROWTH IN GDP IN MAJOR SECTORS

(*Percentage*)

Category	1981–2 to 1990–1	1992–3 to 2001–2	1992–3 to 2002–3	1997–8 to 2001–2	1997–8 to 2004–5
GDP	5.6	6.1	5.9	5.5	5.3
Agriculture	3.8	3.3	2.7	2.0	1.2
Industry	7.0	6.3	6.4	4.6	5.0
Service	6.7	7.8	7.8	8.1	8.0

Source: Parikh and Radhakrishna, *India Development Report* (2004–5), IGIDR and Oxford University Press, New Delhi.

quate food grain stock even after occasional droughts. The sectoral growth compositions show the highest growth rate being achieved by the service sector since 1992. Average annual growth rates in both agriculture and industry were little lower during the post-liberalization period compared to the pre-liberalization period. The service sector has been the prime driver of growth of GDP. It now accounts for about half of the total GDP. Communications was the fastest-growing component of this sector during 1990s. Other sectors which have recorded higher growth after liberalization compared to the 1980s include construction, trade, hotels and restaurant and transport.

Structurally, contributions of agriculture and industry have declined in the GDP growth compared to the service sector. But agriculture is still the dominant source of employment, providing employment for more than 60 per cent of the total workforce though its share in GDP has fallen to about a quarter. This implies that a typical agricultural worker shows one-fourth productivity compared to his counterpart in non-agricultural activities. National Sample Survey (NSS) data has shown that the incidence of open unemployment has increased from 1.96 per cent in 1993–4 to 2.25 per cent in 1999–2000. In absolute terms, the number of unemployed persons was more than 9 million in 2001. Vision 2020, prepared by the Planning Commission, estimated that the total volume of unemployment including substantial under-employment and seasonal variation in work availability was close to 35 million persons in 2002. The NSSO data indicates that employment growth decelerated in the Indian economy in the 1990s. As agriculture and allied sectors account for most of the employment in India, the fall in employment growth was also primarily driven by this sector. Crop output increase has been largely due to yield rather than to area expansion in recent decades, leading to a fall in labour-absorption capacity. Employment volume has fallen in absolute terms in mining and quarrying and public utilities, which are mostly in the public sector. In contrast, there has been a substantial increase in employment in construction, transport, financial services and the real estate business sector, which have also experienced high-income growth.

Employment growth relative to income growth has deteriorated in recent years (Table 2.2). Employment elasticity has fallen for all sectors in the general. In the electricity, gas and water supply sectors, which are largely under the public sector, the introduction of the voluntary retirement scheme and other expenditure curtailment

TABLE 2.2: EMPLOYMENT–INCOME ELASTICITY IN MAJOR SECTORS OF INDIAN ECONOMY

(*Percentage*)

Sectors	1983–93	1993–9
Agricultural and Allied	0.48	0.01
Manufacturing	0.32	0.20
Electricity, Gas and Water Supply	0.48	–0.52
Construction	1.27	1.00
Trade, Hotels and Restaurants	0.67	0.38
Storage and Communications	0.55	0.56
Finance, Insurance and Real Estate	0.49	0.68
Public Administration and Community Services	0.63	0.02
All Sectors	0.36	0.13

Source: Chadha and Sahu, *EPW*, 25 May 2002.

programmes has resulted in a substantial reduction in jobs, while in the private sector there have not been sufficient labour-absorbing activities. Trade, hotels and restaurants, two of the fastest growing sectors dominated by the private sector, has shown a fall in employment elasticity to nearly half. Finance, insurance and real estate, other fast-growing sectors with dominant private sector presence, have shown substantial improvement in employment elasticity but they do not absorb a significant proportion of the labour force. This rise is not sufficient to cover the loss of employment owing to shrinkage in public administration, thereby lowering the overall value of total employment elasticity. India's split development is emerging out of growing income with inadequate redistribution impact. Several studies and NSS data have also revealed another alarming facts an increase in the proportion of casual workers in total employment.

POVERTY ALLEVIATION

Poverty reduction has been a major goal of development policy in India since Independence. The efforts initiated under the five-year plans were aimed at achieving a minimum standard of living for all within a reasonable period. This was to be brought about by attaining higher growth, raising the livelihood opportunities of the poor and supplementing market forces with targeted government interventions.

India's achievement in reducing poverty at the national level during 1956–2000 has been significant. The proportion of people below the poverty line remained above 50 per cent till the mid-1970s but thereafter registered a declining trend with yearly fluctuations. It declined perceptibly in the late 1970s and 1980s from 51 per cent in 1977–8 to 39 pet cent in 1987–8 and further to 26 per cent in 2001. The intensity of poverty has also declined considerably in both rural and urban areas. Yet about 193 million in rural areas and 67 million in urban areas remained below the poverty line in 1999–2000.

There has been a substantial decline in both HCR and PGI in both rural and urban areas leading to the conclusion that the growth process has included the poor, even if marginally (Table 2.3). However, Gini Coefficient figures show that inequality has declined marginally in rural areas but remained almost the same in urban areas. Given the fact that rural income is nearly one-third of urban income, it is clear that the fruits of development have been localized in urban areas much more than in rural areas. This has increased the income difference in urban areas as rural income growth was less than urban income growth.

Poverty indicates multiple deprivations caused by a host of economic, social, political and institutional factors. It mainly connotes low income, inadequate consumption, low human capability in terms of skill, education, health and nutrition, and insecurity. The traditional measure of poverty, which measures only the income deprivation as a proxy of deprivation of the poor, therefore, is considered inadequate to capture its complexity and multi-dimensionality. Poverty measures, associated with the human development index,

TABLE 2.3: INDICES OF POVERTY AND INEQUALITY

	Head Count Ratio (HCR)		Poverty Gap Index (PGI)		Gini Coefficient % at 1993–4 Prices	
Year	Rural	Urban	Rural	Urban	Rural	Urban
1973–4	56.4	49.0	16.24	15.51	28.7	31.9
1977–8	53.1	45.2	17.55	18.35	29.5	33.7
1983–4	45.7	40.8	13.35	12.88	30.0	34.1
1987–8	39.1	38.2	10.09	11.24	29.4	34.5
1993–4	37.3	32.4	7.82	8.36	28.5	34.4
1999–2000	27.1	23.6	5.34	5.02	26.7	34.8

Source: *Oxford Handbook of Poverty in India* (2005).

provide a proper picture of deprivation and inequality. Apart from direct government interventions, private partnership has been a very useful complementary instrument to reduce the level of deprivation and inequality. Private functionaries, including the NGOs, CBOs and self-help groups (SHG), have become important agents of change and good governance. National and local plans and programmes are now designed to be implemented through these agents of change. In many studies and analyses of effective governance, transfer of power and actions then the state organs to these groups have become the indicators of decentralization and development.

In the national five-year plan documents, these perspectives have been considered at length with the objective of enhancing the quality of governance through decentralization of the development process for achieving planned objectives of growth with social justice. PPP is expected to improve the quality of delivery of development goods and in the process make governments more responsive and responsible. The Ninth Five-Year Plan has emphasized social mobilization and empowerment of the socially and economically disadvantaged with the focus on linking them in a cause–effect relationship. The approach to social mobilization ranged from welfare in the Sixth Plan to development in the Eighth Plan and empowerment in the Ninth Plan. The Tenth Plan has carried this approach further by documenting ingredients essential for the social mobilization process for empowerment and poverty reduction, namely, creating an enabling environment, building up the capacities of facilitating agencies and creating opportunities for social and economic development.

Delhi as the state capital, and a city-state, offers a glaring example of the split development process when its growth rate is compared to the national level. Delhi's low level of income poverty, however, cannot capture the nature of the split development associated with enormous progress. It is reflected in the poor living conditions of the slum dwellers, non-availability of education and medical facilities to a significant percentage of the population and gender discrimination.

Delhi enjoys the highest per capita income in the country, has the highest per capita electricity consumption and the highest per capita investment on capital expenditure. Close to 50 per cent of the total Multi-National Corporations (MNC) that entered India since the 1990s, have chosen Delhi as their base. The city-state has more private vehicles than the other three metros combined and enjoys per capita ownership of consumer goods. The wide green landscapes, access to some quality schools and hospitals add to its charm. As a result, migrants add roughly 2,50,000 to its population every year.

Delhi has been able to capitalize effectively on the new growth opportunities that opened up after 1990. Today, 78 per cent of Delhi's State Domestic Product (SDP) comes from a strong and growing service (or tertiary) sector comprising trade, hotels and restaurants, transport, communications, financial and insurance service, real estate, public administration and other business services. Banking and finance, real estate and insurance account for almost 30 per cent of Delhi's SDP.

As a result, Delhi's per capita income today is more than two and a half times greater than the national average (Economic Survey, 2005–6, Govt. of India). Over the past ten years, Delhi, along with West Bengal, Karnataka and Tamil Nadu, recorded the maximum growth rate in per capita income. Delhi's real per capita income grew by 32 per cent during 1981–90. It went up by 60 per cent during the next decade.

Delhi remains an attractive city for jobs. Close to 74 per cent of those working in the organized sector are employed by the government. Of these, however, barely 10 per cent are women. These workers have been absorbed particularly by the unorganized service sector. For a majority of the workers in the unorganized sector, however, irregular and low earnings mark conditions of employment.

The private sector too is contributing significantly in this growth process, providing employment to nearly 26 per cent of the workforce in the organized sector. Private sector employment has been growing in recent years, especially with new employment opportunities opening up in multinational companies and information technology within and on the outskirts of Delhi.

INCIDENCE OF POVERTY

Delhi's record in reducing levels of income poverty has been impressive. In 1999–2000, an estimated 1.15 million people, i.e. 8 per cent of Delhi's population lived below the income poverty line—considerably lower than the average of 26 per cent. Between 1973–4 and 1999–2000, Delhi registered an 82 per cent decline in urban poverty, the largest reduction among India states. The distribution aspect of income growth can be considered in terms of the proportion of persons falling bellow the poverty line, i.e. the incidence of poverty in Delhi is to be far below than the all-India level for each point of time and for each category. In fact, for the rural segment the proportion has been below 10 per cent in Delhi as against the 25–46 per cent range at the all-India level from 1981–2001. The rural segment does not hold much meaning in the case of Delhi. But even in the urban segment, the incidence of poverty is lower than at the all-India level (Table 2.4).

The second aspect of poverty in Delhi, which is a very striking dimension, is the fact that unlike in the rest of India, where there is more rural poverty than urban poverty, in Delhi urban poverty is much more than rural poverty. In fact, the incidence of urban poverty has been roughly four to twenty times higher in the urban segment of Delhi than in its rural segment at the three points of time. For example, according to 1999–2000 estimates, it emerges that the incidence of rural poverty in Delhi is almost as good as being absent with only 0.4 per cent of rural population living below the poverty line whereas in urban Delhi the incidence of poverty is at 9.42 per cent.

The expansion of various farms in rural Delhi, owned by urban holders, largely accounts for very low rural poverty. Villages are changing their characters fast and are being categorized as urban villages with planning implications.

TABLE 2.4: INCIDENCE OF POVERTY: DELHI AND INDIA

	Total Population Below Poverty Line (BPL)					
	Number in Million			Percentage		
Year	Rural	Urban	Total	Urban	Rural	Total
Delhi						
1983–4	0.04	1.79	1.83	0.76	27.89	26.22
1993–4	0.01	1.53	1.51	0.19	16.03	14.69
1999–2000	0.07	1.14	1.14	0.04	9.42	8.23
India						
1983–4	252.00	70.90	322.90	4.5	40.8	44.5
1993–4	244.03	46.23	320.26	3.72	32.36	35.97
1999–2000	193.24	67.00	260.25	2.70	23.62	26.1

Source: Household Consumption Expenditure Survey NSS Rounds.

Delhi's consumption expenditure per capita (Rs. 1,535.60) is more than double the average all-India level (Rs. 648.54) and is second only to Chandigarh (Rs. 1,538.60). The structural characteristics of consumption expenditure also reflect Delhi's affluence. The proportion of expenditure on non-food items is much higher than the national average, compared to that on food items.

SOCIAL INFRASTRUCTURE

The city has one of the most extensive health care facilities in the country. The central, state and local governments spend a heavily on health care services associated with the private sector. Close to 53 per cent of households in Delhi avail themselves of private medical facilities. After Kerala, Delhi has the lowest Infant Mortality Rate (IMR 10 in Kerala and 30 in Delhi) among the states. The state government has allocated 10.35 per cent of its plan outlay for health in Tenth Plan—the highest by any state government in the country.

The state also has an extensive network of education institutions offering some of the finest education within the country. Basic education however, is not widespread in the capital. Nearly 50 per cent of the people above the poverty line have completed secondary school or above and another 27 per cent have studied till class eight. In contrast, a third of Delhi's population below the poverty line has not finished primary schooling. The state has established one of the largest school systems in the world. Even then, the student/teacher ratio remains high. The private sector also plays an important role in this sector. Almost 75 per cent of the children of primary school age attend government schools. But at the high school age it is estimated that more than half of all enrolled children are in private schools. Table 2.5 shows the comparative achievements of Delhi in education and health.

As mentioned earlier, Delhi has established one of the largest school systems in the world, with 93,000 teachers and close to 3 million children enrolled in schools. Yet the student–teacher ratio is much higher than the Planning Commission norms. Close to 7 per cent of children in the age group of 6–14 years are out-of-school children, with almost half of them being girls. Almost the same percentage of out-of-school students was found in the age group of 11–14 years, 48 per cent of them being girls. In some districts, the percentage of out-of-school children is as high as 25.

TABLE 2.5: COMPARATIVE SOCIAL INDICATORS

Item	Delhi	India
Per capita Expenditure on Health (2003–4)	Rs. 492.20	159.46
Per capita Expenditure on Education (2001–2)	Rs. 1,115.76	0.7
Bed/Population Ratio per 1,000	2.2	0.7
Life Expectancy at Birth (years)	69.6	62.9
Infant Mortality Ratio (IMR)	10	62
Literacy Rate (per cent)	82	65

Source: Delhi Human Development Report, 2006.

Another area of concern is discrimination against women. Out of the four major metropolitan cities, Delhi reports the lowest child sex ratio and the largest male-female gap in literacy. The sex ratio among children (0–6 years) declined from 915 in 1991 to 865 in 2001.

A significant proportion of the population (22 per cent) of the Delhi lives in slums, i.e. sub-standard housing and squalor without any physical amenities. Slums and squatter settlements are characterized by densities which are two to three times higher than normal residential settlements, the absence of legal recognition or tenurial rights and the absence of basic services. Unofficial estimates say that close to 1,00,000 people are shelterless in Delhi. The problems of low-end households present a formidable challenge for improving the index of Delhi's human development.

2. Public-Private Partnership in the Social Sector in India

Public-private partnership (PPP) is not a new concept in India. In rural sector activities, even some small-scale judicial decisions have been taken and implemented through community involvement. Voluntary organizations, a common expression for current NGOs, have taken lead roles in spreading education, health services and various social service-related activities including disaster management. Their scale of operation is low, generally confined to local areas. Such organizations played a big role even in India's struggle for Independence.

The voluntary sector in India is constituted under the Society Registration Act, the India Trust Act, the Religious and Charitable

Societies Act, non-profit making companies under the Companies Act and under any other legislation to be recognized by state governments. The services taken up by the voluntary sector are generally included in the 'state list' of the Constitution of India. This sector also includes CBOs and SHGs, which are generally informal or unregistered bodies. It does not, however, include all cooperative societies.

The voluntary sector may broadly be classified as traditional, community-based and government sponsored. The traditional sector comprises various religious and charitable trusts dedicated to spreading education, health care, orphanages, rehabilitation homes, etc. The CBOs include societies for relief from natural disasters, neighbourhood societies, micro-credit societies, women's associations, wildlife protection communities, etc. The government sponsored voluntary sector is comprised of agencies engaged in welfare programmes like rural development, afforestation programmes, watershed management, health and education services including agencies engaged in research and evaluation.

The voluntary sector is classified in the following categories based on their main areas of activity as shown in Table 2.6. Religious and cultural activities dominate almost half (45 per cent) of the total voluntary sectors in India. Government-sponsored voluntary activities, however, are in health, education and community services.

The voluntary sector is quite active in resource generation. More than half (51 per cent) of the total resources generated in this sector are through own source, i.e. fees and charges for the services ren-

TABLE 2.6: CLASSIFICATION OF VOLUNTARY SECTOR

Sl. No.	Category	Number	Percentage to Total
1.	Religious	3,18,000	26.5
2.	Cultural	2,16,000	18.0
3.	Community Service	2,55,600	21.3
4.	Education	2,44,800	20.4
5.	Health	79,200	6.6
6.	Others	86,400	7.2
Total		12,00,000	100.0

Source: Planning Commission, Government of India.

dered. This is followed by grants and donations (29 per cent). Among the various sources of funds, donations and charity are mostly ad hoc and irregular. Private fund-raising is time consuming. Collection of funds from fees and user charges are market determined. Grants-in-aid are the most dependable and regular resource base.

The Government of India has tried to include the voluntary sector in community development since the First Five-Year Plan. Various pilot projects in community development were started in Andhra Pradesh to begin with. It entered other states with different government-sponsored programmes financed through grants. Various central government departments operate welfare programmes with the involvement of voluntary sectors. Table 2.7 provides a glimpse of budget allocations for this sector from different ministries.

The total central sector allocation in the Tenth Plan has been Rs. 89,318,300 million of which the social sector allocation through major ministries accounted for Rs. 2,166,950 million (2.42 per cent), i.e. less than 3 per cent. This money is routed through NGOs and similar groups. The Ministry of Rural Development disperses the maximum amount of money through NGOs followed by the Ministry of HRD and Ministry of Health and Family Welfare.

PPPs in the social sector are very different from PPPs in the infrastructure and real estate sector, which entered the social sector in a

TABLE 2.7: BUDGETARY ALLOCATION TO THE SOCIAL SECTOR BY MAJOR MINISTRIES DURING THE TENTH PLAN

Sl. No.	Ministry	Budgetary Support (Rs. in million)	
1.	Ministry of Agriculture	2,08,500	(9.62)
2.	Ministry of Human Resources Development	5,31,200	(24.51)
3.	Ministry of Environment and Forests	57,500	(2.65)
4.	Ministry of Health and Family Welfare	3,63,450	(16.77)
5.	Ministry of Rural Development	7,99,900	(36.91)
6.	Ministry of Social Justice and Empowerment	74,600	(3.44)
7.	Ministry of Culture	20,000	(0.92)
8.	Ministries of Urban Development and Poverty Alleviation	1,11,800	(5.18)
Total		21,66,950	(100.00)

Source: Tenth Five-Year Plan, Government of India.

big way in the 1990s. PPPs here involved large private firms rather than individual or collective participation by small groups. The infrastructure sector operates on a market mechanism with the objective of maximizing risks within the constraints of ensuring supply to certain deprived sectors or deprived areas. The success of the PPP depends on the efficiency with which the private sector can manage risks. The government sector can raise funds in a variety of ways, but public entities tend to under-price risks and consequently levy low user charges which are not cost-effective. Injection of private capital and management applied with superior technologies sometimes leads to more efficient utilization of resources thus releasing public finances for alternative uses. Major PPPs have been initiated in telecommunications, electricity, civil aviation, roads and highways, railways, shipping and housing. Budget allocations in the infrastructure sector far exceed that of the social sector. The national government has brought several changes in the legal and regulatory framework in order to make PPPs a success. However, their success rates vary from sector to sector. Healthy competitive elements and risk management have played a major role in successful PPPs (Table 2.8).

PPP AND PRIVATIZATION

The key differences between PPP and 'privatization' may be summarized as follows:

1. *Responsibility*: In privatization, responsibility for delivery and funding of a particular service rests with the private sector. PPPs,

TABLE 2.8: PPP MODELS PRACTISED IN INDIA

Option	Asset Ownership	O&M	Capital Investment	Commercial Risk	Duration
Management Contract	Public	Private	Public	Public	3–5 Years
Lease	Public	Private	Public	Shared	8–15 Years
Concession BOT	Public	Private	Private	Private	25–30 Years
BOOT/BOO	Private/Public	Private	Private	Private	20–30 Years

Source: Report on PPP Sub-Group on Social Sector, 2004, Planning Commission, Government of India.

on the other hand, have full retention of responsibility by the government for providing the service.

2. *Ownership:* While ownership rights under privatization are sold to the private sector along with associated benefits and costs; PPPs, may continue to retain legal ownership of assets by the public sector.
3. *Nature of Service:* While the private provider determines the nature and scope of services under privatization, under PPPs the nature and scope of services is contractually determined between the two parties.
4. *Risk and Reward:* Under privatization, all the risks inherent in the business rest with the private sector. Under PPPs, risks and rewards are shared between the government (public) and the private sector.

The potential benefits expected from PPP could be mentioned as below:

1. *Cost-effectiveness:* Since the selection of the developer/service provider depends on competition or some benchmarking, the project is generally more cost effective than before PPPs.
2. *Higher Productivity:* By linking payment to performance, productivity gains may be expected within the programme/project.
3. *Accelerated Delivery:* Since the contracts generally have incentive and penalty clauses *vis-à-vis* implementation of capital projects/programmes, this leads to accelerated delivery of projects.
4. *Clear Customer Focus:* The shift in focus from service inputs to outputs creates the scope for innovation in service delivery and enhances customer satisfaction.
5. *Enhanced Social Service*: Social services to the mentally ill, disabled children and delinquents, etc., require a great deal of commitment rather than sheer professionalism. In such cases it is community organizations (CO)/voluntary organizations (VO) with dedicated volunteers who alone can provide the requisite relief.
6. *Recovery of User Charges:* Innovative decisions can be taken with greater flexibility on account of decentralization. Wherever possibilities of recovering user charges exist, these can be imposed in harmony with local conditions.

NATURE OF COLLABORATION

The government may collaborate with the private developer/service provider in any one of the following ways:

(i) *as a funding agency* providing grant/capital/asset support to the private sector engaged in provision of public service, on a contractual/non contractual basis;
(ii) *as a buyer* buying services on a long-term basis; and
(iii) *as a coordinator* specifying various sectors/forums in which participation by the private sector would be welcome.

The funding pattern and collaboration between the public sector and the private sector could take any one of the following forms:

(i) public funding with private service delivery and private management;
(ii) public as well as private funding with private service delivery and private management;
(iii) public as well as private funding with public/private service delivery and public/private/joint management; and
(iv) private funding with private service delivery and private management.

PPP initiatives supplement government resources through private participation.

PRINCIPLES OF PPPs

PPPs involve a long-term relationship between the public sector and the private sector. While the collaboration between the two may take various forms, like *buyer–seller relationship, donor–recipient relationship*, the most stable partnership is in the form of a *contract* binding on both the parties. The following features broadly characterize PPP.

Contractual Framework

The contract mirrors the basic objective of the programme/project, the tenure of agreement, the funding pattern and the sharing of risks and responsibilities. Therefore the need to define the contract very precisely, becomes paramount under PPP.

Projects/programmes under PPPs may, be broadly classified under three heads, namely, (i) service contract, (ii) operations and maintenance (management) contract, and (iii) capital projects, with operations and maintenance contract.

Selection of Service Provider

Transparency in 'selection' is an essential feature of the PPP. Selection of *the developer* or *the service provider* may be done in any of the following three ways:

COMPETITIVE BIDDING: This involves a well publicized and a well-designed bid process to ascertain the financial, technical and managerial capabilities of the service provider or the developer. Either of the two formats for bidding, namely, single-round sealed bid auction or multiple-round open-outcry (ascending) bid auction, could be adopted. The appropriate bidding process depends on the nature of the valuation that the bidders place on the concession, that is, on the right to do the job.

In some cases the valuation of the project depends on factors which are within the bidder's control, such as the construction and maintenance costs of a building or a road. These are also known as 'private value items'. In other cases, the valuation does not depend just on the bidders own assessment, but also on certain unknown factors which need to be anticipated. These unknown factors are common to all bidders and each bidder may update his/her own assessment based on the assessment of other bidders. These are known as 'common value items' and include factors such as the size of market, willingness-to-pay of consumers, future behaviour of regulators, etc. For private-value items, a single-round auction is appropriate since bidders do not need to learn from the information of other bidders and a sealed bid auction is preferable since it has the least potential for collusion. Concessions with common-value characteristics, on the other hand, are best awarded through multiple-round bids since this facilitates the process of value discovery by bidders, allowing bidders to observe and respond to quotations/prices as they emerge. Multiple-round bids can also be sealed-bids, but there is an opportunity to rebid after the bids are opened. Moreover, wherever there is a two-stage process involving, for instance, mega-infrastructure projects, the bidders are required to obtain from their prospective lenders the financial terms, expectations regarding state support as well as their comments on the concession agreement.

The final selection of the developer/service provider depends on one or a combination of the following:

(a) lowest capital cost of the project;
(b) lowest operation and maintenance cost;
(c) lowest bid in terms of the present value of user fees;
(d) lowest present value of payment from government;
(e) highest equity premium;
(f) highest upfront fee;
(g) highest revenue share to the government; and/or
(h) the shortest concession period.

Where only a sole bid is received, the authorities have the choice of either accepting or rejecting the bid. When a sole bid is rejected, or when no bid is received, the project/programme proposal itself may be modified and the bid process restarted. Alternatively, the selection of the developer/service provider is done through competitive negotiation with private sector participants.

SWISS CHALLENGE APPROACH: The Swiss Challenge approach refers to *suo-motu* proposals being received by the government from the private participant. The private sector thus provides all details regarding (a) its technical, financial and managerial capabilities; (b) the technical, financial and commercial viability of the project/programme; and (c) expectation of government support/concessions.

The government may examine the proposal and if the proposal belongs to the declared policy of priorities, then it may invite competing counter proposals from others (in the spirit of the 'Swiss Challenge' approach) giving them adequate notice. In the event of a better proposal being received, the original propose is given the opportunity to modify the original proposer. Finally, the better of the two is awarded the project/programme for execution.

COMPETITIVE NEGOTIATION: Direct or indirect competitive negotiation is considered a variant of competitive bidding. The government thus specifies the service objective and invites proposals through advertisements. It then negotiates/finalizes the contract with the selected bidders.

The government agency (or the local authority) may select the service provider/developer through competitive negotiation in the following cases:

(a) Social sector projects and programmes involving VOs/NGOs/ Local Community Organizations;
(b) projects involving proprietary technology or a franchise;
(c) linkage projects related to a mega project or a major activity;
(d) projects and programmes which failed to solicit any response to a bidding process; and
(e) *suo-motu* proposals from a private participant.

Negotiation may, however, be 'simple' (direct) or 'complex' (indirect). In the latter, the government negotiates through a 'master contractor'/mother NGO. In other words, contracts for (public) services are contracted out and the master contractor handles all dealings with sub-contractors/franchisees. While the government reviews the works of the master contractor through its monitors (officials) who may visit the site of programme implementation and meet the beneficiaries, the master contractor may monitor the programme (run by sub-contractors) by collecting information from beneficiaries selected randomly, based on questionnaires/interviews.

Advantage of Master Contractors: Some of the advantages of master contracting are:

(a) the government has administrative convenience and better control in dealing with a fewer number of service providers;
(b) funds can be raised from public and private sources, other than the government;
(c) decisions can be taken more quickly, despite political pressures; and
(d) training programmes for the sub-contractors/service provider/ vendors can be organized more innovatively by the contractor.

However, 'master contract' is not always relevant and negotiation *vis-à-vis* the contract ought to be done directly with the community/ beneficiaries, as, for instance, of wildlife conservation with the help of people living in the vicinity of the forests. Competitive negotiations are, however, less transparent than competitive bidding. With a view to ensure fairness, the government auditor may audit such contracts.

PAYMENT MECHANISM

Payments to the private sector could take the form of: (a) contractual payments; (b) grants-in-aid; and (c) right to levy user charges for the asset created/leased-in. Contractual payments may be in the form of advance payment, progress payment, final payment, annuities and guarantees for receivables. Annuities, in turn, could be with respect to recovering the fixed cost or for recovering both variable cost and the fixed cost of the project. In the former case, both the government and the private partner share the risk of running the project. Grants-in-aid, in turn, can take different forms such as a block grant, capital grant, matching grant, institutional support, etc. Lease agreement licence, similarly, may allow the concessionaire to recover the cost of construction/operation and maintenance through levying user charges. Moreover, in the case of lease agreements, the assets revert to the government after the expiry of the contract. The agreement ought to also provide for the condition of the asset that would be returned at the end of the contract.

MONITORING AND EVALUATION

It is quite often thought that the job is over with the signing/finalizing of the 'contract'. However, payments have to be linked to performance, which in turn requires monitoring. Performance measurement can be done by measuring 'efficiency' or measuring 'effectiveness'. While the measurement of efficiency entails comparing the unit cost of providing the service from amongst the various alternatives, measurement of effectiveness involves comparing the desired outcomes from amongst the various alternatives.

Monitoring may be done in either of the following ways:

(i) by government departments authorized to do so based on a standardized scale;
(ii) by independent agencies/regulators based on a standardized scale;
(iii) by the department or independent agencies, based on the simple criteria of 'pass' and 'fail'; and
(iv) by the department or independent agencies, based on the feedback received from the beneficiaries.

The involvement of third party/independent agencies for monitoring appears to be preferable as they minimize government control. A certain percentage of the cost of the project needs to be, therefore, earmarked for contract management. The government and the developer/service provider could mutually decide the third party. The third party involvement could be further supplemented with provision for adjudication by the (higher) judiciary.

RISK AND REVENUE SHARING

PPP involves the sharing of risks and rewards between the partners. The risks involved in project implementation may be of the following types:

1. *Construction/implementation risk, arising from:*
   (i) Delay in project clearance;
   (ii) Contractor default;
   (iii) Environmental damage.
2. *Market risk, arising from:*
   (i) Insufficient demand;
   (ii) Impractical user levies.
3. *Financial risk, arising from:*
   (i) Inflation;
   (ii) Change in interest rates;
   (iii) Increase in taxes;
   (iv) Change in exchange rates.
4. *Operation and maintenance risk, arising from:*
   (i) Termination of contract;
   (ii) Technology risk;
   (iii) Labour risk.
5. *Legal risk, arising from:*
   (i) Changes in law;
   (ii) Changes in title/lease rights;
   (iii) Insolvency of developer/service provider;
   (iv) Change in the security structure.

It is essential that all the generic risks be identified before finalizing the contract.

The assurance of the government to share the risks with the private partner is a significant confidence-building measure. Similarly, if the actual output/returns exceed those contemplated at the start of the project, the windfall is to be shared (equally) between the public and the private sectors.

3. Innovative Elements of PPPs in State Schemes

The Department of Social Welfare (DSW) of the Government of NCT of Delhi is the nodal agency for implementing various social legislations and welfare schemes for the disadvantaged sections of society in the state. The services of the DSW can be broadly categorized as institutional and non-institutional services. The institutional services provided by the department include the running of a number of institutions for beggars, juveniles, the handicapped, women, aged persons, etc. The Delhi government has promoted a partnership (Bhagidari) scheme in various departments for providing better implementation and better utilization of resources in partnership with people-centric organizations. This scheme is instrumental in ensuring transparency in administration, flexibility in approach and effective monitoring of programmes to be implemented in a time-bound manner. One such programme of the DSW is the Stree Shakti (Gender Empowerment) scheme, which aims at empowering the women of the economically weaker section through intervention in health, skill development and income generation. It is a capacity-building project through Bhagidari with NGOs to bringing the marginalized women into the mainstream through an unconventional approach, i.e. bringing the service to the doorstep of the stakeholders and generating awareness. In the conventional approach, the target groups, i.e. women living in slums, come to the institutions for service delivery to get the service. For health care programmes, they have to visit the hospitals and doctors; for skill development, they visit distant places for information and training; for legal problems, they have to visit the concerned places and persons. The Stree Shakti scheme attempts to take all these facilities to their doorstep and under one roof through organizing camps at periodic intervals and establishing Gender Resource Centres (GRC) for the dissemination of information and assistance.

DESIGN OF THE STREE SHAKTI PROJECT

A unique approach is followed by the Sree Shakti Project to extend the delivery system associated with this programme to the target groups to almost their doorstep, rather than the conventional expectation that the target group will come to the institutions where the facilities are available. It is operational in two components: the establishment of GRCs through reliable NGOs and the organization of Stree Shakti camps.

Camp activities focus on health-related activities while GRCs concentrate on skill development, non-formal education and legal counselling along with health issues.

GENDER RESOURCE CENTRES

GRCs are planned as resource centres for women in the following areas:

- Health and Nutrition Awareness
- Skill Development for Economic Empowerment
- Non-formal Education
- Legal Counselling
- Information Sharing and Networking

Activities

The GRC is run at the district level by a nodal NGO identified by a panel of experts including officials from the DSW. The centre works at a public space owned by the government where it runs its programmes in health and legal counselling, vocational training and information facilitation. A nodal officer, assisted by other volunteers, is in-charge of the GRC. The volunteers keep regular contact with the women of that area. They help in disseminating information regarding camp activities.

The GRCs render the following specific services:

HEALTH AND NUTRITION AWARENESS: The four health issues are:

1. Anaemia in adolescent girls and pregnant women.
2. Full immunization of children.
3. High fertility, especially in economically weaker sections.
4. Sexually transmitted infection.

The GRCs provide the services of doctors on their premises. The doctors are available twice a week to meet the beneficiaries. Medicines are generally freely available on the premises, although sometimes they have to be bought from the market. The doctors refer the beneficiaries to nearby hospitals for further check-up if required.

NON-FORMAL EDUCATION: The GRCs provide services in non-formal education in the following areas:

- Improving functional literacy.
- Admitting dropout children on the open schools and to providing financial initiative.
- The GRCs run non-formal educational classes on the premises. The trainers come regularly to help the children and women who did not or could not associate themselves with formal schooling system. They also help dropout children to get admission in the open school.

SKILL DEVELOPMENT TRAINING AND FORMATION OF SHGS: The GRCs provide vocational training near the beneficiaries' residence; increase their knowledge base regarding better marketing techniques; facilitate loans and marketing opportunities; enlarge the scope of traditional/non-traditional trade; and help in getting marketing facilities.

The trainers come to the GRC premises to provide training for a fixed duration course. The number of participants in each batch is around 20–25. They get certificates from the Department of Education of the state government after completing the course and clearing the necessary examinations. GRCs help them to form SHGs and establish proper marketing contacts for selling their products.

FORMATION OF SHGS: MGRCs take twenty-five women from economically weaker communities and help them set-up SHGs. A minimum of eight such groups are to be formed within six months. GRCs provide them with training in community leadership, assist them in opening bank accounts and take loans to cater for necessary expenditures.

LEGAL COUNSELLING: The GRCs help to sensitize women to their rights; spreading legal awareness regarding the girl child; provide legal help in women-related crimes and help the women complainants to follow up their cases. Lawyers visit GRC premises twice a week. The volunteers accompany the beneficiaries to concerned agencies for follow-up of legal cases.

INFORMATION AND FACILITIES: GRCs maintain computerized information regarding several women-related schemes. They keep a record of the women seeking information. They also take up primary surveys of the communities for identifying the health-related needs of poor women in general.

STREE SHAKTI CAMPS

The second component of the project deals with organization of large-scale camps, one in every district in every month. It aims to reach 700–800 beneficiaries in each camp, i.e. 6,300–7,200 in every month (9 camps in 9 districts) reaching a total of 63,000–72,000 beneficiaries annually, assuming a total of 10 camps in a year. These camps are thus spread all over Delhi. The government tries to link the identified beneficiaries to the delivery system through these camps with the active participation of NGOs.

The major focus in the camps is on the health sector. The growth rate of the population and the child sex ratio (0–6 age group) are taken as the major indicators of health deprivation in selecting the areas of the district where camps will be held. However, the camps also cover other areas and other programmes as well.

Objectives

The main objective of the Stree Shakti camps is to make the various programmes under the Stree Shakti project available to the target group at their doorstep. Specific objectives are described as follows:

- Camps are to be held for creating awareness and consciousness among women of the economically weaker sections of society on the issues of health and nutrition, legal rights, opportunities for skill development and non-formal education.
- The delivery system attached to the institution/programme is to be extended to the target group at their doorstep. The identified beneficiaries will be linked to the delivery system through the active intervention of the NGOs.
- The referral cases identified in the camps are to be followed up as the major post-camp activities with NGO participation.
- Proper beneficiaries and the right kind of facilitators are to be identified for success of the programme.

- Establishment of proper linkage through a participatory approach is to be established between the government agencies, the stakeholders and the NGOs.

Activities

Stree Shakti camps are organized in each of the nine districts of Delhi in order to bring the facilities closer to the communities. The programme is operationalized with extensive NGO participation. There is one NGO, known as Mother NGO (MNGO), which supervises the camp activities in whole of Delhi and is involved in designing the programme and providing training to the NGOs that will actually organize the camps. These NGOs, known as Field NGOs (FNGO), are selected after they respond with expression of interest to public advertisements every year. They take charge of one district each for organizing three to four camps in a year. They undertake pre-camp surveys in their respective areas to identify the beneficiaries and explain to them the purpose of the camps in order to link them to the delivery system. These camps offer various health-related services and provide information about a number of opportunities including contact agencies in legal counselling, skill formation, non-formal education for the children, etc. The FNGOs and the officials from the DSW co-ordinate with local hospitals and other health-related government organizations. A team of doctors provides preliminary health check-up facilities to the beneficiaries in the camps. Those who need further medical attention are referred to nearby hospitals with assistance from the FNGOs. Legal counsellors visit the camps to provide legal awareness to the beneficiaries and sensitize them regarding their rights. Workers for non-formal education for children (*Anganwari*) contact the beneficiaries who cannot send their children to formal schools. These workers encourage them to send their children for non-formal schooling. After the camps, the NGOs continue to follow up the cases related to health and legal counselling.

The project design for camp activities involves some specific characteristics:

- A dedicated team of doctors and nurses from government health institutions is contacted to provide health check-ups, medicines and necessary counselling for women.

- These camps are held on Sundays in order to include the maximum number of beneficiaries who, by and large, cannot take leave from their workplace without risking loss of wage.
- Women who need further treatment are issued referrals through 'Stree Shakti cards'. These cards are meant to ensure further treatment for them in preference over others in the linked hospitals in future, free of cost. There are special counters in the specified hospitals for Stree Shakti cardholders to encourage them to avail of health care facilities.
- Camps are jointly managed by the DSW, other government agencies and the NGOs.
- The success of the project is based on a strong link up between the programmes introduced and services provided in these camps and the post-camp referral service for the beneficiaries.

PARTICIPATING DEPARTMENT AND AGENCIES: Several government departments act in coordination to provide wide-ranging facilities to the beneficiaries in the camps. These include the Bhagidari cell of the chief minister's office (CMO), health, education, social welfare and legal departments of the state, autonomous institutes and the NGOs. Their involvement and scope are increasing with the expansion of camp activities.

Monitoring and Evaluation

The project design consists of regular monitoring and checking by a Managing Committee. The Committee is to meet once in a month. The Committee consists of: the Principal Secretary, Health Department; the Principal Secretary, Information Technology; the Secretary, DSW; the Director, Education Department; the Joint Director, Training/Technical Education; the Director, Bureau of Economics and Statistics; the Representative of MNGO; and the Joint Director, DSW.

Stree Shakti projects consisting of both GRCs and Stree Shakti camps are implemented as an overall Bhagidari Scheme of the Government of NCT of Delhi. Accordingly, it is managed by various departments/agencies of the Government of NCT of Delhi, one nodal NGO known as the MNGO and the FNGO, as mentioned earlier.

The GRCs are supposed to directly monitored by the officers of the DSW regarding the maintenance and running of the centre as well as the dissemination of information. They are expected to be well aware of the locality, its women and their problems, and develop a warm relationship and a good rapport with them so as to encourage them to trust the programme and avail themselves of the opportunities provided.

The officers from the DSW as well as the MNGO regularly monitor Stree Shakti camps on the camp day. The MNGO provides training to the NGOs that organize the camps. They are trained to conduct baseline surveys, transport the beneficiaries, maintain referral records and follow up cases after camp day. The MNGO regularly collects progress reports from them and makes comparative analyses of performance in different camps (see Table 2.9). It also monitors the progress in the follow-up cases for one year after each camp activity and sends the reports to the DSW. The FNGOs get their funds after submitting the reports of the follow-up cases.

STREE SHAKTI CAMPS

Stree Shakti camps are more visible of the two components of the Stree Shakti project. These are held all over Delhi with the objective of providing benefits to the doorstep of the target group. The government has tried to ensure that the beneficiaries identified are linked to the delivery system through active intervention of NGOs.

Identification of the Issues

Three areas of intervention are broadly identified for camp activities, i.e. health, literacy and income generation. Four major issues in health are highlighted: anaemia in adolescent girls and pregnant women; full immunization of children; high fertility, specially in economically weaker sections; and sexually transmitted infections.

Under literacy, non-formal education, especially for children, is covered.

Income generation activities consist of traditional and non-traditional skill development training. Actual training is not provided in the camps but beneficiaries are provided with information regarding training activities and contact agencies. The beneficiaries can register their names for different courses.

TABLE 2.9: COMPARATIVE PERFORMANCE OF GRCs (2002–5)

S. No.	Particulars	GRC I	GRC II	GRC III	GRC IV
1.	Name of the GRC	Smarth	B.R. Ambedkar Dalit Uthan Avom Shiksha Samiti	Manav Paropkari Sanstha	Bisnauli Sarvodaya Gramodyog Sewa Sansthan
2.	District	North-West	East	South-West	South
3.	Field NGOs (Nos.)	22	19	9	14
4.	Activities Undertaken During	2002–5	2004–5	April 2004–March 2005	Nov. 2004–Mar. 2005
	(a) Skill Development	Trained: 624 Placed: 189 (30.28%)	Trained: 226 Placed: Figures NA	Trained: 731 Placed: 325 (44.45%) Self-Employed: 306 (41.86%)	Trained: 356 Placed: 144 (40.44%)
	(b) Health and Nutrition Awareness (No. of Beneficiaries)	3,185	2,325	748	3,125
	(c) Training of SHG (Nos.)	Beneficiaries: 189	Beneficiaries: 1,215	Groups: 14 Beneficiaries: 280	45 sessions
	(d) Legal Counselling (No. of Beneficiaries)	882	882	130	394
	(e) No. of SHGs (Beneficiaries)	144 (1,338)	50	20 (Apr. 2003–Sept. 2004)	50
	(f) No. of Beneficiaries Visiting Information Centres	1,554	1,455	663	1,553

(Contd.)

TABLE 2.9: (Contd.)

S.No.	Particulars	GRC I	GRC II	GRC III	GRC IV
5.	Share of FNGOs in Total Grants	7,95,000 for 22 NGOs (24.6%)	1,308,434 for 19 NGOs (18.6%)	*	3,34,150 for 14 NGOs (21.1%)
6.	Total Camps Conducted by FNGOs (Health, Legal and Nutrition)	(2002–5) Camps: 137 Beneficiaries: 19,303	(Sept. 2004–March 2005) Camps: 18 Beneficiaries: 13,722	(Apr. 2004–Mar. 2005) Camps: 35 Beneficiaries: 1,600 (Health & Nutrition only)	(2003–5) Camps: 62 Beneficiaries: 10,229

Source: Primary Survey conducted by IHD, 2006.
Note: *Could not be separated.

Even though there are three major themes for camp activities, gradually many additional activities are also being included in the camps to provide more opportunities to the beneficiaries. In health-related issues, information about and demonstrations in yoga and mental health have been included. In literacy, several programmes for attracting dropout children back to school are taken up. Income generation activities are not restricted to skill training but also provide facilities for the sale of products prepared by SHGs.

Legal counselling is a more recent addition to camp activities. It involves: sensitizing women to their rights; spreading legal awareness; providing legal help to women-related crimes, and helping the women complainants to follow-up their cases.

The officials of the DSW, one nodal NGO identified as MNGO and the FNGOs are jointly responsible for organizing these camps. The specific issues to be taken up in each camp within the overall broad framework discussed above are finalized at a joint meeting of all the organizers before the start of the camps.

Identification of the Area and Venue

The primary focus of these camps remains health-related issues though other diversified themes are being taken up gradually. Population growth rate and the child sex ratio (0–6 age group) are two major indicators of development. Health-related improvement is reflected in lowering the population growth rate and increasing the child sex ratio. Camp areas are identified where both the population growth rate and growth rate of the child population (0–6 years) are very high and the child sex ratio (female/1000 male) is low. The census and National Family Health Surveys provide an important database for the choice of areas. However, these criteria are not followed very strictly. As the camp activities expand, there is increasing demand from other areas. The DSW holds such camps in each of the nine districts to provide a balanced coverage of the programme.

As mentioned earlier, the camps are held on Sundays to ensure maximum participation. Government schools are generally chosen as the venue to accommodate large numbers of participants. The schools provide ten to twenty rooms to accommodate various organizations, various activities and the free movement of 300–400 people at a time.

Identification of FNGOs

NGOs are involved at two levels in Stree Shakti camps. One NGO, known as the MNGO is involved in the overall operation and supervision of the camps. In every month, a series of nine camps is held in nine districts of Delhi. The MNGO is responsible for providing training to the NGOs who will actually conduct the camp activities. It is also involved in designing the pre-registration survey of beneficiaries before such activity and the modalities of such operations. After the camp day, it documents the achievements and keeps track of the follow-up activities of the beneficiaries in association with other NGOs. Society of Voluntary Associations (SOSVA), the MNGO for Stree Shakti camps, has been working with the DSW since the beginning of the programme. It was identified by the DSW on the basis of its previous involvement with various health-related public schemes like the Reproductive and Child Health (RCH) programme of the states.

FNGOs are actually involved in organizing the activities on the camp day. They take up pre-registration surveys before the camp activities in the areas jointly decided on by the DSW, MNGO and the FNGOs. They identify possible beneficiaries and their health problems in the pre-registration survey and inform them about the objectives and activities of the forthcoming event. They even accompany the beneficiaries to the venue on the camp day.

Earlier, FNGOs were selected based on the recommendations of District Officers (DO) and Community Development Project Officers (CDPO) in the districts. The DSW used to receive details of several NGOs working for quite some time in health-related issues in the nearby areas, recommended by the officials in the district. Recently, the DSW has issued advertisements inviting expressions of interest from the NGOs. A selection committee consisting of the Joint Director and other officers of the DSW and one member from the MNGO has been formed to select the FNGOs that will take up direct responsibility of organizing Stree Shakti camps. One FNGO cannot organize more than four camps in a year.

A tripartite agreement is prepared and signed by the DSW, the MNGO and the concerned FNGOs in the beginning of each camp event. A letter of understanding specifies the respective roles of the MNGO and the FNGOs. A series of nine camps (one camp in each of the nine revenue districts of Delhi) are held at a time, whose activities are to be followed up within twelve months from the camp date.

The letter is signed a fresh in each series with a commitment to work together for one year at least.

Camp Activities

Camp activities are aimed at 700–800 beneficiaries in each camp. This requires elaborate arrangements and various pre-camp activities. The FNGO in-charge of each district takes up pre-registrations surveys in order to determine the common health-related problems suffered by local women. The MNGO and DSW officials arrange pre-camp meetings and provide trainings to the FNGOs. The training content focuses on: acquainting the FNGOs about the basic objectives of Stree Shakti camps; promoting interaction between NGOs and participating agencies; providing guidelines regarding pre-registration surveys and follow-up activities; arranging camp participation plans for different agencies; interacting with the beneficiaries on camp day; and training the volunteers regarding individual duties, responsibilities and treatment of beneficiaries.

Camp-day activities take place on Sunday in government schools, and continue through the whole day (9.00 a.m.–5.00 p.m.). Several agencies have different stalls. GRCs also participate in these camps and set-up their own stalls. The FNGO volunteers inform the beneficiaries regarding the activities and venue while conducting pre-registration surveys.

Pre-registration surveys provide some indication of the type of health care treatment needed in different categories. Preventive and curative medicines are distributed as far as possible. On the spot medical check-up facilities like blood tests are provided in the camps. Specialist doctors, legal professionals and other specialists meet the beneficiaries in the camps. The NGO volunteers provide the beneficiaries with Stree Shakti cards. Such cardholders get special facilities when they visit the hospitals, they have been referred to by the doctors in the camps.

Coverage of Activities and Programmes

During the last three years (2004–6), camp activities have covered more than 50 per cent of the area in each district. They have spread to rural areas as well. New Delhi district has been excluded from establishing camps as the majority of the slums in this district have been relocated elsewhere. The spread of camp activities is evident from Table 2.10.

TABLE 2.10: YEAR-WISE BREAK-UP OF THE NUMBER OF CAMPS HELD

	Camps Held	Beneficiaries	Referrals	Availed Medical Services
2002	52	37,252	5,718 (15.34)	5,578 (97.55)
2003	45	32,524	4,936 (15.17)	4,670 (94.61)
2004	45	37,422	5,060 (13.52)	3,764 (74.38)

Source: Primary Survey Conducted by IHD, 2006.
Note: Figures in brackets are percentages corresponding to the total in the previous column.

Camp activity started in February 2002 in only one district (south). Since then five series in each year (5 × 9 districts) have been possible. In 2002, seven series (the maximum till the present) were completed but all districts could not be included. Camp activities were discontinued in some districts while in five cases the results of camp activities were not reported. Hence the number of total camps in 2002 was much less (52) than it would have been had seven series been completed.

Achievements of the Project

The Stree Shakti project has been operational since 2002. It is being implemented under the citizen-government partnership (Bhagidari) with special focus on women. Various departments of the state government and the NGOs, jointly manage the implementation of the project, thereby facilitating new direction in PPP. There is an attempt to integrate other welfare programmes like the Integrated Child Development Scheme (ICDS) with it for maximizing welfare for the target group. Some statistics may be relevant to indicate the coverage of the programme during 2002–5:

- More than 200 Stree Shakti camps have been held to benefit nearly 200,000 women.
- The programme has spread to a catchment area of over 1 million people.
- Approximately 16,000 women have been benefited through health and nutrition awareness camps.
- Approximately, 5000 women have been benefited through legal counselling offered in the GRCs.

- More than 15,000 women have been benefited through skill development programmes.
- Nearly 300 SHGs have been formed.

The project has clearly brought some changes for the better in the lives of deprived women through a decentralized delivery process. It has been able to increase the level of awareness regarding quality of life with increasing coverage and adaptability. The comparative success story is summarized in Table 2.11.

More and more NGOs have been associated with this project during the years since its inception. More and more women are now willing to join the camps and pursue follow-up cases. Skill development training has widened the income generation opportunities for the economically deprived as programmes are now within their reach. Legal awareness has increased and women are coming out in the open to fight against dowry-related, family-related and other injustices.

The increase in the number of SHGs has opened opportunities for accessibility to the market and finance. All these have resulted in an increasing demand for such activities.

GRCs have been set up to provide a 'window of hope' to the deprived women who fail to utilize existing opportunities towards improving their quality of life. The major strength of this set-up is the conceptual acceptance that women find it difficult to leave household chores, even if the opportunities are there, and, therefore the attempt to bring the services to them.

TABLE 2.11: IMPACT OF DECENTRALIZED SERVICE DELIVERY DURING 2002–5

Category	2002	2005	Improvement
Women Willing to go to Hospital	325	1,085	More than 3 times
Association of Camp Volunteers in Referral Cases	92	219	More than 2 times
Employed after Skill Development Training	65	864	More than 13 times
Number of SHGs Formed	25	239	More than 9 times
Number of Participating NGOs	17	85	5 times
Number of Beneficiaries Coming for Legal Aids	235	2053	More than 8 times

Source: Primary Survey, IHD, 2006.

BRIDGING THE GAP IN SERVICE DELIVERY: GRCs' primary focus is on income generation through various skills development programmes. These are provided at the district level in order to bring the centres closer to the beneficiaries' living area. Various kinds of training is provided at the end of which the beneficiaries get certificates from the state education department. These trainings are much cheaper than those available in the private sector. The health and nutrition awareness camps, organized by the FNGOs in different areas of the districts help in taking the facilities to the beneficiaries.

PARTICIPATING AND CO-ORDINATING ELEMENTS: GRCs involve other NGOs in organizing health, nutrition and legal awareness camps. These are generally local NGOs already involved in similar kind of work. They are well acquainted with local people. This helps them in conducting pre-registration surveys and identifying the target groups who are in need of such services. The DO and CDPO of the DSW are involved in these activities creating a model of public-private participation and spreading the coordinating spirit.

MULTIDIMENSIONALITY COUPLED WITH A SINGLE SOURCE FOR DELIVERY: The programme is multidimensional in its goal towards developing all the basic capabilities in women—to be able to live life fully and participate as agents of change in social, economic, political and cultural spheres of their society. This is being done by providing services in all important areas like health, legal, nutrition, education and skill training for income generation initiatives. The multidimensionality coupled with a single source for delivery of services is its greatest potential which needs to be tapped. It also fosters group activities which builds confidence in women through SHGs.

SINGLE WINDOW INFORMATION DISSEMINATION: A new important component of the GRC is its role as an emerging centre of a single window information system. Women are largely not aware of the programmes available to them. They also do not know where to get the information, how and whom to contact, how to prepare the documents and various other important information without which they cannot utilize the benefits due to them. GRCs are developing a database of such information and working towards dessiminating it. The number of information seekers itself is proof of its need and importance.

TARGETED BENEFICIARIES: VAST COVERAGE: The programme is expending in its scope and coverage. It is a complete outreach programme which is targeted at women in economically weaker sections—women who are often left out and are not able to access the opportunities provided by the government.

INVOLVEMENT OF SENIOR GOVERNMENT OFFICIALS: The implementation of any programme depends on the interest and determination of people who initiate and pursue it. The project is directly under the charge of the CMO. The DSW is actively involved in all stages and has shown promising efforts and skills in pursuing it. A determined team and a collaborative effort from the top to the grass-root level, with minimum political intervention, is an asset of the project which if pursued with the same determination will succeed in achieving its goal of women empowerment.

Strength of the Project

The prime thrust of camp activities is on health-related issues, though other programmes are also being added gradually in order to provide wider coverage. The camps provide a bridge between the government agencies who provide the services and the community members using them. The strength of these camps is reflected in the increasing number of participants in the camps as revealed by various statistical figures quoted earlier.

Project Design

There are three important stages in the effective implementation of a project design: concretized and well-defined goals; appropriate and reliable methodology and approach; and consistent evaluation and monitoring of the programme.

The Stree Shakti project, has these three essential components, which gives it a wide scope in terms of its continuation as well as expansion.

The objectives laid down are not only unique in their vision and perspective of the problems of the economically weaker sections of women in the society, but they also endorse a new methodology of making the 'services available at the doorstep' of the needy women, thus leaving out any possibility of inaccessibility. Another unique dimension of this project is the element of accountability with transparency through regular monitoring and periodic evaluation by an independent agency. The involvement of thirteen stakeholders in the project at various stages of implementation ensures mutual accountability and transparency where each stakeholder is answerable to another for its functioning. What also stands out uniquely in this programme is the partnership across the stakeholders in the state, i.e. officials of DSW, the civil society (NGOs/hospital doctors/lawyers) and the local people—which are prominent features strengthening the purpose and fulfilment of the scheme.

Interviews with the beneficiaries reveal that the target group of women needs such intervention and inputs. Thus, in this sense the scope of the programme is unlimited: in its reach and consequence in terms of a better life for women among the economically weaker sections of Delhi. If pursued well, it can open new opportunities for the needy and destitute women of Delhi—and help them in their self-development and capacity building. However, what is constantly needed is growth and modification the changing 'needs' and 'situations', in covering the untouched and newer dimensions of women's empowerment.

Direct Service Delivery

The inputs and goals of the project are oriented towards qualitative improvement in the lives of women through direct service delivery, that is, providing opportunities at their doorstep. It is this feature that makes this scheme different from other women's programmes. There is no dearth of programmes for women in India. However, the most constraining factor is the wide gap between the service providers, or the 'services', and the needy recipients. Stree Shakti camps and Kosh (GRCs) have been designed to bridge that gap as the opportunities are literally to be availed of at the doorstep. This aspect of the programme immediately enhances its reach to the maximum number of women who are in need of it.

Participatory Approach

Camp activities involve participation of government officials, NGOs and beneficiaries, with well-defined responsibilities. NGOs are involved in pre-registration surveys thereby establishing direct contact with the target groups. The MNGO representative is there to help the FNGOs in their work and to keep records of the camp activities.

Government officials from different departments are involved in designing camp activities and are present on camp day to supervise and keep in touch with the beneficiaries, who may approach them directly to discuss their problems. Higher level government officers and political leaders including the chief minister occasionally visit the camps. This sends the message that the government is serious regarding the success of the programme. It also helps in creating confidence among the beneficiaries.

Extended Coverage

Camps are held all over Delhi in each of the districts. In each district, different areas are chosen to include deprived women from every area. The regularity of camp activities creates confidence among the beneficiaries, that this is not a one-day affair. Follow-up activities pursued by camp volunteers are a very novel concept to help the beneficiaries to come out of their shelter and take the required help. Many women do not go for treatment because they are afraid of the unfamiliar hospital environment. Health care facilities have assumed a new dimension with this extended help. The volunteers arrange for transport and accompany the beneficiaries to referral places.

4. Tackling the Problems of Exclusion

The Stree Shakti programme of the state government has brought a new approach to the PPP. Medical camps are common events but they are a one-way supply of services, without the active involvement of the people in assessing need-based services. In Stree Shakti camps, NGOs identify the camp areas through baseline surveys to determine the size of the target groups and their specific needs. The objective of this scheme is not only the provision of service, but awareness generation as well. The women in every family of the slums surveyed are provided a specific identification card, but the men are also encouraged to visit the camps as male awareness is equally important for women empowerment.

Wide coverage of NGOs is another characteristic of the PPP in this scheme. NGOs are identified all over the state and encouraged to participate by turn in order to avoid stagnation in participation. There is short-term involvement of the NGOs in organizing camps in every month and long-term involvement in running a GRC for three years.

The target group in each area knows that all service-related information is available at one place. Sometimes slum dwellers do not have access to very basic information, as where to get certificates, previous and the like. The GRCs provide them informations regarding the welfare schemes available in other government departments as well. The GRC volunteers help them in completing procedural details in availing these facilities.

The NGOs assist the target groups to utilize, the services even after the camps end. A primary survey conducted by, IHD has revealed that women do not want to go to the hospitals alone. Similarly, they do not want to pursue legal problems owing to lack of awareness of the place and process. The NGOs extend these services and help the women to come out of their vicious cycle of poverty.

The involvement of PPPs in this project has helped in cost reduction in significant ways. They use the built-up assets owned by the state or the local bodies. Camps are held in government schools on holidays. Public resources are utilized more extensively to accommodate a large number of beneficiaries. Apart form health, awareness regarding legal issues and skill development opportunities are also provided under the same roof for maximum utilization of time, which is a precious input for the poor.

The NGOs are actively involved in the design and implementation of the project so that services delivery is not a one-way traffic. They hold regular meetings with the officials as well as the stakeholders in order to reduce the gap in the service delivery mechanism. They bring several government departments together in the camps in order to bring the beneficiaries into direct contact with the officials. The state government's initiative for a citizen–government partnership in governance is practised fully in this scheme. This innovative PPP helps to increase accountability and transparency in governance, as the persons responsible are now known to the beneficiaries. This form of the PPP has been able to break the barrier of non-familiarity with the place or the provider. Women who do not find the time to go to hospitals regularly can now avail themselves of those opportunities with minimum time overrun or cost overrun. Public holidays are chosen so that they can come with their family members.

This experiment of the state government is not without difficulties and all the participating agencies know that they are passing through a learning process. However, the increasing willingness among the stakeholders to participate more and more in such events speaks of the growing need for such initiatives. The unique PPP initiative of the state government has tried to tackle the problem of exclusion by taking the services to the doorsteps of those who otherwise would not have access to them.

REFERENCES

Chaddha, G.K. and P.P. Sahu (2002), 'Post-reform Setbacks in Rural Employment: Issues that need Further Scrutiny', *Economic and Political Weekly* (vol. 37, no. 21, pp. 1998–2026).

Delhi Human Development Report (2006), United Nations Development Programme, New Delhi.

Maitra, Shipra and B.S. Mehta (2007), Stree Shakti Project—Reducing Gender Inequality. Report Submitted to Deptt. of Social Welfare, Govt. of NCT of Delhi.

Parikh, Kirit S. and R. Radhakrishna (2004–5), *India Development Report*, New Delhi: Indira Gandhi Institute of Development Research and Oxford University Press.

Vision 2020 (2002), Planning Commission, Government of India, New Delhi.

CHAPTER 3

Patterns of Policy in Public-Private Partnerships: Puzzles, Performance, Problems and Prospects in the Delivery of Health Care Services in India

A. VENKAT RAMAN
JAMES WARNER BJÖRKMAN

Background

PRIVATE SECTOR IN INDIA

It is widely accepted that the deficiencies in the public sector health system require significant reforms. The need for reform in India's health sector has been emphasized by successive plan documents since the Eighth Five-Year Plan in 1992, by the 2002 national health policy and by international donor agencies. The World Bank (2001:12,14), which has been catalytic in initiating health sector reforms in many states, categorically emphasized, 'now is the time to carry out radical experiments in India's health sector, particularly since the status quo is leading to a dead end. . . . But it is evident that there is no single strategy that would be best option. . . . The proposed reforms are not cheap, but the cost of not reforming is even greater.'

Health Sector Reform (HSR) is defined as '. . . a sustained, purposeful change to improve the efficiency, equity and effectiveness of the health sector' (Berman 1995). The World Health Organization (WHO) (1997) defined health sector reform as '. . . a sustained process

*Research study funded by the Indo-Dutch Programme on Alternatives in Development (project 5.3.96).

of fundamental change in policy and institutional arrangements of the health sector, usually guided by the government. . . . It is designed to improve the functioning and performance of the health sector and ultimately the health status of the people.' Reform strategies include (i) alternative financing (user-fees, health insurance, community financing, private sector investment); (ii) institutional management (autonomy to hospitals, monitoring and management by local government agencies, contracting); (iii) public sector reforms (civil service reforms, capacity building, productivity improvement); and (iv) collaboration with the private sector (public/private partnerships, joint ventures) (World Bank 1993; Thomason 2002; Abrantes 2003).

Partnership with the private sector has emerged as a new avenue of reforms, in part due to resource constraints in the public sector of governments across the world (Mitchell-Weaver and Manning 1992). There is growing realization that, given their respective strengths and weaknesses, neither the public sector nor the private sector alone can operate in the best interest of the health system. There is also a growing belief that public and private sectors in health can potentially gain from one another (ADBI 2000; Bloom et al. 2000; Agha et al. 2003). Involvement of the private sector is, in part, linked to the belief that public sector bureaucracies are inefficient and unresponsive while market mechanisms promote efficiency and ensure cost-effective, good quality services (WHO 2001). Mitchell (2000) argues that, given its increasing inability on both fronts, the public sector must reorient its dual role of financing and providing services. Under partnerships, public and private sectors can play innovative roles in financing and providing health care services.

After reviewing the health sector in India, the World Bank (2001) and the National Commission on Macroeconomics in Health (2003, 2005) strongly advocated harnessing the private sector's energy and countering its failures by making both public and private sectors more accountable. The Tenth Five-Year Plan (2002–7) envisioned in detail the need for private sector participation in the delivery of health services.

Collaborating with the private sector and fostering a partnership for providing health services to the underserved sections of the population are crucial in the Indian context. Due to deficiencies in the public sector health systems, the poor in India are forced to seek services from the private sector, often borrowing to pay for them. India has one of the world's highest levels of private out-of-pocket financing (87 per cent estimated in World Bank 2001). Out-of-pocket expenditure at the point of service is about 85 per cent (Kulkarni 2003). Such a mode of financing imposes debilitating effects on the poor. Hospitalization or chronic illnesses often lead to liquidation of assets and indebtedness. It is estimated that more than 40 per cent of hospitalized people in India borrow money or sell assets to cover expenses, and 35 per cent of hospitalized Indians fall below the poverty line because of hospital expenses. In any given year, out-of-pocket medical costs alone may push 2.2 per cent of the population below the poverty line (Selvaraju and Annigeri 2001; Mahal et al. 2002). Approximately 29 per cent of the Indian population (almost 300 million people) live below the poverty line and depend on free health services from the public sector. The inequities in the health system are aggravated by the fact that public spending on health has remained stagnant at around 1 per cent of GDP (0.9 per cent compared to the global average of 5.5 per cent). Yet even the public subsidies on health do not automatically benefit the poor. The poorest quintile of the population uses only one-tenth of the public (state) subsidies on health care while the richest quintile accesses 34 per cent of them (Mahal et al. 2002).

PRIVATE SECTOR IN INDIA

Over the years the private health sector in India has markedly expanded (Baru 1998). At independence the private sector in India had only 8 per cent of health care facilities (World Bank 2004), but recent estimates indicate that 93 per cent of all hospitals, 64 per cent of beds, 85 per cent of doctors, 80 per cent of outpatients and 57 per cent of inpatients are in the private sector (World Bank 2001). Contrary to commonly held views, private hospitals are relatively less urban-biased than public hospitals. Given the overwhelming presence of the private sector in health, various state governments in India have been exploring the option of involving the private sector and creating partnerships with it in order to meet the growing health-care needs of the population.

The private sector is not only India's most unregulated sector but also its most potent untapped sector. Although inequitable, expensive, overly indulgent in clinical procedures and without quality standards or public disclosure of practices, the private sector is perceived to be easily accessible, better managed and more efficient than its public counterpart. It is assumed that collaboration with the private sector in the form of public-private partnerships (PPP) will improve equity, efficiency, accountability, quality and accessibility of the entire health system. Advocates argue that the public and private sectors can potentially gain from one another in the form of resources, technology, knowledge and skills, management practices, cost efficiency and even a make over of their respective images (ADBI 2000). Partnerships are expected to ameliorate the resource constraints of the public sector by reducing investments in expensive tertiary care services.

Public-Private Partnership

There are many ways of defining the terms 'public' and 'private' (Wang 2000). In general, the public sector includes organizations or institutions which are financed by state revenue and which function under government budgets or control. The private sector comprises those organizations and individuals working outside the direct control of the state (Bennet 1991). Broadly, the private sector includes all non-state actors, some explicitly seeking profits (for-profit) and others operating on a not-for-profit (NFP) basis. The former are conventionally called 'private enterprise', the latter 'non-governmental organizations' (NGO). In the health sector, for-profit providers may include individual physicians, diagnostic centres, ambulance operators, blood banks, commercial contractors, polyclinics, nursing homes and hospitals of various capacities. They may also include community service extensions of industrial establishments, cooperative societies and professional associations. The for-profit private health sector encompasses the most diverse group of practitioners and facilities. But likewise, the character of NFP organizations varies in terms of their size, expertise level and geographical spread. NFP services are clustered in charitable clinics or hospitals. Some are established on a financially sustainable basis and are funded from user-charges; most, however, require the support of grants or donations.

Although widely used, the term 'partnership' is difficult to define. Some definitions in the literature are so ambiguous that they cover practically any type of interaction between public and private actors. Yet partnership is often used to describe a range of inter-organizational relationships and collaborations. Some of the useful definitions of PPP are:

> . . . [the] means to bring together a set of actors for the common goal of improving the health of a population based on the mutually agreed roles and principles. (WHO 1999)

> . . . a variety of co-operative arrangements between the government and private sector . . . in delivering public goods or services . . . [which] provides a vehicle for coordinating with non-governmental actors to undertake integrated, comprehensive efforts to meet community needs . . . to take advantage of the expertise of each partner, so that resources, risks and rewards can be allocated in a way that best meets clearly defined public needs. (Axelsson, Bustreo and Harding 2003)

> . . . that both parties have agreed to work together in implementing a program, and that each party has a clear role and say in how that implementation happens. (Blagescu and Young 2005)

> . . . a form of agreement [that] entails reciprocal obligations and mutual accountability, voluntary or contractual relationships, the sharing of investment and reputational risks, and joint responsibility for design and execution. (World Economic Forum 2005)

Three fundamental themes emerge from these definitions: a relative sense of equality between the partners; mutual commitment to agreed objectives; and mutual benefits for the stakeholders involved in the partnership. Partnership is therefore a collaborative effort and reciprocal relationship between two or more parties with clear terms and conditions, well defined partnership structures, and specified performance indicators for delivery of a set of health services in a stipulated time period. In other words, the core elements of a viable partnership are beneficence (joint gains), autonomy (of each partner), joint-ness (shared decision-making and accountability) and equity (fair returns in proportion to investment and effort).

CHALLENGES IN PARTNERSHIP

While the health system as a whole has common objectives of equity, efficiency, quality and accessibility, public and private providers interpret the contents of these objectives differently. Generally, the motive of the government is to provide health services to all at minimum cost or free; it develops policies and programmes to provide equity of access to such services. From the public sector point of view, there are merits and demerits in collaborating with the private sector.

Not-for-profit organizations have special concern for reaching the poor and the disadvantaged but in many states, they account for less than 1 per cent of all health facilities (World Bank 2004). Their sustenance depends on philanthropic donations or external funding. As a result their interventions remain ad hoc, and their 'up-scalability' remains doubtful. But they provide good quality care, need little regulation or oversight from government, are able to attract dedicated staff, and cater to the needs of those otherwise excluded from mainstream health care. Moreover, they are also willing to undertake health care challenges that the for-profit sector is unwilling or unable to take on. Given their non-profit motives and grass-roots level presence, NGOs can play useful oversight roles in the system. Their size and flexibility allows them to achieve notable successes where governments have failed.

Opinion is divided on the motives of the (for-profit) private sector, ranging from outright distrust to strong support for close cooperation with it. One extreme view is that the private sector is primarily motivated by money and has no concern for equity or access. Bennet et al. (1994) identified five main problems associated with private for-profit provision of health services. They are related to the use of illegitimate or unethical means to maximize profit, little concern about public health goals, lack of interest in sharing clinical information, creating a 'brain drain' among public sector health staff, and lack of regulatory control over practices. Rosenthal (2000) cites similar concerns about involving the private sector in delivering public health services. However, Bloom et al. (2000) suggest that the private sector is neither so easy to characterize nor so easy to neglect. Its strengths lie in its innovativeness, efficiency and ability to learn from competition. Management standards are generally higher in the private (for-profit) sector. The private sector can play an important role in transferring management skills and best practices to the public sector. In India, the formal for-profit sector has the most diverse group of facilities and practitioners. Since it accounts for the largest proportion of services and resources in the health sector, it is argued that future strategies to improve public health should take into account the strengths of the private sector (World Bank 2004).

India also has a large number of non-qualified rural medical practitioners in the informal private sector. A conservative estimate puts the number of these practitioners at 1.25 million. The pros and cons of partnering with each subgroup in the private sector are identified in Table 3.1.

TABLE 3.1: PROS AND CONS OF COLLABORATING WITH THE PRIVATE SECTOR IN HEALTH

Sub-sector	Pros	Cons
Informal	Accessible Client-oriented Low cost	Poor quality care Difficult to mainstream Poor educated
Not-for-Profit	High quality Targeted to the poor Low cost Involves the community	Small coverage Lack of resources Cannot be scaled-up Ad hoc interventions
For profit	High quality (in select disciplines) Huge outreach/coverage Innovative Efficient	Ad hoc interventions High Cost Variable quality Clustered in cities

Source: Adapted from World Bank, 2004.

CHARACTERISTICS OF PARTNERSHIP

Despite these differences, the public and private sectors constantly interact with one another. While the government needs the private sector's support in order to attract more resources, expand coverage and provide diversity of services, the private sector has incentives to approach government in order to influence its policies in terms of tax-exemptions, accreditation and fee setting (Wang 2000). Partnerships are more useful when the net benefits of partnership exceed those of independent activities, and when the joint efforts result in more efficient or effective services than through independent action (Bazzoli et al. 1997).

The Ministry of Health and Family Welfare (MOHFW) in India presupposes that partnerships could help in ameliorating the problem of poor health services delivery at two levels: in improving delivery mechanisms and in increasing mobilization of resources for health care (GOI 2005). Other presumed benefits of partnerships are improvements in quality of services, reduced cost of care due either to competition or through economies of scale, redirecting the public resources to other areas, reduction in the duplication of services, adoption of best practices, targeted services to the poor and better self-regulation and accountability.

It is often observed that partnerships are formed between organizations but succeed because of individuals who are strong leaders and who champion the partnership projects with vision, energy and enthusiasm. It is important to emphasize that partnerships are no substitute for good governance and that partnership requires governmental leadership. There is a danger that, wherever governance is weak, partnerships could be projected as an automatic choice rather than improving governance. Partnerships work typically with one providing the financing and the other providing the services (ADBI 2000).

ADBI (2000) identifies the enabling conditions for the success of a partnership as:

- A clear understanding between the partners about mutual benefits
- A clear understanding of the responsibilities and obligations between the partners
- Strong community support
- A need for some catalyst to start the process of partnership (maybe an individual, a donor, a compelling vision or even a political or economic crisis)
- Stability of the political (government) and legal climate (laws)
- A regulatory framework which is followed and enforced
- The capacity and expertise of the government at different levels in designing and managing contracts (partnership)
- Appropriate organizational and management systems for partnerships
- A strong management information system
- Clarity on incentives and penalties.

In many countries, legal and political considerations create obstacles for any partnership with the commercial private sector. Partnership with the private sector can be misconstrued as an attempt at privatization. Such fears about the private sector may have emerged from the perceived social image of the private sector as 'exploitative' and having 'ulterior motives'. Possibly the bureaucracy would be willing to partner with the for-profit sector for administrative efficiency, but political and popular sentiments may prevent overt or enthusiastic collaboration. Though NFP NGOs may be easier to engage as partners, concerns have been raised about the difficulties of NGOs working with the government (Mukhopadhyay 2000) and the financial (survival) motives of the NGOs (Ahmed 2000). In India concerns have been raised about the dubious nature of some NGOs which are often established by political personalities to garner funds from the state. Other concerns about partnerships are the apparent difference between the public sector and the private sector in terms of resource commitment (long-term commitment of the public sector compared to short-term commitment by the private sector), differences in work culture and the notion of efficiency, perceptions about the quality of care, and type of patients seeking services.

SCOPE AND TYPES OF PARTNERSHIP

Based on research literature it is possible to identify varied types and models of PPP in health sectors around the world. Among the types and models of partnerships are contracting (contracting-out and contracting-in); franchising; social marketing; joint ventures; subsidies and tax incentives; vouchers or service purchase coupons; hospital autonomy; build, operate, and transfer; philanthropic contributions; health cooperatives; grants-in-aid; capacity-building; leasing; and social health insurance. Different models are, of course, useful under different circumstances. However, among all the partnership models, contracting has been the most common form. The research literature is replete with examples of contracting as a form of PPP.

CONTRACTING

One of the dominant tools for engaging the private sector in health sector reforms across all types of public health systems throughout the world is contracting, under which the financing and provision (delivery) of health services are clearly delineated between the provider and the purchaser (Ashton, Cummings and McLean 2004). The private providers receive a grant or budget amount from the government for delivering certain services which the latter previously delivered itself. The relationship between the government and the private sector is specified in a written agreement. Bennett and Mills (1998) identified several stages in a contracting process, viz., (a) decision to contract and the services to contract; (b) tendering and selection of the contractor; (c) contract design; (d) implementation; (e) monitoring the performance, and (g) evaluating the implications of contract on the public health system. Other critical issues relate to the objectives and scope of the services to be delivered, costing of the services, performance specifications including quality and expected health outcomes, payment for the services, supervision, access or special privileges to the poor and target population, and the relative capacity of the partners in managing the partnership contract.

Currently several private partnership initiatives are under implementation in the states of India. The scope of these initiatives spans disease surveillance; purchase and distribution of drugs in bulk; contracting specialists for high-risk pregnancies; national disease control programmes; social marketing; adoption and management of primary health centres; co-location of private facilities (blood banks, pharmacies); subsidies and duty exemptions; joint ventures; contracting-out; medical education and training; engaging private sector consultants; pay clinics; discount vouchers; self-regulation; R&D investments; telemedicine; health cooperatives; and accreditation.

The Study

While the forms of partnerships vary, there is little evidence to indicate the relative merits of one form of private partnership over another. Little is known about the scope and coverage of services under partnership with the private sector; less is known about the institutional capacity of government agencies to design, negotiate, implement and monitor such partnerships. Information is required about subsidies, performance and quality of services under partnership arrangements, operational constraints, effect on the public health system, and the stakeholders' perspectives on this policy option. There is no consensus about the appropriate level of private sector involvement in health care or an appropriate public policy towards the private sector.

At the policy level, some issues that need careful analysis are the relative efficiency of one mode of partnership over other. How can partnership deals be specifically designed to target and benefit the poor? What is the institutional capacity of the government or the private partner to manage a partnership? At the operational level, questions that merit in-depth analysis include the conditions for successful partnership; how to ensure that the poor actually benefit from services; mutual responsibilities and commitments of partners; incentives and disincentives; performance indicators; and monitoring the functioning of the partnership.

A range of health services is spanned by case studies conducted by the authors for the IDPAD. Located in rural and urban areas, the health services studied include clinical care services as well as non-clinical support services and stationary establishments as well as mobile services. They specifically include diagnostic services, general curative care, maternal and child health services, community health financing activities, health promotion activities and ICT-based health service provision.

After careful review of various 'partnership models' in different states, the study compiled sixteen cases in nine states of India in order to reflect and assess different models of PPP. The study critically reviewed, in depth, the cases through contract documents, government orders, memoranda of understanding and other documents. The study also compiled the feedback from different stakeholders, including the patients, public and the private partner officials. Operational issues in the management and functioning of schemes were carefully reviewed.

Appendix 3.1 provides a synoptic summary of the sixteen case studies. Partnership initiatives ranged from super-specialty tertiary-care hospitals (Apollo Hospital, Raichur, SMS hospital, Jaipur) to primary care (Karuna Trust in Karnataka) to slum communities (Arpana Swasthya Kendra, Delhi, urban slum care in the district town of Adilabad, Andhra Pradesh). Community health insurance initiatives in two states were also documented (Arogya Raksha Scheme in Andhra Pradesh, Yeshasvini Scheme in Karnataka). In Tamil Nadu, Uttaranchal, and West Bengal the study examined mobile health services: the first provides emergency ambulance services, the second provides diagnostic and general health care and the third combines features of the previous two. Other partnership initiatives studied include telemedicine and tele-health projects in Karnataka and contracting-out cleaning, kitchen and laundry services in West Bengal. Rogi Kalyan Samiti or hospital autonomy in a decentralized context by local self-government in Bhopal, the capital of Madhya Pradesh, was investigated in order to understand whether hospital autonomy fits within the PPP framework.

Analysis and Discussion

The case studies are analysed under two broad frameworks: operational issues in the management of partnerships, and policy perspectives on PPPs. Appendix 3.1 provides a synoptic summary of all the case studies, from which some critical issues are discussed below.

OVERVIEW OF THE CASE STUDIES

Though contracting (contracting-'out' and contracting-'in') is the predominant model of private partnership, our research also studied other forms of partnerships. The private sector was represented in the form of individual physicians, commercial contractors, large private and corporate super-speciality hospitals and NFP agencies (NGOs). Of the sixteen case studies and nineteen partnership agreements, only eight partners were NGOs. Some partnerships dealt with simple contracts (diet, laundry, cleaning) whereas other more complex contracts involved many stakeholders (Yeshasvini is a community-based self-financed health insurance scheme). In almost all partnerships, the principal public partner is the Department of Health and Family Welfare, either directly or through health facility-level committees. In terms of monetary value, the least valued contract provided dietary services at a rate of Rs. 27 per meal for about 30 meals in a day (Bhagajatin Hospital, Kolkata); the most expensive engaged a corporate hospital to run a government-built super-speciality hospital in Raichur, Karnataka (over Rs. 600 million). The oldest partnership (since 1996) is the Karuna Trust, which adopted and manages primary health centres in Karnataka, whereas the Chiranjeevi Scheme, which engages private doctors for deliveries in Gujarat, is the most recent initiative (since December 2005). Except in one case (Birla Institute in Uttaranchal's Mobile Health Clinic), all private partners had prior experience in the health sector. In terms of the scope of services, three partnerships provide super-speciality tertiary-care services, twelve partnerships provide community care and support services, and the remaining few provide non-clinical support services. Of the sixteen partnership projects, five are based in urban areas but most projects are in rural and tribal regions. Although most projects are specific to a geographical region, some partnerships benefit people in the entire state (Yeshasvini Scheme in Karnataka and Arogya Raksha Scheme in Andhra Pradesh).

ENABLING CONDITIONS

Policy pronouncements by government are not sufficient for a PPP to succeed. Except in three partnerships where the government resorted to open-tender bidding, most of the partnerships revealed that the government and the private partner chose to consult each other, formally or informally, before venturing into partnership agreements.

In such partnerships, charismatic leadership and vision of the personalities, both from the private sector and from the public sector, played a critical role. There were also compelling circumstances and relationships based on trust that were critical in triggering partnership initiatives. For example, in the case of Arpana Swasthya Kendra, the Municipal Corporation of Delhi (MCD) had built a maternity health centre with funds from the World Bank's India Population Project-VIII, but the building was not operational due to non-deployment of staff. An NGO that had been working in the slum community approached the IPP-VIII project director in MCD with a request to let the NGO manage the health centre. The project director worked hard to convince the political leaders and administrative heads of the corporation, eventually obtaining their approval for a proposal to transfer the health centre to the NGO under a fixed-term agreement.

In the case of the Yeshasvini Scheme, Dr Devi Shetty, founder-director of Narayana Hrudayalaya and already a highly popular figure in the country for his pioneering work on low-cost cardiac surgeries and charity, was invited to endorse a milk product at a function held by the Karnataka Milk Federation (KMF), a cooperative with more than two million members. During the function Dr Shetty offered to provide services to all KMF members if each paid a monthly fee of Rs. 5. Dr. Shetty made a proposal to Karnataka's then chief minister and to the secretary of the cooperatives department. The proposal was formally approved by the state government which, in turn, contributed half of the subscription for each member in the scheme. Dr Shetty and his staff conducted most of the planning, initial implementation and supervision before an independent trust undertook the responsibility. To make the services available to the beneficiaries all over the state, Dr Shetty used his personal contacts and his persuasive skills to convince more private hospitals across the state to become part of the scheme. Similarly, Dr Shetty played a critical role in the setting up the Karnataka Integrated Telemedicine and Tele-health project. There are, of course, other personalities involved in the project too.

In the case of adoption and management of the primary health centres (PHC) in Karnataka, the role of Dr Sudarshan from the Karuna Trust was crucial. At his suggestion, the Government of Karnataka mooted a proposal for NGOs to manage the PHCs. Dr Sudharshan undertook the task of managing two PHCs as model centres for primary care. The success of this experiment led the government to issue a formal policy on PPP in 2000. Similar initiatives of people like retired Colonel C.S. Pant (Uttaranchal mobile health clinic), Dr K.J.R. Murthy (Mahavir Trust Hospital in Hyderabad), Mr M.A. Wohab (boat-based mobile health services in the Sunderbans of West Bengal), and Dr Haren Joshi (Shamlaji Hospital in Gujarat) have inspired partnership initiatives.

Circumstances which lead to private sector involvement are critical for the success or failure of a partnership. The Rajiv Gandhi super-speciality hospital in Raichur, Karnataka was built at a cost of Rs. 600 million. This economically backward region of the state has no modern health facilities so people are forced to travel long distances to seek specialist medical care. As government was unable to either deploy or retain specialist doctors, the hospital was lying unused. Apollo Hospitals Ltd., a corporate hospital chain, was seeking to establish its own hospitals in the region but it was not sure about building a super-speciality hospital. The respective dilemmas of the Government of Karnataka and Apollo Hospitals Ltd. were highly conducive for establishing this partnership for mutual benefit. Through this partnership, the government is able to provide free services to the poor, and Apollo Hospitals Ltd. is able to establish its business operations without having to invest in constructing physical infrastructure. The corporate hospital is able to pay its staff well so it can retain the desired manpower. Similarly, Chamarajanagar, a predominantly tribal district, had only primary care facilities at its district hospital. For any super-speciality care, people had to travel long distances. Bangalore's Narayana Hrudayalaya came forward to set up telemedicine services in collaboration with the state government and the Indian Space Research Organization (ISRO). In another example, geographical and topographical limitations in accessing health services by the people in Uttaranchal and in the Sundarbans prompted innovative health delivery mechanisms by local private agencies.

Operational constraints also prompted some partnership initiatives. In Jaipur's SMS Hospital, the hospital administration could not properly maintain its radiological equipment. Instead of purchasing and maintaining expensive equipment (CT scan and MRI), the government invited a private contractor to operate his own machine on the hospital premises, with special concessions and even free services for the poor (an example of purchasing services on behalf of the poor rather than provisioning). Similarly, the Life Line Fluid Store in the same hospital is able to negotiate cheaper rates for drugs and supplies and maintain better inventory management of the drug store. Contracting out dietary, laundry and cleaning services in Kolkata's Baghajatin Hospital is another typical example of private partnership for improving hospital efficiency.

Partnerships with the private sector tend to be more successful if the policy is built around the lessons from prior experiments, although contracting-out non-clinical support services seems to be an exception to this principle. For example, in Karnataka and West Bengal, state-level policy on PPP was framed after launching a few pilot projects. In Tamil Nadu, Rajasthan and Gujarat, state policy towards PPPs seems to have been introduced without any prior experimentation. Tamil Nadu is one state where private sector involvement in health services had long been encouraged, especially by industrial houses. Yet it would be fair to say that, as of now, the policy is ineffective. The state of Andhra Pradesh, which had a positive engagement in health sector reforms, does not currently have any private sector partnership initiatives of significance.

EQUITY AND ACCESSIBILITY

Partnership with the private sector presupposes that equity, accessibility and quality of care will be ensured to the targeted beneficiaries, i.e. the poor and deprived sections of the population. However, verification of the authenticity of the poor patients is one of the operational difficulties faced by field managers. Each partnership project gives special privileges to the poor under various contract clauses. Such services range from direct provision of clinical care to providing services via insurance, vouchers, etc. In some projects, upper limits have been placed on the utilization of services. For example, patients in Yeshasvini Scheme are not allowed to avail of any medical treatment (inpatient admission) which does not lead to surgery; and only two unmarried children plus a spouse of a cooperative society member are allowed to avail themselves of benefits under the scheme. In the Arogya Raksha Scheme in Andhra Pradesh, beneficiaries are eligible for free hospital treatment only if sterilization had been carried out in a government hospital.

Relatively few partnership projects—Adilabad's urban slum health project, Arogya Raksha and Chiranjeevi schemes—are exclusively meant for patients from families below the poverty line (BPL). There are no uniform procedures adopted for the identification and verification of authentic BPL beneficiaries. Decisions about who qualifies as BPL patients are left to the interpretation of hospital managers. As a result, complaints often lead to confrontation between patients and hospital management. An observation by one staff member at Raichur's Rajiv Gandhi Hospital sums up the difficulty in verifying the antecedents of BPL patients: 'People drive to the hospital by a Honda City car and claim that they are BPL patients.' Some projects have better systems to verify the antecedents of BPL patients. For example, in the cases of Chiranjeevi Scheme beneficiaries in Gujarat and sterilization in the Arogya Raksha Scheme in Andhra Pradesh, patients are required to get a citation from the local government hospital for an ante-natal check-up. In most of the partnership projects 'user charges' are not permitted. In those projects where a 'user-fee' is allowed, the quantum of collection is too meagre to meet the operational expenses. How the 'user-fee' is to be accounted for during the grant allocation by the government is not made clear in the partnership agreements.

PRIVATE PARTNER SELECTION AND OBLIGATIONS OF THE PARTNERS

Based on our analysis, it is possible to suggest that a competitive process of selecting the private sector partner is less effective than an invited or negotiated partnership. A possible explanation may be that, while competing to win a contract, the private partner's primary concern is to showcase a low cost which would clinch the bid. The public sector managers, on the other hand, are more concerned about satisfying procedural requirements (for internal regulatory systems) than meeting the beneficiaries' needs. In the tendering process, in government invariably chooses the lowest bid. While seemingly economical for the government in the short run, after some time the contractor would expect an upward revision of the tariffs or incentives. In the absence of these, the contractor is unlikely to deliver services at the same level of quality or effectiveness as at the beginning of the contract. Governments may resort to a transparent and competitive process of selecting the private agency to withstand administrative and legal scrutiny. This approach of contracting may be useful in commercial projects but not in the social sector where competitive pricing of services is not the priority; reaching the poor is. Some of the successful partnership projects documented here point to the importance of prior negotiations with the potential partners. In some cases the eligibility conditions were tailor-made or else the prior experience of the agency was used as a basis for choosing the private partner.

Among the core components of any partnership are mutual responsibilities and commitments. In all the partnerships, the public sector is committed to providing the physical infrastructure in the form of building premises, equipment, drugs and supplies, electricity, water connection and in some cases fuel for the ambulance or an equivalent budget item. Otherwise the public sector commits resources by reimbursing expenses incurred or by providing grants-in-aid. The responsibilities of the private partners are clearly stated in most of the projects. A common theme of responsibility is to provide uninterrupted services to the target beneficiaries (BPL patients), employment of qualified staff, maintenance and upkeep of physical infrastructure, payment of rents and taxes, and submission of periodic accounts and reports. Some partnership projects prescribe additional responsibilities for the private partners under certain contingencies. For example, the Rajiv Gandhi Super-Speciality Hospital should be ready to provide free services during natural calamities; Shamlaji Hospital should cater to medico-legal cases as well as treat accident and trauma cases. All the partnership projects are expected to provide services under national programmes, including immunization and family planning. Private partners are allowed to extend the services beyond the scope of the partnership agreement.

PERFORMANCE SPECIFICATIONS

While all the partnership agreements have clear operational guidelines for the private partners, specific performance indicators are conspicuously absent in all projects except Delhi's Arpana Swasthya Kendra, Andhra Pradesh's urban health scheme and West Bengal's mobile health scheme in the Sunderbans. In the AP urban slum project, the performance parameters are explicitly based on a formula which has a weighted score of 200 points. Most of the indicators include health outcomes indices. In the Sunderbans' mobile health scheme, the performance indicators are measured by mortality and morbidity indicators. Some partnerships' agreements mandate the private sector to submit periodic reports but most indicate a monitoring mechanism without specific details. It is widely believed that in government contracts there is a tendency to pay less attention to the performance indicators. This is based on a premise that the public sector itself does not function efficiently and therefore would not be able to identify performance standards and specifications. Another premise is that if those who are in charge can use contracts to obtain appropriate performance from the private contractors, they should use their influence to get the same level of required performance from their own workforce.

RESOURCE IMPLICATIONS

Private provision of health services instantly evokes the image of user-charges. However, in the partnership projects reviewed in our study, there are no uniform policies about user-charges (see Table 3.2). No mention is made about either the basis of fixing the rates of user-charges or how the revenue from the user-charges will be used. Some charges are in the form of direct fees paid by patients; others are in the form of insurance premiums. The funds received by the private agency are in the form of either grants-in-aid or global budgets. Case analysis indicates that government grants under private partnerships are invariably directed towards primary care services. This finding repudiates the claim in some quarters that partnership with the private sector would divert government resources toward specialist care services. Even in primary care services, the argument that private partnership is a route towards privatization does not hold since without government grants the private sector cannot sustain the operations at these locations. Therefore government responsibilities have become more indispensable under PPPs.

One of the critical issues in PPPs throughout the world is the timely release of grants or reimbursements to the private partner. At the core of this issue are the procedural requirements to get funds released. Timely release of funds is inevitably tied to the efficiency of the bureaucracy. In some states the release of funds is timely whereas there are inordinate delays in others. In at least one instance, a state government did not release a grant to an NGO for nearly thirteen months. Since the NGO is large and had long been functioning, the agency was able to withstand the delay. For most agencies, however, such delay would cause closure of the project. The entire issue of timely release of payment appears to be a sensitive one, and the private partners underplayed their difficulties. The existing partner-

TABLE 3.2: TYPE OF PARTNERSHIP AND USER-CHARGES

Nature of Partnership		Primary Care Level	Specialist Care Level
Competitive	User-fee	Emergency Ambulance Services, Theni	CT Scan/MRI, SMS Hospital and LLFS Drug Store, SMS Hospital, Jaipur; Diet, Baghajatin Hospital, Kolkata
	No user-fee	*AP Urban Slum Health Project, Adilabad*	
Non-Competitive	User-fee	*Arpana Swasthya Kendra, Delhi; Uttranchal Mobile Health Clinic, Bhimtal; Mobile Health Clinics, Sunderbans; Shamlaji CHC, Gujarat*	Rogi Kalyan Samiti, Bhopal; Rajiv Gandhi Hospital, Raichur; Yeshasvini Scheme, Karnataka; *KITTH, Chamarajanagar, Karnataka*
	No user-fee	*PHC Management, Karuna Trust, Karnataka*; *Chiranjeevi Yojana, Gujarat*; RNTCP, Mahavir Hosptial, Hyderabad	

Notes: (a) Arogya Raksha Scheme does not fit any of these categories.
(b) Italics indicate projects with full budget support (grant) from the government for operational expenditures.

ship agreements do not mention the timely release of payments or in the event of non-release of payments, the consequences thereof. In some projects (Mahavir Trust Hospital in Hyderabad, Emergency Ambulance in Theni), no financial transaction occurs between the government and the private agency.

Another critical issue is related to the difference between private for-profit agencies and NFP agencies in terms of the quantum of the grant or budgetary support. While the for-profit agencies receive full grants or reimbursement, the NFP agencies (NGOs) are not given full budgetary resources. For NGOs, grants from the government are in fact sustenance for their existence. Interestingly, the government on the one hand is circumspect about granting incentives to the non-profit private sector, while on the other hand there have been excessive concessions to the private for-profit sector. It would be interesting to examine whether this is due to better negotiating skills in the private sector or to a philosophical approach towards NFP agencies by the government. There is also a widespread perception that it is acceptable for a for-profit agency to negotiate financial details and profit margins whereas a similar approach by a NFP agency would be spurned. Such distinct differences could be seen in the manner in which the government of Karnataka supports Raichur's Rajiv Gandhi Hospital and the Karuna Trust in running the PHCs. While Karuna Trust is given a maximum of only 90 per cent of the salary costs of staff and other material support, Rajiv Gandhi Hospital gets full reimbursement of all expenses plus a service fee. There are no explicit incentives stated or agreed in any of the partnership agreements. A positive incentive for private partners is that their experience of working with the government may help them in securing more 'contracts' in the future.

AUTONOMY

One of the cornerstones of partnership is the relative autonomy enjoyed by both partners on day-to-day operations as well as in the overall management of the partnership. Autonomy is seen as non-intrusiveness by the public sector and the freedom of the private agency to take operational decisions without having to resort to cumbersome bureaucratic approvals or being constantly told about do's and don'ts. In the partnership projects analysed, the autonomy of the private agency has not been compromised in the majority of the cases. However, the partnership agreement does provide the government agencies with enormous scope for an active (interventionist) role. Possibly the government agencies lack either the technical skills or the willingness to take an active oversight role. If the government officials were to take a more active role in monitoring and supervising the partnership projects, then a logical question could be, what prevents these officials from taking similar interest in monitoring the functioning of the government hospitals and their functionaries? In most of the projects the private partners are free to decide what additional services to offer, free to generate additional resources except through user-fees, and free to appoint staff and determine their service conditions. In fact, in Karnataka and West Bengal, the private sector has been influential in shaping government policy towards the private sector. Given the degree of autonomy of the private sector, the often expressed fear about loss of autonomy by private organizations if they work with the government is misplaced, at least in this context.

TECHNICAL AND MANAGERIAL CAPACITY

Public-private partnership as a formal policy instrument is at a nascent stage. State governments are still organizing themselves to engage the private sector effectively. Many continue to experiment with the partnership concept. In states where health sector reform projects had been initiated through funding from the World Bank (e.g. West Bengal, Karnataka, Andhra Pradesh, Gujarat), separate health sector reform cells exist. Officials in these cells are trained in PPP concepts and systems. But the efforts of these officers must be complemented by modifications in the legal and administrative systems in the health departments, which is not easy. Despite these limitations the officers have been able to design systems such as tenders, policy guidelines, requisite forms for financial transactions, performance monitoring, etc. But often officers trained in health sector reforms are transferred out of the department, and the new officials are unable to understand or appreciate the systems developed by their predecessors. Furthermore, lower-level functionaries are either unaware of or unskilled in handling the private sector agencies. Similarly the private agency may not be able to understand the more formal and complex rules that bind the bureaucratic system. Bureaucracy requires a great deal of documentation and procedural details which the private sector, especially non-profit NGOs, are unable (or unwilling) to understand. Similarly the NGOs may not be able to calculate the unit cost of their own services or to follow accounting systems as detailed as the government agency would prefer.

QUALITY OF SERVICES

One of the major gaps in partnership agreements has been a lack of specific conditions related to the quality of services to be delivered to the beneficiaries. In most of the projects, the importance of delivering quality services is stated, but not in specific terms. Only the SMS Hospital mentions that the private agency is responsible for improper contrasts in CT scan and MRI images. Although most partnership projects concern primary health care services, specific quality parameters have not been taken into account.

RISK-SHARING

Another critical issue in PPPs is the vulnerability of the partners to risk. Perception of risk depends on two factors: the rule-bound behaviour of the partners with strict disincentives for deviance, and the notion of 'trust' between the partners. The risks vary at different levels of health functionaries and are also based on the scope of services. At the policy level, the risks are rather political in nature. Popular sentiment (media, political parties, health action groups, staff unions, etc.) may forestall the government from making overt gestures towards the private sector, especially its for-profit sector. This constraint is evident in the assumption that the private sector is primarily interested in making profits. Among the poor, the cognitive image of the 'private sector' is that of an 'exploiter'. In the context of liberalization, where public sector commercial activities are slowly divested from government control through disinvestment or privatization, there is a strong suspicion that the government may resort to similar steps in the health sector too.

This suspicion is strengthened by the fact that the government has not been effective in regulating the asymmetrical growth of the private sector in health care and its misdeeds. Some wonder 'why a commercial private health sector organization would be interested in delivering health services to the poor without any motive? The private sector, in turn, has shown enormous enthusiasm to 'collaborate' with the government in providing tertiary care services and in medical education (setting up medical colleges). This proclivity again reinforces the image that the private (for-profit) sector will collaborate with the government only if there are monetary benefits without their having to face any risk. The NFP organizations, on the other hand, are popularly perceived as 'givers' and this image is advantageous for them.

At the operational level, the risks for both the partners are on many dimensions. There are financial risks, performance and accountability risks, risk of confrontation between stakeholders and reputational risks for the private sector. While the for-profit private sector may well be capable of withstanding financial risks in the implementation of the project, any error by a NFP agency could close down the organization. Accounting systems in NFP agencies are usually not sophisticated so errors lead to administrative strictures or unforeseen complications. The government agency may have to delay the release of funds until the error is rectified. A crisis of funds at this stage could lead to stoppage of services to the beneficiaries, further complicating the issue. Also, an administrative stricture may lead to audit inspections by the government agencies, thereby denting the reputation of the agency and inhibiting it from bidding on projects in the future. Another problem is accountability for service delivery because the government is ultimately responsible for the delivery of health services. If deficiencies are committed by the private sector, responsibility for dereliction of services falls on the government health functionaries.

Coordination among stakeholders is another area of potential conflict. Differences in personalities and operating styles could jeopardize the functioning of the partnership. And once the contract expires, would another contractor with similar terms and conditions be ready for such a partnership? In Raichur's Rajiv Gandhi Hospital, if Apollo Hospitals Ltd. does not function effectively, the alternatives available to the government are not evident. At the same time, if the partnership is successful, it is not known if the government would be willing to extend such a partnership to other areas in the state. In the event of the project being unsuccessful, there could be a sense of discomfort, that is to say, 'if Apollo could not, who else could?'

Another notion of risk is whether the partnership is based on rule-bound behaviour or on 'trust'. A relevant hypothesis is whether partnership projects run higher risks if the partners are chosen through competitive tendering or through selectively negotiated agreements. Competitive processes cannot easily distinguish those who can perform better or more effectively from those who cannot. The partnership is therefore based purely on the terms and conditions agreed by the partner agencies without any prior 'intimacy' between the partners. On the other hand, selecting partners on the basis of their prior track records may help in determining the effectiveness of the partners and in making a more judicious selection. Whether non-profit private agencies prefer trust-based partnerships with government or whether the for-profit private sector prefers competitive selection processes requires careful analysis. In the projects documented in this study, many partnerships were generated by 'relationships'. Except in the Andhra Pradesh urban health scheme, almost all

NFP partnerships have been based on prior familiarity and trust-oriented selection.

STAKEHOLDER PERSPECTIVES

Beneficiaries in all the partnership project sites viewed the services received by them in a positive manner, though often they were not aware of any partnership. In general, feedback from the beneficiaries indicated that services are better now than in the past. Very few patients have been turned away from receiving services. Despite an overall positive feedback from the beneficiaries, some concerns require attention from the authorities. Though most of the concerns are project-specific, a common complaint has been the insufficient availability of drugs, thus forcing patients to buy these from the market. Another concern expressed by both beneficiaries and private agencies is a lack of clarity about who should pay user-fees and who is exempt.

The main concern of the staff working under the private partners has been that of heavy workload, long hours of work, lower pay, job insecurity, political interference and staff turnover. The public health staff are not kind in their comments about private partnership projects, although they are willing to work with them. It has been reported that health services are among the most corrupt civic services in India. However, there were no reports of bribery or corruption in any of the projects—although inference of it could be drawn from the now-defunct Arogya Raksha Voucher Scheme in Andhra Pradesh where millions of rupees 'disappeared'.

CONCLUSION

The research study compiled sixteen case studies which spanned diverse forms of PPPs in the health sectors of nine states in India. The case studies represent a spectrum in terms of rural-urban mix, for-profit and NFP partners, primary care *versus* speciality care services, clinical services to insurance schemes, laundry, telemedicine, etc. These case studies provide insights about the manner in which PPPs function in India.

No pattern emerged to indicate whether the PPP as a policy option was primarily guided by donor agencies or due to compulsions of resource constraints or due to competitive bureaucracy. Rather,

PPPs seem to have been prompted by visionary personalities from the bureaucracy and from civil society. Our analysis suggests that states which experimented with partnership ideas before formalizing a policy seem to have been more successful compared to those that promulgated a formal policy without experimentation. Policy pronouncements by government alone are not sufficient for PPPs to succeed. Visionary leadership, social entrepreneurship and relationships based on trust between the stakeholders are equally important for successful partnerships.

There is no uniform pattern to suggest which type of services are to be provided through partnership and what type of services should be 'off limits' to the private sector. Our analysis suggests that some of the most 'successful' partnerships have been with private non-profit organizations. Lack of success in partnerships was often due to insufficient consultations with facility-level managers. Contracting is the predominant form of partnerships, although other forms of partnerships are beginning to attract greater attention. Pre-negotiated partnerships seem to be more effective than competitive bidding. Apparently, wherever the partnerships initiatives have been made by the bureaucracy, their success seems to be limited compared to partnerships initiated by the private sector. Poor patients have benefited from PPP. Revenues generated through user-fees are negligible so there is a need to redesign the services towards more acceptable user-fees or else abolish them altogether.

The capacity of private partners and public sector officials to manage the partnerships is yet to be fully developed. Public sector managers may perceive the new initiative as a burdensome task, requiring them to not only placate their subordinates but also seek better performance from their private partners. This is a daunting task. Private partners, who are known for their informal and flexible systems and organizational processes, are uncomfortable with the rigid organizational and managerial processes and procedures of the public sector. Bureaucracy is yet to become conversant with the principles of New Public Management.

Partnership (contract) agreement design requires sufficient capacity-building measures but central government leadership may not be ideal for achieving this aim. States could create regional resource centres to develop these capacities locally. The approach towards fixing the tariffs for services (both in block grants or in case-based reimbursements) is based only on competitive tendering process rather than on a standard calculation of competitive rates. Similarly the payment system is mired in red tape which is an impediment to successful partnerships.

Policy innovations such as PPPs are, of course, contextual. Partnership with the private sector is not a substitute for the provision of health services by the public sector. Also, PPP initiatives cannot be uniform across all the regions or suitable under all kinds of political and administrative dispensations. While private partnership is an administrative decision, an obvious but important point is that it must enjoy political and community support. In states where the private sector is prevalent, partnership initiatives may be an alternative, not necessarily because of competitive efficiency but to prevent further immiseration of the poor and the deprived sections of society. There has to be a clear rationale for partnering with the private sector. It is important to understand not only what services are to be provided under private partnership but also the basis on which such decisions are made.

Any policy initiative to strengthen the flagging public sector health services in India would be welcome. But a government which fails to deliver quality social services due to lack of basic administrative capacity would not be able to contract either clinical or non-clinical services. The first step must be to improve basic administrative systems.

REFERENCES

Abrantes, A. (2003), 'Contracting Public Health Care Services in Latin America', in *Innovations in Health Service Delivery: The Corporatization of Public Hospitals*, ed. A.S. Preker and A. Harding, Washington DC: The World Bank, pp. 239–62.

ADBI (2000), *Public Private Partnerships in Health*. Executive Summary Series No. S34/01, Executive Summary of Proceedings (30 October–3 November, Ayutthaya, Thailand), Tokyo: Asian Development Bank Institute.

Agha, S., A.M. Karim, A. Balal and S. Sossler (2003), *A Quasi Experimental Study to Assess the Performance of a Reproductive Health Franchise in Nepal*, Commercial Market Strategies (CMS), Country Research Series Paper No.14, Washington, DC.

Ahmed, M. (2000), 'Promoting Public-Private Partnership in Health and

Education: The Case of Bangladesh', in *Public-Private Partnerships in the Social Sector: Issues and Country Experiences in Asia and the Pacific* ed. Y. Wang, ADBI Policy Paper No.1, pp. 219–91.

Ashton, T., J. Cummings and J. McLean (2004), 'Contracting for Health Services in a Public Health System: The New Zealand Experience', *Health Policy*, vol. 69, pp. 21–31.

Axelsson, H., F. Bustreo and A. Harding (2003), *Private Sector Participation in Child Health: A Review of World Bank Projects, 1993-2002*, Washington, DC: The World Bank.

Baru, R. (1998), *Private Health Care in India: Social Characteristics and Trends*, New Delhi: Sage.

Bazzoli, G. et al. (1997), 'Public-Private Collaboration in Health and Human Service Delivery: Evidence from Community Partnerships', *The Milbank Quarterly*, vol. 75, no. 4, pp. 533–61.

Bennett, S. (1991), *The Mystique of Markets: Public and Private Health Care in Developing Countries*. PHP Departmental Publication No 4, London, London School of Hygiene and Tropical Medicine.

Bennett, S. et al. (1994), 'Carrot and Stick: State Mechanisms to Influence Private Provider Behavior', *Health Policy and Planning*, vol. 9, no. 1, pp. 1–13.

Bennett, S. and A. Mills (1998), 'Government Capacity to Contract: Health Sector Experiences and Lessons', *Public Administration and Development*, vol.18, pp. 307–26.

Berman, P. (1995), 'Health Sector Reform: Making Health Development Sustainable', in *Health Sector Reform in Developing Countries: Making Health Development Sustainable*, ed. Peter Berman. Boston: Harvard University Press.

Blagescu, M. and J. Young (2005), *Partnerships and Accountability: Current Thinking and Approaches among Agencies Supporting Civil Society Organizations*, Working Paper 255, London: Overseas Development Institute.

Bloom, D.E., P. Craig and M. Mitchell (2000), 'Public and Private Roles in Providing and Financing Social Services: Health and Education', in *Public-Private Partnerships in the Social Sector: Issues and Country Experiences in Asia and the Pacific*, ed. Y. Wang, ADBI Policy Paper No.1, pp. 17–29.

Government of India (2005), *Concept Note on Public Private Partnerships*, New Delhi, Department of Family Welfare, Ministry of Health and Family Welfare.

Kulkarni, S. (2003), *India Sector Paper: Health—Overview and Prospects*, New Delhi, Centre for Media Studies (submitted to Asian Development Bank).

Mahal, A. et al. (2002), *Who Benefits from Public Sector Health Spending in India*, New Delhi: National Council for Applied Economic Research.

Michell-Weaver, C. and B. Manning (1992), 'Public-Private Partnerships in Third World Development: A Conceptual Overview', *Studies in Comparative International Development*, vol. 26, no. 4, pp. 45–67.

Mitchell, M. (2000), 'Models of Service Delivery', in *Public-Private Partnerships in the Social Sector: Issues and Country Experiences in Asia and the Pacific*, ed. Y. Wang, ADBI Policy Paper No. 1.

Mukhopadhyay, A. (2000), *Public-Private Partnerships in the Social Sector: Issues and Country Experiences in Asia and the Pacific*, ed. Y. Wang, ADBI Policy Paper No. 1, pp. 343–56.

National Commission on Macroeconomics in Health, New Delhi, Ministry of Health and Family Welfare, Government of India, 2005.

Paoletto, G. (2000), 'Public Private Sector Partnership: An Overview of Cause and Effect', in *Public-Private Partnerships in the Social Sector: Issues and Country Experiences in Asia and the Pacific*, ed. Y. Wang, ADBI Policy Paper No.1, pp. 35–54.

Rosenthal G. (2000), *State of the Practice: Public-NGO Partnerships for Quality Assurance*. Boston, LAC-HSR Health Sector Reform Initiative, Family Planning Management Development Project, Management Sciences for Health, 2000. Accessed at http://www.lachsr.org/documentsstateofthepracticepublishingpartershiponsetodecentralisation

Selvaraju, V. and V.B. Annigeri (2001), *Trends in Public Spending on Health in India*, New Delhi, National Institute of Public Finance and Policy. Background paper for the Commission on Macro Economics and Health (India).

Thomason, J.A. (2002), *Health Sector Reform in Developing Countries: A Reality Check*, accessed at http://www.sph.uq.edu.au/acithn/conf97/papers97/thomason.htm

Wang, Y. (2000), *Public-Private Partnership in Social Sector: Issues and Country Experience in Asia and the Pacific*, ADBI Policy Paper No. 1, ADBi, Tokyo.

World Health Organization (1997), *Public Private Sector Partnerships for Health: The Role of Governments*, SEA/HSD/212, WHO Project: ICP ICO 001/ICP RPS 002, New Delhi: WHO Regional Office.

——— (1991), *WHO Guidelines on Collaborations and Partnership with Commercial Enterprise*, Geneva, WHO.

——— (2001), 'Making a Public-Private Partnership Work: An Insider's View', *Bulletin of the World Health Organization*, vol. 79, no. 8, pp. 795–6.

World Bank (1993), *The World Development Report, 1993*, Washington DC, The World Bank.

——— (2001), *India: Raising the Sights: Better Health Systems for India's Poor*, Washington DC, HNP Unit-India, Report # 22304.

——— (2004), *India: Private Health Services for the Poor*, Draft Policy

Note, accessed at http://www.sasnet.lu.se/EASASpapers/11Ismail Radwan.pdf

World Economic Forum (2005). *Building on the Monterrey Consensus: The Growing Role of Public-Private Partnerships in Mobilising Resources for Development*, Geneva, United Nations high-level plenary meeting on financing for development (September)

APPENDIX 3.1: SYNOPTIC SUMMARY OF CASE STUDIES

Type of Partnership	Case/State	Type of Services	Private Partner(s)	Objectives	Benefits to the poor
Conventional 'Contracting Out'	SMS Hospital Jaipur, Rajasthan	Radiological diagnostics (CT Scan and MRI)	Private company	Operate CT Scan/ MRI facility; Provide high-tech diagnostic services at low cost	Free for all BPL patient, those above 70 years age, freedom fighters
		Drugs and medical supplies store	Individual entrepreneur	Quality medicines and supplies at lowest possible rate compared to market prices	Provision of 20% services to the poor patients is not clear
	Baghajatin Hospital, Kolkata, West Bengal	Three serices: • Dietary and Kitchen • Cleaning/Scavenging • Laundry	Two individual entrepreneurs and a private company	Improve the quality of diet of indoor patients; improve the cleanliness and hygiene; Establish mechanized laundry	BPL (free bed) patients are supplied diet free of charge; all others pay 50% of the charges
Performance Management Contracts	Arpana Swasthya Kendra, Delhi NCT of Delhi	Management of a maternity health centre	Non-profit NGO	Provide mdical and diagnostic services, build referral system, provide RCH and child-care services	Lab tests, select surgeries are free for poor patients
	Karuna Trust, Bangalore Karnataka	Management of primary health centres (PHCs)	Non-profit NGO	Provide round-the-clock helath services, maintain and manage the primary health centre and its official sub-centres	All patients are provided health services free of cost for diagnosis, treatment, drugs or for any other purpose

	Shamlaji Hospital Sabarkantha District, Gujarat	Management of a community health centre (CHC)	Non-profit NGO	Prvide quality health care to tribal population through community health centre	No user-fee on immunization; sterilization; maternal and child health services, diagnosis and treatment of poor people
	Rajiv Gandhi Super-Speciality Hospital, Raichur, Karnataka	Super-specialty clinical care services	Large corporate hospital	Provide super-specialty clinical care services and management of the hospital	Free outpatient services for BLP patients; 40% beds are for BPL inpatients free of cost
'Contracting in'	Urban Slum Health Care Project, Adilabad, Andhra Pradesh	Providing maternity and child-care and RCH services	Non-profit NGO	Provide health and family welfare services to slum dwellers; reduce morbidity and mortality among women and children; ensure safe deliveries and child survival	Services are meant for only the people (women and children) in urban slum community. All services are free
	Chiranjeevi Yojana, Sabarkantha District, Gujarat	Enrolment of the private obstetricians and gynaecologists for conducting deliveries	More than 45 individual private doctors	Increase the proportion of institutional deliveries, reduce the maternal mortality rate and infant mortality rate	Free services for the BPL women beneficiaries. Scheme is primarily targeted at pregnant women of BPL familes

(Contd.)

APPENDIX 3.1: Contd.

Type of Partnership	Case/State	Type of Services	Private Partner(s)	Objectives	Benefits to the poor
	Emergency Ambulance Services, Theni District, Tamil Nadu	Providing ambulance services to emergency cases	Non-profit NGOs (2)	Provide round-the-clock emergency transport to pregnant women for obstetric care, improve institutional deliveries	10% of the cases provided ambulance services free of cost. Other pay Rs. 5 per km
	Mobile Health Services in Sunderbans, West Bengal	Providing mobile (boat-based) health services	Non-profit NGO	Improve access to health services in remote and inaccessible areas through mobile boat clinics, regular health camps	No explict statement about any specific benefits to poor patients
Technology Demonstration Project	Uttaranchal Mobile Hospital and Research Centre, Bhimtal, Uttaranchal	Mobile health vans delivering diagnostic and health care services	Non-profit research institute Autonomous GOI agency	Provide clinical and diagnostic services in the hilly region in the form of health camps	Free services for patients with BPL card, including OPD consultation, radiological diagnostics, and pathological tests
Collaborative Partnership	Karnataka Integrated Telemedicine and Tele-health Project, Karnataka	Tele-consultation and inpatient services for cardiac and other specialist care	A large private hospital Autonomous GOI agency	To provide tele-diagnosis and consultation for coronary care	Free diagnostics, medicines and treatment for BPL patients and Yeshasvini cardholders. Medicines are free

Community Based Co-operative Health Insurance	Yeshasvini Health Insurance Scheme, Karnataka	Health insurance to the members of farmers cooperatives	A large private hospital A corporate TPA More than 160 private hospitals in the state	Provide access to clinical care to farmers, who are members of farmer cooperative societies through health insurance	Scheme is principally targeted towards the poor farmers
Voucher Scheme	Arogya Raksha Scheme, Andhra Pradesh	Hospitalization services for those who undergo sterilization after two children	Public sector company One private clinic per block	Low-cost insurance to provide hospitalization benefits and personal accident benefits to patients below poverty line	Beneficiaries are restricted to only those below poverty line with only one or two children
Hospital Autonomy	Rogi Kalyan Samiti (RKS), JP Hospital Bhipal, Madhya Pradesh	Decentralized management of hospital and improving the quality of care	Stateun district hospital	Improve the patient facilities through augmenting alternate sources of financing	All services free for BPL patients, ex-defence personnel and physically handicapped patients
Public-Private Mix	RNTCP, Mahavir Trust Hospital, Hyderabad	Surveillance and treatment of tuberculosis patients, under disease control programme	A large private hospital Number of private doctors and nursing homes	Create network of private doctors for surveillance, diagnosis, and drugs delivery	The entire programme is covered under the national (RNTCP) programme, and no charges are asked from any of the patients

THEME 3

ACCESS TO PUBLIC AND CORPORATE SECTOR EMPLOYMENT: RURAL AND URBAN DYNAMICS

CHAPTER 4

Employment, Exclusion and 'Merit' in the Indian IT Industry

CAROL UPADHYA

INTRODUCITON

The Indian information technology (IT) industry has been frequently hailed by the media and the state as a significant new source of high quality and well-paid employment for the educated youth of India.[1] With the rapid growth of the industry and expansion of the workforce since the 1990s, the sector already employs more than one million people and is projected to provide many more jobs over the next few years. More importantly, the IT industry is often represented as providing employment opportunities to wider sections of the population than has been the case for most managerial, professional and white-collar jobs. This argument is based on at least two claims: that employment does not depend on social connections (influence) or 'ascriptive' social status (socio-economic class—through the influence of money, or caste—through reservations), and that it is based entirely on 'merit'. The dominant industry discourse asserts that 'merit'-based recruitment, together with the spread of higher education (especially engineering colleges) in semi-urban and rural areas, has created new employment opportunities for rural youth and for the socially and economically disadvantaged, as well as for women.

While icons of the IT industry—such as the co-founder and former chairman of Infosys, N.R. Narayana Murthy (through his famous rags-to-riches story of a boy from a poor village family)—symbolize

* A shorter version of this paper has been previously published in the *Economic and Political Weekly*, 42(20): 1863–8, 19–25 May 2007. I am grateful to the editor for granting permission to reproduce this paper here.

the economic opportunities that the IT industry has provided to the disadvantaged, the social reality appears to be somewhat different. In this chapter, data from a study of the IT workforce in Bangalore is presented to show that the social composition profile of IT workers is largely urban, middle class and high and middle caste. The processes that create this social homogeneity in the workforce are also delineated, including the education system, the recruitment process and the industry's customer-driven requirement for a certain type of 'global' IT professional. The final section will focus on the ideology of 'merit' that dominates the industry in the context of the debate on reservations.

Social Composition of the IT Workforce

The emergence of the software and services outsourcing industry in India is one of the most visible outcomes of globalization and the spread of modern information and communication technologies (ICT) and the restructuring of global capitalism since the 1980s. The new ICTs have not only facilitated the emergence of transnational production networks, but also altered the way in which production and services are carried out, in that work has become increasingly 'dematerialized', 'disembodied', and hence geographically dispersed (Aneesh 2006). The Indian IT and IT enabled services (ITES) industries[2] have emerged to take advantage of this trend, in which companies located in the advanced industrial economies are outsourcing and offshoring an increasingly large proportion and range of their activities to locations where skilled human resources are more easily available at lower cost.[3]

The advent of the 'informational economy' (Castells 1996) has transformed the labour market, generating demands for certain information goods and services, and therefore for specific kinds of skills and specialized labour, worldwide—especially software and IT enabled services. A wide range of jobs, types of work and employment conditions are encompassed within the category of 'IT'—from 'high-end' computer science research to very 'low-end' services such as data entry and back office processes.[4] The discussion in this chapter is confined only to software workers, most of whom are engaged on relatively low-skilled software services, and is based primarily on research conducted in Bangalore.[5]

Till date no large-scale study of the social-economic background of IT professionals has been carried out, hence one is forced to rely on smaller and partial studies such as the one described here. It must be emphasized that the sample size of this study, of 132 software engineers is much too small to be representative of the larger picture, and one does not make any claims about the social profile of the IT workforce as a whole on this basis. Moreover, the sample may be further skewed due to the fact that it was drawn mainly from MNCs and large and medium-size Indian companies in the export sector, while smaller, 'informal sector' and domestic sector firms may have more diverse workforces. However, in the absence of larger data sets, the data presented below provides some kind of indication of the socio-economic background of the IT workforce, and the conclusions are supported by other studies and by the more extensive qualitative data collected during this study.[6]

SOCIO-ECONOMIC CLASS

Because family income data is usually not available or reliable, most studies have taken parents' education and occupation as a proxy for the socio-economic class. In present study's Bangalore survey, 80 per cent of software professionals were found to have fathers who are graduates or above, and only three respondents had fathers with less than SSLC level education. In addition, 56 per cent of respondents' mothers were graduates or above. Another survey of 102 software engineers in Bangalore yielded similar findings: 77 per cent of respondents' fathers had graduate or postgraduate degrees and all of the remainder were at least high school graduates. The mothers in this sample were similarly highly educated, most to high school level and half with graduate degrees (Krishna and Brihmadesam 2006: 3309-10).[7] With regard to occupation, fully 84 per cent of the fathers in the sample were engaged in occupations which can be identified as 'middle class': they were managers or executives in public and private sector companies (21 and 10 per cent, respectively), government officers (21 per cent), professionals such as doctors and university professors (18 per cent), and businessmen (13 per cent). Only 9 per cent had fathers in lower level clerical (white-collar) or blue-collar jobs, and 3 per cent were from agricultural families.

These figures imply that most software engineers come from middle-class, educated families, a conclusion which is supported by several other studies. A survey of 100 software professionals in Chennai,

Bangalore, Hyderabad and Trivandrum found that 97 per cent had parents who were graduates and three-fourths of the fathers had post-graduate or professionals degrees (Oommen and Meenakshisundararajan 2005). Almost all of the fathers in this study were in middle-class professional or managerial occupations. Anirudh Krishna and Vijay Brihmadesam (2006), who also collected information on consumption as an indicator of economic status, found a somewhat more diverse socio-economic profile, with about 15 per cent coming from 'lower' economic backgrounds, 40 per cent from 'lower-middle', 28 per cent from 'upper-middle', and 19 per cent from the 'upper' category (according to their classification scheme). But they conclude, nonetheless, that the majority of software engineers come from the middle class, although some people from lower and lower-middle class backgrounds have also entered this profession. This pattern is not surprising, for it is primarily the middle class that possesses not only the economic means but also the social and cultural capital necessary to equip their children to enter this profession, as discussed further below.

REGIONAL AND RURAL-URBAN ORIGINS

With rgard to regional origin, the majority of respondents in the present study—67 per cent—were from south India: the largest proportion were born in Karnataka (35 per cent), followed by Tamil Nadu (17 per cent), Kerala, and Andhra Pradesh (AP). Despite the bias in favour of south India, the data also points to a fair degree of regional diversity in the IT workforce. Taking mother tongue as a better indicator of regional identity than birthplace, it was found that 27 per cent of respondents were Kannadigas, 24 per cent Tamils, 17 per cent Hindi speakers, and 10 per cent Telugu speakers. In all, twelve different languages were represented in the sample and respondents came from fifteen different states.

A claim often made by representatives of the software industry is that a large proportion of the software workforce is drawn from rural and semi-rural areas. For instance, in a recent newspaper column, one of the founders of the Bangalore-based software company MindTree, Subroto Bagchi, argued that IT

> . . . is an industry that has a very high number of people who have been children of significant economic and social disadvantages but have broken

free from their background and are treated at par by their employers. Not a surprise, because this is an industry that values what you know as against who you know. (Bagchi 2006)

Bagchi cites a survey carried out in his own company which found that 33 per cent of new recruits were from 'rural, agricultural backgrounds', while 20 per cent were from small business families. But he also refers to the study by Anirudh Krishna and Vijay Brihmadesam (2006), to shore up his argument, and his interpretation of their data is sharply different from their own. In fact, the authors argue that having a rural background operates as a major constraint on entry into the software industry because of the poor standard of education (including teaching of English), the relatively lower level of education of parents and lack of access to information on career paths (Krishna and Brihmadesam 2006: 3312). This discrepancy clearly points to the dominance of the ideology of 'merit' and the myth of inclusivity in the IT industry, even in the face of substantial countervailing evidence (discussed further below).

The standard industry discourse is called into question by our survey results: 36 per cent of the sample were born in one of the five metros (including Bangalore), 29 per cent were from Tier Two towns and cities such as Mysore and Pune, but only 5 per cent came from rural areas. However, an interesting finding is that a substantial proportion—31 per cent—came from Tier Three towns, including district and *taluka* headquarters such as Tumkur, Guntur or Madurai, and smaller, semi-urban towns. The study by Krishna and Brihmadesam (2006: 3309) yielded similar results, but a somewhat smaller proportion of their respondents were from metro cities, while 32 per cent were from state capitals, 23 per cent from district capitals, and 11 per cent grew up in villages. U. Oommen and A. Meenakshisundararajan (2005) also found that only 12 per cent of their respondents were from rural areas. Similarly, an ILO survey of 143 IT professionals in Bangalore and Delhi, carried out a few years earlier, found that 44.1 per cent were from the metros and 43.4 per cent from other urban areas, while 8.4 were from semi-urban and 4.2 per cent from rural areas (Rothboeck et al. 2001: 36). These figures challenge the contention that the IT industry is opening up new opportunities for people from rural and semi-urban areas. This may be true for the lower end of IT work (such as in small firms catering to the domestic market), which was not well captured by this study, but in the case of the large Indian companies and MNCs—which offer the most lucrative and prestigious jobs—the social background of the workforce appears to be fairly homogeneous, albeit internally stratified.[8]

Even within the category of software engineers who come from rural and semi-urban areas, closer investigation of their background usually reveals that most are from relatively well-off agricultural families and have entered this profession after being educated in one of the many private engineering colleges located especially in the smaller towns of the southern states. While again there is no comprehensive data to substantiate this statement, ethnographic studies and anecdotal reports suggest that it is primarily the nouveau riche class of the more developed rural regions who have been able to take advantage of these new opportunities. The reasons are not difficult to find: education up to the level required to work in the IT industry requires access to the appropriate institutions and substantial investment of resources. The flow of people from the wealthier class of rural society into IT represents only the latest phase of an older pattern which has been well documented in the more agriculturally developed regions. In AP and Karnataka, especially, the rural rich since the 1980s have been sending their children to professional colleges by paying 'capitation fees' (donations), such that upward socio-economic mobility via professional education is quite common in these regions.[9] The interlinked processes of rural-urban migration, upward mobility and urbanization observed especially in the Green Revolution areas of the country also helps to explain the fact that a significant minority of IT professionals come from small towns rather than state capitals and metros.[10]

While this process has opened up a new avenue for the entry of people from rural and semi-urban backgrounds—especially the dominant (landowning) agricultural castes—into the urban middle class, thereby expanding the size and to some extent the social heterogeneity of this class, the available evidence suggests that it still has not become a significant means of social and economic mobility for the poor and the lower castes in rural areas. But because there are a number of IT professionals from this caste/class/regional background in the industry, the impression has been created that IT has opened up employment opportunities to the deprived sections of rural society. To the contrary, IT appears to have reinforced the process of consolidation and integration of what I has been called the new regional rural-urban dominant classes (Upadhya 1997), which are primarily 'dominant castes' who control land but are usually of middle ranking or other backward class (OBC) caste status. While many IT professionals from rural and semi-urban areas probably belong to this caste/class category, the industry has also provided significant opportunities for students from higher caste and middle-lower middle-class families in small towns (symbolized by the archetype of the 'poor Brahmin'), who have been able to avail themselves of the educational opportunities that are now widely available outside of the larger cities.

CASTE AND RELIGION

This brings one to the question of the caste and community composition of the IT workforce. While 88 per cent of the respondents were Hindus, only 5 per cent were Christians and 2 per cent Muslims, reflecting the pattern of marginalization of Muslims observed elsewhere in formal sector employment and higher education. With regard to caste identity, Brahmins constituted 48 per cent of the present sample. The predominance of Brahmins is not surprising given their historical monopoly over higher education and formal sector employment, especially in south India (Fuller 1999; Fuller and Narasimhan 2007).[11] If others belonging to 'twice-born' castes are included, the figure for all upper castes comes to 71 per cent. Those belonging to dominant agricultural castes (including some OBCs) constituted 15 per cent, bringing the proportion of respondents from upper- or middle-dominant caste groups to 86 per cent.[12] If one further includes some of the Christian respondents, such as Syrian Christians (a relatively wealthy landowning community in Kerala), the proportion of those from the higher and dominant castes is even greater. Only one respondent said that he belonged to a scheduled community. Other studies have thrown up the same pattern: in the survey by Oommen and Meenakshisundararajan (2005), three-fourths of the respondents were from forward castes and the rest were OBCs; none were from the Scheduled Caste/Scheduled Tribe (SC/ST) category. C.J. Fuller and Harpriya Narasimhan's (2006, 2007) study of software professionals in Chennai also found that they come overwhelmingly from Brahmin or forward castes.

These findings call into question the dominant industry position that entry into the IT industry is completely based on 'merit' and that factors such as caste, region, gender and class are irrelevant. Industry leaders frequently argue that because of its requirement for technically qualified people, they have had to look far and wide for workers, in the process drawing in many people from non-middle class/upper-caste backgrounds. To the contrary, the available evidence suggests that the IT workforce is quite homogeneous socially, in terms of class (middle class), caste (upper and middle caste), and regional (urban) background. However, this statement must be qualified by highlighting two features of its social composition: first, the large proportion who are from small towns, and second, the significant minority of workers from non-Brahmin middle- to high-ranking and dominant (including some OBCs) castes.

SOCIAL PROFILE OF IT PROFESSIONALS

The fact that a substantial proportion of the IT workforce hails from small- and medium-size towns (which are often labelled as 'rural' by city-bred Human Resource [HR] managers) is often taken as evidence of the IT industry's inclusiveness, but this picture is misleading because most of such employees are from the upper- and middle- (dominant) caste groups—especially Brahmins and landowning agricultural communities—which historically have benefited most from the spread of educational opportunities. Again, there should be nothing surprising in these findings, for given the pattern of inequality of opportunity in education that prevails in the country, any occupation which requires a high level of education and training—especially such a highly competitive one as IT—is bound to draw on the more privileged sections of society. But it is not only inequalities in the education system that produce this social profile; it is also an outcome of the IT industry's requirement for workers with a certain kind of cultural capital, who are capable of being moulded into 'global professionals', as is argued in the next section.

Production of the IT Workforce

Examination of the recruitment practices of IT companies reveals that there are several mechanisms that have the effect of privileging candidates with a certain social background. Of course, existing inequalities and exclusionary mechanisms in the higher education system produce a skewed pool of potential hires, over which the industry does not have control, but this is exacerbated by several of the selection procedures used.

THE EDUCATION SYSTEM

The first important factor is that software companies recruit primarily engineering graduates—although they also hire graduates and post-graduates with other computer-related degrees such as Master's in Computer Applications (MCA). Studies show that the percentage of students from the OBC, SC and ST categories graduating from engineering colleges (and from other professional and graduate courses) continues to be much lower than their percentage in the population, and that of higher castes correspondingly much higher. Further, upper-caste Hindu youth is two to four times more likely to have graduate degrees than is the youth from the OBC, SC, ST categories and Muslims (Deshpande 2006; Deshpande and Yadav 2006; Mohanty 2006). Since Hindu upper castes constitute almost 67 per cent of engineering and technology graduates (Deshpande 2006: 2439), it would not be surprising to find that upwards of 70 per cent of the IT workforce is upper caste.[13]

The data from the present survey of software professionals in Bangalore reflects the preference for enginnering graduates: 76 per cent had graduate or postgraduate engineering degrees—28 per cent had degrees in computer science and related subjects and 43 per cent in other branches of engineering, while 13 per cent had postgraduate degrees in computer-related subjects such as MCA. It is important to note here that IT companies prefer to hire engineering graduates not because their training is necessarily related to the work they will be doing (unless they have studied computer science or related streams), but because they believe that they have already been pre-selected for a certain level of intelligence and aptitude. These companies hire engineers from any stream and then train them in computer programming.[14] This means that it would be possible for IT companies to hire more ordinary graduates (in science or computer fields) and then train them, just as they train fresh engineering graduates—a strategy that might widen the pool of potential employees.

The advantageous position of the upper castes in higher education largely flows from historical factors and their class status. (We know that the Indian 'middle-class', although it is becoming more heterogeneous, is predominantly upper caste in composition, although the reverse may not be true.) Given the mushrooming of private engineering colleges and coaching classes designed to help students get admission to the premier institutions, students from middle-class and wealthy families have a clear advantage in higher education. Students from lower-caste, rural, and working-class families, on the other hand, are more likely to study in government schools and in the vernacular medium, have less well-educated parents, and also lack the economic and cultural resources to develop their 'merit' (high marks in examinations). This creates a barrier to entry into IT-related professions due to poor examination results and lack of access to English and other forms of cultural capital. All these factors work together to create a bias in the social composition of potential IT employees.[15]

THE RECRUITMENT PROCESS

Apart from the inherent inequality in the pool of candidates that is created by the education system, there are certain features of the recruitment process that tend to favour middle-class (and upper-caste) candidates. In this section, the focus will be only on the campus placement process, which is the major source of new recruits for IT companies, rather than recruitment as a whole.[16]

The first such filtering mechanism is the college ranking system that is used by all companies. Each company maintains a rating of engineering colleges and visits only certain ranked colleges for placement each year. The large services companies such as Infosys and TCS usually visit fifty to sixty campuses, while the MNCs and the medium-sized Indian products or services companies may visit about ten select campuses. The rankings of the top fifty colleges are more or less the same for all the companies, so they are competing for a limited pool of well-qualified engineering graduates.[17] The vast majority of engineering colleges are not even ranked by the major companies, which means that their students are not recruited from campus (although they may apply to IT companies directly after they graduate). This limits the pool of candidates at the outset.

Second, only those students with a certain cut-off percentage throughout their course (ranging from 60 to 70 per cent aggregate marks in most cases) are allowed to apply. In fact, many IT companies require candidates to have had a consistent average of 70 to 75 per cent marks from the 10th standard onwards, and not only in college (Fuller and Narasimhan 2006). This requirement tends to exclude engineering students who got seats on government quotas

(SC/ST or OBC) but were not able to score well in previous examinations because of their educational and social backgrounds.

The students who make the cut-off are given a written test of their logical, analytical and problem-solving skills, as well as English and maths, and those who pass this round go on to the next level of assessment, which is usually a group discussion designed to evaluate communication skills, personality and spontaneous thinking abilities. Candidates who are short-listed after the group discussion are then individually interviewed. Candidates who have entered engineering colleges through government quotas, and who have the requisite marks and pass the initial tests, are likely to be 'weeded out' in these subsequent rounds. The requirement for good spoken English acts as yet another filtering mechanism because, given the well-known differential access to private English-medium education across India, it tends to exclude those from lower caste, rural, and less privileged backgrounds.

The final stage of recruitment consists of individual interviews, of which there are usually two types—technical and HR. Apart from 'learnability' and technical aptitude, software companies place great emphasis on attitudes and values, personality and 'soft skills'. The HR interview is designed to assess these non-technical attributes—including the candidate's career aspirations, family background, and personality—and to determine whether s/he will 'fit' into the company's culture and (in some cases) into the group or team for which s/he is recruited. The most important 'soft skill' that is assessed during the HR interview is communication. Because most software jobs, especially in services companies, are 'client-facing', good communication skills (especially oral) are considered to be essential and a candidate who is otherwise well qualified may be rejected purely on this basis. While fluency in English is a basic requirement, 'communication skills' refers more broadly to the ability to converse and interact easily in different social and cultural situations. A common refrain among HR managers is that Indian software engineers are very good technically but do not communicate well with clients, and the ability to socialize with people from different backgrounds is considered necessary for most IT jobs. The candidate's general appearance, demeanour and 'ability to mingle' are assessed during the HR interview.

The close attention that is paid to this stage of the recruitment process suggests that as much importance is given to the personality, communication skills and social attributes of potential IT professionals as to their aptitude for computer work or technical skills. Such assessment operates as yet another mechanism of exclusion. Good communication and social skills, confidence and the right kind of personality are elements of cultural capital which students from urban middle-class families are most likely to possess. C.J. Fuller and Haripriya Narasimhan (2006), in their study of IT professionals in Chennai, similarly conclude that recruitment practices tend to select only the best students from a few engineering colleges, because the majority of engineering graduates lack the required cultural capital. They point out that the gap is not so much in their knowledge of English as in the unfamiliar cultural style of interaction and communication required by software companies—a style which those from urban, middle-class, and higher-caste families are more likely to have or be able to acquire. With the industry giving increasing emphasis to soft skills, candidates from non-metropolitan, non-middle-class, and lower-caste backgrounds are even more likely to be passed over.

CULTURE AND EXCLUSION

The relationship between cultural capital, language ability and social background requires further elucidation. The remark frequently made by HR managers that Indian software engineers lack communication skills appears to contradict the argument presented here that IT professionals come primarily from more privileged social backgrounds, because those who had studied in good English-medium schools would be expected to be conversant with the language as well as good communicators. However, this contradiction is resolved if one takes into account the fact, as noted earlier, that a large number of IT professionals come from medium and small towns. Although most have studied in private English-medium schools they may not be accustomed to speaking regularly in English or with a standard accent. Several HR managers drew this connection between language and social background, identifying those from small towns as the ones with 'communication problems' because of their heavy mother tongue influence (MTI).[18]

Here it must be pointed out that many HR managers, most of whom are probably from the larger cities, tend to identify anyone who is not from larger towns and cities as 'rural'. This identification is linked not only to lack of fluency in English but also to differences in cultural style between the youth from small towns and there from the metros. While middle-class metropolitan youth tends to possess the kind of demeanour and social skills required by the industry, those from smaller centres have to acquire them. One HR manager explained the poor communication skills of Indian software engineers in terms of the changing 'demographics' of the workforce, which in turn is due to the pressure on margins. While earlier they would recruit only from the top institutions, whose students automatically had good knowledge of English, now they have gone down the hierarchy of colleges to recruit in order to get 'cheap labour'. Although they complain about the cultural skills of these 'cheap' workers, they are nonetheless selected out of a much larger pool of people, most of whom are excluded.

The sharp disparities in the higher education system and the IT industry's methods of recruitment together have not only produced mechanisms which tend to exclude the majority of potential hires, they have also created a system of stratification within the IT workforce. A software engineer's position and career prospects in the industry are largely determined by his or her educational background. At the top are graduates from the IITs and other premier institutions, who are able to land the best jobs in the overseas development centres (ODC) of multinational companies. The next layer consists of those from the 'Tier Two' colleges, who are heavily recruited by the MNCs and the large Indian companies for more routine jobs, followed by those from lower-ranked private and government engineering colleges. At the lowest end are those with degrees from unranked engineering colleges, degree colleges, or diplomas from private computer training institutes, most of whom never make it into the large Indian companies or MNCs, but find jobs (if they do at all) in smaller companies and low-end 'informal sector' operations.

Because of the routinized and low-end nature of much of the work in the large Indian software services companies, they prefer to hire students from Tier Three campuses rather than from the top-ranking colleges because, as on HR manager put it, they require 'guys who can just sit and code and not ask questions', or people who 'know English and can work and learn', rather than the extra-bright and ambitious IITians. This remark suggests that there is a filtering mechanism in place which not only excludes certain social types from the IT industry but also (re)produces within it the social hierarchy or class fractions that characterize the middle class in general. Given the nature of the education system and the easier access that students from middle-class/high-caste backgrounds have to the IITs and the better engineering colleges, this means that the higher management positions and more challenging technical jobs within the IT industry are likely to be monopolized by people from more privileged social backgrounds, while greater 'diversity' may be found at the lower end of the job market.

In sum, the IT industry looks for certain social types to fill its ranks of 'knowledge workers' and designs recruitment procedures to filter out those who do not 'fit'. Hiring practices also slot recruits into the workforce at different levels, according to not only their educational qualifications and technical skills but especially to their social (caste/class/urban-rural) background. At the same time, given the great demand for human resources, software companies are often forced to hire people who are not completely 'suitable', who are then subjected to extensive 'soft skills' training programmes (Upadhya and Vasavi 2006; Upadhya 2007).

The Ideology of 'Merit' and the Reproduction of Privilege

One of the distinctive features of the IT industry, according to many of the present survey's informants, is that recruitment and promotion are based purely on 'merit', and ascriptive identities based on gender, region, caste or religion are irrelevant. This argument of course ignores the social and economic factors that produce 'meritorious' candidates in the first place, and the continuing monopoly over a certain kind of cultural capital that is enjoyed by the middle-class (which is mainly upper-caste) due to their greater access to the best educational institutions and other processes of social closure. It is no one's case that the industry *deliberately* practises caste discrimination, but, as argued above, the requirements of a global outsourcing business make it more difficult for people from non-urban and lower caste/class backgrounds to enter this profession because certain social and cultural attributes are thought to be necessary to work in a 'global' environment. This situation has been acknowledged by industry leaders, who have repeatedly urged that appropriate 'soft skills' be taught in schools and colleges and that English be introduced at the primary level in government schools, in order to expand the pool of qualified candidates. Of course, IT companies need to hire people with the requisite skills for the jobs, and they cannot be faulted for having to choose from a limited and skewed pool of candidates. But there is an apparent contradiction between the limited recognition that processes of exclusion do operate in the industry, and the official position that upholds 'merit' and individual achievement as the sole criterion for recruitment. For this reason it is important to examine closely the operation of the ideology of 'merit' in the industry and its role in the production of the IT workforce.

Although there is some recognition on the part of industry leaders of the filtering that takes place during recruitment, they have been staunchly opposed to proposed corrective policies. IT industry leaders have been at the forefront of opposition to the recently revived proposal for reservations in the private sector, as well as the new policy of reservations for OBCs in premier institutions of higher education. In response to the recent debate on reservations, the former chairman of Infosys, N.R. Narayana Murthy, made the following statement:

> I firmly believe that there is considerable social injustice in the country and that we have to help the disadvantaged people to overcome this. The solution is not reservations in education or in employment. The solution is to make the disadvantaged people more competition worthy than they are today.[19]

The industry's position on this question flows in part from its growing requirement for large numbers of highly educated and 'learnable' young people: the spectre of reservations, what threatens to open the doors of premier institutes to masses of 'unmeritorious' students, in their view, would further reduce the pool of 'employable' engineers. The standard argument is that reservations, or affirmative action, would adversely impact the industry's competitiveness (and hence its ability to provide more employment for India's youth). Instead, steps should be taken to make young people from rural areas and lower castes more competitive in the job market, especially by improving the quality of school education. To this end, and also in order to be seen as 'good corporate citizens', several IT companies have funded and led initiatives in the area of primary education. Industry leaders have also repeatedly blamed the government's poor performance in education for the dearth of qualified candidates and 'poor quality' of most engineering graduates, and the industry has taken steps to upgrade and re-orient engineering education to better suit its needs.[20]

While industry spokespersons decry the poor quality of education, which is limiting the supply of qualified IT workers, they do not recognize the problem of *access* to education that is faced by students from rural poor and lower-caste backgrounds, especially to the premier institutions of higher learning. It is this inequality of access, and the monopoly that the middle classes and the Hindu higher castes have had over elite education, that the recent policy initiative on reservations is intended to address. However, as with the proposal for reservations of jobs in the private sector, the IT industry has opposed this move. As stated earlier, industry leaders have made public statements opposing the extension of reservations in the premier higher education institutions to OBCs, arguing that other mechanisms should be found to enhance their competitiveness—especially by improving the quality of primary education. At the same time, most are careful to appear socially conscious, and recent statements by industry leaders suggest that they wish to be seen as taking steps to increase the diversity and inclusiveness of their workforces. Several companies have floated internship schemes and training programmes for rural youth, but the primary response to the problem has been to target the primary education system through charitable foundations and partnership programmes with the government.

The staunch opposition to reservations or affirmative action that is the dominant position of most IT (and other) industry leaders is closely linked to their support for liberalization. It is this connection that has elevated the ideology of 'merit' to an article of faith. Industry spokespersons often claim that the IT industry has flourished in India primarily because of the *absence* of state interference or control, and that it would not have grown as fast as it has if it had been subjected to the kind of bureaucratic controls that typified the Nehruvian planned economy. This provides the basis for their argument against any kind of government 'interference' (including, for instance, application of labour laws), and allows them to insist that IT companies must be left free to hire the most 'meritorious' people in order to maintain their competitive edge (without interference by the state in the form of reservations). The notion that the IT industry has grown because of liberalization ignores the fact that it has all along received substantial support from the state, both directly in the form of various subsidies, tax holidays, provision of land and infrastructure and other policy measures, and indirectly in the form of the large pool of 'knowledge workers' that has been produced through state investments in higher education over several decades (Balakrishnan 2006; Parthasarathy 2005). Given this history, from a policy point of view one could make a case that the industry should give something back to the state and to the wider society. Yet, because of its central symbolic position in the current discourse on India's new development path under liberalization, the IT industry has been able to sustain a large degree of autonomy from state regulation, in part by promoting its image as a 'new' kind of industry—meritocratic, open, and socially committed—which is providing ample (and equal) opportunities to anyone willing to work hard enough to take advantage of them.

In view of the fact that most IT companies represent themselves as socially responsible 'corporate citizens', it would be in their interest to formulate or accept some kind of positive discrimination policy (statutory or voluntary) to make the workforce more inclusive. For instance, although the pool of qualified OBC and SC/ST engineers may be smaller than that of engineering graduates from upper castes, given the large number of graduates overall it should be possible for companies to evolve preferential hiring policies (together with training programmes) to ensure the inclusion of employees from more diverse backgrounds. However, given the bias against any kind of protective discrimination on the basis of caste among most of the elite and the middle classes (on the grounds that it would perpetuate caste and be unfair to people of other communities), proposals for caste-based reservations are usually firmly opposed.

The Corporate Sector and Social Responsibility

The discussion in this chapter suggests that one of the reasons for the IT industry's success is that it has been able to tap into the existing cultural capital of the urban middle classes (which consist primarily of high and middle castes)—including educational attainments, knowledge of English and some degree of Westernized social orientation and habitus. The IT workforce is drawn mainly from this section of society and by providing new and lucrative employment opportunities is contributing to the reproduction and consolidation of middle-class/upper-caste domination. The middle-class is certainly expanding in size and diversity, and the IT industry is contributing to this process by providing new forms of cultural capital and employment to highly educated workers and pulling at least some people from non-dominant social groups into the 'new middle-class'. Yet in the final analysis, the industry cannot be said to have contributed to overcoming the deep social and economic divisions that continue to characterize Indian society, despite its faith in the ideology of 'merit' and individual achievement.[21]

As the IT industry has become a major vehicle for the reproduction and consolidation of middle-class hegemony, it is all the more necessary for its leaders to issue periodic affirmations of their social conscience, their concern for the poor and the marginalized and their conviction that IT is going to provide hitherto unimaginable opportunities to those who are willing to work hard enough, regardless of their caste, class, gender or religion.[22] But while supporting programmes to improve primary education in order to create a 'level playing field' for all students, both IT industry leaders and employees are staunchly opposed to the idea of positive discrimination.[23] This continual emphasis on the inadequacy of the labour pool has the effect of deflecting attention away from the question of exclusionary processes in employment. It is also based on the individualist liberal assumption that all that is required is to provide every child with an education which will enable him or her to 'compete' on an equal footing. This notion, like the ideological opposition to positive discrimination, reflects a complete denial of the unequal distribution, by class and caste (and other divisions such as gender and religious community), of the cultural, social and economic capital required to become an IT professional.

NOTES

1. This paper is based on a sociological study of the Indian IT/ITES workforce in India and abroad that was carried out by A.R. Vasavi and me along with a research team at the National Institute of Advanced Studies, Bangalore. The research project was funded by the Indo-Dutch Programme on Alternatives in Development, The Netherlands, and was carried out in collaboration with Peter van der Veer. Fieldwork for the study was conducted for eighteen months, between January 2004 and June 2005, in Bangalore and in three countries in Europe. For a comprehensive report on the study's findings, see Upadhya and Vasavi (2006), available on the NIAS website (www.iisc.ernet.in/nias).

An earlier version of this paper was presented at the IDPAD End Symposium, 'India's Split Development: Reflections on Development Theory and Practice', Hyderabad, 1–3 November 2006. I thank A.R. Vasavi and conference participants for their comments, while the remaining errors are of course my own.

2. The software and services industry is often referred to generically as the 'IT industry', although technically 'IT' includes hardware as well as software. Following common usage, I use the terms 'IT' and 'software' interchangeably to refer to this industry and to 'IT' or 'software professionals'. ITES is often categorized as 'low-end' IT services although it is a very different kind of business.
3. The software industry generated total earnings of $13.5 billion in 2004–5, of which $10 billion were from exports (NASSCOM, 'Indian IT Industry – Factsheet', www.nasscom.org, accessed May 2006). Accurate employment figures are difficult to obtain, but NASSCOM estimates that the total direct employment generated by the industry came to 1.3 million in 2005–6—representing a rapid expansion from the figure of 284,000 for 1999–2000 (NASSCOM, Knowledge Professionals—Factsheet, www.nasscom.org). Of the estimated one million IT employees, about 345,000 are in the software exports sector, 348,000 in the ITES-BPO sector, and the rest are in the domestic sector or are 'in-house' IT professionals.
4. Existing surveys of IT professionals have failed to capture the heterogeneity of the job market, which includes the low-end 'informal sector' of the IT industry, so there is not have adequate data on the size, composition and stratification of the IT workforce. NSSO data for 1999–2000 shows that 38 per cent of 'IT occupation workers' are employed in small, informal enterprises (proprietorships or partnership firms), 25 per cent in public limited companies, and 28 per cent in private limited companies—indicating that small firms participate in the labour market in a significant manner (Basant and Rani 2004: 5324).
5. It may be unwise to generalize, from findings in one city, the entire IT sector in India, but I assume that many of the features described here are common throughout the industry. Bangalore is widely regarded as the premier centre for the IT and ITES industries in the country and attracts IT professionals from across the country. Hence, the IT workforce in Bangalore may be more diverse than in other cities. The number of IT and ITES employees in the city in 2005 was probably around 2,00,000 to 2,50,000, out of a population of about 7 million.
6. Fieldwork for the study was conducted over eighteen months, between January 2004 and June 2005, in Bangalore and in three countries in Europe. Research methods were primarily qualitative and ethnographic in nature, including informal interviews and interactions with a large

number of IT and ITES employees, managers, their family members and others connected with the industry, at workplaces and elsewhere; observations in IT/ITES companies and at other sites; and interviews and discussions at other relevant sites such as engineering colleges. In order to generate some amount of quantitative data, we also conducted structured interviews with a purposively selected sample of IT employees. To construct this sample, we attempted to select companies which represent a cross-section of the IT export industry: the final sample was drawn from two large Indian software services companies, two medium-size Indian companies (one product, one services), five multinational (MNC) software development centres, and six small companies (both Indian and foreign owned, and a mix of products and services). The study had targeted a larger sample size, but could not achieve it due to difficulties in getting permission to conduct interviews. Also, we could not access HR data from most of the sample companies that might have helped us to paint a more comprehensive picture of the workforce.

Within each company, we conducted interviews with a small number of employees (relative to the size of the company—ranging from 20 to 40 each in the medium and large companies to 5 in the small ones)—who were a randomly selected but structured the sample reflecting the demographics of the workforce, i.e. in terms of age, gender, years of experience and position. However, because we had to depend on HR managers for sampling we had little control over the selection process. Completed formal interviews in software companies totalled 132, obviously much too small a sample from which to generalize. However, other studies mentioned here with similarly small sample sizes indicate similar trends. Moreover, this survey formed only a small part of the entire research project, and information collected from informal interviews and qualitative data also supports the argument presented here.

7. The authors of this study argue that education of parents is the most critical 'limiting factor' to entry into the software profession—more so than economic background. The exclusionary effect of this is clear: given the small percentage of all Indians who have two highly educated parents, only '. . . between 4 and 7 per cent of rural Indians will qualify to gain entry' (Krishna and Brihmadesam 2006: 3310).
8. In the present survey, 45 per cent of MNC employees were from the metros compared to 32 per cent of engineers employed by Indian services companies. MNCs are able to attract the cream of engineering graduates, and these figures suggest that students from the metros are more likely to make it to the good engineering institutes and later into the best jobs.
9. Between 1995–6 and 2000, 75 private engineering colleges were established in AP alone, largely to cater to the demand for degrees leading to jobs in the IT sector (Xiang 2002: 82).

10. Wealthy agricultural families often send their children to nearby towns to study in private schools, even from the primary level, and then up to college and beyond. This pattern accounts for Krishna and Brihmadesam's (2006: 3309) finding that 18 per cent of their respondents had spent the first five years of their lives in rural villages, but over the next five years only 11 per cent remained in their villages and completed their education there. Xiang (2002: 95) notes: 'My observation suggests that, at least in the Andhra region, many software professionals are the second generation of well-off rural-urban migrants. While their fathers moved from villages to towns, they are moving from towns to metropolitans and the West'.
11. As C.J. Fuller (1999) argues, even though Tamil Brahmins lost their monopoly over public sector employment due to the non-Brahmin movement and reservations, they were able to shore up their cultural capital through education and entry into private sector employment and the professions.
12. Several caste groups that are classified as OBCs are actually 'dominant castes' in that they are the primary landowners in their regions as well as often the most wealthy and politically powerful groups; for example, Vokkaligas and Lingayats in Karnataka.
13. After all, the argument usually made with regard to the gender ratio of the workforce is that it reflects the proportion of women graduating from engineering colleges (about 22 per cent in both cases). This means that other social inequalities in the pool of potential hires would be reflected in the workforce as well.
14. Suma S. Athreye (2005: 159) suggests that the preference for engineers is a way in which software companies signal quality to customers.
15. A survey of 100 software professionals in south India (cited above) found that *all* the respondents had studied in private schools, and 96 per cent in English medium schools (Oommen and Meenakshisundararajan 2005) and 72 per cent of the respondents in the study had scored above 80 per cent marks in their Higher Secondary examinations. However, another study found that 27 per cent of respondents had studied in government schools and 13 per cent had attended high schools in rural areas (Krishna and Brihmadesam 2006: 3308).
16. The discussion of recruitment practices in this section is based on interviews with HR managers from sixteen companies, and placement officers of several engineering colleges in Bangalore.
17. Campuses are usually graded into three 'tiers', with premier institutions such as the IITs in Tier One and the government-run NITs, the top-state campuses, and a few of the better private institutes in Tier Two. Tier Three colleges include the less well-known campuses but ones that are still considered to produce 'employable' engineers.

18. While the concept of 'MTI' is heard primarily in the call centre industry, where accent training is devoted to erasing Indian accents and inculcating American, British or 'neutral' accents, it is of concern even in the software industry, although here training is not explicitly designed to address this 'problem'.
19. *Times of India*, 23 April 2006, quoted in Assadi (2006: 3146).
20. Concerns are frequently expressed by the industry about the dearth of qualified people, and spokespersons often quote a report that found that only 25 per cent of the 290,000 engineering degree and diploma holders that enter the workforce annually are suitable for employment in the offshore IT industry (Summary of NASSCOM-McKinsey Report 2005, in NASSCOM Newsline No. 50, December 2005, www.nasscom.org). Commissioned studies have highlighted the poor quality of education imparted by many of the engineering institutes and the need to produce more graduates with the appropriate technical and 'soft' skills, and both the industry and the state have initiated programmes aimed at improving engineering education (GOI 2003, NASSCOM 2004). However, statements by HR managers suggest that what makes most engineers 'unemployable' is the lack of 'soft skills' suited to the industry, discussed above, more than technical deficiencies.
21. This in itself would not be cause for criticism—for one may argue that it is not the role of the corporate sector to remedy social ills—were it not for the continual litany that emanates from IT industry leaders about the opening up of employment opportunities, which in turn is attributed to their commitment to 'merit'. In this context, it is not unfair to examine closely the production and composition of the IT workforce, rather than accepting the industry's representations of itself at face value.
22. There is no space here to tackle the thorny but crucial question of the relationship between caste and class. I will only suggest that to the extent that historically the middle class—especially in south India—has been largely Brahmin in its make-up, it could be argued that middle-class-ness has become a new media through which Brahmin status and domination are being reproduced, albeit in a transformed shape (Fuller 1999). Further, as Ramesh Bairy (personal communication) has argued, the espousal of secular, anti-caste, egalitarian values by the middle class (as seen in the dominant discourse about the IT industry as well as the 'merit' argument) represents the affirmation of Brahmin status in the very denial of caste. What needs to be added to this argument is that it is not only *caste* that is denied in the dominant ideology of the middle class, but also *class* itself and the privileges that are accorded by middle-class status.
23. At the height of the anti-reservation agitation in 2006, a number of IT professionals came out on the road near Electronic City in Bangalore (the campus that houses Infosys as well as several other software com-

panies) to protest. These protests extended even to Indian students and professionals in the U.S., where anti-reservation demonstrations were organized in the Bay Area in June 2006 under the banner of 'Indians for Equality'. The liberal argument made by many of these protestors was that affirmative action on the basis of 'class' or economic status might be acceptable, but not on the basis of caste. The denial of the upper caste monopoly over higher education and jobs in the private sector is intrinsic to the anti-reservation position.

See http://www.youth4equality.org/aspx/pastevents.aspx; http://www.tribuneindia.com/2006/20060606/world.htm.

REFERENCES

Aneesh, A. (2006), *Virtual Migration: The Programming of Globalization.* Durham: Duke University Press.

Assadi, Muzaffar (2006), 'Karnataka: The Muted Anti-reservation Agitation', *Economic and Political Weekly*, 22 July: 3146-50.

Athreye, Suma S. (2005), 'Human Capital, Labour Scarcity and Development of the Software Services Sector', in A. Saith and M. Vijayabaskar (eds.), *ICTs and Indian Economic Development; Economy, Work, Regulation,* New Delhi: Sage, pp. 154–74.

Bagchi, Subroto (2006), 'Bunti Aur Babli', *Times of India*, Bangalore, 13 January 2006.

Balakrishnan, Pulapre (2006), 'Benign Neglect or Strategic Intent? Contested Lineage of Indian Software industry'. *Economic and Political Weekly*, 41: 3865-72.

Basant, Rakesh and Uma Rani (2004), 'Labour Market Deepening in India's IT: An Exploratory Analysis', *Economic and Political Weekly*, 39: 5317-26.

Castells, Manuel (1996), *The Information Age: Economy, Society and Culture,* vol. I: *The Rise of the Network Society*, Oxford: Blackwell.

Deshpande, Satish (2006), 'Exclusive Inequalities: Merit, Caste and Discrimination in Indian Higher Education Today', *Economic and Political Weekly* 41, 17 June: 2438-44.

Deshpande, S. and Y. Yadav (2006), 'Redesigning Affirmative Action: Castes and Benefits in Higher Education', *Economic and Political Weekly*, 41, 17 June: 2419-24.

Fuller, C.J. (1999), 'The Brahmins and Brahminical Values in Modern Tamil Nadu', in R. Guha and J.P. Parry (eds.), *Institutions and Inequalities: Essays in Honour of Andre Beteille*, Delhi: Oxford University Press, pp. 30–55.

Fuller, C.J. and Haripriya Narasimhan (2006), 'Engineering Colleges, "Exposure" and Information Technology Professionals in Tamil Nadu', *Economic and Political Weekly*, 41: 258-62.

——— (2007), 'Information Technology Professionals and the New-rich Middle Class in Chennai (Madras)', forthcoming, in *Modern Asian Studies*, 41(1): 121–50.

Government of India (2003), Report of Task Force on 'Meeting the Human Resources Challenge for IT and IT Enabled Services', Ministry of Communications and Information Technology, Dept. of Information Technology.

Krishna, Anirudh and Vijay Brihmadesam (2006), 'What Does it Take to Become a Software Professional?' *Economic and Political Weekly*, 41: 3307-14.

Mohanty, Mrithunjoy (2006), 'Social Inequality, Labour Market Dynamics and Reservation', *Economic and Political Weekly*, 41: 3777–89.

NASSCOM (2004), 'Strengthening the Human Resource Foundation of the Indian IT Enabled Services/IT Industry. KPMG-NASSCOM. Report (under the aegis of the Department of IT, Ministry of Information Technology and Communications, Government of India).

Oommen, U. and A. Meenakshisundararajan (2005), 'Social Structuring of Human Capital of the New Global Workforce', paper presented to International Conference on New Global Workforces and Virtual Workplaces: Connections, Culture, and Control, National Institute of Advanced Studies, Bangalore, 12–13 August.

Parthasarathy, B. (2005), 'The Political Economy of the Computer Software Industry in Bangalore, India', in A. Saith and M. Vijayabaskar (eds.), *ICTs and Indian Economic Development: Economy, Work, Regulation*, New Delhi: Sage, pp. 199–230.

Rothboeck, S., M. Vijaybaskar and V. Gayathri (2001), *Labour in the New Economy: The Case of the Indian Software Labour Market*, New Delhi: International Labour Organization.

Upadhya, Carol (1997), 'Social and Cultural Strategies of Class Formation in Coastal Andhra Pradesh', *Contributions to Indian Sociology* (n.s.), 31(2): 169–93.

——— (2007), 'Management of Culture and Management through Culture in the Indian Software Outsourcing Industry', in Carol Upadhya and A.R. Vasavi (eds.), *New Global Workforces and Virtual Workplaces: Connections, Culture, and Control*, New Delhi: Routledge.

Upadhya, Carol and A.R. Vasavi (2006), 'Work, Culture, and Sociality in the Indian IT Industry: A Sociological Study (Final Report submitted to IDPAD)', Bangalore: National Institute of Advanced Studies.

Xiang, Biao (2002), 'Global "body shopping": A New International Labour System in the Information Technology Industry', D.Phil. dissertation, Oxford University.

CHAPTER 5

Access to Employment in India: The Case of Public and Corporate Sector Jobs

ALAKH N. SHARMA

It is widely believed that while the process of globalization has led to significant growth in trade, capital flows and foreign direct investment and in the world income as a whole, unemployment and precarious employment, inequality and poverty have all been either on the rise or stagnated at a high level.[1] Apart from the deceleration in employment growth and the rise in open unemployment, there has been increasing informalization of employment and deterioration in its quality. There are growing disparities in wages and incomes between skilled and unskilled workers, owners of capital and workers, and workers in the informal sector and the formal. Except for a few countries, this has been the global experience, both in developed as well as in developing countries.

In India too there has been an upward trend in inequality in income and wealth and the exclusion of disadvantaged areas (rural, inaccessible, less developed) and groups Scheduled Castes (SC) and Scheduled Tribes (ST) from the gains of the high rates of economic growth of the last several years. Such a concern is well reflected in the very subtitle of the approach paper to the Eleventh Five-Year Plan—'The Challenge of Inclusive Growth'. The recent moves to expand the reservations policy to private sector jobs and the reservation of seats in educational institutions for Other Backward Classes (OBC) also originate from the same concern regarding unequal access to assets, skill, education and employment opportunities.

The main objective of this chapter is to analyse the extent of unequal access of various social groups to 'quality jobs' and discuss the factors behind the unequal access. This analysis has been done on the basis of the unit-level household data of the NSSO 55th Round

(1999–2000). The availability of the NSSO 61st Round-data for 2004–5 along with the data for 1993–4 will provide information on the trend over time and may help in discussing some dynamics of the trend. The present study does not go into the issue of the implications of globalization for inequality and access to employment. The structure of the chapter is as follows. The first section reviews the recent trend of increasing inequality in income and employment with respect to various groups, rural *vs.* urban and regions. The next section briefly discusses the nature of the Indian labour market in the context of access to 'quality jobs' as well as the framework of this chapter. This is followed by the details of access to 'quality jobs' of various social groups. Next is an analysis of the segmentation of sub-groups within the social groups and the so-called 'creamy layer' cornering the major share of jobs. Finally, the broad conclusions and policy implications are discussed.

Increasing Trend of Inequality in India

INEQUALITY ACROSS VARIOUS GROUPS

Although the aggregate data shows a decline in the incidence of poverty, albeit at a decreasing rate in the post-liberalization era, there is near unanimity on the conclusion that there has been a the rise in inequality or relative deprivation since the start of that policy. The estimates of the growth rates of per capita expenditure between 1993–4 and 1999–2000 point to a significant increase in rural-urban inequalities not only at the all-India level, but also in most of the states. There has been a significant increase in the differences in wage/salary incomes between those in rural and urban sectors (Deaton and Drèze 2002). Further, if the data is disaggregate gender-wise and caste-wise, the picture is even more worrisome (Thorat 2001). The people belonging to SCs and STs preponderantly fall into the net of poverty. In 1999–2000, the percentage of the population below the poverty line among SCs and STs was 36 and 44, respectively as against 16 in the case of other categories of the population. It is also important to note that the decline in poverty over the years has been slower among STs and SCs, particularly among the former, in comparison to other groups. STs and SCs have also been traditionally disadvantaged in terms of property and education—the two most important endowments that enable one to cope with the exclusionary process of the market.

Women workers form another category, for whom evidence points to their relative deprivation. With regard to female labourers, the downtrend in the labour market further worsens their condition because of the gender-specific exclusionary processes. Although some studies highlight the increasing feminization of labour, the overall trends in the growth of employment of women in rural and urban areas point to the contrary. The overall rate of growth of employment declined in the post-reform phase, but the decline was greater for women than for men. For rural males, it declined from 1.94 per cent during 1983/1993–4 to 0.94 during 1993–4/1999–2000 and for females it went down from 1.41 to a mere 0.15 per cent. In urban areas, the decline was from 3.22 per cent to 2.61 per cent for males and from 3.44 to 0.94 for females (Chadha and Sahu 2002). Whatever addition to female employment has taken place during this period has largely been confined to the informal sector.

It will be interesting to see the share of labour *vis-à-vis* capital in the development process of India. A recent study found that labour's income share in the aggregate economy of India has been declining since 1993–4 (Mohan 2003). The share of labour income was higher than that of capital income throughout the period of 1970–1 to 1999–2000, but the gap widened considerably during the period from 1987–8 to 1992–3 (0.66 to 0.68). But after that, the share of labour income has been steadily declining and that of capital income increasing, resulting in nearly equal shares for the two categories (0.49 and 0.51 respectively). This fall in the labour income share has occurred while the share of agriculture in national income and the proportion of labour force employed in it have been declining. This could be due to the emergence of new sub-sectors of low-wage subsistence segments, probably in the services sector. Another reason could be the slowdown in the growth of real wages in the organized manufacturing sector, a fall in employment in the high wage income share activities and growing labour flexibility (outsourcing and informalization). All these require more detailed analysis, but they clearly show that liberalization and globalization policies have played important role in the decline.

RURAL-URBAN DIVIDE AND EMPLOYMENT[2]

Over time there has been a distinct and deepening rural-urban divide, particularly during the 1990s, in terms of income and access to employment. The share of rural areas in national income has been falling much faster than its share in population. During 1970–1, 62 per cent of India's national income was generated in rural areas, and only 38 per cent of it came from urban areas. During 1999–2000, the urban share became about half of the national income. The vast majority of workers (71.6 per cent), however, continue to be in rural areas. As a result, urban per capita income in 1999–2000 had risen to about two and half times that of rural per capita income. During the 1970s and 1980s, the rural-urban per capita income gap had actually narrowed but it widened considerably during the second half of the 1990s.

Most rural income is still generated by agriculture, although its share has gone down by more than 28 percentage points since 1970–1. Agricultural income now accounts for only half of all rural incomes. The share of services, on the other hand, has risen from more than 9 per cent to more than 17 per cent, and that of manufacturing from about 5 to about 9 per cent during 1970–1 to 1999–2000. There has also been a rapid expansion of income in rural transport, storage and communications (Table 5.1). Among all the rural sectors, agriculture records the slowest growth of income, although it employs the majority of workers.

As a whole, for all sectors combined, the urban Net Domestic

TABLE 5.1: SHARES OF EACH SECTOR IN RURAL INCOME (NDP AT FACTOR COST): 1970–1, 1980–1, 1993–4 AND 1999–2000

Sector	Year			
	1970–1	1980–1	1993–4	1999–2000
1. Agriculture, forestry and fishing	73.44	65.77	56.99	51.06
2. Mining and quarrying	1.49	1.58	2.60	2.63
3. Manufacturing	5.34	7.68	8.15	8.90
(i) Registered	(2.67)	(2.64)	(5.22)	(5.62)
(ii) Unregistered	(2.66)	(5.03)	(2.94)	(3.28)
4. Electricity, gas & water supply	0.44	0.57	0.88	1.13
5. Trade, hotels and restaurants	4.59	5.22	4.61	4.29
6. Transport, storage and communications	1.42	2.09	3.41	4.47
7. Services	9.59	10.79	16.57	17.29
NDP at factor cost	100.00	100.00	100.00	100.00

Source: Bhalla, 2004.

Product (NDP) per worker presently is about 3.5 times that of rural NDP per worker: in 1999–2000, NDP per rural worker was Rs. 16,621 as against Rs. 55,088 per urban worker; it was Rs. 12,951 and Rs. 39,028 respectively in 1993–4. Within rural areas, the gap between NDP per worker in agriculture and NDP per worker in the non-farm sector is also large and growing. Today the NDP per worker in the rural non-farm sector is about three times than of the farm sector.

Rural employment growth rates have significantly declined in recent years, which has pulled down the overall growth rate of employment (rural plus urban) to unacceptably low levels. During the 1990s, rural employment growth rates fell to less than half of what they had been in the 1980s, and to less than one-third of the growth rate in urban India during the 1990s. The major reason for this has been the decline in the growth rate of agricultural employment. As compared to the 1970s and 1980s, non-farm employment growth rates have also gone down in recent years. But at least they remain above the population growth rate. The biggest decline in the non-farm workforce was recorded by rural manufacturing. That is why the late 1980s and early 1990s have been described as the 'de-industrialization' of the rural workforce.

Because of these reasons, the rural employment elasticities, which were already low by the usual standards even during the 1980s, became even lower during the 1990s. The rural employment elasticities in the 1990s were about half than that in urban areas. This implies that the rural economy would have to grow at twice the rate of the urban economy in order to generate the same percentage increase in employment.

Over the last three decades or so, rural workers have experienced unequal access to employment *vis-à-vis* the new jobs that were created in the economy. During the entire period, from 1972–3 to 1999–2000, the rural employment growth rate was considerably lower than the urban one; consequently the share of the rural workers in the new jobs created has been proportionately smaller than their urban counterparts. The situation was far worse in the 1990s compared to the earlier period due to a very slow growth of rural non-farm employment during the early 1990s and almost zero growth of agricultural employment in the latter half of the 1990s. During 1972–3, the share of rural workers in the workforce was about 84 per cent, but their share in the additional employment generated over the next five years was only 70 per cent (Table 5.2). In 1993–4, the share of rural areas in the workforce was 78 per cent, but their share in the new employment created had declined to only 51 per cent. The access of rural workers to additional non-farm employment was even lower than their access to employment in the farm and non-farm sectors combined. There was, however, an improvement in their relative position during the 1980s as contrasted to the decline in their share in new non-farm jobs in the early 1990s. Further, till the late 1980s, the share of rural workers in new non-farm employment was always higher than the rural areas' share in existing non-farm jobs. However, from the end of the 1990s, rural workers lost their early advantage. Thus rural workers have always suffered from unequal access to whatever employment opportunities were created in the Indian economy. During the 1990s their relative position *vis-à-vis* urban workers further deteriorated.

Regional Disparities

One of the major fears of globalization in India has been its adverse implications in terms of accentuating the already uneven regional development in the country. While the growth rate in the State Domestic Product (SDP) at the all-India level was higher in the 1990s (about 6.5 per cent) as compared to the 1980s (about 5.5 per cent), the disparities in growth rates across various states have also increased. While the poor states of Bihar, Orissa and Uttar Pradesh have registered very low rates of growth, states like Gujarat, Maharashtra and Karnataka have done exceptionally well with a growth rate of approximately 7 per cent or more. The growth rate of Gujarat was about three-and-half times higher than that of Assam and two-and-half times higher than that of Bihar during the 1990s.

Notwithstanding the poor quality of human and physical resources as well as governance in the backwards states, the forces generated by liberalization and globalization have further accentuated these variations in performance. As a whole, the backward states have not been able to generate adequate resources for their development as against the richer states. While their own efforts to generate resources have been extremely limited because of their widespread poverty, the transfer of resources to them from various sources have also been much lower compared to the richer states. Not only has the plan size of these states been very low, but the transfer of resources from finan-

TABLE 5.2: UNEQUAL ACCESS: SHARE OF RURAL AND URBAN WORKERS IN THE UPSS TOTAL (R+U) WORKFORCE, AND THEIR SHARES IN NEW JOBS: 1972–3, 1977–8, 1983, 1987–8, 1993–4 AND 1999–2000

Category/Location	Year/Period										
	1972–3	1972–3 to 1977–8	1977–8	1977–8 to 1983	1983	1983 to to 1987–8	1987–8	1987–8 to 1993–4	1993–4	1993–4 to 1999–00	1999–00
	Share in Work-force	Share in in New Jobs	Share in Work-force	Sahre in New Jobs	Share in Work-force	Share in New Jobs	Share in Work-force	Share in New Jobs	Share in Work-force	Share in New Jobs	Share in Work-force
1. Rural Area's Share in											
(i) Existing jobs (workforce)	83.63	*	81.91	*	80.62	*	79.43	*	78.15	*	76.47
(ii) New Jobs	*	69.99	*	70.23	*	63.21	*	69.76	*	50.58	*
(iii) New Non-farm Jobs	*	49.53	*	49.16	*	59.40	*	28.47	*	40.53	*
2. Urban Areas' Share in											
(i) Existing Jobs (workforce)	16.37	**	18.09	*	19.38	*	20.57	*	21.85	*	25.53
(ii) New Jobs	*	30.01	*	29.77	*	36.79	*	30.24	*	49.42	*
(iii) New Non-farm Jobs	*	50.47	*	50.84	*	40.60	*	71.53	*	59.47	*
3. Rural Areas' Share in Existing Non-Farm Jobs	46.35	*	47.04	*	47.42	*	49.66	*	46.85	*	45.92

Source: Bhalla, 2003.

cial institutions has also been highly uneven. For example, during 1999–2001, the per capita public and private investment in Gujarat and Tamil Nadu was respectively, 12 and 9 times higher than that of Bihar; the per capita plan outlay in Karnataka, Gujarat and Punjab was more than four times higher than in Bihar. Similarly, per capita per annum for externally aided projects during 1997–2002 was Rs. 11 in Bihar, while it was Rs. 221, 138 and 125 in Andhra Pradesh, Gujarat and Karnataka respectively. The same is true for credit utilization (Table 5.3). Because of the poor state of infrastructure and lack of any promotional and protective policies in backward regions, even the resources of these regions are increasingly being diverted to better performing ones, as reflected in the decline in the already low levels of credit-deposit (C-D) ratios of banks in the era of liberalization.

It is also revealing that the trend in the growth of Foreign Direct Investment (FDI) in different states is strongly associated with the process of globalization as is borne out from the growth of FDIs in the 1990s. The three relatively more developed states—Maharashtra, Karnataka and Tamil Nadu—together account for more than one third of the total FDIs (till April 2003). Apart from Delhi, FDIs is mostly concentrated in the two western states of Maharashtra and Gujarat and the southern states of Karnataka, Tamil Nadu and Andhra Pradesh. Significantly, some of the most backward states of the country—UP, Bihar, Chhattisgarh, Jharkhand, Orissa, Assam and Rajasthan—together account for just 4 per cent of this investment (Table 5.3).

Thus, the inter-state inequalities were increasing in the 1990s and there are signs of divergence rather than convergence. Due to this the backward states have witnessed very low levels of growth in per capita SDP and a slower decline in the incidence of poverty. In the 1990s, the poorer states like Bihar, Madhya Pradesh, Rajasthan, Uttar Pradesh and Orissa showed a smaller reduction in poverty while the richer states such as Andhra Pradesh, Gujarat, Karnataka, Maharashtra, Tamil Nadu and Punjab recorded a much higher decline (Mahendra Dev 2004). The six states of Bihar, Uttar Pradesh, Madhya Pradesh, West Bengal, Orissa and Assam alone account for 74.4 of the total number of poor in India (in 1999–2000). The share of these states in all-India poverty increased in 1999–2000 as compared to 1993–4 when it was 68.8 per cent.

TABLE 5.3: STATE-WISE PER CAPITA FLOWS AND SHARE IN FDI: 1999/2000/2001

States	Per capita NSDP (Rs.) 1999–2000	Per capita public and private investment (Rs.)	Per capita plan-oulay (Rs.)	Per capita institutional investment (Rs.)	Per capita total credit utilization (Rs.)	Per capita per annum externally aided projects (average 1997–2002) (Rs.)	Share in total FDI approved (August 1991 to April 2004) % to total all India*
Andhra Pradesh	14,715	21,447	1,032	910	4,668	221	4.71
Bihar	6,328	2,852	319	546	669	11	0.25
Chhattisgarh	N.A.	12,209	631	32	1,803	N.A.	0.22
Goa	N.A.	56,057	3,423	1,821	14,489	25	0.34
Gujarat	18,685	33,875	1,285	720	5,827	138	6.43
Haryana	21,551	9,201	861	827	5,098	106	1.33
Jharkhand	N.A.	9,105	836	37	1,759	N.A.	0.05
Karnataka	16,343	24,775	1,499	688	6,420	125	8.24
Kerala	18,262	12,235	710	1,173	5,872	19	0.53
Madhya Pradesh	10,907	7,287	652	725	2,528	62	3.16
Maharashtra	23,398	17,556	1,120	660	14,890	52	17.62
Orissa	9,162	25,525	627	1,049	1,706	118	2.81
Punjab	23,040	12,688	1,244	1,078	7,707	68	0.83
Rajasthan	12,533	6,763	822	914	2,419	35	1.03
Tamil Nadu	19,141	26,292	837	709	9,194	83	8.56
Uttar Pradesh	9,765	3,304	293	619	1,638	47	1.68
West Bengal	15,569	7,113	710	662	3,674	89	3.18
Delhi	–	–	–	–	–	–	12.05

Source: *SIA Newsletter, May 2004; rest from Planning Commission, 2003.

The Nature of the Indian Labour Market and Access to Employment

The huge inequality in wealth and income in India is because of several factors, but the three most important ones the very skewed distribution of assets (land and capital), extremely unequal access to education and skill endowment and, finally, discrimination in the labour market. These factors lead to unequal access to good and 'quality jobs' in the labour market. This section examines the extent of access to 'quality jobs' in the background of the nature and structure of the labour market. 'Quality jobs' includes two kinds of jobs which are most sought after: one is public sector jobs (government and semi-government and various government controlled/owned organizations), and the other corporate sector jobs (private limited companies and other jobs in the large private sector).[3]

Such a categorization of 'quality jobs' is appropriate in a poor country like India where access to employment *per se* does not necessarily denote well-being. A significant proportion of those who are employed are part of the 'working poor'. This is well reflected from the fact that the incidence poverty in India (27 per cent in 1999–2000) is much higher than the incidence of unemployment, even when measured on the most comprehensive (CDS) basis (around 7 per cent). Paradoxically, often in the Indian context, the incidence of poverty and unemployment rates are inversely related. Some states with high poverty have lower unemployment rates and vice versa. Further, most poor people are not unemployed and the incidence of poverty is higher among the employed than among the unemployed. In fact, most people are employed in low-productivity activities which bring low incomes. Consequently, the incidence of poverty is inversely related to productivity, not to employment *per se* (Table 5. 4). That is why the poverty incidence is highest among casual labour and lowest among regular workers.

Thus there exists considerable dualism in the labour markets and there are sharp differences in the quality of employment between three categories of employment status. Regular workers are the best placed and casual workers worst. The self-employed are a heterogeneous category but a large majority of them with meagre capital have very low income levels. But at the higher end, the self-employed also includes large landholders and owners of other productive assets and highly qualified professionals. The category of

TABLE 5.4: POVERTY AND UNEMPLOYMENT RELATIONSHIP

Poverty and Unemployment in Selected States, 1999–2000

High Poverty States	Poverty Rates	Unemployment Rates
Orissa	47.2	2.6
Bihar	42.6	2.4
MP	37.4	1.1
UP	31.2	1.4
Low Poverty States		
Kerala	12.7	8.6
Punjab	6.2	2.1

Poverty and Labour Productivity Among Rural Households, 1999–2000

Sectors	Poverty (HCR %)	Labour Productivity (NDP per worker at 1993–4 base)
Construction	27.9	21,519
Trade	16.8	23,991
Transport	18.9	36,015
Services	15.6	55,745

Poverty Ratio Among Employment Categories, 1999–2000

Employment Category	Rural	Urban
Self-employed	20.76	23.09
Regular/Salaried	12.38	10.78
Casual Labour	38.66	43.72
Total Workers	26.93	21.90

Poor Among Employed and Unemployed

Year	Poor Among the Employed (UPSS)	Poor Among the Unemployed
1983	44.18	36.45
1987–8	37.82	36.17
1993–4	34.29	18.53
1999–2000	29.35	19.15

Source: NSSO, 2000, 2005.

regular workers is also not a homogeneous category and, at the lower end, there are a large number of workers employed in the smaller private sector enterprises, mostly in the informal sector. The best 'quality employment' in this category is decidedly the public sector (government, semi-government and similar organizations) and the corporate sector (mainly larger private enterprises). In fact, these 'quality jobs' are most sought after. While central and various state governments have reserved a maximum of 50 per cent of jobs in the public sector, there is a strong demand for extending the reservation to the corporate sector also.[4] In this context, it will be insightful to see the access of various social groups to these 'quality jobs'.

The Indian labour market is considered to be a highly segmented one. In spite of increasing urbanization and mobility of people, there exist large differentials between various social groups, regions, gender and location (rural/urban). As such, the present study attempts to analyse the access to employment of different groups with respect to these criteria. Caste and religion are widely discussed social categories in India which we have also taken up. Here it is proposed to analyse access to employment for the three official categories of SC, ST and OBC that come under the affirmative policy of reservation. These three groups have population categories from several religions, albeit with considerable variations. The categories of upper caste Hindus and upper Muslims have been derived by excluding the ST, SC and OBC from the all-Hindus and Muslims. The category of 'others' comprises other religions, but mainly consists of Sikhs and Christians and, to a smaller extent, Buddhists and Jains. Thus, the classification includes the following six categories: ST, SC, OBC, upper caste Hindu, upper Muslim and 'Others', whose account for 8.9, 19.6, 35.8, 25.0, 8.5, 2.2 per cent respectively of the total population as per the 55th Round of the NSSO (Table 5.5). Upper caste Hindu, Upper Muslim and 'Others' are much more urban-based than the three other groups, especially the STs, and SCs. Little less than nine-tenths of the STs and more than nine-tenths of the SCs are Hindus. Again, 88 per cent of the OBCs are Hindus and about one-tenth are Muslims (Table 5.5).

Apart from these social groups, an attempt has also been made here to introduce the income criterion. In view of the lack of income data, consumption expenditure has been taken as a proxy for income, although an imperfect one, and consumer expenditure classes as economic categories. Access to jobs considering the regional location of the various social groups has also been analysed.

TABLE 5.5: POPULATION DISTRIBUTION OF SOCIAL GROUPS

	Rural	Urban	Total
ST	10.63	3.88	9.91
SC	21.35	14.56	19.62
OBC	37.36	31.35	35.84
Upper Hindus	21.38	35.77	25.03
Upper Muslims	7.72	11.13	8.44
Total	100.0	100.0	100.0

Religious Composition of SC, ST and OBC

	Rural	Urban	Total
ST			
Hindus	88.35	75.14	86.89
Muslims	0.65	3.57	0.97
Christians	7.57	14.18	8.31
Others	3.43	7.11	3.83
SC			
Hindus	92.04	88.56	91.39
Muslims	0.71	1.77	0.91
Christians	1.41	1.77	1.47
Sikhs	3.0	2.64	2.94
OBC			
Hindus	89.66	80.89	87.71
Muslims	8.54	15.89	10.17
Christians	0.97	1.99	1.20
Others	0.83	1.23	0.92
All	100	100	100

Source: NSSO, 2000, 2005.

Access to Quality Jobs by Social Groups

Before analysing the access of the various social groups to 'quality jobs', it will be useful to look at their sectoral distribution as well as distribution across employment status categories. Of the six groups—ST, SC, OBC, upper caste Hindus upper Muslims and 'Others'—the proportion of SCs and STs in low-paid agriculture and related activities is much higher than among the other four groups. The upper caste Hindus are less in agricultural activities compared to OBCs and their proportion is much higher in white-collar occupations such as finance and real estate and public administration (Table 5.6). Further, the 'upper Hindus' have a much higher pro-

TABLE 5.6: DISTRIBUTION OF WORKERS BY SOCIAL GROUP AND INDUSTRY (15–59 AGE GROUP), 1999–2000

Sector	Industry	Social Group						
		ST	SC	OBC	Upper Hindus	Upper Muslims	Others	Total
Rural	Agriculture, Forestry & Fishing	84.70	75.22	73.02	72.20	60.75	67.20	74.08
	Mining & Quarrying	0.80	0.51	0.71	0.29	0.33	0.79	0.57
	Manufacturing	3.59	7.36	8.67	6.10	13.29	4.61	7.42
	Electricity	0.17	0.17	0.16	0.34	0.05	0.48	0.20
	Construction	4.37	5.50	3.40	2.28	3.84	4.07	3.81
	Trade, Hotels & Restaurants	1.54	3.64	6.11	7.48	11.15	9.31	5.57
	Transport, Storage & Communication	1.21	2.67	2.26	2.74	4.14	5.07	2.46
	Finance., Real Est. & Business	0.16	0.26	0.35	0.88	0.32	1.76	0.43
	Pub. Admn., Edu., Health & Others	3.44	4.66	5.32	7.70	6.13	6.70	5.46
	Total	100.00	100.00	100.00	100.00	100.00	100.00	100.00
Urban	Agriculture, Forestry & Fishing	16.26	11.03	9.74	4.18	3.96	3.27	7.44
	Mining & Quarrying	3.15	1.31	0.71	0.59	0.44	0.47	0.82
	Manufacturing	14.70	17.95	25.10	22.14	27.12	17.50	22.51
	Electricity	0.64	0.55	0.58	1.20	0.33	0.69	0.78
	Construction	14.30	14.83	9.73	4.51	7.57	3.96	8.42
	Trade, Hotels & Restaurants	15.84	18.21	26.40	28.16	35.49	31.67	26.45
	Transport, Storage & Communication	9.21	11.07	9.02	8.33	11.51	9.54	9.35

	Finance., Real Est. & Business	2.95	1.94	2.57	7.12	1.68	6.20	4.14
	Pub. Admn., Edu., Health & Others	22.96	23.10	16.15	23.78	11.87	26.70	20.09
	Total	100.00	100.00	100.00	100.00	100.00	100.00	100.00
Total	Agriculture, Forestry & Fishing	78.91	64.31	59.90	48.04	41.41	41.16	58.52
	Mining & Quarrying	1.00	0.65	0.71	0.40	0.37	0.66	0.63
	Manufacturing	4.53	9.16	12.08	11.80	18.00	9.86	10.95
	Electricity	0.21	0.24	0.25	0.64	0.14	0.57	0.33
	Construction	5.21	7.08	4.71	3.07	5.11	4.02	4.89
	Trade, Hotels & Restaurants	2.75	6.12	10.32	14.82	19.45	18.42	10.45
	Transport, Storage & Communication	1.89	4.10	3.66	4.72	6.65	6.89	4.07
	Finance., Real Est. & Business	0.39	0.55	0.81	3.09	0.78	3.57	1.29
	Pub Admn., Edu., Health & Others	5.10	7.80	7.56	13.41	8.09	14.85	8.88
	Total	100.00	100.00	100.00	100.00	100.00	100.00	100.00

Source: NSSO, 2000, 2005.

portion as regular workers compared to other groups like SC and ST. Almost three-fourths of the SC workers and half of the ST workers are casual workers, as against only one-sixth among the 'upper Hindus', one-third each of OBCs, and upper Muslims. The best placed seem to be the 'others' who are much less dependent on agricultural activities and have the largest share in white-collar jobs and business activities[5] (Table 5.7).

As a whole STs, SCs and OBCs have an overwhelmingly larger concentration of their workforce in the lowest paid 'other' type of employment (mostly agriculture and related) than do other groups (Table 5.8). Despite job reservation, the proportion of their workforce

TABLE 5.7: PERCENTAGE DISTRIBUTION OF WORKERS BY SOCIAL GROUP AND WORK STATUS, 1999–2000

Sex	Social Group	Work Status			
		Self-Employed	Regular	Casual	Total
Males	ST	53.26	16.80	29.94	100
	SC	33.86	18.83	47.31	100
	OBC	54.95	19.49	25.56	100
	Upper Hindus	55.58	33.44	10.98	100
	Upper Muslims	56.37	20.82	22.81	100
	Other	60.87	29.20	9.93	100
	Total	51.94	23.47	24.60	100
Females	ST	58.60	8.77	32.63	100
	SC	31.34	10.60	58.06	100
	OBC	56.75	10.99	32.26	100
	Upper Hindus	56.55	27.98	15.47	100
	Upper Muslims	60.94	14.06	25.00	100
	Other	36.96	52.16	10.88	100
	Total	52.22	14.85	32.93	100
Persons	ST	45.53	7.87	46.59	100
	SC	30.53	11.83	57.64	100
	OBC	53.24	13.29	33.47	100
	Upper Hindus	55.69	27.45	16.85	100
	Upper Muslims	53.86	15.52	30.62	100
	Other	55.07	30.84	14.09	100
	Total	48.38	16.18	35.44	100

TABLE 5.8: PERCENTAGE DISTRIBUTION OF REGULAR WORKERS BY SOCIAL GROUP AND ENTERPRISE TYPE, 1999–2000

Sex	Social Group	Enterprise Type			
		Public Sector	Private Sector	Corporate	Total
Males	ST	69.56	22.01	8.43	100
	SC	50.57	36.29	13.14	100
	OBC	38.13	46.86	15.00	100
	Upper Hindus	48.76	33.79	17.44	100
	Upper Muslims	32.54	55.42	12.04	100
	Other	45.89	34.76	19.35	100
	Total	46.29	38.45	15.26	100
Females	ST	74.46	18.65	6.88	100
	SC	50.07	37.27	12.66	100
	OBC	38.47	42.99	18.54	100
	Upper Hindus	57.03	28.06	14.91	100
	Upper Muslims	38.01	43.89	18.10	100
	Other	45.13	26.84	28.03	100
	Total	51.68	32.57	15.75	100
Persons	ST	70.72	21.21	8.06	100
	SC	50.48	36.46	13.06	100
	OBC	38.19	46.24	15.57	100
	Upper Hindus	50.07	32.88	17.04	100
	Upper Muslims	33.06	54.32	12.62	100
	Other	45.69	32.66	21.65	100
	Total	47.19	37.47	15.34	100

Source: NSSO, 2000, 2005.

employed in the public sector is less then half of the upper caste Hindus. Muslms fare worst with almost as low a percentage as STs. In the corporate private sector, the disparity is more glaring with upper Hindus and 'the "other" having a much larger share. OBC and upper Muslims are almost equally placed and only slightly better then the SCs. When one looks at the distribution of only regular workers in enterprises, both SCs and STs (particularly the latter) have a large proportions of their workers in the public sector, but upper Muslims and OBCs have larger proportions in the low-paid small private sector enterprises. As can be seen from Table 5.9, there is a

TABLE 5.9: PERCENTAGE DISTRIBUTION OF REGULAR WORKERS BY SOCIAL GROUP AND ENTERPRISE TYPE, 1999–2000

Sex	Social Group	Public Sector	Private Corporate
Males	ST	6.63	3.05
	SC	16.52	11.24
	OBC	24.88	27.25
	Upper Hindus	44.33	49.58
	Upper Muslims	4.88	5.13
	Other	2.76	3.75
	Total	100.00	100.00
Females	ST	9.60	3.95
	SC	15.82	11.99
	OBC	22.94	35.99
	Upper Hindus	43.80	32.04
	Upper Muslims	2.75	4.10
	Other	5.09	11.93
	Total	100.00	100.00
Persons	ST (18.9)*	7.12	3.19
	SC (19.6)*	16.40	11.36
	OBC (35.8)	24.56	28.63
	Upper Hindus (25.0)	44.24	46.80
	Upper Muslims (8.4)	4.53	4.97
	Others	3.14	5.04
	Total	100.00	100.00

Source: NSSO, 2000, 2005.

considerable gap between various groups with respect to access to these quality jobs. It seems that the reservation policy has helped the SCs and STs in getting jobs in the public sector, although the share even now is somewhat less than their population share. However, the gap is large among the OBCs and Muslims who have got a much smaller share in public sector jobs as compared to the others. On the other hand, upper caste Hindus have got a discretionally much larger share (44.2 per cent) *vis-à-vis* their population share (25 per cent). The picture is similar in corporate sector jobs, but the gap widens in for the SCs and STs. Thus, it seems that the reservation policy has a played positive role in their case.

It appears, then, that among the major social groups, the SC and ST workers are the worst placed and upper Hindus and 'the other' best placed. The OBCs and other Muslims are in the middle, with almost similar characteristics in the labour market with respect to access to good quality jobs.

Not much difference is observed across the three reservation groups in the public sector jobs in terms of their distribution by occupation. Here again, upper caste Hindus and 'others' are relatively greater in number (around three-fourth of the total workers in these categories), concentrated in professional, technical and administrative jobs, than workers of the other four groups (Table 5.10). The 'lower groups' have a larger concentration than the 'upper groups' in sales and service and production related works. More than half of the SC workers are in these two kinds of somewhat inferior jobs. However, the difference is glaring in corporate sector jobs. Here, about two-thirds of 'others' and about half of the 'upper Hindus' are in professional, technical and administrative jobs, compared to the less than one-fourth of SC and ST workers, and around one-third OBCs and Muslims who are in such job. These groups are mostly concentrated in production related work and to a lesser extent in sales and service work (Table 5.10). The high proportion (60.74 per cent) of professional and managerial category among ST in the public sector may also be due to a very small number, and that too because of positive discrimination.

On the whole, it seems that the affirmative policy has helped the three groups—SC, ST and OBC—in the access to public sector jobs, although their participation in proportion to their total workforce is still very low. Clearly, in the absence of a reservation policy, even this would not have been achieved. This is reflected in their small presence in corporate jobs, that too in the more inferior jobs.

Affirmative Policy and 'Creamy Layer'

It has been pointed out by several experts that the benefits of the reservation policy have been cornered by certain elite sections—the so-called 'creamy layer' among them. There have been equally strong positions against it citing arguments such as deep-rooted prejudices of the society towards them. Even the uniform reservation policy has been advocated for the sake of solidarity of these groups. This controversy has taken centre stage now in view of the recent judge-

TABLE 5.10: PERCENTAGE DISTRIBUTION OF WORKERS BY SOCIAL GROUP AND JOB TYPE, 1999–2000

Job Type	Occupation	Social Group						
		ST	SC	OBC	Upper Hindus	Upper Muslims	Others	Total
Public Sector	Professional, managerial, administrative	60.74	47.96	58.56	71.87	65.43	74.80	63.42
	Sales & service workers	15.93	28.28	13.87	10.76	8.39	8.76	14.74
	Production & related workers	22.09	22.68	26.08	16.02	25.65	15.85	20.57
	Others	1.24	1.08	1.48	1.35	0.53	0.59	1.27
	Total	100.00	100.00	100.00	100.00	100.00	100.00	100.00
Corporate	Professional, managerial, administrative	18.84	18.50	30.27	47.96	32.91	62.61	36.43
	Sales & service workers	14.97	19.43	10.86	13.34	7.94	9.63	13.11
	Production & related workers	64.41	59.73	56.97	36.67	57.20	27.73	48.52
	Others	1.78	2.34	1.90	2.03	1.95	0.03	1.94
	Total	100.00	100.00	100.00	100.00	100.00	100.00	100.00

Source: NSSO, 2000, 2005.

ment of the Supreme Court to exclude the 'creamy layers' among the beneficiaries of reservation.

An attempt is made here to deal with the 'creamy layer' issue by analysing the access to quality jobs, particularly the public sector jobs, by the various strata of the reservation beneficiary groups (SC, ST and OBC). As pointed out earlier, in the absence of income data, their study relies taken on consumption expenditure which is considered to be a proxy of income. An attempt has been made to analyse the regional spread/concentration supplemented by educational endowment.

Table 5.11 gives the share of workers belonging to the highest consumption expenditure class (CEC) (richest) and the lowest CEC (poorest) of the various social groups with respect to access to public and corporate sector jobs. The results are quite revealing. The richest 20 per cent in all groups—either beneficiaries of affirmative policy or the rest—have cornered a very large share of all public sector jobs, much greater than their population share. The proportions are in fact much higher in the general category (except upper

TABLE 5.11: PERCENTAGE SHARE OF WORKERS IN THE POOREST AND RICHEST EXPENDITURE CLASS (QUINTILES) BY PUBLIC AND CORPORATE JOBS, 1999-2000

Caste	Quintiles	Job type	
		Public Sector	Corporate
ST	Poorest	5.02	20.01
	Richest	56.95	24.02
SC	Poorest	8.12	18.22
	Richest	45.90	30.47
OBC	Poorest	2.65	8.30
	Richest	58.14	40.07
Upper Hindus	Poorest	1.17	1.77
	Richest	74.70	70.36
Upper Muslims	Poorest	3.73	19.74
	Richest	50.92	30.76
Others	Poorest	0.92	0.19
	Richest	90.18	82.86
Total	Poorest	3.12	8.12
	Richest	63.71	51.06

Source: NSSO, 2000, 2005.

Muslim) as compared to the reserved categories—around 75 and 90 per cent respectively, among the Hindus and 'others' have cornered the public sector jobs. The share of the richest SC (47 per cent), ST (57 per cent) and OBC (58 per cent) are lower compared to the share of the richest 'upper Hindu' (74.70 per cent) and 'others' (90.18 per cent). However, the shares of poorest 20 per cent among the reserved categories are higher compared to the shares of upper Hindu or others. The picture for reserved groups is very different in corporate sector jobs where they are much more evenly spread. Only 5 and 8 per cent of the poorest among the STs and SCs, respectively, have access to public sector jobs, whereas in the corporate sector their proportions are 20 and 18 per cent respectively. In the case of OBC, the poorest 20 per cent have access to less than 3 per cent of public sector jobs as against 58 per cent in the case of the richest 20 per cent, the proportions being 8 and 40 per cent respectively for corporate sector jobs.

Thus, it seems that among the SCs, STs and OBCs, a very large share of public sector jobs have been cornered by the elite in their group. As such, the poorest among them have consequently tried hard to access corporate sector jobs, although their share of such jobs is small in this sector. It is also quite revealing that the poorest among the upper Hindus as well as the 'others' have negligible access to both public sector as well as corporate sector jobs.

In this context, it will be interesting to see the distribution of various social groups *vis-à-vis* the expenditure groups, as provided in Table 5.12. The proportion of the poorer groups among the SCs and STs is higher than in the richer groups and somewhat lower than the OBCs and upper caste Hindus (with respect to their population shares). But the picture is not smooth, with 10 per cent of the richest belonging to the SCs and 28 per cent to the OBCs, although both are lower than the upper Hindus (45 per cent). However, it points to the fact that over the years the policy of positive discrimination may have also contributed to this situation. But it appears that in the reserved groups also there have emerged somewhat richer sections.

An analysis of access to self-employment may also throw light on the issue. Self-employment still represents the highest proportion compared to the regular or casual status of employment. It is a very heterogeneous category with poor artisans and others with meagre capital on the one extreme and high income-earning businessmen on the other. Table 5.13 gives some of the well-being of the various

TABLE 5.12: PERCENTAGE OF POPULAITON IN VARIOUS SOCIAL GROUPS IN DIFFERENT CEC (QUINTILES GROUPS), 1999–2000

Quintiles	Social Group						
	ST	SC	OBC	Upper Hindu	Upper Muslim	Other	Total
Poorest	16.53	27.15	35.55	10.45	9.98	0.33	100.00
Poor	10.28	23.67	39.62	16.59	9.23	0.61	100.00
Medium	8.12	20.31	39.04	22.44	9.05	1.05	100.00
Rich	5.64	16.80	36.69	30.54	7.79	2.54	100.00
Richest	3.98	10.19	28.30	45.16	6.12	6.25	100.00
Total	8.91	19.62	35.84	25.03	8.44	2.16	100.00

Source: NSSO, 2000, 2005.

social groups, where the self-employed (non-agricultural workers aged between 15 and 59 years) are classified by social groups and expenditure groups (quintiles). The percentages of the OBC and upper Hindus among the rich and the richest are quite high, more so of the upper caste Hindus; but a significant percentages of the OBCs and upper castes, particularly the former, also belong to the poor groups. It can also be seen that even among the SCs there are some relatively some well-off self-employed persons—12 per cent of the rich and 7 per cent of the richest belong to the SCs. This further reinforces the fact that, like paid jobs, among the self-employed also, there exist large gaps between the incomes of various groups. The even spread of the share of OBCs at around 40 per cent in all categories poses a much bigger challenge for any purely caste-based positive discrimination.

It is now well recognized that education is the principal means of accessing quality jobs, either public or private. The role of educational endowment is shown in Table 5.14 by the distribution of graduates and above in the various consumption expenditure classes across social groups. Here again, the two top classes—upper Hindus and 'others'—show extreme inequalities: 77 per cent of graduates or above among the 'upper Hindus' belong to the richest class, while the poorest having less than even 1 per cent. Similarly, among 'others', 90 per cent of graduates and above are from the richest, while the poor and the poorest account for less than 0.5 per cent. The inequal-

TABLE 5.13: DISTRIBUTION OF SELF-EMPLOYED INDIVIDUALS NON-AGRICULTURAL ENTERPRISES (AGE 15–59 YEARS) BY SOCIAL GROUPS AND EXPENDITURE QUINTILES

Identity	Expenditure Quintiles					
	Poorest	Poor	Middle	Rich	Richest	Total
RURAL						
ST	7.2	3.8	3.8	3.7	3.0	4.5
SC	22.8	20.9	20.2	16.1	10.2	18.7
OBC	44.2	47.8	43.4	43.1	40.8	44.1
Upper Hindu	11.3	13.9	20.1	25.1	32.7	19.4
Upper Muslim	14.3	13.0	11.7	10.3	8.4	11.9
Others	0.3	0.5	0.9	1.7	5.0	1.5
Total	100.0	100.0	100.0	100.0	100.0	100.0
URBAN						
ST	3.8	2.6	2.4	1.7	2.0	2.6
SC	19.1	14.1	10.0	8.5	4.1	11.5
OBC	41.5	42.1	34.7	31.2	17.9	34.0
Upper Hindu	14.4	25.8	37.4	43.0	60.2	35.1
Upper Muslim	20.2	14.3	12.0	10.5	6.7	13.0
Others	1.0	1.1	·3.6	5.1	9.1	3.8
Total	100.0	100.0	100.0	100.0	100.0	100.0
RURAL + URBAN						
ST	5.7	3.2	3.1	2.7	2.5	3.6
SC	21.1	17.7	15.2	12.2	7.1	15.2
OBC	43.0	45.2	39.2	37.1	29.2	39.3
Upper Hindu	12.6	19.4	28.5	34.1	46.6	26.9
Upper Muslim	16.9	13.6	11.8	10.4	7.5	12.4
Others	0.6	0.8	2.2	3.4	7.1	2.6
Total	100.0	100.0	100.0	100.0	100.0	100.0

Source: NSSO, 2000, 2005.

ity in the distribution of graduates across expenditure classes is much less among the SCs, STs and OBCs, particularly the first group, where the poor and the poorest among them also have 10 per cent to 18 per cent of persons with graduates and above degrees, although the richest among them have very high shares. Obviously this is because of the policy of reservation of seats for these groups in educational institutions; because of such a policy, the poorer groups have had some

TABLE 5.14: PERCENTAGE GRADUATES AND ABOVE AMONG SOCIAL GROUP AND QUINTILES WISE, 1999–2000

Social Group	Quintiles					Total
	Poorest	Poor	Medium	Rich	Richest	
ST	4.74	5.59	7.51	14.75	67.40	100
SC	7.60	10.49	12.07	20.12	49.72	100
OBC	3.72	6.79	10.60	20.06	58.83	100
Upper Hindus	0.94	2.52	4.89	14.79	76.86	100
Upper Muslims	2.72	5.44	12.32	20.70	58.83	100
Others	0.10	0.36	1.45	8.39	89.71	100
Total	2.13	4.06	6.77	16.14	70.91	100

Source: NSSO, 2000, 2005.

access to higher education, although a disproportionately large share has gone to the richest class.

Thus it would appear that segmentation in the labour market is not only in terms of caste but also in terms of income and wealth which is reflected in the possession of educational endowment. The segmentation on an economic basis is much more among the upper Hindus and 'other' groups than among the STs and SCs. Among the OBCs also, there is high inequality in terms of income and access to education, but it is lower than for the upper Hindus and the 'others'.

Further, the inequalities among the social groups also vary widely region-wise in a diverse and unevenly developing country like India. The present study examines the regional distribution of access to jobs in terms of various groups as well as total jobs. Table 5.15 shows that the central and eastern regions of India, which have the highest incidence of poverty, account for only 31 per cent and 27 per cent in the share of public and corporate sector jobs respectively, although they account for about 45 per cent of the country's population. On the other hand, the southern and western regions together, with 40 per cent of the country's population, account for 58 per cent of the corporate jobs. This pattern is also reflected in the access to jobs by different groups in different regions (Tables 5.16 and 5.17). Among the STs, those belonging to the north-east have a significant presence in both public and corporate jobs, which is higher than their population share. This is obviously because of the higher human development indicators in these states compared to other regions. Among the

TABLE 5.15: REGIONAL DISTRIBUTION OF QUALITY JOB BY SOCIAL GORUP, 1999–2000

Job Type	Location	Social Group						
		ST	SC	OBC	Upper Hindus	Upper Muslims	Others	Total
Public Sector	North	8.34	20.19	11.07	20.06	10.50	45.26	17.27
	Central	24.85	16.86	17.44	18.04	20.05	7.85	17.97
	East	13.92	13.89	10.23	16.27	14.03	1.64	13.62
	North-East	14.38	1.65	2.59	3.31	9.34	0.84	3.85
	West	28.32	22.34	18.27	23.09	26.34	17.65	22.11
	South	10.19	25.07	40.40	19.23	19.74	26.76	25.18
	Total	100.00	100.00	100.00	100.00	100.00	100.00	100.00
Corporate	North	21.41	12.44	6.12	15.18	6.08	19.06	11.99
	Central	21.46	23.34	17.47	10.28	23.63	4.21	15.50
	East	14.37	12.62	6.98	15.16	21.86	3.17	12.13
	North-East	10.16	1.43	1.24	2.36	5.74	0.41	2.40
	West	24.77	20.49	15.97	35.82	21.74	25.13	25.68
	South	7.83	29.69	52.21	21.21	20.95	48.03	32.30
	Total	100.00	100.00	100.00	100.00	100.00	100.00	100.00

Source: NSSO, 2000, 2005.

TABLE 5.16: SHARE OF WORKERS IN PUBLIC SECTOR JOBS AMONG THE POOREST AND RICHEST (QUINTILES) SOCIAL GROUPS BY REGIONS, 1999–2000

Location	Quintiles	Social Group						
		ST	SC	OBC	Upper Hindus	Upper Muslims	Others	Total
North	Poorest	0.00	1.34	0.04	0.18	1.64	0.00	0.41
	Richest	52.94	56.13	71.77	85.01	55.11	91.85	75.72
Central	Poorest	5.49	5.26	4.68	2.38	5.97	11.75	4.02
	Richest	63.77	40.37	42.56	67.99	42.76	82.52	55.83
East	Poorest	14.38	5.82	4.81	1.62	3.51	0.00	3.99
	Richest	36.85	40.22	41.75	65.72	31.64	88.54	53.09
North-east	Poorest	0.45		1.76	0.25	3.39	0.00	0.88
	Richest	64.87	43.50	43.93	54.12	43.80	62.08	53.48
West	Poorest	4.81	14.83	0.53	1.66	4.22	0.00	4.07
	Richest	53.87	46.95	56.37	75.71	56.66	92.50	64.05
South	Poorest	2.26	11.34	2.96	0.25	2.25	0.00	3.35
	Richest	68.39	43.75	67.00	80.19	66.38	89.06	68.11
Total	Poorest	5.02	8.12	2.65	1.17	3.73	0.92	3.12
	Richest	56.95	45.90	58.14	74.70	50.92	90.18	63.71

Source: NSSO, 2000, 2005.

TABLE 5.17: SHARE OF WORKERS IN CORPORATE SECTOR JOBS AMONG THE POOREST AND RICHEST (QUINTILES) SOCIAL GROUPS BY REGIONS, 1999–2000

Location	Quintiles	Social Group						
		ST	SC	OBC	Upper Hindus	Upper Muslims	Others	Total
North	Poorest	16.48	4.75	3.27	0.47	0.01	0.01	3.01
	Richest	4.97	48.94	52.02	80.31	43.56	78.02	62.82
Central	Poorest	34.63	30.16	16.35	2.92	10.17	0.01	16.52
	Richest	3.62	22.80	30.09	61.56	30.55	69.87	35.30
East	Poorest	18.59	13.00	17.15	1.52	34.89	0.01	10.51
	Richest	29.93	26.67	28.27	60.37	19.84	55.38	43.43
North-East	Poorest	42.70	30.50	31.95	18.39	48.93	0.01	31.03
	Richest	23.01	5.79	19.65	22.00	8.47	5.40	18.44
West	Poorest	5.79	2.06	4.83	1.44	22.48	0.01	3.33
	Richest	51.60	48.72	52.36	71.65	43.52	92.99	63.79
South	Poorest	7.77	27.25	5.51	1.02	9.58	0.40	7.18
	Richest	35.20	18.96	40.31	77.82	31.54	83.10	49.42
Total	Poorest	20.01	18.22	8.30	1.77	19.74	0.19	8.12
	Richest	24.02	30.47	40.07	70.36	30.76	82.86	51.06

Source: NSSO, 2000, 2005.

SCs, those belonging to the eastern and central regions, with a population share of around 50 per cent in the country, have access to only 30 per cent of public sector jobs, although, contrary to expectations, they have a reasonable share in corporate jobs. Here, again, those belonging to the south and west, with a population share of 35 per cent, have access to more than 47 per cent and around 50 per cent of the public and corporate sector jobs respectively. The regional disparity is more obvious in case of the OBCs, where those belonging to central and eastern India with a population share of around 45 per cent, account for just 27 per cent of the public sector jobs and as low as 24 per cent of the corporate jobs. OBCs belonging to southern and western regions with a population share of 45 per cent, account for around 60 per cent of the public sector jobs and 68 per cent of the total corporate sector jobs. Among the upper Hindus and Muslims, there is not much regional disparity with regard to access to public sector jobs, but there is large disparity among the upper Hindus when corporate jobs are concerned.

The differential in access to jobs is observed in all the regions. Even in the region of the north-east which has a relatively high human development, the poorest tribals have been entirely bypassed in access public sector jobs while the richest 20 per cent have cornered almost two-thirds of the jobs. Among the SCs, those belonging to the northern region have hardly any access with 56 per cent of the richest cornering all the jobs—only in the south and west is there some reasonable access by the poorest. The story of the OBCs is even worse with the poorest group of the northern and western states having a 0.5 per cent or less share; while in other regions—east, central and south—the percentages range between less than 3 and less than 5. The picture for the upper Hindus is more alarming, with zero share of the poorest in the northern and southern states—in other regions too the percentages range between 1 and 2.

Although the picture is less uneven in the case of access to corporate sector jobs, the large disparity between the poorest and the richest toes exist. The poorest SCs of the western region are the worst off with only 2 per cent access to jobs followed by the north with about 5 per cent. In the case of OBCs, only in the eastern and central regions is it reasonably distributed. The poorest OBCs belonging to the northern, western and southern regions have only meagre access (ranging from 3 to 5 per cent) with the bulk going to the richest. The poorest among the upper Hindus seem to be worst off in almost all regions, ranging from 0.2 to 2.3 per cent in various regions.

The above pattern is clearly due to the varying levels of economic and human development in the different regions of the country. But it also throws up some questions which need to be probed. The question is whether over the years, some groups among the OBCs which were earlier lagging behind the development ladder climbed up and now have come to disproportionately share the benefits of the affirmative policy. Or whether because of competitive politics, a few prosperous groups have been added to the list of OBCs enabling them to grab the benefits of reservation that should have gone to the deserving ones.

Towards Explaining Unequal Access to Quality Jobs

In this section an attempt has been made to capture the probability of getting 'quality jobs' through a logit model. In this model good quality job is defined as regular employment in the public, semi-public and corporate sectors. The description of the model is as follows:

Let y be a binary dependent variable, where

$$y = 1 \text{ if quality of job is good, 0 otherwise}$$

It is assumed that the probability of a getting good quality job is dependent on age, sex, education, social group, location (rural/urban), region and the expenditure quintile class (defined on the basis of household monthly per capita expenditure). Symbolically,

$$\text{Prob}\,(y = 1) = f(x),$$

where x is the vector of the above-mentioned explanatory variables. The *binary logistic regression* model is used to estimate the coefficients of the independent variable. In the logit model the parameters to be estimated are non-linear in nature. As a result the estimated coefficients cannot be used to infer the extent of influence of each variable on the probability of getting a good quality job. Here the predicted probability of each of the dependent variables has been used for discussion. In Appendix 5.1, a detailed description of the model and estimation of the independent variables are provided. The logistic regression model results are presented in Appendix 5.2. Table 5.18 provides the predicted probabilities of the independent variables.

TABLE 5.18: PREDICTED PROBABILITIES OF GETTING (AND NOT GETTING) GOOD QUALITY JOBS

Independent Variables	Prob (y = 1)	Prob (y = 0)
Sex		
Male	0.0400	0.9600
Female	0.0532	0.9468
Education		
Not literate	0.0059	0.9941
Literate & up to primary	0.0093	0.9907
Up to Secondary	0.0209	0.9791
Higher secondary	0.0323	0.9677
Graduate & above	0.2156	0.7844
Social group		
Scheduled tribe	0.0599	0.9401
Scheduled caste	0.0751	0.9249
Other backward castes	0.0437	0.9563
Upper Hindu	0.0370	0.9630
Upper Muslim	0.0343	0.9657
Others	0.0340	0.9660
Location		
Rural	0.0322	0.9678
Urban	0.0709	0.9291
Region		
North	0.0362	0.9638
Central	0.0304	0.9696
East	0.0323	0.9677
North-east	0.0363	0.9637
West	0.0549	0.9451
South	0.0355	0.9645
Expenditure quintiles		
Poorest	0.0110	0.9890
Poor	0.0163	0.9837
Middle	0.0223	0.9777
Rich	0.0296	0.9704
Richest	0.0957	0.9043

Source: NSSO, 2000, 2005.

It is seen that the level of education has a significant impact on the probability of getting a good quality job. Keeping all other variables constant, the results show that individuals who are graduates or above have a 21.5 per cent chance of getting a good quality job. In contrast, an illiterate person has merely a 0.6 per cent chance (37 times lower than a graduate). In all other educational categories, the predicted probabilities of getting a good job are quite low compared to the graduates. They are 23, 10 and 7 times lower for the primary, secondary and higher secondary educated persons respectively, a graduate's chance.

Location (rural or urban) is another characteristic that has a great bearing on the chances of getting a good job. The results show that in urban areas the probability of getting a good job is 7.1 per cent. In rural areas the probability is only 3.2 per cent (2 times lower than in urban areas). This is quite expected as there is the dominance of agriculture in the rural areas and diversification is limited. Further, the quality of education is also generally lower in rural areas as compared to urban areas.

The expenditure quintiles have been used here to classify the households at different levels of standard of living. The results show that individuals from the richer sections have greater access to good quality job (9.6 per cent), keeping all the variables constant. In contrast, the poorest sections of the population have the least chance of getting a good job (9 times lower than the richest). Comparing with other levels of standard of living it was found that the poor, the chances of the middle-class and the rich are 6 times, 4 times and 3 times lower respectively of getting good quality jobs as compared to the richest section of the society. This result is not surprising. As individuals from well-off families have access to better educational endowments and other necessary training, their chances are better. In contrast, the illiterate and inadequately educated people belong to the poorer sections of the society; as result, do not possess adequate education or have enough skills.

The results for the predicted probabilities of getting a good job across different social groups present a very interesting picture. The upper-class Hindus and Muslims have a 3.7 per cent and 3.4 per cent chance respectively of getting a good quality job. The probability for the 'other' social category is 3.4 per cent. On the other hand, SCs and STs have a 7.5 per cent and 6.0 per cent chance respectively of getting good employment. This clearly indicates that, keeping all other explanatory variables constant, SCs and STs have a better chance of getting a good job. Obviously, this is because of the positive discrimination policies and the relatively limited educational endowments as a whole in their favour. Thus, the policy of reservation has played a positive role for these groups so far as access to quality jobs is concerned. Individuals belonging to the OBC category have 4.4 per cent probability of getting good employment. This is not much higher than that of the upper castes but way below the levels for the STs and SCs. This is possibly because of the higher educational endowments among the social sub-groups of OBCs and the lower quota of reservation as compared to their population shares.

Finally, with regard to getting a good job in different regions the predicted probabilities do not vary much across the regions, except for the western part of India. In west India, the probability of getting a quality job is 5.5 per cent. The chances in the other four regions are two times (on an average). The western region covers states like Maharashtra, Gujarat, Goa, etc., which have a large concentration of quality jobs because of higher levels of economic development with a concentration of financial and service sector occupations.

Conclusions and Implications

The above analysis shows that there still exists considerable segmentation in the Indian labour market across social groups, locations (rural/urban), educational endowments, gender and income groups. It seems that the positive discrimination policy has played a positive role in empowering the disadvantaged groups by enabling their accessibility to quality public jobs, although the share is still somewhat lower as compared to their population shares. Further, their access to these jobs is more in inferior jobs as compared to the general categories.

In the absence of the reservation policy, it would not have been possible for groups like the SC and ST to access these jobs. It is also found that while the 'other' group, comprising small religious minorities (Christians and Sikh), are better placed than all the other groups, the so-called upper Muslims are in disadvantageous position in this regard. In fact, although about 29 per cent of Muslims have been designated as OBCs, a large section of the rest of the community is also very backward and that is why the upper Muslims have got a small share in both public sector and corporate sector jobs.

It is also evident that over the years there have been developments due to which some sections within the hitherto deprived and backward communities have moved up the ladder, particularly among the OBCs. Further, there is a section among the upper castes, and more so among the Muslims which has had hardly any access to public sector quality jobs. This group has attempted to access jobs in the corporate sector, but with little success. Then, within each social group there is considerable segmentation with respect to accessing jobs.

It is also found that endowment of education is a very powerful factor in getting a quality job. Reserved category classes, particularly the SCs, STs and to a smaller extent the OBCs and the Muslims, are still at a great disadvantage in this regard. Persons belonging to rural areas are also much less fortunate in accessing good quality jobs. Moreover, it seems that income also plays an important role in accessing jobs. Poorer classes, particularly the deprived groups, are very unfortunate in this respect.

In the above scenario, what should be the direction of the reservation policy. The following are some questions which need debate:

- Can there be positive discrimination for the more deprived subgroups within the reserved groups, particularly among the OBCs where segmentation is very large?
- Should not some thought be given to designating some other sections of the Muslims as OBCs?
- Should positive discrimination not be introduced at least for the poorest strata of the upper-caste Hindus?
- In view of the acute regional disparities in accessing jobs by various groups, should there be some mechanism for the backward regions as well as the remote rural areas to help then access education as well as better employment?
- Should access to education and improving its quality, especially for the reserved and deprived groups, which has not been done so far, not be pursued vigorously?

All these are important issues which, however, may cause controversies due to their emotional embeddedness. The need of the hour is to debate objectively without passion and with positive politics.

NOTES

1. For a comprehensive account of these trends, see ILO (2003), Sharma (2004), Stigtliz (2003), etc.
2. This section is based on Bhalla (2004).

3. This category in this chapter also includes jobs in the cooperative sector.
4. Some states such as Tamil Nadu have a higher level of reservation, to the extent of 69 per cent.
5. This group, accounting for about 2.16 per cent of the total population, is largely urban-based and is comprised of 0.86 per cent Christians; 0.93 per cent Sikhs, and 0.36 per cent others.

REFERENCES

Chadha, G.K. and P.P. Sahu (2002), 'Post-reform Setbacks in Rural Employment: Issues that Need Further Security', *Economic and Political Weekly*, Review of Labour, vol. 37, no. 21, 25–31 May, pp. 1998–2026.

Deaton, Angus and Jean Drèze (2002), 'Poverty and Inequality in India: A Re-examination', *Economic and Political Weekly*, 7 September, pp. 3729–48.

Mahendra Dev, S. (2004), 'Post-Reform Regional Variations', *Seminal*, 537(24), pp. 24–8.

Mohan, R. (2003), 'Factor Income Shares in India, 1970–71 to 1999–2000: What do the Trends in the 1990 Reveal?', *Journal of Indian School of Political Economy*, vol. 15, no. 3, p. 647.

National Sample Survey Organisation (2000), *Consumer Expenditure, Employment & Unemployment and Non-agricultural Enterprises in the Informal Sector in India NSS 55th Round (July 1999–June 2000)*, Department of Statistics, Ministry of Planning and Programme Implementation, New Delhi: Government of India.

National Sample Survey Organisation (2005), *Employment-Unemployment NSS 61st Round (July 2004–June 2005)*, Department of Statistics, Ministry of Planning and Programme Implementation, New Delhi: Government of India.

Thorat, S. (2001), 'Economic Status of Social Groups in Maharashtra: Emerging Issues', in Sukhadeo Thorat, ed., *Rural Development: Problem and Prospect*, Maharashtra: Pravara Rural Development Association, p. 317.

APPENDIX 5.1: SUMMARY OF THE VARIABLES

Independent Variables	Number of Observations	Frequency
Sex		
Male	145,116	75.73
Female (base)	46,496	24.27
Education		
Not literate	64,476	33.65
Literate and up to primary	44,895	23.43
Up to Secondary	53,250	27.79
Higher secondary	12,003	6.26
Graduate and above (base)	16,988	8.87
Social identity		
Scheduled tribe	25,410	13.26
Scheduled caste	31,334	16.35
Other backward caste	64,401	33.61
Upper Hindu (base)	50,352	26.28
Upper Muslim	14,336	7.48
Others	5,779	3.02
Sector		
Rural	122,922	64.15
Urban (base)	68,690	35.85
Location		
North	27,487	14.35
Central	36,935	19.28
East	32,191	16.80
North-east	20,349	10.62
West (base)	27,674	14.44
South	46,976	24.52
Expenditure quintiles		
Poorest	36,758	19.18
Poor	40,520	21.15
Middle	38,091	19.88
Rich	37,635	19.64
Richest (base)	38,323	20.00
Age (in completed years)	191,612	–

Note: Base-indices reference category for the dummy variable.

APPENDIX 5.2: THE REGRESSION MODEL RESULTS

Independent Variables	Probability (y = 1) = f(x)	Logic Estimation of the Independent Variables Quality
ln_age	2.051	(67.39)*
Male	-0.299	(12.86)*
Iltrt	-3.058	(76.59)*
Primary	-2.049	(67.07)*
Secondry	-1.025	(45.16)*
HS	-0.316	(11.18)*
ST	0.406	(11.97)*
SC	0.711	(24.83)*
OBC	0.029	(1.30)
Muslim	-0.251	(6.49)*
Other	-0.249	(6.09)*
Rural	-0.830	(43.80)*
North	-0.208	(7.41)*
Central	-0.445	(14.52)*
East	-0.353	(11.36)*
North-east	-0.196	(5.78)*
South	-0.261	(9.84)*
Poorest	-1.721	(35.63)*
Poor	-1.260	(36.69)*
Middle	-0.845	(31.46)*
Rich	-0.480	(22.26)*
Constant	-6.718	(59.73)*
Observations	1,91,612	–

Notes: Absolute value of z statistics in parentheses;
*significant at 1%.

CHAPTER 6

Labour Under Stress: An Assessment Based on Primary Information

SUNANDA SEN
BYASDEB DASGUPTA

INTRODUCTION

The logic of economic reforms in India has been growth-centric, which subscribes to the interests of corporate global capital. It has been contended in mainstream economics that the spill-over effects of growth would usher in a better world by making everybody better off. It is further held that 'competitive capitalism' is the means to achieve growth as well as its spill-overs, by providing an institution which links local production to the circuits of global capital. Viewed from this perspective, the growth-centric logic of economic reforms can be treated as a shift from the long protected 'non-competitive' to competitive markets, which reduces the 'wasteful' utilization of resources including that of labour.

Liberalization in the Indian economy started in 1991 with the formal inception of the economic reforms. The main targets of the latter included (a) inflows of foreign capital on a larger scale, (b) strength of the market *vis-à-vis* state, and (c) competition and efficiency in production in place of market rigidity. Economic reforms in India were expected to lead the economy onto a higher growth path. A host of policy initiatives have been implemented since then, covering, among others, the industrial sector, fiscal and monetary

*This study is part of the ICSSR-IDPAD funded project on 'Political Economy of Labour in a Globalized Economy'. We acknowledge the financial assistance received from IDPAD for this study.

management, financial institutions, trade and the labour market. Given the current emphasis in the country on achieving a growth track with at least an 8 per cent GDP growth rate, these reforms in different spheres of the economy are considered by the policy-makers to be of paramount importance.

Competitive pressures which arise, with the opening up of an economy are usually expected to initiate shifts in the country's industrial structure, from the high-profit low-output scenario of the pre-reform years to scale expansions and low-profit margins in the post-reform period. The process logically entails cost reduction, quality improvement, and productivity growth. However, at the same time, these competitive pressures are expected to weaken the implicit social contract in the economy, and, in particular, in its formal sector. In its defence it is even held in mainstream theory that the implicit social contract had been a part of the autarchic industrialization strategies which in the past were responsible for the slow growth in these autarchic economies.

As competitive capitalism relies on the removal of barriers to entry, the process demands exit routes for capital from what is considered as inefficient use to more productive, cost-effective and better quality operations. The resulting shifts in the utilization of labour and capital are considered as the basic prerequisites for rapid growth on a sustained basis. However, the process involves stressful adjustments, with occupational dislocation and unemployment for labour and industrial restructuring and obsolescence of capital. The consequences include the rising disparities in terms of performance between fast-growing and slow-growing industries and considerable stress for those, including labour, who are dislocated in the process. For political and social stability, these may necessitate cost-sharing and conflict resolution mechanisms which are also socially credible.

The status of labour needs to be situated in the above context of industrial restructuring and occupational dislocation. Industrial restructuring is capable of contributing to de-industrialization in some cases and the creation of new *sunrise* industries in others. The process is basically rivetted around cost-cutting devices with labour as well as the less competitive industries bearing the burden of adjustment. The channels of cost-cutting adjustments across industries with high and low growth include the use of (i) productivity augmenting technology and (ii) flexible labour by recruiting more labour on a contractual basis.

The implications of these reforms have been far-reaching for Indian labour, particularly in the organized manufacturing sector. As shown in a recent study.[1] Foreign Direct Investment (FDI) inflows have affected the structure of the Indian industries that tried to cope with the challenges of competitive pressure in the market by opting for labour-displacing and productivity enhancing technologies. Further, as the subsidiaries of foreign firms are usually vertically integrated even the additional employment effect of FDI flows often remains conjectural.

Information available at the secondary level from official sources does not enable an in-depth enquiry into the conditions of labour under globalization. To overcome these lacunae, a field survey was undertaken of organized labour employed in manufacturing industries in a few states of the country. While at an aggregate level the analysis of secondary data, as provided in a previous study[2] indicates a rather unfavourable picture for factory labour employed in manufacturing, field surveys undertaken for the present study reveal the qualitative dimensions of work including the wide dissimilarities as well as adverse conditions in terms of wages, working hours, institutional voice representation and skill at a disaggregated level. Given below are the main findings of the survey for the present study, and an analysis of the results.

The Primary Survey

A field survey of labourers in the organized manufacturing industry was undertaken in selected pockets of West Bengal, Delhi, Haryana, Gujarat and Maharashtra over a period of fourteen months during 2004–6. A total of 615 factory labourers were underviewed. These workers were selected at random from the industrial clusters of different areas in these states, which include Mayapuri, Okhla and East Delhi in Delhi; Ghaziabad, NOIDA and NOIDA Special Economic Zone in Uttar Pradesh; Faridabad and Gurgaon in Haryana; Kolkata, Kalyani, Howrah, Hooghly and Falta Special Economic Zone in West Bengal; Surat in Gujarat; and Santa Cruz Special Economic Zone and other areas of Mumbai in Maharashtra. It is important to point out that the survey was conducted in three Special Economic Zones (SEZ) of the country: Falta in West Bengal, NOIDA in the National Capital Region of Delhi located in Uttar Pradesh and Santa Cruz at Mumbai in Maharashtra. A structured questionnaire was used in the field survey to gather information from the industrial labourers. To avoid bias in the sample not more than five workers were selected from a single factory. Besides, in some areas a few management surveys were also conducted. As is typical in field surveys, for the interviews, female workers, for various reasons, were not easily accessible. The research team had to contend mainly with male workers and make an attempt to understand the plight of the women workers indirectly by talking to the males. In addition to the use of questionnaires, an intensive survey was undertaken of workers in the labour-intensive tobacco manufacturing (*bidi* making) industry at Aurangabad in the district of Murshidabad in West Bengal.

An analysis of the data obtained from these surveys is provided in the following sections. It involves the grouping of data according to one or other characteristic considered important for analysis. These characteristics include job tenure, age, education, skill, migration, trade union membership, trade orientation and locations of industries. The device allows for a comparative analysis of different areas, different industries and different categories of workers interviewed in the survey.

These groupings of labourers in the sample as are related to the specific attributes can be used to answer the following queries:

1. As for *job contracts*, one can distinguish between permanent and casual workers. Are casual workers more hard-pressed than their non-casual counterparts? Is the disparity between the workers significant in terms of nature of job tenures or contract?
2. *Education* plays a crucial role in skill formation. Do the differences among the workers in the sample vary with their education level, with the less educated workers being marginalized in comparison to the more educated ones?
3. *Caste* is a social institution in Indian society which stratifies the labourers. Caste identity may be crucial for skill, education and earning levels. Can one hypothesize that worker in the non-general category (which includes SCs, STs and OBCs, and for that matter minorities) are unfavourably placed (as compared to the general category workers comprising higher castes) in terms of wages and other amenities?
4. *The trade orientation of industries* may matter in differentiating labour according to wages, hours of work, savings, non-wage benefits, voice representation, savings, a growing fear of losing

jobs and of security levels in general. Trade orientation is introduced here as an attribute by grouping the industries into exportables and importables and then testing the above hypothesis.

5. *The structure of industries* and the changes also matter significantly in explaining the gaps among workers in terms of wages, working hours, voice representation, non-wage benefits, security levels as well as fear of job loss, if any. This study identifies the labour and capital intensive industries in the sample to test the relevance of the industrial structure in terms of the above-mentioned aspects. Industries in the sample are classified according to the changes in labour/capital intensity over the post-reform period as compared to the pre-reform years.
6. *Migration* of labour across different parts of the country in search of new jobs and means of earnings may be relevant in explaining the levels of their current earnings and job insecurity. Workers who migrate are often engaged in factory jobs on contractual or casual basis while permanent regular workers show less interest in migrating unless they are offered better prospects elsewhere or if they face a sudden deterioration in living conditions in their present locations with no immediate alternative options available in the neighbourhood. Are there differences between these who are migrant workers and those who are not in terms of wage earnings and non-wage benefits, hours of work, voice representation, fear of job loss and savings? Does migration decrease with an increase in the number of earning members in the family of the concerned labourer?
7. *Globalization* changes the notion of work and employment under competitive capitalism. On the one hand, the so-called 'labour redundancies' warrant drastic downsizing of the workforce in a factory, and on the other, the nature of job contracts offered to the labourers is drastically changed, particularly for new entrants in the job market. Thus new recruitments are increasingly on a short-term contractual basis, which hardly provides any non-wage benefits or earned leave. The scope for voice representation in trade union activities is getting eroded day by day with the labour market reforms on the anvil. These reforms with legalize and institutionalize the flexible norms characterized by the easy hire-and-fire policy of the employers. Do entry-level young workers face an uncertain, bleak future in comparison to workers who entered the labour force in the past and is this reflected in the

significant divergences between the entry-level workers (up to 25 years of age) and workers older than them, in terms of wages, working hours, non-wage benefits, voice representation?

8. *Divergent growth patterns* of different industries at the disaggregated level influence labour features in the respective industries. These affect average earnings, average working hours, voice representation and non-wage components of earnings, savings and the fear of jobs loss.
9. *SEZ workers* are more hard pressed than their non-SEZ counterparts, again in terms of hourly wage levels, hours of work, savings, voice representation (union membership), fear of losing their job, non-wage benefits such as provident fund (PF), gratuity and bonus. These SEZs are set-up as enclaves where production units officially enjoy special incentives, tax concessions and the right to have flexible labour rules. It has been held that the primary concern for setting up a unit in the SEZ is the relaxation in the labour laws of the land. It is also held that SEZs provide tax havens which attract many business firms. While this may be true the primary concern here is to explore whether SEZ workers are more under duress than their non-SEZ counterparts.
10. *Trade unions* provide for voice representation which had been a part of conventional labour rights. These institutions provide an organized base for workers to register their protest when situations demand it. But with the introduction of the flexible labour market and with shifts from Taylorist types of production processes in the post-globalization era, the significance of trade unions has rapidly declined. With the declining unionization trend, particularly among the new workers and the new production lines (initiated by foreign capital, SEZs, and contractual casual appointments), workers can be meaningfully grouped according to whether they are members of trade unions or not. The study will try to find out non-members face harsh terms and conditions of work including wages, hours of work and other relevant aspects of job contracts. It will also evaluate their saving propensities.

The ten attributes mentioned above provide us the possibilities of grouping workers under the respective heads in terms of binary classification. This will include all 615 workers interviewed in different industries located in different parts of the country. The next section presents the results of the exercise in arriving at the classification of workers in specific groups.

Grouping of Workers According to Specific Attributes

The overall picture of the surveyed areas taken together is given in Appendix 6.1. It shows that of the 615 workers interviewed 271 are permanent workers with tenured job contracts with a fixed age of retirement and 344 are casual or contractual on a short-term basis with temporary attachment to their current job. The sharp contrast between the two groups of workers is visible in the wage gaps, with the respective average hourly wages for all workers, permanent and casual workers at Rs. 14.46, Rs. 18.77 and Rs. 11.07 respectively. The wage gap between the permanent and casual workers of Rs. 7.70 is quite significant at a 1 per cent level. While 40 per cent of the 615 workers are union members, 51 per cent of them are employed on a permanent basis. Thus the union presence is relatively higher among the permanent workers.[3] Workers on an average work for 9.06 hours a day, which is above the stipulated 8 hours. Permanent workers work for 8.58 hours a day, whereas casual workers work 9.45 hours a day. As for their educational level, 90 per cent are literate or have some education with a mean schooling period of five years. Of these 40 per cent are permanent workers while 60 per cent are casual workers. The incidence of migration is most pronounced among the casual workers because of the temporary nature of their job contracts and low earning which is below the minimum wage level prevailing in many industries in different locations. Dif-ferent social categories of workers also matter in terms of the mean hourly wage, and mean hours of work can be seen with the 324 workers in the general category earn Rs. 1.24 more per hour than the non-general category of workers (numbering 291). The former category also works 0.53 hours less on an average than the latter.

The references to the workers in the sample when grouped according to specific attributes indicate their vulnerabilities, both at an aggregative level and in terms of the specificity within the respective groups, each centred on a specific attribute. Given below are the details of the exercise, which speaks of the differentiation among workers within each group. Groupings are done according to the specific attributes of the workers and include job tenures (permanent/casual), age of workers, education level (skilled/unskilled), migratory status, social background (SC, ST, OBC), and pattern of industry in terms of trade orientation (export/import intensity), factor intensity (labour/capital intensity), SEZs and otherwise and finally labour absorbed in different industries at a two-digit level of classification. Workers in each group are further sub-divided under each of the seven to eight heads that indicate their economic status of in terms of wages and other amenities, etc.

JOB CONTRACTS—PERMANENT OR CASUAL

Table 6.1 indicates the casual and permanent worker divide. As expected, casual workers are more hard-pressed than the permanent and regular workers in every respect of the job-related features that include wages, hours of work, PF and gratuity. They are naturally insecure in terms of job prospects and have less to do with union membership. This dampens the saving propensity of these casualized workers as compared to permanent workers.

AGE-WISE DISTRIBUTION

The sample does not clearly indicate that entry-point workers (aged up to 25) are worse off than the workers in higher age groups (Table 6.2). In fact, workers aged below 25 years receive higher hourly wages as compensation for working longer hours daily. But unionization among the entry group of workers is much lower and they are mostly deprived of non-wage benefits like PF, gratuity and bonus.

EDUCATIONAL LEVEL AND SKILLS

Education plays a crucial role in skill formation. The economic status of the workers in the sample varies with their level of education (Table 6.3). As it can be expected, the less educated workers who are also unskilled get marginalized in comparison to their relatively educated counterpart having some skill. The present survey found very few workers to be completely illiterate and some basic level of literacy (with at least up to the level of 4th standard) was visible among those interviewed. In the sample skilled workers (judged in terms of education above the basic minimum of 8th standard) are better off than the unskilled workers in that they have a better economic status. Possibly the evolving post-reform industrial situation is creating more space for skill-absorption and less for unskilled occupations. Again, the differences speak for the differentiated labour force, with the unskilled having lower access to the basic amenities than to the skilled.

TABLE 6.1: LABOUR IN TERMS OF JOB TENURE

		N	Mean Hourly Wage (Rs.)	Mean Hours of Work	Savings (%)	Union Membership (%)	Fear of Losing Job (%)	PF (%)	Gratuity (%)	Bonus (%)
Casual	Mean	344	11.07	9.45	19	32	43	08	0	51
	Variance		27.34	2.55	0.16	0.22	0.25	0.07	0.00	0.25
Permanent	Mean	271	18.77	8.58	34	51	59	91	46	66
	Variance		76.81	0.60	0.22	0.25	0.24	0.08	0.25	0.22

Source: Based on the primary survey data.

TABLE 6.2: LABOUR IN TERMS OF AGE COMPOSITION

		N	Mean Hourly Wage (Rs.)	Mean Hours of Work	Savings (%)	Union Membership (%)	Fear of Losing Job (%)	PF (%)	Gratuity (%)	Bonus (%)
Below 20	Mean	21	10.59	10.05	52	24	48	10	00	19
	Variance		42.18	1.85	0.26	0.19	0.26	0.09	0.00	0.16
Age 21–5	Mean	133	8.96	9.31	17	24	54	19	01	43
	Variance		20.26	1.93	0.14	0.18	0.25	0.16	0.01	0.25
Age 26–30	Mean	134	9.92	9.07	17	33	49	38	7	60
	Variance		30.70	1.78	0.14	0.22	0.25	0.24	0.07	0.24
Age 31–5	Mean	117	10.81	9.17	27	43	51	46	16	56
	Variance		31.49	2.10	0.20	0.25	0.25	0.25	0.13	0.25
Age 36–40	Mean	94	10.95	8.83	23	53	51	61	36	74
	Variance		27.16	1.67	0.18	0.25	0.25	0.24	0.23	0.19
Age 41–5	Mean	66	13.07	8.82	38	58	45	73	52	65
	Variance		34.04	1.75	0.24	0.25	0.25	0.20	0.25	0.23
Age 46–50	Mean	30	14.15	9.11	48	56	48	74	52	63
	Variance		38.96	2.33	0.26	0.26	0.26	0.20	0.26	0.24
Above 51	Mean	20	16.76	8.10	50	75	50	85	75	85
	Variance		52.91	0.09	0.26	0.20	0.26	0.13	0.20	0.13

Source: Based on the primary survey data.

TABLE 6.3: LABOUR IN TERMS OF EDUCATION

		N	Mean Hourly Wage (Rs.)	Mean Hours of Work	Savings (%)	Union Membership (%)	Fear of Losing Job (%)	PF (%)	Gratuity (%)	Bonus (%)
Illiterate & literate	Mean	68	12.44	9.26	31	38	59	32	18	57
	Variance		47.21	2.56	0.22	0.24	0.25	0.22	0.14	0.25
Others	Mean	545	14.71	9.05	25	41	49	46	21	58
	Variance		65.25	1.79	0.19	0.24	0.25	0.25	0.17	0.24

Source: Based on the primary survey data.

MIGRATION

By grouping the sample of workers according to their migratory status one can see that migrant workers receive lower wages, work more hours, are hardly unionized and receive less non-wage benefits than workers who do not migrate. It is clear that migrant workers are mostly casual and therefore the fear of losing their job is greater more amongst them (Table 6.4).

SOCIAL BACKGROUND

Workers in the sample can further be grouped in terms of their social background which includes caste among the Hindus and other minorities (Table 6.5). The 'general category' workers (which includes all workers except the 'others' category which includes SCs, STs and minorities) are relatively better placed. However, it appears that caste does not play an important role at the time of recruitment in the private sector. But SCs, STs and minorities come with a background which adversely affects their education and skill. Hence, at a time when demand for skilled labour is rising it is quite plausible that the 'others category' of workers are losing out.

UNION MEMBERSHIP

Next the workers are grouped according to whether they are unionized or not (Table 6.6). The results indicate that while unionized workers put in fewer hours of work per day they also receive lower hourly wages. It was also found that among the unionized members, the fear of job loss is greater than among the non-unionized workers. Even in terms of non-wage benefits, non-unionized workers are better off than the unionized workers. This seems to indicate that voice representation had almost no effect in improving the status of workers in the sample.

TRADE ORIENTATION OF INDUSTRIES

Trade reform is an integral part of economic reform programmes in India, with its two-pronged thrust on export promotion and import liberalization. The first pertains to gaining a competitive edge for Indian goods in the global market while the second is geared towards achieving cost-competitiveness for Indian industry by permitting free

TABLE 6.4: LABOUR IN CONTEXT OF MIGRATION

		N	Mean Hourly Wage (Rs.)	Mean Hours of Work	Savings (%)	Union Member-ship (%)	Fear of Losing Job (%)	PF (%)	Gratuity (%)	Bonus (%)
Non-migrant	Mean	308	15.32	8.75	24	47	55	48	31	65
	Variance		79.73	1.55	0.18	0.25	0.25	0.25	0.22	0.23
Migrant	Mean	307	13.60	9.39	27	34	46	41	09	51
	Variance		46.30	2.00	0.20	0.22	0.25	0.24	0.08	0.25

Source: Based on the primary survey data.

TABLE 6.5: LABOUR IN CONTEXT OF SOCIAL BACKGROUND

		N	Mean Hourly Wage (Rs.)	Mean Hours of Work	Savings (%)	Union Membership (%)	Fear of Losing Job (%)	PF (%)	Gratuity (%)	Bonus (%)
Others	Mean	291	13.81	9.35	26	37	49	38	12	50
	Variance		57.22	2.05	0.20	0.23	0.25	0.24	0.10	0.25
General	Mean	324	15.05	8.82	25	43	52	50	28	65
	Variance		68.94	1.59	0.19	0.25	0.25	0.25	0.20	0.23

Source: Based on the primary survey data.

TABLE 6.6: LABOUR IN TERMS OF UNION MEMBERSHIP

		N	Mean Hourly Wage (Rs.)	Mean Hours of Work	Savings (%)	Fear of Losing Job (%)	PF (%)	Gratuity (%)	Bonus (%)
Non-member	Mean	367	13.29	9.40	0.26	0.65	0.37	0.04	0.48
	Variance		7.10	1.51	0.44	0.48	0.48	0.20	0.50
Union member	Mean	348	16.19	8.58	0.25	0.29	0.56	0.44	0.73
	Variance		8.87	0.94	0.44	0.45	0.50	0.50	0.44

Source: Based on the primary survey data.

imports of inputs from abroad. Trade liberalization measures started off in the mid-1980s, and since their FDI inflow have also been made much easier. Indian firms with foreign collaboration as well as those set up by MNCs as subsidiaries today rely heavily on raw materials and technology, mostly imported from their foreign subsidiaries and/or parent firms abroad. This limits the backward linkage effects of these firms in the domestic economy.[4] Against this backdrop, one can identify certain domestic industries that compete with the finished and semi-finished products imported from abroad. Export-intensive ones can be defined as those having 10 per cent or more firms are those exports as a proportion of their sale values, and import-intensive with a share of importables of 10 per cent or more as a proportion of their sale values. These industries are in the 2-digit level of classification, as indicated in Tables 6.7 and 6.8. In the areas covered one can identify computing (30), wood (20), pharmaceuticals (35), machinery (29), furniture (36) and paper (21) as industries producing importable items. The rest are non-importable.[5] Exportable industries include food and beverages (15), textiles (17), leather (19), chemicals (24), computing machinery (29) and gems & jewellery (36). All those industries export a certain proportion (20 per cent or above) of their output. Table 6.7 delineates the conditions of labourers according to whether they work in importable or non-importable industries. While hourly the wage rate happens to be relatively higher in industries producing importables, the average number of hours worked is also higher. Despite a lower percentage of unionization, workers in the above industries have less fear in terms of losing their jobs; their non-wage benefits are lower than those engaged in non-importable goods industries. On the whole, workers engaged in industries producing importables seem to be marginally better off as compared to others. Possibly this is because these industries are better organized and more competitive in the home market as compared to others and are thus able to offer jobs on slightly better terms.

Labourers in exportable industries, however, are not much better off as compared to labourers engaged in non-exportable industries (Table 6.8). The export orientation of industries has thus not benefited labour engaged in these industries. Thus the trade orientation of industries seems to hardly impact the economic status of workers engaged therein. The present study's findings are similar to other researches in the area which are based on secondary data.[6] It is thus

TABLE 6.7: LABOUR IN INDUSTRIES PRODUCING IMPORTABLES

		N	Mean Hourly Wage (Rs.)	Mean Hours of Work	Savings (%)	Union Membership (%)	Fear of Losing Job (%)	PF (%)	Gratuity (%)	Bonus (%)
Importable	Mean	15.41	9.79	0.3	0.07	0.43	0.13	0.07	0.34	15.41
	Variance	65.93	1.90	0.21	0.06	0.25	0.12	0.07	0.22	65.93
Others	Mean	14.26	8.92	0.25	0.47	0.52	0.51	0.23	0.63	14.26
	Variance	63.04	1.74	0.18	0.25	0.25	0.25	0.18	0.23	63.04

Source: Based on the primary survey data.

TABLE 6.8: LABOUR IN EXPORTABLE INDUSTRIES

		N	Mean Hourly Wage (Rs.)	Mean Hours of Work	Savings (%)	Union Member-ship (%)	Fear of losing Job (%)	PF (%)	Gratuity (%)	Bonus (%)
Exportable	Mean	185	14.45	8.97	34	48	42	53	32	72
	Variance		74.69	1.96	0.23	0.25	0.25	0.25	0.22	0.20
Others	Mean	430	14.47	9.11	22	37	54	41	15	52
	Variance		74.69	1.96	0.23	0.25	0.25	0.25	0.22	0.20

Source: Based on the primary survey data.

found that the present analysis based on a primary sample of 615 workers corroborates the conclusion drawn in those studies regarding the insignificant contribution of trade in the post-reform period on labour in trade-oriented industries *vis-à-vis* those in the non-trade-oriented industries.

STRUCTURE OF INDUSTRIES

Economic reforms have significant effects on the technological structure of industries, and especially so in industries which adopt labour-displacing technologies. This has been pointed out in many studies.[7] It has been held that 'The surge in competitive pressures prompts enterprises to focus more and more on efficiency consideration which forces them to cut their overall costs of production. Minimization of labour costs is often a natural response in such a situation.'[8] Consequently, the adoption of labour displacing-technologies becomes a preferred option for the entrepreneurs. Thus 'If FDI inflows assume more importance, there could be an intensification of this tendency as multinationals would generally bring in technologies of this nature. Therefore, in the age of heightened consciousness for quality and competitiveness, a rise in unemployment becomes a misgiving of the modernization process.'[9]

In the present analysis, two groups of industries have been identified—capital-intensive and labour-intensive (Table 6.9). In terms of the present estimates, an industry showing a ratio of 1.03 or more, capital to labour is identified as capital-intensive and the rest as labour-intensive. Thus defined, capital intensive industries, at a 2-digit level, include basic metal (27), chemical (24), computing (30), paper (21), electrical (31), machinery (29), motor vehicles (34) and electronics (32), while labour-intensive industries are food and beverages (15), textiles (17), wearing apparel (18), leather (19), paper (21), chemicals (24), rubber and plastic (25), non-metallic mineral (26) and fabricated metals (28). In terms of the employment pattern, roughly 30 per cent of the workers seem to be with the capital-intensive industries where the wage rate on an average is relatively higher and workers put in more labour hours per day as compared to those who are employed in the labour-intensive industries. The appropriation of surplus labour, therefore, takes place through *both* labour-displacing technological changes as well as by increases in average work time. However, while labourers in the

TABLE 6.9: LABOUR IN THE CONTEXT OF STRUCTURE OF INDUSTRY

		N	Mean Hourly Wage (Rs.)	Mean Hours of Work	Savings (%)	Union Member-ship (%)	Fear of Losing Job (%)	PF (%)	Gratuity (%)	Bonus (%)
Capital intensive industrties	Mean	471	14.74	9.24	27	39	49	40	17	51
	Variance		65.61	2.07	0.20	0.24	0.25	0.24	0.14	0.25
Labour intensive industires	Mean	144	13.54	8.53	21	46	56	58	33	80
	Variance		56.65	0.87	0.17	0.25	0.25	0.25	0.22	0.16

Source: Based on the primary survey data.

capital-intensive industries receive higher wages than those in the labour intensive groups, the second group receives relatively more of the non-wage benefits, whatever these may be. However, despite a higher rate of unionization, workers in these labour-intensive industries are found to be subject to higher degrees of fear in terms of losing their jobs.

From this it appears that industries which are going in for more capital-intensive technologies are offering higher wages and lower non-wage benefits to their workers as compared to the labour-intensive industries. The new recruitments in these capital-intensive, high-tech industries are mostly on contractual basis, and because of this, the proportion of non-wage benefits are naturally lower. Capital-intensive technologies require more skilled work effort and hence wages tend to be higher in these industries in relation to the wages offered in the labour-intensive industries.

In the present survey, it was also noticed that the incidence of workers in capital-intensive technologies who can save is more common than it is in the labour-intensive ones, an outcome, once again, which is related to the relative wage levels in the two industries. However, in the final analysis, with an increasing number of industries adopting capital-intensive lines of production, the labour content of output may tend to go down further thus creating more pressures in the labour market in terms of unemployment.

Labour-Intensive Industries

The industries are further classified in terms of changing labour-use which is defined as the ratio of wages and salaries to value of output net of wages and salaries. In a similar study the notion has been[10] identified as registering labour intensity in the liberalization period. The post-reform period registers declines in the above ratio in the present sample for all industry groups. Three categories of industry groups have been identified—those with steep declines in the ratio (SD), those with moderate declines (MD) and the rest with an increasing trend (INC). It was seen in from Table 6.10 that while the hourly wage on an average are less, working hours are relatively more in these SD units when compared to the MD and INC units. Labour-displacing has thus gone hand-in-hand with a worsening labour status for the 511 workers employed with SD units, which tune for the majority of workers in the sample. As for union membership, it

TABLE 6.10: LABOUR IN THE CONTEXT OF DIFFERENT RATIOS BETWEEN WAGE-SALARY COMPONENT AND OUTPUT (NET OF WAGES AND SALARIES)

		N	Mean Hourly Wage (Rs.)	Mean Hours of Work	Savings (%)	Union Member-ship (%)	Fear of Losing Job (%)	PF (%)	Gratuity (%)	Bonus (%)
SD	Mean	511	14.52	9.03	0.26	68	0.36	0.52	0.43	0.21
	Variance		63.45	1.69	0.19	0.28	0.23	0.25	0.25	0.17
MD	Mean	48	16.35	8.98	0.29	26	0.69	0.42	0.69	0.35
	Variance		116.43	2.11	0.21	0.23	0.22	0.25	0.22	0.23
INC	Mean	56	12.31	9.50	0.16	6	0.52	0.43	0.39	0.00
	Variance		15.18	3.31	0.14	0.22	0.25	0.25	0.24	0.00

Source: Based on the primary survey data.

is surprising that SD workers are better organized, which also helps them to have better non-wage benefits and they love less fear of losing their jobs.The increased union membership is difficult to reconcile in the context of post-reform attempts to flexibilize labour market rules and regulations. However, the percentage of workers with savings is highest in the MD category. This may be related to the higher earnings as wages.

One can also distinguish the workers in the sample in terms of their age so as to differentiate between entry-level workers and other workers in the sample. A further grouping is made in terms of migration, social background, education level and industry-wise variations.

LABOUR IN SEZs OR OTHER INDUSTRIES

As mentioned earlier, of the sixteen areas selected for interviewing industrial labour, three were SEZs. These included Falta in West Bengal, NOIDA in the National Capital Region of Delhi (which is actually located within the administrative jurisdiction of UP) and Santa Cruz (SEEPZ) at Mumbai in Maharashtra.[11] Of the 615 workers in the sample, only 60 belong to these three SEZ areas. Industrial units set up within a SEZ need not pay the minimum wages that prevail in industries located in the neighbourhood of the SEZs. In SEZs labour laws as the well as the taxation norms of the country are not applicable. Flexible hire-and-fire practices, therefore, are even easier to implement. This further deprives labour of its due share of production in terms of both wage and non-wage benefits as well as other amenities normally available elsewhere in the country. This is reflected in Table 6.11 which delineates this disparity between SEZ and non-SEZ workers. The gap between the average hourly wage between non-SEZ and SEZ workers is Rs. 5.08, which is significant at the 1 per cent level. SEZ workers, on an average work 0.48 hours more a day than their non-SEZ counterparts. Besides, the variance in the mean hours of work is more in the case of SEZ workers, indicating flexible working time and very long daily working hours in the case of few workers in the sample.

As for unionization, those outside SEZs are relatively more organized as members of trade unions with a higher percentage of SEZ workers (almost three-fourths of SEZ workers in the present sample) fearing job loss and thus living with uncertain job prospects as com-

TABLE 6.11: LABOUR IN SEZ AND NON-SEZ AREAS

		Sample Size	Mean Hourly Wage (Rs.)	Mean Hours of Work	Savings (%)	Union Membership (%)	Fear of Losing Job (%)	PF (%)	Gratuity (%)	Bonus (%)
Non-SEZ	Mean	555	14.96	9.02	28	40	48	45	22	61
	Variance		66.24	1.78	0.20	0.24	0.25	0.25	0.17	0.24
Others	Mean	60	9.88	9.50	2	40	73	37	5	28
	Variance		63.68	1.88	0.19	0.24	0.25	0.25	0.16	0.24

Source: Based on the primary survey data.

pared to their non-SEZ counterparts. Similarly, a lower percentage of SEZ workers receive retirement benefits in the form of PF and gratuity and earn a yearly bonus. As expected under such a situation, only 2 per cent of the SEZ workers in the sample have savings as against 28 per cent of non-SEZ workers. Thus the SEZs, which are supposed to be the leading enclaves of export-oriented growth in this country, derive their comparative advantage by offering labour at a level which is even less than what is available ouside these zones. Labour processes in both SEZ and non-SEZ areas are exploitative in varying degrees as the case studies of Falta, SEEPZ and NOIDA indicate.

Labour in SEZ is exploited to an extent that is only comparable to the experiences of industrial labour in England at the beginning of the Industrial Revolution in the eighteenth century. Growth, which takes place on account of the export initiatives of these SEZs, is thus biased and asymmetric. Thus, welfare loss in terms of labour deprivation is not compensated by adequate welfare gain through the redistribution of social surplus from the process. The plight of labour in the SEZs therefore requires the immediate attention of the policy-makers to build-up a strong social safety network as has been argued in several studies and is being currently debated. In an era when labour efficiency is the buzzword of reform and development, the real test will lie in combining efficiency with safeguarding the legitimate demands and authentic interests of labour.

ANNUAL AVERAGE GROWTH RATES OF INDUSTRIES

Referring back to the basic tenets of the neo-liberal theory of economic reforms, it would be intending to guage the impact of industrial growth rates on labour (Table 6.12). The present sample includes 16 industry groups at the ASI 2-digit codes. These can be ranked in terms of their annual average growth rates (AAGR) of output over the post-reform period (1991–2003). Grouping the workers in the sample according to the growth rates of the industries where they are employed, one can see that industry-level growth rates hardly matter in terms of the mean hourly wage rates (the AAGR of industries has a range of 15.97 per cent to 2.51 per cent). Labour does not have a better deal in terms of other attributes when industry-growth rates are higher and the fear of job loss happens to be even greater in those with higher growth rates. There is not much of a correspondence

TABLE 6.12: LABOUR IN TERMS OF INDUSTRIAL GROWTH

Industry Code	AAGR (%)		N	Mean Hourly Wage (Rs.)	Mean Hours of Work	Savings (%)	Union Membership (%)	Fear of Losing Job (%)	Gratuity (%)	Bonus (%)
34	15.97	Mean	20	14.31	8.55	20	60	70	40	75
		Variance		45.16	0.26	17	25	22	25	20
36	15.70	Mean	66	13.74	10.17	39	5	41	3	32
		Variance		32.08	1.59	24	4	25	3	22
28	14.92	Mean	12	9.62	8.42	25	58	33	8	75
		Variance		28.67	0.27	21	27	24	8	21
18	14.88	Mean	56	9.54	9.50	16	52	43	0	32
		Variance		7.66	3.31	14	25	25	0	22
25	11.66	Mean	69	7.56	9.22	6	49	68	12	42
		Variance		17.07	2.58	6	25	22	10	25
26	9.31	Mean	10	11.17	8.40	20	70	40	50	100
		Variance		35.76	1.60	18	23	27	28	0
19	9.05	Mean	15	13.33	9.13	47	13	40	27	80
		Variance		32.99	1.70	27	12	26	21	17
35	8.62	Mean	20	11.64	8.15	30	65	100	40	100
		Variance		19.09	0.24	22	24	0	25	0
24	8.51	Mean	78	9.36	8.31	26	49	54	38	85
		Variance		33.69	0.48	19	25	25	24	13
17	6.96	Mean	56	10.18	9.73	45	39	25	16	48
		Variance		18.02	2.56	25	24	19	14	25

29	6.64	Mean	41	10.69	9.20	15	10	46	15	37
		Variance		55.50	1.86	13	9	26	13	24
31	6.19	Mean	64	12.75	8.48	42	42	42	25	64
		Variance		42.72	0.25	25	25	25	19	23
27	6.07	Mean	40	10.60	8.68	20	42	63	25	77
		Variance		15.60	0.33	16	25	24	19	18
21	5.85	Mean	16	6.67	9.31	0	25	63	13	50
		Variance		6.79	3.03	0	20	25	12	27
15	5.84	Mean	36	12.44	9.17	31	72	44	44	81
		Variance		57.69	2.60	22	21	25	25	16
22	2.51	Mean	16	10.29	9.00	0	19	69	0	38
		Variance		12.59	0.00	0	16	23	0	25

Source: Based on the primary survey data.

between industry growth and other labour features (including union membership, fear of job loss, non-wage benefits including PF, gratuity and bonus, savings, etc.). Thus the growth-centric reform process does not seem to have much of a favourable impact on the economic status of labour, as conveyed in terms of the present primary survey statistics.

In a way, these findings contest the logic of the growth-centred, neo-liberal globalization process when judged in terms of labour. It is possible that growth has been the result of labour compression forced by competitive capitalism.

Conclusion

The present study's primary survey of selected industrial units in the organized industrial sector of the country bears testimony to the fact that labour had an unfair deal in the process of economic liberalization and reforms over the preceding decades. Contesting the trickle-down doctrine of the neo-liberal policies, one can find no evidence of an improved labour status in terms of employment, wages, other benefits, hours of work, job security or the ability to save. One cannot also find any positive impact of industrial growth, trade intensity or technological upgrading (in terms of capital intensity) on the economic status of industrial workers in the present sample. As for the young workers who are new entrants in the labour market, their deprivation is even greater in terms of long hours of work, casual status and other related aspects. Skill, as judged by education beyond the basic level, compensates to some extent in the earnings of workers and related aspects. Those with job skills as well as those who are young seem to be subject to the changed work atmosphere of contractual and casualized recruitments which offer very few non-wage benefits (PF, bonuses) or opportunities to participate in union activities. Workers with a migratory and/or casual status (which often go together), resulting from lack of job opportunities and/or uncertain job situations, are naturally subject to prospects which are even worse. As for industries subject to higher capital intensity, the higher output growth that results is matched by longer working hours and higher wages (but less or none of the other benefits) compared to what prevails in labour-intensive industries. The pattern is similar for the relatively younger workers (aged less than 25) who seem to be relatively well off in terms of wages but lack opportunities in terms of non-wage benefits and trade union participation.

The present survey thus throws light on the new generation of workers in India, young, casualized, with no options for trade union activities which could provide them with a bit of bargaining power to fight for their due share in industry. Workers will permanent jobs in this day of labour flexibility are not much better off. In capital-intensive industries with higher growth, presumably with higher labour productivity, labour employed is both displaced and expropriated, with wages disproportionately low as compared to their performance, which includes long working hours. There are records from the SEZ areas, rated highly as lead sectors of the economy, where labour is even more expropriated. Neither are the workers better off when industries are generally trade-oriented, especially in terms of export orientation.

With increased casualization under labour market flexibility, with the use of labour-displacing technology and enhanced work pressure on an average worker in high growth industries, there appears to be a steady deterioration in the well-being of labour in the age of competitive capitalism. Clearly it is labour which bears the brunt of structural adjustments under economic reforms in order to make room for capital.

NOTES

1. Panchmukhi, Kumar and Das (2004).
2. See Sunanda Sen and Byasdeb Dasgupta, 'Political Economy of Labour under Globalization: A Study of Labour in India's Manufacturing Sector' (mimeo) (2006).
3. During the course of this survey, it appeared that unionizing casual, contractual or temporary workers is more difficult than unionizing permanent workers as the former category of workers is footloose in nature, who frequently move from one job to another in the absence of any long-term employment, contract unlike permanent workers.
4. Panchmukhi et al. (2004).
5. The list of industries at the 2-digit level in which 615 workers interviewed by us includes food and beverages (15), textiles (17), wearing apparel (18), leather (19), wood (20), paper (21), printing, etc. (22), chemicals (24), rubber and plastic (25), non-metallic mineral (26), basic metals

(27), fabricated metals (28), machinery (29), computing (30), electrical (31), motor vehicles (34), other transport (35), and furniture which includes gems and jewellery (36).

6. Panchmukhi and Das (1999); and Panchmukhi et al. (2004).
7. Chaudhuri (2002); Panchmukhi (2000), Panchmukhi and Das (1999); Panchmukhi, Das and Kumar (2004); and Sharma (2004).
8. Panchmukhi, Das and Kumar (2004).
9. Agarwala, Kumar and Riboud (2004: 139–40).
10. Panchmukhi and Das (1999).
11. A separate profile of each one of these SEZs is provided on the profiles based on the field survey for their study in the ICSSR-IDPAD Report.

REFERENCES

Agarwala, Ramgopal, Nagesh Kumar and Michelle Riboud (eds.) (2004), *Reforms, Labour Markets, and Social Security in India*, New Delhi: Oxford University Press.

Annual Survey of Industries (various issues), Central Statistical Organization, Government of India.

Chaudhuri, Sudip (2002), 'Economic Reform and Industrial Structure in India', *Economic and Political Weekly*, 12 January, pp. 155–62.

Panchmukhi, V.R. (2000), 'Trade, Technology and Employment: A Profile of Systemic Dilemmas and Paradoxes', *The Indian Journal of Labour Economics*, 43(1), pp. 59–94.

Panchmukhi V.R. and Ram Upendra Das (1999), *Economic Reforms, Regional Integration and Labour Markets in the SAARC Region*, New Delhi: ILO-SAAT.

Panchmukhi, V.R., Nagesh Kumar and Ram Upendra Das (2004), 'Economic Reforms and Implications for Labour Markets', in Ramgopal Agarwala, Nagesh Kumar and Michelle Riboud (eds.), *Reforms, Labour Markets, and Social Security in India*, New Delhi: Oxford University Press.

Sen, Sunanda and Byasdeb Dasgupta (2006), 'Political Economy of Labour under Globalization: A Study of Labour in India's Manufacturing Sector' (mimeo).

Sharma, Alakh N. (2004), 'Employment Generation Policy and Social Safety Nets in India', in Ramgopal Agarwala, Nagesh Kumar and Michelle Riboud (eds.), *Reforms, Labour Markets, and Social Security in India*, New Delhi: Oxford University Press.

Standing, G. (1999), *Global Labour Flexibility—Seeking Distributive Justice*, New York: Macmillan Press Ltd.

APPENDIX 6.1: DISTRIBUTION OF SAMPLE ACCORDING TO STATE, AREA AND WORKERS' TYPE

State	Area	Worker	Number
Delhi	East Delhi	Casual	5
		Permanent	9
		Total	14
	Mayapuri	Casual	11
		Permanent	30
		Total	41
	Okhla	Casual	19
		Permanent	19
		Total	38
	Total	Casual	35
		Permanent	58
		Total	93
Gujarat	Surat	Casual	64
		Total	64
Haryana	Faridabad	Casual	2
		Permanent	6
		Total	8
	Gurgaon	Permanent	11
		Total	11
	Total	Casual	2
		Permanent	17
		Total	19
Maharashtra	Mumbai	Casual	25
		Permanent	22
		Total	47
	Total	Casual	25
		Permanent	22
		Total	47
Uttar Pradesh	Ghaziabad	Casual	5
		Total	5
	Noida	Casual	42
		Permanent	16
		Total	58
	Noida SEZ	Casual	9
		Permanent	8
		Total	17

(Contd.)

APPENDIX 6.1: Contd.

State	Area	Worker	Number
	Total	Casual	56
		Permanent	24
		Total	80
West Bengal	Falta	Casual	26
		Permanent	17
		Total	36
	Hooghly	Casual	3
		Permanent	16
		Total	19
	Howrah	Casual	24
		Permanent	5
		Total	29
	Kalyani	Casual	57
		Permanent	64
		Total	121
	Kolkata	Casual	52
		Permanent	48
		Total	100
	Total	Casual	162
		Permanent	150
		Total	312
All states in the sample	All areas in the sample	Casual	344
		Permanent	271
		Total	615

THEME 4

UNEVEN ECONOMIC GROWTH AND ENVIRONMENTAL IMPLICATIONS

CHAPTER 7

From the Other End: Tribals and Democratic Decentralization in Kerala

ABEY GEORGE AND JYOTHI KRISHNAN

INTRODUCTION

Kerala stands out as a 'model' in the development history of independent India. There has been wide appreciation for its achievements in social development (particularly with respect to education, health, literacy, sex ratio, women's status, implementation of land reforms, and so on (Ramachandran 1997).[1] These achievements, however, have not adequately filtered down to the weaker sections of society, particularly the tribals who have remained as 'outliers' to the development process (GOK 2003). Even the much celebrated decentralization process in Kerala has not been able to deliver development benefits to the tribal population. The lack of tribal participation in the development process has been pointed out as one of the important factors that contributes to the ineffectiveness of tribal development programmes in the state (Vijayanand 1996). The first section of this chapter gives a picture of the tribal position *vis-à-vis* the achievements of the state in various realms of social development. The second section discusses the decentralization process underway in the state since 1997, and the provisions therein for

*This paper is an abridged version of the report submitted to IDPAD titled 'From Degradation to Regeneration: Issues of Power, Governance and Participation'.

ensuring tribal participation in development activities. The third section gives a detailed case study of the Attappady Tribal Development Block. It discusses the operationalization of the decentralization agenda in Attappady from the mid-1990s onwards, and the extent to which it ensured the participation of the tribal people in local decision-making processes. The focus in this section is on the process of democratic decentralization through the panchayati raj institutions (PRI), as well as the participatory eco-restoration programme implemented through the Attappady Hills Area Development Society (AHADS). We argue that the decentralization initiative was not sensitive to the social realities of Attappady, in particular to the existing skewed nature of resource access. As a result, disempowered tribal communities remained at the peripheries of 'participatory programmes'. The final section contains the concluding remarks.

Tribals and the Kerala Model

As of 2001, the tribal population of 3.64 lakhs comprises only 1.14 per cent of the total population of the state. A total of 38 tribal communities comprise the total tribal population in the state. These tribal communities are distinct from one another in terms of their cultural patterns, diversity of habitats, lifestyles, languages and livelihoods. In addition, they are spread over almost all the fourteen districts in the state. Hence, numerically, culturally and socially, tribals constitute a very weak force in the state of Kerala.

A close look at some of the indicators of social development show that tribals have been largely left out of the overall achievements of the state in this regard. For instance, while a high level of literacy is one of the defining features of the 'Kerala model', the tribal situation is markedly different. While the average literacy rate for the state is 89.81 per cent, it is only 57.22 per cent for the tribal sections, with female literacy amongst tribals amounting to only 51.07 per cent (GOK 2005), as against the state average of 75.25 per cent (Gulati and Ramalingam 1997). Education is another sector which distinguishes Kerala from many other parts of the country, with the state exhibiting high levels of enrolment in schools and colleges. Once again the tribal situation is different. The enrolment of Scheduled Tribes (ST) in the lower and upper primary levels is relatively higher than their population share. This indicates a high degree of willingness on the part of the tribal population to enrol their children. However, a falling enrolment rate and a high dropout rate from the high school level onwards indicate the inability of the government system to provide the necessary support to tribal students to continue their education. So much so that only 0.58 per cent of their population share is enrolled at the higher secondary level.

The incidence of poverty among the STs is about three times that of the total population of the state. According to the NSSO, 24.2 per cent of the tribals are below the poverty line, which constitutes 3 per cent of the total BPL population in the state, while the proportion of the ST population to the total population is only 1.14 per cent (GOK 2005). The tribals are also deprived of the health care facilities available to the general public in the state (GOK 2003).

Landownership is another issue that sets the tribals apart from the general population. Land alienation is a serious problem encountered by the tribal communities across the state. The customary nature of tribal land rights made it easy for the land hungry migrants to grab their land in very many ways. In addition, the connivance of the settlers with the bureaucrats and the political lobby nullified many of the legal provisions that aimed to prevent land alienation (Menon 2001). Since the 1990s, the severity of the situation has led to a few court cases and agitations in different parts of the state. All of the above culminated in the constitution of a high-power committee, the Tribal Rehabilitation and Development Mission (TRDM), by the government of Kerala. However, locating suitable land for rehabilitating the tribals proved to be a difficult task, as a result of which rehabilitation has covered a very small section of the total tribal population in the state. Till 2005, there existed a total of 22,052 landless tribal families in the state, and another 32,131 families with less than one acre. Out of this cumulative total of 54,183 families, the TRDM was able to give land to only 3,802 families (GOK 2005).

The Decentralization Process and Tribals

The 73rd Amendment to the Constitution of India in 1993 formally recognized the authority of district, sub-district and village level elected bodies (the PRIs) (Johnson, Deshingkar and Start 2003). The Eleventh Schedule of this amendment identified twenty-nine areas, which fell under the legitimate jurisdiction of the panchayats. These included many of the key sectors of the rural economy;[2] it also covered areas related to the provision and maintenance of rural infrastructure,[3] key rural services[4] as well as the provision of targeted welfare benefits for the SC and ST, women, children and the handicapped (ibid.). In keeping with the spirit of the same, the Government of Kerala passed the Kerala Panchayati Raj Act in 1994, which enhanced the power of the grama sabha (the village electorate) and the accountability of the grama panchayat (the village assembly). According to the Kerala Panchayati Raj Act of 1994,

> The village panchayat shall place before the grama sabha a report relating to the developmental programmes relating to the constituency during the previous year and those that are proposed to be undertaken during the current year, and the expenditure therefore, the annual statement of accounts and the administration report of the preceding year. If in any circumstances, any decision of the grama sabha could not be implemented, the president shall report the reason therefore, before the grama sabha.

The grama sabha was also empowered to 'formulate the proposals and fixing of priority of schemes and development programmes to be implemented in the area of village panchayat' (ibid.). A statewide campaign for decentralized planning was launched by the Left Democratic Front in the state in 1996, and 35–40 per cent of the plan expenditure (excluding salaries) was devolved to local bodies. As a result, since the commencement of the Ninth Five-Year Plan, PRIs in the state were strengthened with enhanced financial and administrative powers.

In tune with the spirit and process of the decentralization campaign in the state, the concept of *oorukootam* (*ooru* refers to the hamlet) was introduced into the tribal development sector. The *oorukootam* refers to the general assembly of all adult members of a tribal hamlet. This is comparable to the concept of the grama sabha which consists of adult members of a panchayat ward. In the case of the *oorukootam*, all the members are tribals. The emphasis on the *oorukootam* was in order to give the tribal members an opportunity to have a say in the development activities implemented in their area. Unlike the grama sabha, where the recommendations made by the grama sabha are accepted or rejected by the executive council of the panchayat (consisting of elected members), in the *oorukootam*, the recommendations made by it are binding on the executive council of the panchayat. Such an exclusive tribal assembly was envisaged in order to redress the prevailing situation wherein tribal opinions were not given a voice.

As a part of the Ninth Five-Year Plan Campaign for Decentralization in the state, 100 per cent of the Tribal Sub-Plan (TSP) money was transferred to the PRIs. However, it was soon realized that the PRIs were not able to deliver the TSP benefits to the tribal community. Subsequently, the TSP component was taken back from the PRIs and entrusted once again to the Tribal Development Department. In 2003–4, the government issued further detailed guidelines for the implementation of the TSP, recommending this time that 50 per cent of the TSP funds be devolved to the PRIs. The guidelines also recognized the extreme levels of poverty and deprivation within the tribal communities and the extremely low levels of empowerment in the political, social and economic spheres. It also acknowledged the existing exploitative relations between tribal communities and others, with tribals enjoying very low levels of access to entitlements. The government took particular note of the alienation of land. With regard to government interventions in tribal areas, the guidelines took note of the siphoning of developmental resources and benefits due to tribals by middlemen, the weak delivery system of public services and the absence of proper planning, implementation and monitoring systems (GOK 2003).

In addition, the guidelines also emphasized the strengthening of the *oorukootam* as a 'democratic niche for tribal communities within the local government system' (ibid.). Also envisaged was a process wherein the tribal people would make an attempt to understand the development situation themselves through a process of analysis, reflection and action (ibid.). The guidelines also stressed the strengthening of the role of 'tribal promotors' (trained grass-roots workers from the tribal community) to implement the guidelines in letter and spirit.

The following case study explores the gap that exists between policy prescriptions and field realities.

THE CASE OF ATTAPPADY

The Attappady Tribal Development Block in the Palakkad district of Kerala has been selected for a detailed study and analysis of the process of decentralization and the extent of tribal participation therein. The implementation of decentralization through the PRIs and through AHADS makes it a compelling case for an understanding of the dynamics of tribal participation.

Attappady is an eastern sloping plateau in the Western Ghats, in the Mannarkad taluk of Palakkad district of Kerala. This 750 sq. km. area is inhabited by a total of 66,171 people, of which tribals comprise 27,121 (AHADS 2002). Once it was an almost exclusively tribal dominated area, inhabited by three distinct tribal communities, viz., the Irulas, the Mudugas and the Kurumbas. Once heavily forested, this area faces severe ecological degradation today. The intervention of the government in the forested parts of the valley since the turn of the twentieth century, coupled with the process of inmigration triggered a long-drawn-out process of resource degradation and alienation.

The influx of migrants from the neighbouring plains of Kerala and Tamil Nadu has reduced the tribal population in Attappady to a mere 40 per cent (AHADS 2002). The organized land grabbing by the non-tribals, and the resultant land alienation during the post-Independence period has removed from the tribals much of the fertile cultivable land. Continuing land alienation has transformed their once prosperous agricultural systems into a relic of the past, so much so that today the tribals are totally dependent on the poor quality food rations made available through the Public Distribution System of this area. Increasing malnutrition, particularly amongst women and children, is highly prevalent amongst the tribals today giving rise to a range of preventable health disorders like anaemia.

Having lost much of their customary rights to the use of forest and agricultural land, the edifice of the tribal community has been shaken. Traditional systems of governance, along with the kinship ties which had maintained the cohesiveness of the tribal hamlets, have weakened. The period between the early 1950s and the 1990s marked the establishment and strengthening of the development administration in Attappady. Through the Integrated Tribal Development Programme (ITDP) and the forest, soil conservation, public works and agriculture departments, a range of government programmes aimed at tribal development have been implemented in this area. None of these programmes have paid attention to the existing skewed access to natural resources, and hence have done little to ameliorate the worsening livelihood crisis of the tribals.

DECENTRALIZATION IN ATTAPPADY

The participatory era had its manifestations in Attappady as well, with the reform of governance structures being viewed as a remedy for many of the complex problems that the area and people faced. Two forms of decentralization have been underway in the area since the mid-1990s. The first is the process of democratic decentralization, which was initiated as part of the statewide Ninth Plan campaign for decentralization (1997–2002). Around the same period, the Japan Bank for International Corporation- (JBIC) funded the Attappady Comprehensive Eco restoration project was implemented by the AHADS in the area. A large variety of user associations were constituted by AHADS to ensure a participatory mode of project implementation. During this period, the issue of people's participation was voiced loudly at all pubic forums. In Attappady, this implied eliciting the participation of the tribal communities who had been exploited and subordinated by the non-tribal sections since the latter half of the twentieth century.

It must be noted that the tribal community was largely sceptical about the emphasis on people's participation as part of the decentralization campaign in Attappady. This was because the very same group of people (local politicians and contractors, largely from the migrant sections of society) who had protected non-tribal interests and who had played an important role in the systematic destitution of the tribal community were now championing the cause of tribal participation. Contractors and politicians who had built their fortunes in this land by partaking of the benefits of the contractor system, were now decrying the very same system, and were asking for a participatory processes to be put in place. It was clear that their intentions were focused on making profits, and not on service to the people. Some of them were a notorious for leaving house and road constructions incomplete and of misappropriating funds. Even the emerging tribal leaders were groomed by the politician-contractor lobby. This dissuaded many tribal leaders from contesting elections, a trend that has been reported amongst indigenous groups from other parts of the world as well (Larson 2005: 47).[5] Similarly, many of the individuals who emerged as leaders of the various participatory committees constituted by AHADS had been engaged in contract work of various kinds. This created immense suspicion in the minds of the tribals and they were never optimistic about the promises of decentralization in Attappady. At the same time, they were forced to depend on these various new institutional structures in order to get the benefits of various welfare measures and employment opportunities.

The following sections review the functioning of the constitutionally empowered panchayats as well as the user groups constituted by AHADS from the angle of participation and accountability. We argue that both these forms of decentralization ignored the specific social realities of the area. By paying scant attention to the existing claims over resources such as land, forests and water, and to the underlying iniquitous power dynamics, these forms of decentralization were not able to ensure justice for the tribal communities.

PARTICIPATION IN NUMBERS

One of the commonly applied methods of ensuring participation of the local people was through the system of electoral reservations. Reservations for women and tribal representatives was made manadatory in the panchayat elections as well as in the elections to the numerous user associations (UA) constituted by AHADS. The 73rd and 74th Constitutional Amendments had made it mandatory for marginalized sections of society to be adequately represented on elected bodies, according to which one-third of all seats in local bodies had to be reserved for women. In the case of SC and ST, the reservation was to be proportional to their population (Johnson et al. 2003: 6). Similarly, AHADS, while formulating an implementation strategy focused on UAs, made it mandatory for about 45 per cent of the seats on the elected councils of these associations to be reserved for the tribal community. While four out of nine seats in the elected body were to be reserved for tribals, this reservation of seats was to be made proportional to the tribal population. Hence in areas where tribals constituted a majority in numbers, the minimum reservation of seats would extend beyond the mandatory four. In addition, one among the three main office-bearers, viz., the president, secretary and treasurer, was to be a tribal.

With AHADS constituting a range of UAs, namely, the watershed-based UAs, the hamlet-based Ooru Vikasana Samitis (OVS), as well as the Joint Forest Management Committees (JFMC), a large number of tribals and women came to the forefront of development activities (Table 7.1).

TABLE 7.1: DETAILS OF USER GROUPS CONSTITUTED BY AHADS AND THEIR OFFICE-BEARERS

Name of the Community Beneficiary Group Constituted by AHADS	Number of Units	Number of Office-bearers
User Association	93	837
Ooru Vikasana Samiti	166	2,158
Joint Forest Management Committee	54	486
Taikula Sangam	111	1,332
Income Generation Group	157	1,884
Total	581	6,697

Out of the total number of 6,697 functionaries, 63.44 per cent were women and 82.25 per cent were tribals. The high percentage of tribals was because some of the committees such as the OVSs and the taikula sangams were exclusively tribal associations. Similarly, taikula sangams, being exclusively women's groups, contributed to the high percentage of women's presence on these committees. This apart, as mentioned earlier, there was a specific reservation for women and tribals on the general committees such as the UAs and JFMCs. It needs to be noted that unlike the elected representatives in the panchayat system, the latter group included a large number of people who bore no strong affiliations to political parties. During the initial stages of project implementation, the issue of giving adequate representation to the tribal members was used by AHADS to secure the trust of the tribal community.

NUMBERS AND THE POWER GAMES

It has been observed in many parts of the country and the world that while representation is supposed to ensure the empowerment of the marginalized sections of society, formal institutions are often usurped by the more informal patterns of domination and power (Blair 2000; Johnson et al. 2003). Rural elites have been known to manipulate candidacies, electoral processes and so on (Ribot 1999). This has been clearly illustrated in the case of women's representation on elected local bodies in many parts of the country, wherein women fill up the required quota, but do not engage actively in council affairs, their husbands playing that role on their behalf (Blair 2000: 24). The outcome of decentralization in Attappady was not very different, proving that numerical representation in an area marked by socio-economic inequalities needs to be taken with a pinch of salt. When it was clear that the issue of tribal representation was mandatory in PRIs, the existing politician lobby in the area focused on how to circumvent these constitutional provisions. While abiding by the numerical quota laid down by the constitution, they went about the selection of candidates in such a way that the existing *status quo* would not be disturbed. While filling in the non- tribal women's quota, for instance, many of the candidates fielded by the Left and Right wing alliances were the wives of contractors or politicians. From the very beginning, therefore, women candidates were not expected to take an active role in issues related to panchayat governance. Similarly, while filling the quota of tribal seats, both political alliances selected people who were unlikely to assert their views or advocate the tribal cause. Hence, tribal representatives who emerged after the election largely fell into the category of 'silent nodders'.

As part of the implementation of the 73rd and 74th Amendments in the state, in 1996, for the first time in the history of Attappady, an Irula tribal woman was elected as president of the Attappady Block Panchayat. It needs to be noted that it was only because of the new policy of reserving seats for women candidates from minority communities that the Irula tribal woman was able to come to power.[6] While the tribal community was sceptical of the promises of decentralization, they began to look hopeful when a member of their community became president. Over a period of time it became evident that the newly elect president could do little within the boundaries laid out by the political party that she represented. In many cases, therefore, tribal representatives were reduced to mere rubber stamps despite the rhetoric of participation. For instance, Koya Moopan from Mele Manjikandi was elected as president of the Pudur Panchayat for three consecutive terms, as a result of which he held the office of president for close to twenty-five years. Once again, his election to the post of president was possible only due to the fact that the post was reserved for a tribal person, Pudur Panchayat being the only panchayat with a tribal majority in the entire state of Kerala. Koya Moopan himself admitted that he was unable to do anything significant for his people during his long tenure, as he was politically overpowered by the vice-president and the contractor lobby. The vice-president in this case was a Malayalee migrant who had built his career in Attappady, first as a contractor and later as both a politician and a contractor.

Box 7.1: Contractor-cum-politician

Most of the political leaders of Attappady belong to the migrant class. They moved into the valley during the 1960s and 1970s. Most of them came as refugees. Some others came seeking to hide their criminal record. Like most other migrants they would try to get some land from the tribal chieftain, either by begging or by cheating. All of them have a history of accumulating tribal land through various illegal means. Some of them were found to have worked as supervisors or assistants with an existing small contractor. Some others used their religious or communal background to come up as local leaders. Many of them slowly moved into a position which enabled them undertake contract work on their own. This they did after building closer relations with the government officials in the ITDP, the Soil Conservation and the Forest Departments. In the process they would mobilize a group of workers who were dependent on them for wage labour. Over a period of time they would involve themselves in local political activities and get a party ticket to contest elections in the panchayats or cooperative banks. Local elections were always a show of money power, with the candidates distributing *arrack* and food in the hamlets to buy votes. This often resulted in a competition between rival candidates as to who would spend more on elections.

All the first-time elected tribal representatives had as their colleagues well-seasoned politicians, most of whom were non-tribals with a contracting background. Hence, though they were represented in numbers, in day-to-day decision-making they were silenced by the latter group.

WAS AHADS DIFFERENT?

It was into such a socio-political context that AHADS made its entry as an advocate of peoples' participation in development and eco-restoration activities. From the very outset, AHADS had made clear that all project activities would be implemented through democratically elected user associations constituted on a watershed basis. It had also made clear that these elected bodies would give equal representation to both tribals and non-tribals. By portraying itself as an advocate of tribal welfare, the project had alienated itself from the migrant lobby in Attappady, and in particular from the politicians and contractors of the area. The migrants of Attappady initiated a counter-campaign through the politicians of the area, accusing the project of promoting divisions amongst the people. While AHADS firmly adhered to the principle of adequate tribal representation on the elected councils, it took a rather naïve approach towards the issue of tribal representation. Assuming that numerical representation was the be all and end all, it paid scant attention to the existing iniquitous power relations that governed interactions between the tribal and non-tribal sections of the society. Being put on the defensive by the accusations of the non-tribal lobby, AHADS was always eager to convince them that though the project has a distinct tribal emphasis, the needs of the non-tribals would be given due consideration. The non-tribals in turn used this as an emotional argument in all negotiations with the project authorities.

This kind of politicking was evident right from the beginning, and became clearly manifest when elections to UAs were held in many parts of Attappady. During the process of elections, it was noted that wherever tribals constituted a numerical majority and were capable of organizing themselves into a pressure group within the UAs, the counter-forces attempted to subdue them in every possible way. The functioning of the Nackupathy UA illustrates this dimension. When it became clear that the tribal votes would outnumber the non-tribal votes, and that there existed an organized tribal group in the area, the non-tribal lobby managed to defer the elections by creating law and order problems. They were able to defer the elections more than once and tried to create an impression that if their discontent was not taken seriously they would be able to cause such bottlenecks in future as well. In such conflicting situations, when the AHADS officials were forced to take a stand they shied away from doing so. In yet another example, of the Cheerakadavu UA, the tribals, owing to their majority status in terms of population, were well represented on the UA. After two years, when elections were held for the second term, the non-tribal lobby skilfully manipulated the situation such that the tribals lost their majority status.[7] Power play was evident were visible even while deciding the proportion of tribals and non-tribals on elected councils. While AHADS endorsed a policy of positive discrimination in favour of women and tribals, the policy of reservation was often misinterpreted as a maximum rather than a minimum representation. Never was there an instance where there were more than four women on any elected council. In the case of tribal representation, instances of more than four tribals on elected councils were highly rare.[8]

COMMITTEE FORMATION AS PARTICIPATION

As mentioned earlier, the grama sabhas and the *oorukootams* under the panchayati raj system, and the UAs and the OVSs under the AHADS system were the principal institutional mechanisms through which the participation of the local people in decision-making processes were to be ensured. However, in both cases, it was thought that the act of constituting the grama sabha or the committee of the UA would ensure participation. While the pressure to put in place these institutional structures before a pre-determined date was a factor which contributed to the speed with which they were constituted, one cannot ignore the disinclination on the part of both the panchayat and AHADS to engage in a 'slow and arduous' (Baviskar 2002) process of social conscientization. Hence there were plenty of instances when a panchayat member and president would convene four to five grama sabhas in different panchayat wards in a single day. Their primary objective was to somehow wind up this process, and hence there was no 'process', only the act of constituting the necessary committees. This was manifest in the preliminary phase of the implementation of the eco-restoration project, when AHADS was conducting a large-scale 'awareness generation campaign' to convince the people of the need for a participatory eco-restoration programme. The aim of such meetings was to communicate the seriousness of the problems of ecological degradation witnessed in the area, the need for ecological restoration, as well as the need to ensure the participation of all sections, in particular the tribal sections of society. Discussions which elicited significant response from the people were gradually done away with, with project officials focusing more on the issue of committee formation. The focus was on to somehow get these committees in place. At the same time, officers were keen for a large turn out of people in order to provide evidence of the participatory process being followed. Hence, in many such meetings, the convening officer was more inclined to collect the signatures of all those who had attended the meeting, to create an 'instant record of participation', a record of participatory institutions at work, a record that which was 'created and authenticated for posterity' (Baviskar 2002: 5).

SCUTTLING PARTICIPATION

While the existing literature on participation dwells much on its potential and the various tools that can be used to facilitate participation, much less is written about how marginalized groups can be left out (Gupte 2004). All implementation programmes, however, should be cognizant of the fact that social stratification hinders real participation for the powerless and the marginalized groups in society, despite policy programmes which promote participation (ibid.). In the context of Attappady, where iniquitous power relations prevail, even the most rudimentary forms of participation are likely to threaten the existing socio-economic relations, inviting immediate resistance from the powerful lobbies (Vijayanand 1996). In such a situation the agency that promotes social participation, be it the panchayat or AHADS, assumes critical importance. Participation in this sense can take place only through a systematic process of providing positive encouragement to the weaker sections, particularly when a tribal/ethnic group is involved. We examine the role played by the panchayat and by AHADS in this regard, by taking two cases from the field.

One of the declared objectives of the implementation of decentralization through the panchayats in Attappady was to do away with the contractor system of project implementation. As mentioned earlier, the implementation of projects under the ITDP and other department programmes was totally contractor-managed. When this mode came under criticism, beneficiary committees were formed, but again stage-managed by the contractors. Such a move proved to be beneficial to the contractors as in the event of non-completion of or poor quality of work, it was the beneficiary committee that was held responsible and not the contractor as he was not directly in the picture. The decentralization initiative aimed to get rid of this *benami* contract system by entrusting the work directly to a group of stakeholders who would benefit from the programme or project. But in Attappady, the predominance of the contractor lobby and its close links with the political lobby (in many cases the contractor and the politician were one and the same) scuttled such a move as well. Where such peoples' committees tried to assert their powers and rights by doing away with the contractor, they were discouraged in every possible way. In many cases, bureaucratic red tape, in connivance with the contractor lobby, stubbed the very spirit of participation. In some others, physical assault by the local political lobby was used to deter the committees.

An example of the contractor lobby's interference is the roadwork undertaken by the people's committee in the Nackupathy hamlet. The committee, consisting of tribals, alone came forward to undertake the work directly. This antagonized the contractor lobby who threatened that they would neither allow the work to be completed nor the payment to be made. Despite these threats, the committee completed the work. The engineers concerned, however, danced to the tune of the contractors and deferred payment of the bill on the grounds of poor quality of work. Non-payment of the bill for a considerably long period of time (more than three months) precipitated internal conflict amongst those who had undertaken the work on the basis of personal loans. What could have emerged as a model for other committees to emulate turned out to be a bitter lesson which discouraged future replications of such an attempt.

The functioning of the 'taikula sangams' illustrates similar dynamics within AHADS. As mentioned earlier, a significant amount of wage labour was generated as part of the activities undertaken by AHADS. For the first time in Attappady, the entire amount of wages reached the labourers directly, as the contractor system was done away with. Coupled with higher wage rates,[9] this led to a situation where the tribals had a significant amount of money in their hands. In the absence of an effective saving scheme, which should have been a part of the design. The result was that most of the money went to the *arrack* lobby in the area. The levels of alcohol addiction rose leading to an increase in the incidence of domestic violence. This resulted in the emergence of a spontaneous resistance on the part of the tribal women. AHADS facilitated, this process, and mothers' groups (taikula sangams) were formed all over Attappady in an extremely short period of time (two to three months).[10] When the taikula sangams became actively involved in clearing up illicit brewing centres, they met with strong opposition from the brewing lobby, which was in turn supported by the local politicians and even the media in some cases. The counter-campaign accused the members of the taikula sangams of being arrogant women who broke up 'happy homes'. When taikula sangam members brought up issues of corruption within the UA, the UA office-bearers turned against them as well and retaliated by excluding taikula sangam members from wage-labour opportunities. In cases where they were employed as supervisors of fieldworkers, they were arbitrarily removed from their position. Those of the taikula sangam members who had contested elections during that time were cornered and defeated.

Perhaps the most damaging impact on the emerging taikula sangams was the response from the field-level implementing officers of AHADS. These officers were directly responsible for the generation of work for and payment to labourers. Hence, they exercised an important influence on the office-bearers of the UAs who implemented the work in the field. These officers were apathetic about the discriminatory practices initiated against the taikula sangam members. Once again, they took the side of the UA office-bearers in order to ensure a favourable situation for them. In the ensuing conflict between two different institutional structures (UAs and the taikula sangams), both of which were created by AHADS, the latter chose to take the side of the more powerful. This was justified on the grounds that a peaceful situation in the field was necessary for field-level implementation to progress without delay so the annual expenditure could be on target. Insensitivity to both tribal and gender issues led to the stifling of a possible corrective move by the tribal women against a social evil, which had enormous negative economic implications as well. A positive intervention from the part of AHADS in every conflicting situation would have helped in reinforcing the faith of the tribals in such a process and encouraged them to come forward. In practice, however, AHADS officials turned a blind eye to power struggles in the name of ensuring a 'peaceful and conflict-free' situation.

These two cases also illustrate the importance of orientating and training the functionaries of project implementing agencies and the panchayat in the nuances of unequal power relations particularly when a disempowered tribal community is involved. In an evaluation of participatory watershed projects, Kerr, Pangare and Pangare (2002), emphasize on the importance of such projects devoting time and resources to social organization as well as to incorporating the interests of various groups into the project design. They cite the example of some NGOs in Andhra Pradesh who organized communities for watershed development by working separately with each interest group they could identify, helping them to become organized and then in mediating negotiations between groups (Kerr, Pangare and Pangare 2002: 77). While the relevance of such an approach is high in an Attappady-like context, neither the panchayat nor AHADS have contemplated engaging in such a process. As an outcome the guidelines for decentralization and people's participation promulgated at higher levels read like a book of rules, where procedures rather than the people become the central focus (Shah 2001). Ensuring the participation of the tribal members in this case necessitates a highly pro-tribal stance on the side of the panchayat/AHADS.

PLANNING PROCESS LARGELY NON-PARTICIPATORY

On paper, both the panchayat and the UAs were to come forward with locally devised development/management plans. It was considered that such an internally generated plan would ensure the representation of local interests and local problems in the planning process. Conducting grama sabhas and development seminars at the panchayat level, it was assumed, would ensure the participation of people in identifying the areas of priority. Towards this end working groups were constituted by the panchayats in different sectors such as agriculture, minor irrigation, housing, SC-ST welfare, and so on. These working groups were comprised of officials as well as knowledgeable people available in the area. The projects recommended by the people were forwarded to these working groups which were entrusted with the task of making them technically viable. In practice, however, as the periodic convening of grama sabhas was not treated seriously people had little say in the formulation of projects in these various sectors. At the same time, the transfer of a significant amount of money to the panchayats put pressure on them to formulate projects in order to spend the money. The politicians and contractors decided what kinds of projects were to be implemented in each ward. Things came to such a pass that close associates of the contractors and politicians formulated projects, which were then passed on to the working groups for approval.

It was same with the eco-restoration activities implemented by AHADS. While AHADS advocated the participation of the people in both planning and implementation, the larger plan for eco-restoration in the area had already been drawn up by Centre for Water Resource Development and Management (CWRDM),[11] a state-level scientific institution. This plan proposed a series of interventions in the four broad sectors of soil conservation, water resource development, agriculture and forestry, and income generation. The broad boundaries for eco-restoration activities in Attappady had therefore been drawn up by 'technical experts' much before the people of the area had even to heard of such a project. When AHADS got into implementation, it proposed breaking up this large plan into smaller plans, in order to make them locally specific. Hence, they sought to break up the larger plan into smaller micro-plans based on micro watersheds. This, however, did not change the nature of the plan, or the planning process which continued to be focused on technical interventions. Assuming that local people would be incapable of drawing up plans for their respective micro watersheds, particularly such technically-oriented plans, AHADS appointed technically qualified external consultants to draw up micro plans for each micro watershed in Attappady. Such a technical view of eco-restoration left very little room for people to be involved in the planning process.[12]

The consultants who were asked to do the job were either institutions or freshly qualified professionals with limited or no work experience. They had no prior working experience in Attappady and therefore were not aware of the social and political undercurrents in the society. They viewed the process of micro-plan formulation as a technical affair which comprised selecting sites for various project activities such as a location for a check dam, or an agro-forestry site, or a contour bund, and so on. The outcome was a miniature version of the earlier plans prepared by the CWRDM. Consultations with local people in such a process of micro-plan formulation was of ornamental value only. Such a micro-plan did not reflect the existing socio-economic inequities and the livelihood problems faced by the marginalized sections.

Since a micro-plan was mandatory before any work was undertaken in the micro watershed, the local people also wanted the plan to be ready as soon as possible. Since AHADS and the external consultants had focused on technical solutions, particularly on civil structures, the local people understood this to be the main mode of activity. They also realized the inherent potential for wage-labour generation in such activities. Hence, in the process of micro-plan formulation, the local people would 'voice' the need for check dams, contour bunds and other civil structures. AHADS on its part, under immense pressure to come out with tangible results in a short period of time, was inclined to implement projects that could produce immediate results. So the intended participatory process of microplan preparation was reduced into a mere listing out of proposed works such as check dam construction, gulley plugging, digging of compost pits and contour trenches, tree planting and constitution of user committees.[13] Thus, the slow and painstaking work of ensuring the participation of all sections of society in the planning and implementation process, particularly that of the silent tribal populace, was compromised.

Once the micro-plans were prepared, the next level of people's participation was only in terms of implementing the work designed by AHADS, i.e. in the construction of structures or in the raising and planting of seedlings. Though the micro-plan could be implemented only when approved by the UA, this approval carried only ritual value. The normal procedure was that AHADS would finalize the micro-plans drawn up by the consultants and pass them on to the UA for mandatory approval. There was not a single case where the UA expressed dissent with the micro-plans passed on from AHADS, largely because they did not understand the language in which the plan was formulated.

Participation in this case was therefore a mere 'add on'(World Bank 2005: 32; Cernea 1989: 1) to a technical programme, an afterthought to a project design, an 'ancilliary ritual' (ibid.). Participation took place only to the extent that local committees were constituted in a hurry, land-use plans formulated and implemented (Huijsman and Sevenije 1991), with AHADS playing a leading role in all the stages. The move towards decentralization was 'tightly leashed' (Baviskar 2002: 4) by ensuring that every proposed plan required the sanction of the technical committee of the panchayat or the technically qualified staff of AHADS. Stage-by-stage approval of the work by the implementing officer of AHADS, for instance, was necessary before funds could be released. On its part AHADS justified retaining such control to ensure quality work and prevent possible misappropriation of funds. However, over a period of time, bureaucratic rent-seeking has crept in, though it is not as widespread a practice as it is the case with the panchayat. It needs to be noted that AHADS had always kept its distance from the panchayat system in order to avoid the possibility of political corruption creeping into the AHADS system. 'Politics' soon crept into the functioning of the UAs, with local political leaders deciding on the selection of UA committee members. Attempting to keep the UAs within the fold of AHADS, however, strengthened bureaucratic control allowing for corruption, and facilitated collaboration between state officials and particular individuals and social groups (Ferguson in Baviskar 2002).

DIFFICULTIES OF PARTICIPATING ON UNFAMILIAR TERRAIN

A factor which contributed to ineffective participation by the tribals was their inability to relate to this new mode of conducting affairs. It was often naively assumed that holding a meeting and discussing matters would ensure participation. The inability of the tribals to tune into this new mode of operation was not taken into account. Consider this example: a tribal woman well-versed in cultivating, harvesting and processing a range of food grains as well as capable of collecting and processing a variety of medicinal plants would find it extremely difficult to draw up a proposal for a 'nutritional garden'[14] in her hamlet and provide an estimate for it. Neither would she be able to sit through a meeting convened by the user association, and make a report or minutes of the meeting. Similarly, if local people felt the need for soil conservation at a particular site they would have to formulate a proposal, giving technical specifications, financial estimates and so on. Naturally the tribals shied away from such participation. On the other hand, members from the non-tribal society were more familiar with such a mode of operation. Hence, over a period of time, the presence of non-tribals in implementation activities increased, whereas tribals were largely relegated to the role of coolie labourers. For instance, when trained youths from the area were selected as 'technical volunteers' in order to assist the technical officers in AHADS, most of them were from the non-tribal community. It has been rightfully argued that in the process of environmental decentralization, it is the socially and economically better-off sections of society who are more likely to participate in user groups; that those who have access to and visit government offices are more likely to participate in user groups created by state officials (Agrawal and Gupta 2005).

TIME FRAME: A FACTOR IN NON-PARTICIPATION

Another factor that contributed to the half-hearted participation of the tribal populace was the short time frame imposed by the Project Implementing Agency (PIA). While the traditional institutions conform to what can be called a 'lifetime approach', the newly created ones adhere to a 'project approach'. The latter emphasizes on completing a given work within a stipulated time frame. Since these time-bound meetings were more of a procedural requirement, often tribals were not able to relate to this mode. In contrast, traditional institutions organized activities within a much larger time frame. While taking decisions on matters related to the use of land, or forests or choosing a site for the hamlet, they kept in mind issues which were likely to emerge over a longer period of time (covering the lifespans of one or two generations). The land-use patterns they followed in the past illustrates this dimension. The method of cultivating a patch of land carved out from the surrounding forests for agriculture for a period of time and then leaving it fallow so that it would regenerate, and he used again reflects this approach. In addition, the very process of decision-making was spread over a larger period of time, enabling all members of the community to participate in the process.

In the traditional system, all major issues in the hamlet were discussed and resolved collectively. A common assembly was called to deliberate upon the issue (what they refer to as *nyayam peshal* meaning discussions to resolve issues in a just manner). In some cases, elders from other hamlets would be called to act as observers and judges. Such deliberations could go on for a whole day or even longer, depending on the nature of the problem. While there was no official protocol, there existed an accepted way of resolving issues through such a process. The head of the hamlet, the *moopan*, coordinated the process in such a way that all members had an opportunity to express their opinion and get actively involved in the deliberations. The uniqueness of the process was that it would last till a consensus was arrived at. Such a consensus would be arrived at through an open process with no back door deliberations or political compromises. On the other hand, the new forms of governance imposed by the government exhibited a totally different style of functioning. Meetings in the new scheme of things, being more of a procedural requirement, are often convened at a time suitable to the implementing officers and not to the people themselves. The 'committee-mania', as it is often referred, to is oblivious to the numerous constraints that local people face (Messer 2001). Women have complained that the time schedules of the meetings convened by the UAs make it inconvenient for them to attend (see Box 7.2).

Box 7.2: Is There a Right Time for Meetings?

Most implementing officers are inclined to hold meetings between 10 a.m. and 5 p.m., which is their official duty hours. This is inconvenient for a tribal who has to take his herd of goats and cows to the hills during the day for grazing. It is equally inconvenient for people engaged in manual labour who would have to give up a day's work to participate in a meeting. When meetings were held in the evenings, it was found to be an inconvenient time for women who were cooking the evening meal after a day's work. In the context of enhancing women's participation, it has been argued that special efforts need to be made to schedule meetings keeping in mind women's domestic chores and childcare responsibilities (Kerr, Pangare and Pangare 2002: 57). This implies that there cannot be a fixed time for holding meetings. A great deal of flexibility is required in fixing the time for a meeting if one really wishes to make it participatory. In many of the *oorukootams* held in tribal hamlets as part of the decentralization campaign, four to five such meetings would be convened on a single day, to suit the convenience of the elected representative and the officers concerned. Naturally the turnout for such meetings was very poor. Once again the tribals would be accused of showing disinterest in the whole programme.

PARTICIPATING IN MULTIPLE COMMITTEES

The decentralization drive in the country and the states has led to the creation of a number of local-level user committees by different government agencies. In Attappady, AHADS itself has constituted five different kinds of stakeholder groups in the area, namely UAs, OVSs, JFMCs, Income Generation Groups (IGG), and the taikula sangams. In addition, there exist the water-user association of the Jalanidhi Drinking Water Programme, the self-help groups constituted by the grama panchayat and the block panchayat, the neighbourhood groups of the Kudumbashree Programme (Poverty Eradication Mission) and the Vana Samrakshana Samities (Forest Protection Committees) set up by the Forest Department. In addition to these government initiatives, non-governmental organizations functioning in the area have set up their own local associations. For example, the Attappady Social Service Organization (ASSO), the Kallamala Multipurpose Charitable Society, and so on, have set up SHGs to implement their rural development/social welfare programmes in the area. This has given rise to problems of integration, effectiveness and legitimacy.

The problems with the conventional run-of-the-mill approach of creating multiple local development and natural resource management institutions have lately received considerable attention (Messer 2001; Larson and Ribot 2004: 6; Vasavada, Mishra and Bates 1999; Cleary et al. 2003). Village-based committees now form the basis of all development interventions in villages, justified on the grounds that they ensure participation of all local members, including the hitherto excluded (Vasavada, Mishra and Bates 1999: 156), so much so that 'people's participation' is envisaged as having a committee in the village (ibid.). The current trend is that each government department constitutes a local-level committee to facilitate the implementation of project activities. Since most of the judicial and financial powers remain with the patron departments, this often leads to a 'I Manage, You Participate' situation (Saxena in Vasavada, Mishra and Bates 1999). This has been manifest in the functioning of the numerous UAs constituted by AHADS, which is considered to be the 'most participatory' effort in recent times. In addition, the proliferation of local institutions ensures very little coordination between the institutions themselves and between their patron departments.[15] Each department is disinclined to recognize and work with committees formed by other departments.[16] What is often overlooked is that ultimately the efforts of various government departments percolate down to the same village, creating parallel structures in the process (Vasavada, Mishra and Bates 1999). Parallel hierarchies of traditional leaders, local government and line-department-sponsored committees create unclear and overlapping boundaries (Shackleton et al. 2002). In Attappady, people of a single tribal hamlet are represented on a large number of such committees. Each implementing agency focuses its attention exclusively on the group/association it has constituted. Viewed from the other end, the tribal is faced with an onslaught of organizations, their meetings and activities. Contrary to the assumption of government officials that the multiplicity of committees facilitates the broadening of the leadership base (ibid.: 178), in most tribal hamlets in the area only a few people are represented on all the committees. They are found to be too tied down with completing procedures and organizing people for one committee after another. In some others, the functioning of so many committees has split the hamlets into various factions.[17] Conflicts intensify when these factions are influenced by political alliances. In this quagmire, people lose interest in all the committees, mostly because they have no real powers, and do not respond to peoples' concerns (Larson 2005). They value the committees only to the extent of the wage labour generated through their activities. The issue of active and informed participation is lost amidst this 'destructive proliferation of local institutions' (Larson and Ribot 2004: 6).

THE OLD AND THE NEW

An equally damaging impact of the new institutional structures imposed upon the people is their disassociation with the traditional institutional matrix of the area. The traditional hamlet-based governance system, which comprised the roles played by traditional community leaders,[18] coupled with norms and rules-in-use looked into various aspects of social living. Traditional resource management was embedded in everyday relations and in networks of reciprocity, with relations of trust and cooperation contributing to the collective management of natural resources (Cleaver 2001). None of the new institutions imposed through various government and non-government agencies considered this traditional set-up to be of any relevance. Most importantly, they ignored the fact that this area and people had a long history of community management of natural resources. Traditional rules and customs regarding access to and use of natural resources, along with the related hamlet-based power structures, were not deemed to be of importance. On the contrary, this hamlet-based system of governance was often referred to as a relic of the past. The fact that this hamlet-based system continued to play a role in the people's common activities was forgotten. While it is true that traditional leaders exert little power over issues related to resource management (largely due to their alienation from land and forests), they continue to retain power and influence in the conduct of social rituals in the event of marriage, death, birth and so on, which are dictated by customary practices. These traditional authorities continue to act 'under cover' in community life (Lundin in Messer 2001: 30). Such social practices may have little political or economic value, but they continue to shape the tribal identity in a world increasingly dominated by an alien culture.

THE PROMISE OF ACCOUNTABILITY

Along with promoting participation, the other laid-out objective of decentralization policies is to enhance the accountability of local governance mechanisms. A multitude of recent studies in this field indicate that no decentralization strategy is likely to work without institutions which tie local political actions to the preferences of their constituents (Manor 1999; Crook and Manor 1998; Blair 2000). Downward accountability in particular is considered to be the cornerstone of successful decentralization (Ribot 2003). Downwardly accountable local institutions would be driven by mandates from below, being held accountable to local constituencies in numerous ways. While elections are the most commonly cited means, non-electoral mechanisms such as legal recourse through courts, third-party monitoring by the media, NGOs, auditing and evaluation, social movements, widespread participation (ibid.: 58), and so on are some of the other means through which a 'counter power' is exercised to control possible 'arbitrary action' (Agrawal and Ribot 1999). In Attappady the issue of ensuring accountability in general has received very little attention in the unfolding efforts at decentralization (through the panchayat as well as through AHADS). The long history of under-the-table manipulations by contractors and politicians and bureaucrats coupled with the rent-seeking behaviour of bureaucrats demands that the issue of accountability be given special emphasis.

THE ELECTORAL PROCESS AND ACCOUNTABILITY

Local-level elections are the most commonly explored form of accountability, with the assumption that regular, fair and competitive elections would compel the formulation and implementation of policies which ensure efficient and equitable outcomes. Time and again, however, it has been proved that elections alone will not ensure accountability to the people (Ribot 2003). In Attappady, both the panchayat as well as the UAs set up by AHADS have been put in place through an electoral process. All of them are therefore representative and accountable in the electoral sense.

With regard to the panchayat, since the elections to the panchayats across the state are organized by the State Election Commission, the electoral process is bestowed with greater credibility and authenticity. However, since only those selected by the mainstream political parties can come into the fray, elected candidates remain accountable to their respective parties rather than to the people at large. Candidate selection by political parties has been consistently reported in a recent review of the process of democratic decentralization in about twenty countries in Asia, Africa and Latin America (Larson 2005). This trend is accepted even by the local people as a normal practice in the democratic process. In Attappady, the silent understanding between the Right and Left wing political parties has obviated the possibility of dissent being voiced in an open forum. As political parties are controlled by the non-tribal lobby, tribal elected representatives are silenced from taking up a pro-tribal stance. Irrespective of the fact that tribals constitute 50 per cent of the total number of elected members in the three-tier panchayat system of Attappady, they have not been able to steer policies and programmes in the tribals' favour. While reservations for women and members of the scheduled tribe community were intended to enhance representation of the marginalized sections, these provisions too have been nullified. In order to ensure representation and accountability Larson argues that elections, must be made transparent, with third-party monitoring, credible oppositions, a vibrant local media, an active civil society and vigilant local citizens (Mandondo and Mapedza in Larson 2005). Attappady is wanting in all of these factors.

ACCOUNTABILITY THROUGH THE EMPOWERMENT OF THE GENERAL BODY

The 73rd and the 74th Constitutional Amendments emphasized the role of the grama sabha, which consists of all eligible voters within a grama panchayat area, in serving as a principal mechanism for transparency and accountability (Johnson et al. 2003: 6). The grama sabha was therefore legally empowered to ensure the accountability of the panchayat system to the people. Similar to the grama sabha, the *oorukootams* has the authority to formulate development programmes in their hamlet (G.O. [MS] No. 40/2001 dt. 8 October 2001). In addition, the decisions taken by the *oorukootam* in terms of fixing a priority of schemes to be implemented and finalizing the list of beneficiaries could not be overwritten by the panchayat committee. In the case of the various user committees constituted by AHADS (such as UAs, OVSs and JFMCs), the general body of these committees was entrusted with similar powers. In addition, they were also empowered to recall the appointment of office-bearers found guilty of malpractices, provided their decision to recall was endorsed by two-thirds of the general body.

In practice, the powers of the grama sabha as a forum to ensure downward accountability have been largely unutilized in Attappady. Since the 1960s, the government has created an image of itself as a provider of welfare measures, particularly to the tribals. The power of the grama sabha to decide the priority of the beneficiaries of various welfare measures has been twisted around by the elected representatives and political leadership to portray the grama sabha as a forum for the distribution of welfare measures. On the other hand, the people who were accustomed to receiving government benefits are not complaining about the limited role of the grama sabha. As a result, the grama sabha never evolved into a responsible body which would undertake local-level planning and ensure downward accountability. Grama sabhas in Attappady, for instance, never demanded that the panchayat accounts be presented to them. Neither did they object when decisions taken at the grama sabha were not adhered to in practice. In the case of the *oorukootams*, the situation was even worse. As reported by the tribal promoters employed by the tribal development department to organize the *oorukootams*, in most of the cases, the panchayat has disregarded the decisions taken by the *oorukootams*. In many cases the panchayat has implemented programmes and projects on behalf of the *oorukootam*. In short, the powers of both the grama sabha and the *oorukootam* were taken over by the elected members of the panchayat. With most of the elected representatives representing the powerful migrant and contractor lobby in the area, decentralization could do little to change the existing *status quo*.

As far as the user committees constituted by AHADS are concerned, although the law entrusted them with the power to plan and prioritize programmes to be taken up in their jurisdictions, in practice the plans were formulated by the officers of AHADS or consultants employed by AHADS. As a result, the general body as well as the executive committees of the UA/OVS/JFMC were reduced to bodies for approving the micro-plans prepared by AHADS for each micro watershed, and for implementing various projects and programmes suggested in the plan. The financial allocation for a particular project were transferred to the UA only after it was approved by AHADS. In addition, the countersignature of the implementing officer in AHADS was required to withdraw money from the bank account of the UA. Through this process AHADS maintained a very strict control over the financial autonomy of the UA and other committees. As a result the elected council of the UA was found to be more accountable to the officers from AHADS than that to the people whom they represented.

A formal meeting of all UA/OVS/JFMC members where a majority decision of the executive committee in favour of withdrawing funds for a particular project was necessary for the release of funds from AHADS. Over a period of time this became a routine affair, so much so that decisions were taken without the actual convening of the executive committee. This was done by circulating the 'minutes book' amongst the members and securing their signatures to support the decision. Once this was done so, the officer in AHADS would release the funds. Such practices demeaned the democratic spirit of such institutional arrangements and made a mockery of the intended objective of accountability.

SOCIAL AUDIT AND ACCOUNTABILITY

Apart from the measures to ensure accountability, discussed earlier, the system of social audit was also introduced in both the panchayat and the AHADS systems. In the panchayat system it was a total non-starter. In the AHADS system, social auditors were selected by the general body of the UA to ensure that the goals of social equity and justice were fulfilled in the functioning of the UA. The primary mandate of these auditors was to ensure that the programmes implemented benefited the most marginalized sections, viz., the tribal communities. However, since both tribals and non-tribals were selected as social auditors, in most of the cases the non-tribal auditors dominated the views of the social audit group. In addition, the non-tribal auditors were not sensitive to the issue of social justice. Over a period of time, the entire process of social auditing was reduced to a process of verification of financial accounts. Since AHADS had its own system of financial auditing in place, the financial auditing by these social audits carried little relevance. Hence the entire system died down.

ACCOUNTABILITY AMIDST A MULTITUDE OF INSTITUTIONS

With numerous local-level user committees being constituted by various government departments, apart from the elected local bodies (the panchayats), it is unclear as to whom they are actually accountable. As discussed above, since most of the non-panchayat elected bodies have been formed at the initiative of government departments, many of these committees remain accountable to the senior officials in the bureaucracy. As in the case of the UAs constituted by AHADS, these committees' inability to participate in the formulation of 'scientific' management plans, along with the control that AHADS enjoys over financial matters, makes them more accountable to AHADS. To be more precise, local UA or JFMCs are found to be accountable to a particular official within AHADS. In effect, they are totally subservient a kind of total subservient to the officer concerned.

The inability to hold 'local groups' accountable to their constituents has prompted the argument that accountability in the decentralization process can be achieved only if it is routed through elected bodies (Larson and Ribot 2004). It has been argued that in attempting to go straight to the people, participatory approaches have avoided the state, failing to make the institutions of the state serve the purpose of greater participation in governance (Ribot 2001) and creating a discourse that diverts attention from the real issue of how the entire system of representative democracy can be transformed to give more powers to the people (Sundar 2000: 269). J.C. Ribot therefore argues that various committees and groups which come about in the absence of a democratic structure may not be democratic in themselves, and hence local governments should be entrusted with greater powers and resources so such that they become effective vehicles of democratic decentralization (ibid.).

What does this imply in the context of Attappady? As in other parts of the state, the panchayats in Attappady are represented by people nominated by political parties. What makes the Attappady situation unique is that most of the political party leaders are former or present contractors, with a proven track record of engaging in rent-seeking and an anti-tribal stance. One can be nominated to the post of a panchayat representative only if she or he toes this line of thinking. Hence, while the panchayat can be said to be the most readily available institution for ensuring local participation, in Attappady the panchayat does not represent the interests of the marginalized. While Ribot's argument is valid in general, it cannot be used in the specific Attappady context. Unless, of course, an exclusive tribal assembly is entrusted with the power of the panchayat. The *oorukootam* and the OVSs constituted by AHADS assume extreme significance here.

As has been mentioned earlier, the *oorukootam* (general assembly of all adult members of a tribal hamlet) was conferred a special status within the panchayati raj system. With regard to tribal affairs, the *oorukootam* was more powerful than the panchayat, with its recommendations being binding on the executive council of the panchayat. Similarly, the OVSs constituted in each tribal hamlet by AHADS were entrusted with decision-making powers in their respective hamlets. While the *oorukootam* has been rendered defunct as a result of political manipulations, the OVS reduced itself to an upwardly accountable institution. The possibility of the *oorukootam* transforming itself into a vibrant democratic institution, and the OVS becoming accountable to the *oorukootam* rather than to senior officials will likely ensure downward accountability in the Attappady.

Conclusion

A close look at the ongoing efforts to ensure participation of tribal people in decision-making processes shows that fulfilling the organizational infrastructure for the exercise of democratic decentralization (by holding elections and upholding principles of reservation for marginalized sections) without addressing the existing power structures reinforced by disempowering social and cultural norms (ODI 2002) will not be very successful. In an Attappady-like context, wherein social relations are highly skewed, a positively enabling environment is required if tribals are to participate. In other words, a level playing field is needed if the marginalized are to bene-fit from decentralization reforms aimed at ensuring participation and accountability. A level playing field is not visible in the near future in Attappady, where non-tribals have the upper hand in all governmental initiatives. Any change requires a special effort from mediating agencies like the panchayat or AHADS. Only if they engage in a conscious process of hand-holding will the tribals be able to assert their rights with confidence. To the contrary, wherever tribals have organized themselves to take the benefits of the statutory provisions in their favour, the panchayat or AHADS have shied away from supporting them. In the case of the roadwork undertaken by the people's committee of the Nackupathy tribal hamlet, the panchayat and the bureaucrats silently supported the contractor lobby, thereby discouraging the people's committee. Similarly, when the tribals asserted their majority status in many of the elections to UAs constituted by AHADS, the latter, sensing the underlying tensions generated by an agitated non-tribal lobby, never came out in clear support of the tribal position. This lack of support was also evident in its treatment of the taikula sangams, as discussed earlier in the chapter. A pro-tribal stance would have communicated the message to all quarters of society, that the agency would do everything possible to encourage tribal participation. To the contrary, many of the officials within AHADS showed a closer affinity for non-tribals, who often took advantage of such personal proximities.

Another issue of importance is that participation is not ensured by merely laying the organizational foundations of devolution (Shackleton et al. 2002), i.e. through the constitution of grama sabhas, UAs, and so on. The overall design of activities should be such that people are able to relate to them. While AHADS declared itself to be participatory, the entire eco-restoration programme was designed in a highly technical fashion, which precluded the participation of tribals in a meaningful manner. Participation was therefore confined to attending meetings, which soon acquired a ritual value. Moreover, the imposition of numerous institutional structures without recognizing the existing *ooru* (hamlet)-based institutional systems has also created problems. Outside interventions, including the most recently implemented governance reforms, have failed to acknowledge that the tribal community has clear views on how to 'govern' their respective hamlets and the resources on which they were dependent. While the panchayat and AHADS set out to ensure the participation of the tribal people, they did not endorse a healthy appreciation of the existing systems of governance. As a result, the newly introduced 'committees' and their time-bound functioning failed to elicit the participation of the tribals.

While the above analysis pertains to Attappady, it is largely true of most other tribal pockets in the state. Like Attappady, almost all other tribal areas in the state are sites of intense resource contests and power conflicts. The Attappady experience with decentralization throws light on the numerous ways in which statutory provisions can be subverted by vested interests and power lobbies. The minority (numerical) status of tribals and their inability to collectively assert their rights also explains their low levels of pariticpation in decision-making processes. Only an enlightened and vibrant leadership from amongst the tribal community can take the constitutional support given to the *oorukootam* to its logical next step. The democratically empowered *oorukootam* and the emerging community leadership should be able to reinforce each other.

NOTES

1. For a critical view of this model, see K.K. George (1993).
2. Such as agriculture, minor irrigation, animal husbandry, fisheries, social forestry, small-scale industries and implementation of land reforms (Johnson et al. 2003).
3. Such as rural housing, rural electrification, transportation and communication linkages.
4. Such as health, sanitation and primary, secondary and vocational education.
5. Larson observes that some indigenous groups shy away from political participation partly because running for office requires political party affiliations. To some groups, such as the Guarani in Bolivia, party politics is seen as meaning political favouritism and providing jobs to party members, and there is little cultural fit with the Guarani's decision-making traditions (Beneria-Surkin in Larson 2005: 47).
6. Democratic decentralization has been observed to have increased the representation of minority ethnic groups on local government bodies in many different parts of the world. Harry Blair, in a study of decentralization in six different countries, reports, that following the implementation of the Popular Participation Law in Andean Bolivia, the Quechua and Aymara community representatives now sit on municipal councils, something that did not exist before the implementation of the law. Similarly, in the Philippines' Cordillera region, indigenous groups such as the Kalingas and Gaddangs now enjoy membership on local government bodies, as do the new rural communes in Mali which demonstrate a heavy representation from ethnic groups such as the Songhai and Dogon in areas where they are numerically strong (Blair 2000: 23).
7. Landownership or residence were the two criteria by which a person could become a member of a UA. If a person owned land in more than one UA, he or she could choose the association in which he/she wished to become a member. In the case of tribals, while their hamlet may be located

in one UA, their lands may be located in another, as was the case with the tribals of the Cheerakadavu hamlet. This was made use of by the non-tribal lobby, who persuaded a significant number of the tribals to take membership in the adjoining UA, which led to their losing their membership in the Cheerakadavu UA. Hence, during the second round of elections, the non-tribal representatives increased their share of seats.

8. Adrian Martin and Mark Lemon note similar power plays with regard to women's representation in the Village Forest Committees constituted under the Joint Forest Planning and Management Programme of the Karnataka Forest Department. They report that while the Karnataka legislation positively discriminates in favour of women through two reserved places, this is interpreted as a maximum representation (Martin and Lemon 2001: 589).
9. When AHADS commenced its operations in the area in 2000, the prevailing daily wage rate in Attappady was Rs. 30–40 for women and Rs. 40–50 for men. AHADS offered a wage rate of Rs. 80–90 for women and Rs. 120 for men. AHADS, however, did not do away with the system of discrimination in wage rates for men and women.
10. Such a fast pace of group formation indicated the severity of the *arrack* problem. The spontaneity with which women came forward to write petitions and initiate group actions, including raiding the illicit brewing centres, enabled the formal constitutions of these taikula sangams.
11. The CWRDM is an autonomous institution of the Government of Kerala based at Kozhikode. When the eco-restoration project was being formulated in 1994–5, the CWRDM was asked to draw up a detailed proposal for a watershed-based eco-restoration programme in Attappady. They divided the entire Attappady valley into 15 watersheds and drew up watershed-based plans for each of them. The micro-plans discussed above were drawn up after dividing the 15 large watersheds into 143 micro watersheds.
12. Sheona Shackleton et al. argue that 'scientific management' is often used to justify continued central control over valuable resources . . . ensuring a dominant role for officials in designing and approving management plans, which are often unnecessarily complex (Shackleton et al. 2002).
13. Amita Baviskar makes a similar observation of the participatory watershed programmes implemented in Madhya Pradesh (Baviskar 2002).
14. One of the programmes implemented by AHADS.
15. In Orissa, the district rural development agency, social forestry and the territorial forest department all had funds for plantation work but all work in their own areas with no coordination over the employment of workers. Planning is carried out department-wise, based on independently laid out targets and policies (Vasavada et al. 1999: 162).
16. Vasavada et al. in their critique of microplanning exercises, which they

feel had become the fashion of the 1990s, observe that in Madhya Pradesh, separate micro-plans had been prepared for the same village under the JFM project, the Rajiv Gandhi watershed mission and by the panchayat as well. 'Is there and will there be any link between these three?', they ask (Vasavada et al. 1999: 173).

17. Dervla Cleary et al. report a similar phenomenon in Burkina Faso, wherein numerous local-level institutions in the Yatenga province functioned in an isolated and competitive manner. This was partly because many of the groups performed similar and overlapping functions within a single village (Cleary et al. 2003).
18. For a detailed discussion, see A. George and J. Krishnan (2006).

REFERENCES

Agrawal, Arun and Krishna Gupta (2005), 'Decentralization and Participation: The Governance of Common Pool Resources in Nepal's Terai', *World Development*, 33 (7): 1101–14.

Agrawal, Arun and Jesse Ribot (1999), 'Accountability in Decentralization: A Framework with South Asian and West African Cases', *Journal of Developing Areas*, vol. 33, pp. 473–502.

AHADS (2002), Attappady Wasteland Comprehensive Environmental Conservation Project.

——— (2006), Consolidated Progress Report submitted to the Minister of Local Self Government, Government of Kerala (in Malayalam).

Baviskar, Amita (2002), 'Between Micro-Politics and Administrative Imperatives: Decentralization and the Watershed Mission in Madhya Pradesh, India', paper presented at the Conference on Decentralization and the Environment, Bellagio, Italy, 18–22 February.

Blair, Harry (2000), 'Participation and Accountability at the Periphery: Democratic Local Governance in Six Countries', *World Development*, 28(1): 21–39.

Cernea, Michael M. (1989), 'User Groups as Producers in Participatory Afforestation Strategies', Development Discussion Paper No. 319, Harvard Institute for International Development, Harvard.

Cleary, Dervla, with contributions from Pari Baumann, Marta Bruno, Ximena Flores and Patrizio Warren (2003), 'People-Centred Approaches: A Brief Literature Review and Comparison of Types', FAO.

Cleaver, Francis (2001), 'Institutional Bricolage, Conflict and Cooperation in Usangu, Tanzania', *IDS Bulletin*.

Crook, Richard C. and James Manor (1998), *Democracy and Decentral-*

isation in South Asia and West Africa, Cambridge: Cambridge University Press.

George, Abey and Jyothi Krishnan (2006), 'From Degradation to Regeneration: Issues of Power, Governance and Participation', Report Submitted to IDPAD.

George, K.K. (1993), 'Limits to Kerala Mode of Development: An Analysis of Fiscal Crisis and its Implications', Centre for Development Studies, Trivandrum.

GOK (1994), Kerala Panchayati Raj Act.

——— (2003), G.O. (MS) No. 54/2003/Plg. Planning and Economic Affairs Dept., Trivandrum.

——— (2005), The Economic Review, Kerala State Planning Board, Trivandrum.

Gulati, Leela and Ramalingam (1997), *Gender Profile: Kerala*. Trivandrum: Centre for Development Studies.

Gupte, Manjusha (2004), 'Participation in a Gendered Environment: The Case of Community Forestry in India', *Human Ecology* 32(3).

Huijsman, Bram and Herman Savenije (1991), 'Making Haste Slowly', in H. Savenije, and A. Huijsman, *Making Haste Slowly: Strengthening Local Environmental Management in Agricultural Development*. Amsterdam: Royal Tropical Institute.

Jeffrey, Roger and Bhaskar Vira (eds.) (2001), *Conflict and Cooperation in Participatory Natural Resource Management*, New Delhi: Palgrave Publishers Ltd.

Johnson, Craig, Priya Deshingkar and Daniel Start (2003), 'Grounding the State: Poverty, Inequality and the Politics of Governance in India's *Panchayats*', ODI Working Paper 226.

Kerr, J.M., Ganesh Pangare and Vasudha Lokur Pangare (2002), 'Watershed Projects in India: An Evaluation', Research Report 127, International Food Policy Research Institute, Washington, D.C.

Larson, Anne M. (2005), 'Democratic Decentralization in the Forestry Sector: Lessons Learned from Africa, Asia and Latin America', in Carol Pierce, J. Colfer and Doris Capistrano (eds.), *The Politics of Decentralization. Forests, People and Power*, London: Earthscan.

Larson, Anne M. and Jesse C. Ribot (2004), 'Democratic Decentralisation through a Natural Resource Lens: An Introduciton', *European Journal of Development Research*, 16(1): Spring, 1–25.

Manor, James (1999), *The Political Economy of Democratic Decentralisation*, Directions in Development Series, Washington, DC: World Bank.

Martin, Adrian and Mark Lemon (2001), 'Challenges for Participatory Institutions: The Case of Village Forest Committees in Karnataka, South India', *Society and Natural Resources* 14: 585–97.

Menon, Mukundan C. (2001), 'Landless in their own land', *Humanscape*,

8(8), September. Downloaded from http://www.humanscape. org/ Humanscape/new/sep01/landless.htm

Messer, Norman M. (2001), 'Mapping Traditional Structures in Decentralisation Policies: Illustrations from three Countries in Sub-Saharan Africa and the Near East', Working Paper No. 12, Rural Development Division, FAO.

ODI (2002), 'Panchayati Raj and Natural Resource Management: How to Decentralise Management over Natural Resources'.

Ramachandran, V.K. (1997), 'On Kerala's Development Achievements', in J. Dreze and A. Sen (eds.), *Indian Development: Selected Regional Perspectives*, Delhi: Oxford University Press, pp. 205–365.

Ribot, Jesse C. (1999), 'Decentralisation, Participation and Accountability in Sahelian Forestry: Legal Instruments of Political-Administrative Control', *Africa* 69(1).

——— (2001), 'Integral Local Development: "Accommodating Multiple Interests" through Entrustment and Accountable Representation', *International Journal of Agricultural Resources, Governance and Ecology* 1(3–4), 2001.

——— (2003), 'Democratic Decentralisation of Natural Resources: Institutional Choice and Discretionary Power Transfers in Sub-Saharan Africa', *Public Administration and Development* 23, pp. 53–65.

Shackleton, Sheona, Bruce Campbell, Eva Wollenberg and David Edmunds (2002), 'Devolution and Community-Based Natural Resource Management: Creating Space for Local People to Participate and Benefit?' *Natural Resource Perspectives*, no. 76, March, ODI.

Shah, Amita, 'Who Benefits from Participatory Watershed Development? Lessons from Gujarat, India', Gatekeeper Series No. SA97.

Sundar, Nandini and Roger Jeffrey (1999), 'Introduction', in Roger Jeffrey, and Nandini Sundar (eds.), *A New Moral Economy for India's Forests? Discourses of Community and Participation*, New Delhi: Sage.

Sundar, Nandini (2000), 'Unpacking the "joint" in Joint Forest Management', *Development and Change* 31(1) (January).

Vasavada, Shilpa, Abha Mishra and Crispin Bates (1999), 'How Many Committees Do I Belong To?' in Roger Jeffrey, and Nandini Sundar (eds.), *A New Moral Economy for India's Forests? Discourses of Community and Participation*, New Delhi: Sage.

Vijayanand, S.M. (1996), 'People's Participation in Poverty Reduction Programmes: A Case Study of the Integrated Development Programme (ITDP) Attappady, Kerala', M.Phil. diss., Centre for Development Studies, Trivandrum, Kerala.

CHAPTER 8

Livelihood Security in the Marine Fisheries Sector of Gujarat State

JYOTHIS SATHYAPALAN AND
DEREK JOHNSON

INTRODUCTION

It is a fact that deprivation and vulnerability are integral to the lives of many people in developing countries. These constitute a chronic state arising from the absence of sufficient assets or resources to ensure adequate livelihood. Therefore, the crucial policy issue is how lives and livelihoods can be made secure against adversity and deprivation (Burgess and Stern 1991: 43). The food security literature of the 1980s identified cyclical and acute food insecurity as central features of rural poverty in tropical countries (Chambers et al. 1981; Sen 1981) while the poverty literature of the 1990s characterized 'the poor' as a static, identifiable group (Ravallion 1998).

Today livelihood insecurity is a re-emerging issue in development literature. The social security literature suggests that 'market failure' is the root cause of social insecurity. Robin Burgess and Nicholan

*This study was developed at MARE, University of Amsterdam during the visit of the Jyothis Sathyapalan under the Exchange of Scholars (EOS) programme of the IDPAD during September–October 2005. The Data for the study has been collected under the IDPAD Project 5.2.11 entitled 'Co-operation in the Context of Crisis: Public Private Management of Marine Fisheries in South Asia'. The authors are grateful to IDPAD for providing financial support for this work. We are also grateful to Maarten Bavinck, Jeena T. Srinivasan, M. Venkitanarayana, and all participants of the IDPAD end-symposium for their valuable suggestions and comments. However, the usual disclaimers apply.

Stern (1991: 49) identify three markets where failures are of particular importance for the security of the less well off: capital markets, insurance markets and labour markets. A properly functioning capital market allows people to transfer spending power from one period to another, thus freeing them from being constrained in a period by the income that they receive in that particular period. Someone who has low income in one period may borrow and repay in a period when income is high. This allows individuals to remove fluctuations in income or, in more formal terms, engage in consumption smoothening. When capital markets function poorly, uncertainty and seasonal periods of poverty combine to significantly worsen the position of the poor. Similarly, poorly functioning capital markets also make the poor highly vulnerable to ill health, injury and death in their households. They are unable to take advantage of insurance schemes which in other circumstances allow individuals to save in a productive way for their retirement or for periods of ill health or injury. The third type of failure is associated with the labour market where no effective means of protection are provided against short-term employment risks. With this background, the present chapter tries to examine the factors that lead to livelihood insecurity among the fishing communities of Gujarat state in India.

FACTORS THAT LEAD TO LIVELIHOOD INSECURITY

The literature on fisheries in India shows that the majority of the fishing population earns a livelihood under risky and insecure conditions (Kurien 1998; Johnson 2001; Bavinck et al. 2005; Srinivasan 2005, 2006). The factors that determine high insecurity in livelihood are partly associated with various risk factors. These may be generic to specific groups of people who are connected geographically or by shared risk characteristics (exposure) or they may be specific to individuals or individual households. Although an entire community might face exposure to a livelihood threat such as drought or food price inflation, susceptibility or resilience is differentially distributed across households depending on relative wealth and access to alternative income sources including support from extended family or social networks (Devereux 2001: 509). Fishermen as a group have long been regarded as being especially exposed and vulnerable to livelihood shocks and variability (Allison and Ellis 2001). The causes of shocks and insecurity can be categorized in various ways.

Small-scale fishermen face production risks because they often have little income diversification and may have few options to improve their fishing technology. The nature of fishing in general is itself risky, with fishing households facing a constant threat of loss of gear or injury or death due to inclement weather. The relative ease with which fisheries can be overexploited with modern technologies also poses a serious risk to fishermen. In the case of marine fisheries, those who have gained access to the most productive technologies, such as trawlers, can put a significant cost on others by overfishing. A few fishermen with access to capital strategically capture a disproportionate share of the fish, depriving others and thereby often provoking inter-sectoral conflicts between fishermen (Bavinck et al. 2005). Current trends of intensified resource use and high possibility of resource depletion worry many fisherfolk, especially those who do not have any supplementary livelihood options.

The current conditions of resource overexploitation in the Gujarat fishery (Bhathal 2005; Johnson 2001, 2002; Johnson and Sathyapalan 2006; Kizhakudan and Kizhakudan 2005; Nayak et al. 2006; Mathew 2000) have become a major source of insecurity for the state's fishermen. Resource depletion has been attributed to specific factors such as the increase in the number of trawl boats, the entry of foreign vessels, industrial pollution, catching of undersize fish (trash fish) and use of small-size mesh in fishing nets, but also to more general factors of which the production-oriented development strategy of the state is the most significant (Johnson and Sathyapalan 2006; Nayak et al. 2006). Mechanization also has reduced opportunities for women in traditional areas like processing, marketing and the making of nets (UNDP 2000).

The vulnerability of fishing communities is compounded by the lack of adequate infrastructure facilities and pricing mechanisms to enable them to sell their catch at a reasonable market price. These market imperfections give opportunities to traders and middlemen to act strategically to exploit fish market. The opportunity arises when fishermen seek advances of money from traders during the monsoon not only for repairs of crafts, purchase of gear, advances to be paid to their crew, but also for money to cover household subsistence costs during that largely closed season. As a result, fishermen are bound to sell their catch to the traders or middlemen who extended the credit. When fishermen are confronted with small or even zero catches, they take further advances from fish traders without settling earlier borrowings, to meet their operating cost. Altogether, this system tends to perpetuate long-term debt traps for the fishermen (Amarsinghe 2005), which work adversely against their livelihood security (Johnson 2003).

COPING STRATEGIES

How do rural people, especially fisherman, prepare for and respond to livelihood insecurity? Platteau (1991) explains various coping strategies of fishing communities with fluctuations of income. Informal insurance against hunger through reciprocal credit was common among traditional maritime communities (ibid.: 149). Reciprocal credit is based on the solidarity that exists within the community arising from the mutual desire to insure oneself against the risk of catch failure (Platteau and Abraham 1987). Jean-Philippe Platteau (1991: 143) identifies three different strategies of hunger insurance: adjustment in the timing of non-recurrent (consumption or capital) expenditures, which are not subject to strict timing constraints; movement in cash holdings; and changes in the household net indebtness position through the use of consumption credit facilities. The former two strategies are considered as 'self-insurance' mechanisms while the latter belongs to the category of 'mutual insurance arrangements'.

In support of this view, John Kurien (2000: 11) points out that sharing of the fish harvest and the income derived from its sale is an efficient mechanism for spreading risk between capital and labour. He reports that the first claim on the fish brought ashore from a fishing trip is for those in the fishing communities who cannot go to sea. These include persons such as widows, the physically and mentally disabled, those temporarily or permanently maimed from accidents at sea and those who provide community services, like the barber, etc.

Another classic example of self-insurance against hunger through providing access to productive natural resources is beach-seine fishing, the rotational system of access to beach-seine sites in southern Sri Lanka. P. Alexander (1977) illustrates the sharing of risk associated with the use of community-controlled marine resources. The distribution of access has long occurred at the individual level as well for beach-seine fishermen communities of Asia and Africa where a common practice consists of permitting all fishermen from the same community who wish to participate to join in the hauling operations to claim access to a portion of the catch. This kind of customary rule benefited old fishermen, fishermen without adult sons, or male adults who fear the open sea (Amarasinghe 2006; Kraan 2006).

Since most fishermen eke out a living from the marine public commons, their livelihood security lies in providing them guaranteed equitable access to the resource, work opportunities, protected market channels and infrastructure support. As a result, the concept of livelihood security acquires a new dimension in the present study, which is not only as a source of assistance when in need through different public actions to safeguard them from persistent deprivation and vulnerability to deprivation, but also through provisions of safeguarding their continued guaranteed access to the use of natural resources (marine fish resources) in a sustainable manner.

The Gujarat Fishery: An Outward-Oriented Pattern of Development

India has a continental shelf of about 508,000 sq km and a coastline with an approximate length 8,118 km, which indicates the richness of the marine resources in the country. Gujarat's share of this coastal endowment is significant. It has the longest coastline of any Indian state, and the largest continental shelf by area at 184,000 sq km within the 200 m depth contour. This represents fully 32.54 per cent of India's total continental shelf area. In recent years, Gujarat's marine catch has fluctuated in the 600 to 750,000 tonne range. This is an important proportion of India's total catch, which in 2004 was 3.6 million tonnes (FAO 2006).

The history of the development of the Gujarat fishery since Indian Independence has emphasized production, with a strong focus on exports from the state to drive growth. This particular development history has given the fishery an outward, globalized orientation, which has shaped the contours of livelihood security for the state's fishing communities.

Fisheries' development policy in India is formulated in broad terms at the national level, but states have primary responsibility for fisheries legislation and development, with state-level fisheries departments being the most important implementing agency. Despite India's natural advantages fisheries have received a comparatively low priority in development planning (Johnson 2002). In the early years after India's Independence, the national policy priority for fisheries emphasized their social benefits. In the First Five-Year Plan, they were highlighted as being a promising means of improving the protein component of the diet of the Indian masses. During this early period of fisheries development, emphasis was given to expanding the annual marine fish catch, mechanizing indigenous craft and developing offshore trawling capacity. In order to achieve these objectives, the country drew on international assistance through such interventions as the Indo–Norwegian Project and the American Technical Cooperation Mission.

With the Third Five-Year Plan, from 1961 to 1966, a new context of growing international demand for shrimp led Indian maritime states, including Gujarat, to recognize the export potential of fisheries. The period saw the intensification of efforts to introduce new technologies of production, including trawler technologies adapted to coastal fisheries. In 1976 the Indian government declared an exclusive economic zone of 200 miles, which cleared the way for the exploitation of Indian offshore waters, confirming the shift to intensified mechanization of fishing to encourage production for export.

As a result of state support and favourable market conditions, the marine fish production of Gujarat has increased at a rate of 5.26 per cent per annum, while exports have increased at a rate of 17.88 per cent per annum since 1972.[1] The outward-orientation of the state's fisheries development is evident from export numbers. In absolute terms, Gujarat exported 208 tonnes of fish in 1972, which grew to 1,19,951 tonnes in 2004–5. The share of Gujarat in the marine export from India is about 28.69 per cent in terms of quantity, although only about 11.05 per cent in value terms (GOG 2004). As Gujarat's domestic demand has been low,[2] growth has come from international and Indian domestic demand for fish.

While national and state authorities made considerable efforts in the period from the 1950s to stimulate production in the fishery of Gujarat, concomitant attention was not paid to the management of effort in the fishery. In the absence of formal state regulations and state support to traditional institutions, the Gujarat fishery has had relatively open access. Since there was no effective rule to govern the effort of the fishery sector till the passing of the Gujarat State Fisheries Act in 2003, the mechanized sector grew at a very high rate. Today, 60 per cent of the 31,000 fishing crafts in the state are mechanized (ibid. 2006). This compares to the India-wide proportion of mechanized boats of about 20 per cent. Among the major maritime states, the figure is less than 18 per cent of the total number of fishing craft.[3] These circumstances are related to the outward-orientation of the fishery sector, particularly its significant export focus. In such a situation, the chapter examines to what extent outward-oriented development in Gujarat fishery reinforced technological externalities and market imperfections, which in turn adversely affected the livelihood of non-trawler fishermen through deprivation and vulnerability. The chapter also highlights the various strategies adopted at the individual and community levels to cope with the Gujarat pattern of high-growth-oriented fishery development.

Study Area, Data and Method of Analysis

As per the Government of Gujarat estimates, there are 1,72,359 active fishermen in the state. The total number of fishing villages is 970, with 88,358 fishermen households. There are ten major marine fish landing centres in the state, which together contribute to more than 70 per cent of the total marine production of the state (ibid. 2006).

Junagadh district has the largest fishing population and fish production of any district in Gujarat. Considering the significance of Junagadh district on these parameters, the research underpinning this study focused on it and the Union Territory of Diu (see Johnson and Sathyapalan 2006). According to the Indian Census of 2001, the population of the coastal blocks (*talukas*) of Junagadh district was 1,265,909 while that of Diu was 44,215.[4] The largest fishing port along the Junagadh and Diu coasts is Veraval, with a fishing population of almost 28,000 people. Veraval is the most significant fishing centre in Junagadh, and indeed in Gujarat. It is the centre for the supply and processing of fish for the whole district, has the largest fishing harbour in Gujarat and is the most significant trawler fishing base in the state. Veraval itself contributes about 26.3 per cent of the total fish production of the state.[5] Vanakbara, Navabandar, Mangrol, and Rajpara are other significant fishing centres in this area. All told, Junagadh and Diu together have 22 fishing ports and fishing hamlets. Figure 8.1 gives the location of the Junagadh district study area.

In Gujarat fishing as an occupation is even more socially marginal than in other parts of the world due to the predominance of

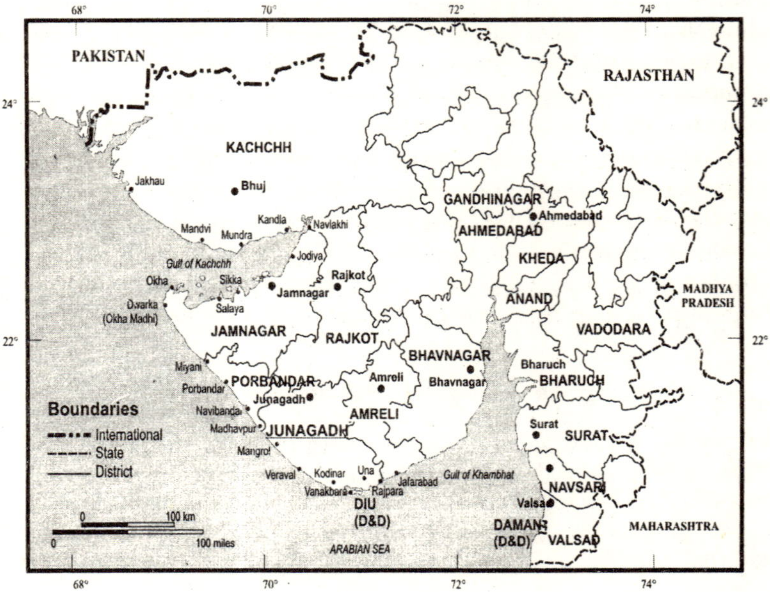

Source: Johnson and Sathyapalan (2006).

FIGURE 8.1: COASTAL DISTRICTS OF GUJARAT STATE

vegetarianism in the state. This has meant that fishing culture and the fishing economy are further removed from the awareness of most Gujaratis than they are in India's other coastal states with significant fisheries. Among Hindus, only two castes are thus involved in marine fishing in Junagadh district: Ghediya Kolis and Kharvas. These two broad caste groups are divided into several sub-castes, reflecting various historical and geographical divisions. Kharvas, for example, have a smaller subdivision known as Goghaliya Kharvas, which is the group that has its origins in Ghoghala. The Koli Kharvas are another sub-caste; in this case a group of Kolis from Vanakbara who broke off from the main Ghediya Koli branch as they accrued wealth from working as sailors and then fishermen. Muslim involvement in fishing is less concentrated by caste, as Muslims do not have the religious injunctions against meat-eating of Hindus. The major fishing caste in Junagadh is the Machhiyaras, who are the only true fishing-specific caste in the district. Numerous other Muslim castes are involved in fishing in one capacity or the other, including Bhadelas, Khureshis, Memons, and Patnis.

To a significant degree, the technological organization of fishing is associated with caste. Junagadh district is divided into two primary ecological zones: an area of intense current action in the east of the district that supports an extremely rich bag-net demersal fishery and a less biologically rich area of lower current amplitude in the western two-thirds of the district. The latter zone has important pelagic and demersal resources which support trawling and gill-netting fleets. Bag-net fishing is largely a Ghediya Koli affair, with some small Kharva and non-Machhiyara Muslim fisherman involvement. Trawling is dominated by Kharvas from Veraval and Mangrol, but the Koli Kharvas from Vanakbara and the suburbs of Veraval also undertake trawling. Gill-netting is the most widely practised form of fishing in the district in terms of caste, with all groups being involved in it. Machhiyaras are uniquely present in this sector and are widely respected for their gill-netting and hook-and-line acumen.

Gill-netting and bag-netting primarily service the domestic market, although the most valuable species from each may also be exported. Trawler fishing is particularly targeted at the export market, with its most important species in terms of volume—croakers, ribbonfish, and cuttlefish—going to the Chinese market. The predominance of Kharvas in trawling means that they also have a great deal of control and influence over the export market. The domestic market, in contrast, is dominated by Memon and Patni merchants in Veraval, the families of whom have been important players in the fish trade for generations.

Data for the present study has been collected through ongoing qualitative interactions with stakeholders (1997 to the present) and a household survey during May–July 2005 using a structured interview schedule. The survey team interviewed 1,056 representatives of households which had at least one member directly involved in fishing. Where possible, the individual actively involved in fishing was interviewed. The surveys were administered in twenty-two coastal settlements in Junagadh district and the Union Territory of Diu. These settlements include all of the major and minor fish-landing sites in the district. In the absence of reliable sample frames, the team adopted what it has labelled as the 'random walk method' to collect data for the study. Survey enumerators selected households for collecting data by moving in different directions in the fishing villages in a systematic manner until the pre-determined size of each sub-sample was reached.

A structured interview schedule was used to collect data from the households that were selected. The qualitative field notes that were prepared as part of this study were used as the basis to formulate appropriate questions related to topics such as the caste and class compositions of fishing settlements, labour and capital market issues and livelihood and institutional aspects related to the use and management of fishery resources.

Asset Base

Fish production depends on the type and amount of capital assets available to fishermen. The sustainable livelihood framework is useful for portraying how various types of capital shape rural livelihoods. It recognizes that in rural communities the capacity to resist vulnerability to livelihoods often depends on the opportunities offered by natural resource-based production systems, conditioned by the wider economic, institutional and political environment. Livelihood analysis prompts assessment of assets used for existence and how they are used in livelihood activities. It shows that household vulnerability is a function of the number, diversity and value of assets they own (Moser 1998). In the case of small-scale fisheries, the important assets that constitute the production base are physical assets like crafts and gear, human capital and financial capital. The following section examines the type and distribution of physical productive assets fisherfolk own and the characteristics of human capital they possess.

OWNERSHIP OF PHYSICAL ASSETS

The main livelihood activity of fisherfolk—fishing—depends on a certain minimum level of fishing assets. Ownership of productive assets like fishing crafts and gear plays an important role in ensuring their livelihoods. The major fishing assets include different kinds of fishing crafts and gear, which can be categorized based on capacity (from higher to lower), that is, trawlers, inboard motor boats (IBM), *dol* netters, outboard motor boats (OBM), and non-motorized boats (*tendiya*). The distribution of the ownership of these assets shows that 23.8 per cent of fishing households own trawlers, 4.5 per cent own IBMs, 5.6 per cent own *dol* netters, 22.4 per cent own OBMs and 1.5 per cent own non-motorized boats. The remaining 42.1 per cent of households do not have any fishing assets. The distribution of each type of fishing craft across different fishing communities is presented in Figure 8.2. The chart shows that the distribution of different types of productive assets is skewed towards certain fishing communities. For example, the most productive technological type, that is, trawlers, is skewed towards the Kharva community, while IBMs are owned by Koli Kharvas. The *dol* netters are mostly used by the Ghediya Koli community. The OBM crafts are distributed among the Ghogaliya Kharvas, Kharvas and Machhiyara communities. Fishing households that do not have any fishing crafts work as crew members in boats.

Another important asset that decides the quality of life is the ownership of a house. During the survey three kinds of houses (*kachcha*, semi-*pukka*, and *pukka* houses)[6] were observed with different ownership status, that is, owned, rental and temporary tents. It was found that 5.1 per cent of the total sample households live in *kachcha* houses of which 0.7 per cent are rented *kachcha* houses. The total number of households living in semi-*pukka* house is around 25.5 per cent, of which 5.5 per cent live in rented houses. It was found that 61.4 per cent of the households live in *pukka* houses of which 7.9 per cent are rented. Some households have vehicles and consumer durables like cars, motorbikes, telephones, televisions, video

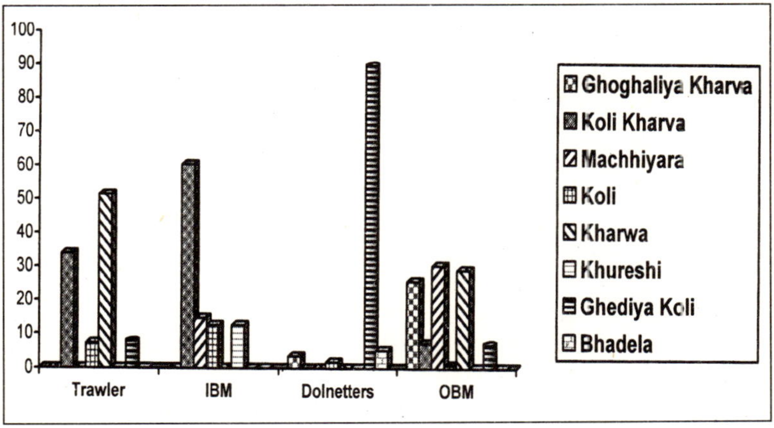

Source: Survey data.

FIGURE 8.2: DISTRIBUTION OF FISHING CRAFTS ACROSS FISHING COMMUNITIES (PERCENTAGES)

cassette recorders, radios, cupboards, cookers, cooking gas connections, grinders, refrigerators, tape recorders, etc. Ownership of cultivable land and domestic animals like goats provides an alternative income source for a small number of fishermen. The survey data shows that 4.4 per cent of the fishermen own cultivable land. A skewed distribution of productive and other physical assets in favour of the dominant Kharva fishing community was evident. Machhiyara and different Koli communities were weak in terms of asset holdings.

HUMAN CAPITAL

In relation to human capital, the literacy level of the household merits attention. In this regard, the Machhiyara fishing community is by far the worst off, with more than 90 per cent illiteracy. At a greater than 61 per cent literacy rate, the Ghogaliya community is the most literate fishing community. The overall literacy rate for the survey sample population is low, with only some 42.4 per cent of the population claiming literacy (Table 8.1). Lack of adequate education hampers the fishermen's ability to diversify their livelihoods. Low literacy and inadequate health provision hamper their ability to save, thus increasing the pressure on resources and raising their vulnerability to exploitation (Johnson and Sathyapalan 2006).

Table 8.2 shows that the fishing population also scores poorly in terms of the sex ratio. The urban rate for Gujarat is 920 females per 1,000 males while the rural rate is 945. For Junagadh, the figures are

TABLE 8.1: DISTRIBUTION OF POPULATION BY EDUCATIONAL STATUS AND CASTE (PER CENT)

Fishing Castes	Functional Literates	10th Standard Pass (SSC)	High School Graduate	Total Literates (Crude Literacy)
Ghogaliya Kharva	49.27	10.17	1.98	61.43
Koli Kharva	37.52	7.35	1.98	46.85
Machhiyara	8.10	0.45	0.09	8.64
Koli	38.40	7.41	3.51	49.32
Kharva	41.56	7.46	2.44	51.45
Ghediya Koli	30.51	5.31	0.68	36.51
Total	34.45	6.30	1.68	42.42

Source: Primary survey data.

TABLE 8.2: SEX RATIOS OF THE FISHING POPULATION BY CASTE

Fishing Castes	Total Female Population	Total Male Population	Female Sex Ratio
Ghoghliya Kharva	361	396	912
Koli Kharva	904	956	942
Machhiyara	516	607	850
Koli	256	257	996
Kharva	1,181	1,365	865
Ghediya Koli	895	1,006	889
Total	4,113	4,587	896

Source: Primary survey data.

955 and 961. As Table 8.2 shows, the sex ratio for the fishing population in Junagadh is only 896. Here again there are considerable gaps between different groups within the fishery. The Kolis and Koli Kharvas score best; indeed the Kolis score well above both the Gujarat and Junagadh levels, while the Koli Kharvas score close to the Junagadh mean sex ratio.

Education and sex ratio are an indication of the relative socio-economic status of the different caste groups in the fishery. The clear outlier by these two standards is the Machhiyara caste, which has an appalling literacy rate of 8.64 per cent and a very poor sex ratio of only 850 females per 1000 males.

RISK FACTORS THAT LEAD TO LIVELIHOOD INSECURITY

Conventionally risks and uncertainty are defined as stochastic events with a known and unknown probability distribution respectively, while vulnerability is a concept which refers to exposure to contingencies and difficulty in coping with them (Chambers 1989). The poor face greater exposure to livelihood threats and are more sensitive to shocks since their asset base is low. There are various ways of evaluating risks and vulnerability to livelihood in developing countries. Jean Drèze and Amartya Sen (1991) advocate an approach focusing on individual capabilities to perform certain basic functioning which is a departure from the traditional way of counting pleasures and desires (as in utility-based accounting) or by focusing on commodities or incomes (commodity-based accounting) to identify the poor and deprived. They state that, 'If life is seen as a set of "doings and beings" that are valuable, the exercise of assessing the quality of life takes the form of evaluating these functioning and the capability to function.' Devereux (2001: 509), categorizes shocks and insecurity according to three variables:

- *Scale*—Macro-level (national to international) economic shocks such as global recession or terms of trade volatility, meso-level (subnational to community) covariant shocks such as civil war or extreme weather events, micro-level (individual or household) idiosyncratic shocks such as ill health.
- *Predictability*—Cyclical variability (economic cycle such as seasonality) and stochastic risk (e.g. drought).
- *Trigger*—Illness and injury, old age, crime and domestic violence, unemployment and other labour market risks.

Against this background, the present study identified three risks which have direct bearing on the livelihood security of small-scale fisherfolk. These include resource depletion associated with the diffusion of modern fishing technology; credit market imperfections and scope for underpricing fish at beach level, and institutional failure to protect fishermen's rights to equitable access and allocation of fishery resources.

TECHNOLOGICAL DEVELOPMENT AND PRODUCTION RISKS

The most productive technological type of fishing craft in terms of total catch is the trawler, which is well suited to the gently sloping and vast muddy continental shelf of the Gujarat fishery. However, overcrowding of trawler boats constitutes a threat to the livelihoods of many poor fishermen. The largest fishing port Veraval, for example, has more than 3,000 trawlers even though it was originally designed for only 800 boats. Small crafts like OBMs and non-motorized boats face the risk of their nets being damaged when big trawlers pass over them. Such incidents, which can be labelled as technology-induced production risks, often provoke inter-sectoral conflicts in the fishery.

The present survey data shows that nearly 85 per cent of the fishing population in Junagadh district supported the view that there has been a considerable decline in the catch over the past ten years. It was pointed out that, although there has been a steady increase in mechanization, catches have been flat at best and catch per boat has actually declined. The bright spot is that fish prices have increased after a decline in the late 1990s, which probably accounts for why fishermen have been able to continue to purchase new mechanized vessels. This shows the risk of promoting modern fishing technology without building institutions for controlling the fishing effort. Falling fish catches have long-term repercussions on the livelihoods of fishing communities. At present poorly capitalized trawler owners have been worst hit, but in the long-run, small-scale fishermen with little income diversification and limited access to improved technology could also be threatened.

Interestingly, the majority of fisherman, irrespective of the ownership of fishing crafts, attributed the basic reason for the decline in the fish catch to the increase in trawling, technological advancement and the opening up of the sea to exploitation by foreign vessels (refer to sub-totals in Table 8.3). Although they were unanimous in their opinion that fishery is in trouble today, a more detailed look at the data across asset ownership shows that the fishermen are divided on trawling as a major reason for the decline in fish catches. Trawler owners saw the origins of overfishing in a different manner than owners of small crafts like *hodis* or OBMs. The latter were convinced that declining catches were due to the destructive technique of trawling itself. Trawler fishers were less inclined to take a negative view of the technology of trawling as it assures their wealth. Therefore, the majority of them attributed the basic reason for catch decline to the opening up of the sea to exploitation by foreign vessels. More frequent fishing, increase in the fishing population, climatic changes and monsoon fishing are some of the reasons included in the 'other reasons' category of Table 8.3.

In addition to this, seasonality in fish production also affects the livelihood security of small-scale fishermen. The cyclical variability in fish production (seasonality) is a more predictable production risk in terms of its timing but not in terms of its severity. During the research, fishermen frequently said that it was difficult to find alternative sources of income other than loans from fish merchants during the monsoon when fishing is risky. As fishing is officially banned during the monsoon season, this is thus the most difficult time for the vulnerable fisherman in this regard.

TABLE 8.3: FISHERSMEN'S OPINIONS REGARDING THE MAJOR CAUSES OF THE DECLINE IN FISH CATCH, AS COMPARED TO CATCHES OF 10 YEARS AGO, BY CRAFT OWNERSHIP

Craft Ownership	Increase in Trawling	Entry of Foreign Vessels	Technological Change	Sub-total	Other Reasons	Total
Asset less (no crafts)	126 (28.31)	91 (20.45)	88 (19.78)	–	–	–
Trawler	44 (17.53)	90 (35.86)	25 (9.96)	272 (67.66)	92 (36.65)	251 (100)
IBMs	12 (25.00)	3 (6.25)	15 (31.25)	169 (65.25)	18 (37.50)	48 (100)
Dol netters	29 (49.15)	7 (11.86)	10 (16.95)	725 (68.66)	13 (22.03)	59 (100)
OBMs	81 (34.18)	41 (17.30)	52 (21.94)	284 (71.90)	63 (26.58)	237 (100)
Tendiyu	5 (31.25)	2 (12.50)	4 (25.00)	272 (67.66)	5 (31.25)	16 (100)
Total	297 (28.13)	234 (22.16)	194 (18.37)	169 (65.25)	331 (31.34)	1,056 (100)

Source: Primary survey data.
Note: Figures in parentheses are percentages to raw total.

ADVANCE SYSTEM AND MARKET RISKS

A second facet of fishermen's vulnerability is the lack of adequate infrastructure facilities and pricing mechanisms to enable them to sell their catch at a reasonable market price. As mentioned earlier, these market imperfections give opportunities to traders and middlemen to act strategically to exploit the fish market. The opportunity arises when fishermen seek cash advances from traders during the lean season not only to smoothen their consumption but also to cover the cost of maintaining fishing assets or buying new ones. As a result, fishermen are bound to sell their catches to the trader or middleman who extended the credit. When fishermen are confronted with small or even zero catches, they take further advances from fish traders without settling earlier borrowings to meet their operating costs.

The product market of the Gujarat fishery is characterized by few buyers and many sellers. The important buyers are fish processors, wholesale suppliers and retail buyers. The wholesale suppliers act as middlemen between fish processors and fishermen. The survey data shows that more than 60 per cent of the fishing population depend on wholesale suppliers to sell their fish. Commonly they are required to sell fish to wholesale suppliers since they take credit from them for fishing operations. Fishermen generally draw credit from fresh fish suppliers (47 per cent), dry fish suppliers (19 per cent), retailers (16 per cent), and pawn brokers (15.4 per cent).[7] Table 8.4 shows the magnitude of credit amounts across different asset-owning classes. These credits vary from Rs. 500 to Rs. 12,50,000 in a year. In the absence of a perfect credit market, fish suppliers exploit this opportunity by keeping the right to determine the purchase price of the fish. Due to collusion between fish suppliers, fishermen are bonded to supply fish at lower than market price which acts as a threat to their livelihoods.

The labour market of Gujarat fishery works on both the cash and the share systems. Trawler boats generally employ labourers (crew members and boat captains) on a cash basis while smaller boats take labourers on share systems. The survey found that the labour market for crew members in trawler boats is quite competitive. As a result of this, they get reasonably good wage rates. However, they are exposed to risks like accidents and hardships due to working conditions and long days away from shore. Protective measures against accident risk are almost entirely absent in the Gujarat fishery. Therefore,

TABLE 8.4: MAGNITUDE OF CREDIT ACCESSED BY DIFFERENT CRAFT-OWNING GROUPS

Craft Ownership	Mean	Minimum	Maximum
No crafts	19,354.76	900	75,0000
Trawler	1,66,070.80	7,000	12,50,000
IBMs	1,02,421.10	10,000	6,00,000
Dol netters	1,51,224.10	6,000	5,00,000
OBMs	56,235.60	500	3,50,000
Tendiyu	73,333.33	5,000	2,00,000
Total	85,931.78	500	12,50,000

Source: Primary survey data.

it is important to mention that organized and controlled product and labour markets, and protection to workers on the beach and at sea merit considerable attention in providing livelihood security to fishing communities

INSTITUTIONAL FAILURE

Fishermen's vulnerability is also influenced by the institutional context. Vulnerability in relationship to the resource is reduced when institutions for resource management are strong and particularly when state and non-state institutions cooperate.

The Gujarat fishery does not have a history of strong institutions for resource access and management at the state or non-state levels,[8] even though coastal social organizations, and particularly caste councils, are powerful (Johnson and Sathyapalan 2006). Caste councils, known locally as *samajs*, act like courts in that they seek to maintain law and order among fishing communities and to settle disputes, including those in fishing. *Samajs* also create and enforce rules of social conduct. While the *samajs* are the ultimate arbiters of social life for many fishing communities, their role in the management of fishing has been limited. They are not uniformly significant along the coast and in some cases are rendered ineffectual due to internal divisions within the caste group. Caste councils are strong in Koli Kharva- and Kharva-dominated ports, but weaker in Koli-dominated ports. Along with caste councils, Boat Owners' Associations (BOA) are the other major indigenous institution for the fishing population. Although in theory the BOAs should be involved in resource management, in practice their activities centre on securing resources for their clienteles, which are normally trawler-owning groups in the larger centres.

Part of the reason for the limited role of fishermen's organizations in management relates to the lack of state recognition as valid actors for fisheries regulation. As the various agencies of the state themselves have been primarily concerned with fisheries development rather than management (see Johnson and Sathyapalan 2006), this oversight is explicable. The reasons behind the surprisingly low level of the fisheries management capacity of fishermen's institutions are likely to be found more in the specific social and cultural conditions of the coast than in the historical development of the fishery (Johnson 2007).

The first significant formal evidence of state-level interest in resource management came with the passing into law of the Gujarat Fisheries Act on 15 August 2003. The Act establishes the basis for increased state control over the harvesting sector by limiting the overall fishing effort through various fishing regulations and licencing systems (GOI 2003). The Act also addresses the excess capacity issue through licencing of crafts and by regulating the mesh size of various gears. The basic presumption of the mesh-size regulation is that it will help to control excessive catch of juvenile fishes so that the recruitment base remains sufficient for the next season. The Act also imposes a ban on fishing during the monsoon season since it is the breeding season for many fish species and because of the physical danger monsoon fishing entails. Although these rules are intended to promote resource conservation, their success and enforcement depend upon fishermen's attitudes towards them. A significant concern in this regard is that the rules are enforced through the Department of Fisheries with scant recognition of non-state organizations and institutions in the fisheries sector. Most strikingly, in Gujarat, there is only a weak interaction between the traditional fisher-caste organizations, the *samaj*, and the Fisheries Department with respect to resource conservation. The lack of an explicit role in fisheries management of the *samaj* is surely an important reason for the missing interaction between it and the Fisheries Department. The other, and more important reason is that the official recognition of non-state institutions in the fisheries regulation goes against accepted governance practice in Indian departments, which is top-down and not inclusive. In practice, however, fisheries department officials who wish to be effective have to cultivate informal relations with leaders of the fishing communities in order to try to ensure the effectiveness of their policies. The strength of fisher organizations is too great for them to be able to implement policies otherwise. As participatory models of governance become more widespread, it will be interesting to see whether they will make it possible for the informal relationships between fisheries department officials and local leaders to become more formalized.

Vulnerable Groups

In this section the effort is to identify the fishing communities that are relatively vulnerable in terms of assets, per capita monthly food expenditure, number of people gainfully employed, cultivable land and household literacy level using a relative achievement index.[9] Each household is ranked according to its index value and the bottom quartile is taken as comprising deprived fishermen as far as living conditions are concerned. The household-count in the bottom two deciles of the distribution of the relative achievement index has been taken as the threshold level and defined as the most vulnerable group. The survey showed that 37.41 per cent of the total sample households fall in this group. The incidence of livelihood vulnerability is quite high among the Machhiyara and Ghediya Koli communities. The index shows that 51.14 and 49.18 per cent of the Machhiyara and Ghediya Koli communities are in the bottom two deciles of the indices.

Machhiyaras are the largest Muslim fishing caste, originally being river fishermen who migrated from Sindh and Kachchh perhaps 200 to 300 years ago. They are the only group who are unambiguously identified as a fishing community. Their language remains Kachchhi, reflecting their ancestral migrations. Machhiyaras are settled in the belt from Chhara to Shil and only employ OBM vessels. In order to supplement their livelihood Machhiyara communities also practise beach-based fishing, as do the Kolis, the Kharvas, and other fishing communities. Beach-based fishing is most common among the Machhiyaras, which is not surprising given their historical association with small-scale river and estuarine fishing. It is reasonable to suppose that Machhiyaras may have been the main source of knowledge of how to engage in beach-based fishing. However, given the frequency of the study team's encounters with the Kolis, it seems reasonable to suppose that there may also be a very deep history of beach-based fishing by Kolis as a livelihood supplement (Johnson and Sathyapalan 2006).

Among the numerous coastal communities that make a living from agricultural labour, only the Ghediya Kolis have a significant role in fishing, perhaps because they have a relatively inferior economic position on the coast. Livelihood integration between farming and fishing is only significant for the Ghediya Kolis, and for some Scheduled Caste members. The Ghediya Kolis of the Navabandar and Rajpara area are the only group in the district who own fishing assets and agricultural land. This reflects their relatively recent entry into fishing as an alternative to farming and their connection with their much larger group of caste fellows who are farmers. Ghediya Kolis also work as crew in both the gill-net and trawler fleets that become an important source of income for these lower castes along the coast. The female members of the Ghediya Koli community play an important role in retail fish marketing.

The third deciles from the bottom of the distribution of the relative achievement index have been taken as the threshold level of people who are moderately vulnerable. This group includes 38.07 per cent of the total fishing households (Table 8.5). Machhiyaras, Ghoghliya Kharvas, and Koli Kharvas are prominent in this category. Kharva is the dominant fishing community in the Gujarat fishery and has a

TABLE 8.5: RELATIVE POSITION OF FISHING COMMUNITIES OF GUJARAT COAST IN TERMS OF VULNERABILITY

Fishing Communities	Most Vulnerable	Moderate Vulnerable	Not Vulnerable	Total
Ghoghliya Kharva	34 (29.57)	52 (45.22)	29 (25.22)	115 (100)
Koli Kharva	66 (30.69)	88 (40.93)	61 (28.37)	215 (100)
Machhiyara	45 (51.14)	37 (42.05)	6 (6.82)	88 (100)
Koli	24 (35.82)	26 (38.81)	17 (25.37)	67 (100)
Kharva	106 (32.42)	120 (36.70)	101 (30.89)	327 (100)
Ghediya Koli	120 (49.18)	79 (32.38)	45 (18.44)	244 (100)
Total	395 (37.41)	402 (38.07)	259 (24.53)	1,056 (100)

Source: Primary survey data.
Note: Figures in parentheses are percentages to raw total.

population uniformly distributed across the three-achievements classification. It is also important to mention that they are the largest group in terms of absolute numbers. The households in the bottom strata of the index pursue different coping mechanisms at the individual and household levels in order to sustain their livelihoods. The following section narrates some of these measures.

Prevailing Coping Strategies

The different coping strategies of traditional fishing communities with fluctuations of income such as informal insurance against hunger through reciprocal credit have already been discussed. These strategies indicate that livelihood security can be achieved when vulnerability is reduced or eliminated through social means. The social means or 'public action' includes measures at state, community and household levels. In the context of social security, these measures are also viewed as promotional and protective measures (Drèze and Sen 1991: 13), the former being concerned with the short-term task of preventing a decline in standards of living and the latter with enhancing the long-term general living standards by raising the basic capability of a person or population. In Gujarat minimal formal livelihood security measures exist beyond the basic public service provisions in education and health. State assistance to the fishery sector is largely confined to development assistance which includes assistance for technological improvements in both the capture and the processing sectors.

As observed earlier, livelihood integration between agriculture and fishery is significant only in the case of the Ghediya Koli communities. As far as safety at sea is concerned, some wealthy fishermen purchase formal accident insurance, accounting for 6 per cent of the total number of households. People who have not opted for vessel insurance attributed the main reason for not doing so to high premiums and complicated procedures. But 21 per cent say they would like to take insurance against the various risks involved in fishing. As far as informal insurance mechanisms are concerned, one way of spreading risk is fishersmen's willingness to share their knowledge about the fishing grounds likely to produce better catches with friends and relatives. In a multiple-response question related to their willingness to share the knowledge about the fishing ground, it was found that 46 per cent of the responses were valid. Out of the total valid responses, 35.7 per cent said they share knowledge with family members, friends and members belonging to the same community. Reciprocal credit during contingency situations is also common among them. This may happen between households, as when members of extended families provide small amounts of money or goods to help their kin in moments of need. When individuals fall ill, for example, extended family members and friends may contribute for medical expenses. Another important self-insurance mechanism is the diversification of livelihood options or migration. But very few fishermen opted for these strategies which account for only 2.7 per cent of the sample data.

Conclusion

Fisheries development in the Gujarat fishery has been a process of commercialization and outward-oriented growth. The quantum of fish traded outside the state as a proportion of the catch has increased considerably. In this context, the present study identified three risks which have direct bearing on the livelihood security of small-scale fisherfolk. These include resource depletion associated with the diffusion of modern fishing technology; credit-market imperfections and scope for underpricing fish at the beach level; and institutional failure to protect fishermen's rights to equitable access and allocation of fishery resources. The new income generated from exports has been important in meeting the cost of technological change and mechanization. In Kerala a similar trend of technological intensification contributed to a decline in levels of caring and sharing, which had once characterized the low level economic equilibrium of marine fisheries. High mechanization and increase in the number of fishermen have affected the physical productivity of workers per unit of capital invested (Kurien and Paul 2001).

In Gujarat, the historical pattern of growth-oriented development has exacerbated a relatively open-access situation with ill-specified property rights in the trawler and gill-net fishing zone. Caring and sharing co-exist with intense competition for marine resources. In such a situation, technological externalities and market imperfections have reinforced insecure livelihood options for vulnerable sectors within the fishery. At present the greatest impact has been felt by poorly capitalized trawler boats, but given that many fishing communities are poorly endowed in terms of productive assets, basic household amenities and education, non-mechanized and poorer OBM fishers, particularly among the Machhiyara and Ghediya Koli castes, could also become vulnerable in the near future. In addition to this, we observed that seasonality, lack of adequate education, low literacy and inadequate health provision hampers their ability to diversify livelihoods. Further, the study noted that laboures are exposed to risks like accidents and hardships due to working conditions and long days away from shore. Protective measures against accident risk are scanty in the Gujarat fishery. Therefore, it is important to mention that organized and controlled product and labour markets, and protection to workers on the beach and at sea merit considerable attention in providing livelihood security to fishers.

Formal transfer mechanisms at the state level to support fishers' social security are virtually absent in the Gujarat fishery. Ideally, considerably more attention needs to be paid to habitat and housing, sanitation and health, literacy and education and finally safety at sea. It is also important for the state to work with traditional fishers' organization like the *samaj* when attempting to tackle livelihood insecurity. Since most fishers depend on marine resources for their livelihood, their livelihood security lies in strengthening the present institutional base for resource allocation and conservation, protecting product and factor markets from imperfections, seeking new areas for work opportunities, and infrastructure support. This is a tall agenda for the future, but without significant efforts to meet it by a coalition of state and non-state groups, livelihood security for fishers in Gujarat will only weaken.

NOTES

1. Authors' estimate using time-series data published by the Government of Gujarat from 1972 to 2004–5. The semi-logarithmic growth rates are at a 1 per cent level of significance.
2. Gujarat reports the lowest per capita consumption of fish both in rural and in urban areas (0.02 kg and 0.04 kg respectively) while it is 1.35 kg in rural and 1.62 kg in urban Kerala. The number of households per thousand reporting fish consumption is 79 for rural and 98 for urban Gujarat while it is 857 and 828 in rural and urban Kerala respectively.

3. Percentages are estimated from secondary data published by the Department of Animal Husbandry and Dairying, Ministry of Agriculture, Government of India (GOI 2003).
4. Throughout this chapter, any reference to Junagadh district includes the Union Territory of Diu, unless specifically noted otherwise.
5. Authors' estimate.
6. These terms refer to construction quality. *Kachcha* refers to temporary structures made of bamboo frames and jute cloth; semi-*pukka* are low quality permanent structures; and *pukka* are high quality permanent structures.
7. The percentages do not add up to 100 since multiple responses are possible.
8. The exception to this general statement is the bag-net fishing zone of eastern Junagadh district. As bag-net fishing is a fixed gear where certain fishing spots are particularly advantageous, bag-net fishermen have worked out strong institutions for the allocation of fishing spots. This is certainly an effective example of access management but it is not designed for resource conservation. Bag-net fisher institutions, for example, have not been able to constrain the growth in numbers of bag-net fishing boats in recent years despite evidence that the increase in numbers is leading to more conflict with other sectors and damaging the resource base.
9. The relative achievement index is summation of the 'Z-scores' of each of the above-said indicators. The Z-score computation is a common technique used to standardize data on one variable to combine them with data on another variable when the two variables have different units of measurement and different scales. The Z-score is defined by the following formula: Z-score = (x - m)/s, where 'x' is the individual household's value of an indicator, 'm' is the indicator average for the household, and 's' is the standard deviation of the indicator for the households. The sum of a household's Z-scores for the seven indicators (weighted equally) is that household's achievement index.

REFERENCES

Alexander, P. (1977), 'Sea Tenure in Southern Sri Lanka', *Ethnology*, 16: 3.

Allison, E and F. Ellis (2001), 'The Livelihoods Approach and Management of Small-scale Fisheries', *Marine Policy*, 25: 377–88.

Amarasinghe, Oscar (2005), *Modernisation and Change in Marine Small Scale Fisheries of Southern Sri Lanka*, Kamburupitiya, Sri Lanka: Navamaga Printers.

——— (2006), 'Cooperation in a Context of Crisis: Public Private Management of Coastal Fisheries in Sri Lanka', *Indo-Dutch Program for Alternatives in Development Working Paper Series 2005–6*: www.idpad.org. IDPAD: The Netherlands.

Bavinck, M. et al. (2005), *Interactive Fisheries Governance: A Guide to Better Practice*, Delft: Eburon Publishers.

Bhathal, B. (2005), 'Historical Reconstruction of Indian Marine Fisheries Catches 1950–2000 as a Basis for Testing the Marine Tropic Index', Vancouver: Fisheries Centre, University of British Colombia, p. 122.

Burgess, Robin and Nicholas Stern (1991), 'Social Security in Developing Countries', in *Social Security in Developing Countries*, ed. Jean Drèze et al., New York: Oxford University Press.

Chambers, R. (1989), 'Vulnerability, Coping and Policy', *IDS Bulletin*, 20(2): 1–7.

Chambers, R., R. Longhurst and A. Pacey (eds.) (1981), *Seasonal Dimesions to Rural Poverty*, London: Frances Printer.

Devereux (2001), 'Livelihood Insecurity and Social Protection: A Re-emerging Issue in Rural Development', *Development Policy Review*, 19(4): 507–19.

Drèze, Jean and Amartya Sen (1991), 'Public Action for Social Security: Foundations and Strategy', in *Social Security in Developing Countries*, ed., Jean Drèze et al., New York: Oxford University Press.

FAO (2006), 'State of the World Fisheries and Aquaculture 2006', FAO: Rome.

Government of Gujarat (2004), 'Gujarat Fisheries Statistics', Department of Fisheries, Government of Gujarat: Gujarat.

——— (2006), 'Gujarat Fisheries Statistics', Department of Fisheries, Government of Gujarat: Gujarat.

Government of India (2003), 'Statistical Abstracts' Department of Animal Husbandry and Dairying, Ministry of Agriculture, Government of India (www.indiastat.com)

Johnson, Derek (2001), 'Wealth and Waste', *Economic and Political Weekly*, 31 March.

——— (2002), 'Emptying the Sea of Wealth: Globalisation and the Gujarat Fishery 1950 to 1999', Department of Sociology and Anthropology: PhD thesis, University of Guelph, Canada.

——— (2003), 'The Persistence and Transformation of Merchant-client Relations in the Rapidly Globalising Marine Fishery of Gujarat State', Canadian Sociology and Anthropology Association Congress: Halifax, 1 June.

——— (2007), 'The Conservation Imperative and Caste and Religions Belonging in Indian Fisheries', Workshop on 'Caring for the Environment: The Role of Religion and Identity in South Asia': International Institute of Asian Studies, Leiden, 22 June.

Johnson, Derek and Jyothis Sathyapalan (2006), 'Legal Pluralism in the Marine Fishery of Junagadh District and the Union Territory of Diu'. *Indo-Dutch Program for Alternatives in Development*, Working Paper Series 2005–6: www.idpad.org, 80 pages. The Netherlands: IDPAD.

Kizhakudan, J.K. and S.J. Kizhakudan (2005), 'Role of Fishermen in Conservation and Management of Marine Fishery Resources in Gujarat, India—Some Case Studies', *People and Sea III: New Directions in Coastal and Maritime Studies*. Amsterdam: Centre for Maritime Research, 7–9 July.

Kraan, M. (2006), 'One Man no Chop: Brach Seine Fishing in Ghana (West Africa)', *Maritime Studies (MAST)*, 5(1): 117–27.

Kurien, John (1998), 'Small Scale Fisheries in the Context of Globalisation', Working Paper No. 289, Thiruvananthapuram: Centre for Development Studies.

——— (2000), 'Factoring Social and Cultural Dimensions into Food and Livelihood Security Issues of Marine Fisheries: A Case Study of Kerala State India', Working Paper No. 299, Thiruvananthapuram: Centre for Development Studies.

Kurien, John and Antonyto Paul (2001), 'Social Security Nets for Marine Fisheries', Working Paper No. 318, Thiruvananthapuram: Centre for Development Studies.

Moser, C. (1998), 'The Asset Vulnerability Framework: Reassessing Urban Poverty Reduction Strategies', World Development 26(1), pp. 1–19.

Mathew, S. (2000), 'Gujarat Fisheries: Time to move from Exploitative to Conservation and Management Regime', Workshop on Current Situation in Fisheries Sector in Gujarat. Ahmedabad: Gujarat Institute of Development Research, p. 22.

Nayak, N.D. Nandakumar and A.J. Vijayan (2006), 'Coastal Population Dynamics and Ecosystem Changes, How Market, Technology and Institutions Affect this Process Along the West Coast of India', Thiruvananthapuram: Protsahan, p. 298.

Platteau, Jean-Philippe (1991), 'Traditional System of Social Security and Hunger Insurance: Past Achievements and Modern Challenges', in *Social Security in Developing Countries*, ed. Jean Drèze et al., New York: Oxford University Press.

Platteau, Jean-Philippe and A. Abraham (1987), 'An Enquiry into Quasi Credit Contract: The Role of Reciprocal Credit and Interlinked Deals in Small Scale Fishing Communities', *Journal of Development Studies*, 23(4).

Revallion, M. (1998), 'Poverty Lines in Theory and Practice: Living Standards Measurement Study', Working Paper 133, Washington DC: World Bank.

Sen, Amartya (1981), *Poverty and Famines*. Oxford: Clarendon Press.

Srinivasan, Jeena T. (2005), 'State Regulation Versus Co-management: Evidence from the Cochin Estuarine Fisheries in India', *Environment and Development Economics*, 10(1): 97–117.

——— (2006), 'The Differential Impact of User Heterogeneity in Resource Management: A Case Study from India', *Ecological Economics* 59(4): 511–18.

UNDP (2000), 'Conservation and Sustainable use of Gulf of Mannar Biosphere Reserve's Coastal Biodiversity', *Project Document*, www. gefweb.org/documents/.../indiamannar.pdf.

THEME 5

GENDER AND GENERATION AS DIVISIONS IN INDIA'S DEVELOPMENT

CHAPTER 9

Gender, Poverty and Transfer of Water Management: Case Study of the Tank Rehabilitation Project Pondicherry

LOES SCHENK-SANDBERGEN

1. Introduction: Managing-Irrigation-Together?

Liberalization and privatization policies and 'state *versus* market' ideologies are very much reflected in the policies and strategies of irrigation development projects. There is an almost universal effort in India and in the world to 'hand over' or 'to transfer' water management—operation and maintenance of irrigation schemes—from the state to the 'community' (Sengupta 1991; Maloney and Raju 1994; Gulati, Meinzen-Dick and Raju 2005; Shivakoti et al. 2005). The privatization of state irrigation systems has become a widespread global trend since the mid-1980s, which is not restricted to irrigation but applies also to other 'common property' sectors, as, for example, joint forest management (Viegas and Menon 1993; Sarin 1998, Schenk-Sandbergen 1986) and wasteland development (Singh and Burra 1993). The devolution of control over resources from the state to the 'community' was dovetailed with the renewed emphasis on panchayati raj as an alternative to the monopoly of the nation state, which has got a definite space in the Constitution since the early 1990s.

These reforms in institutions and organizations reflect policy trends witnessed globally as the withdrawal of the state, building of civil society organizations, democratic decentralization, privatization, participatory user management of resources, emphasis on efficiency, transparency, accountability, etc. (Gupta and Srivastava 1999; Meinzen-Dick and Zwarteveen 1998; Gulati et al. 2005; Shivakoti et al. 2005).

Farmers' direct involvement in irrigation under the label of Participatory Irrigation Management (PIM) is the most common type of reform in the Indian irrigation sector (Gulati et al. 2005). 'Managing irrigation together' became a powerful message in common property irrigation interventions (Maloney and Raju 1994; Sengupta 1991). PIM and all resulting reforms were prompted by what later Mollinga (2000) terms the 'threefold crisis': financial crisis, technical crisis and public image crisis of the irrigation sector under public management. 'Community participation' became the rediscovered magic solution to support, with a prominent role of NGOs and Participatory Rural Assessment (PRA) methodologies, the formation of Water Users' Associations (WUA) and the 'privatization' of common goods.

Concomitant with these trends, gender development policies formulated by donors worldwide, in line with Gender and Development (GAD) strategies, focus on 'mainstreaming' women in the core activities of development projects (Kelkar 2005; Rao and Kelleher 2005). 'Gender mainstreaming' has become the global gender rhetoric with the theoretical goal to achieve gender equality.[1] What are the results of 'mainstreaming' women, in particular poor rural women, in the new 'managing-irrigation-together' type of irrigation organizations and projects? Much can be said on what 'mainstreaming' entails in the practice of PIM irrigation projects (Schenk-Sandbergen 2002), but to keep it short, experience has shown that that the favourite gender mainstreaming policy and approach adopted by the majority of donor agencies and governments is not working. Improvements in livelihood security and empowerment of women, in particular of landless Dalit women, do not fit in the 'men-streaming' fixed and rigid log-frames (activity charts) of 'managing-irrigation-together' projects. A legitimate programme process approach to include reduction of poverty and gender equality is, in practice, ruled out. 'Women-streaming', which can open a wide potential of promising dimensions for a successful and sustainable project, is ignored. A policy commitment of gender 'mainstreaming' by gender advocate donor in embassies and ministries in the formulation of PIM land-and-water projects is not enough to ensure the participation and empowerment of poor and landless women. In practice 'mainstreaming' burns often down to bare 'men-streaming'.

Therefore it is no surprise that it is widely documented that women's participation in WUAs all over the world is very low, despite the high involvement of women in irrigated agriculture and agricultural decision-making (Meinzen-Dick and Zwarteveen 1998, 2001; Zwarteveen 2006; Schenk-Sandbergen and Choudhury 2003). An overview in Meinzen-Dick and Zwarteveen (2001: 73) shows that it is 0 per cent in Nepal and Pakistan, 6 per cent in India and 15 per cent in Sri Lanka. WUAs have much less official and legal gender backing than the panchayati raj where state intervention has ensured women's formal political entitlement by the reservation of seats (one-third with the existing reservation provision for SCs/STs) (Anandhi 2002).

Since 1987 I have participated in three large irrigation projects in India, a small-scale irrigation project in West-Bengal Terai (1987–94), a canal irrigation project in Karnataka (1995–8) and the Tank Rehabilitation Project in Pondicherry (1999–2004), in which I worked as a gender specialist. IDPAD gave me the opportunity to write a book on the Terai project (Schenk-Sandbergen and Choudhury 2003) and papers on the other two projects (Schenk-Sandbergen 2002, 2004). In view of the main theme of the IDPAD seminar, 'India's Split Development: Reflections on Development Theory and Practice', I decided to present a case study of the Tank Rehabilitation Project Pondicherry (TRPP) as it illustrates very well the negative impact on the gender and poverty of a 'managing-irrigation-together' project aiming to transfer the management of water resources from the 'state' to the 'community'. Despite all the initial sincere and intense community participation work, pro-poor and pro-women alternative strategies by NGOs and Community Organizers (CO), in the end the large farmers dominate the WUAs and are the winners. They have double benefits while the poor and landless Dalit women gained hardly anything, or even worse, were robbed of their small share in the public 'common good' which provided some livelihood security before the project was initiated.

The composition of this chapter is as follows. Section 2 gives a brief overview of irrigation research, relevant for my main focus on management transfer, tanks, gender and poverty. The history, background, institutional set-up and objectives of the TRPP are given in Section 3. In Section 4 the stark reality of the 'approaching tragedy of the commons', as foreseen by Vandana Shiva (1988), is discussed. The tank project had already very serious negative consequences for the poor and landless women, even before any bulldozer could start the rehabilitation work. The social context is described in Section 5. In Section 6 the set-up and rise of the community participation process is the central theme. The negative impact of the tank rehabilitation by evicting poor encroachers and not creating employment opportunities for the poor and landless women is presented in Section 7. Section 8 shows the gender dimensions of the membership and representation of women in the Tank Associations (TA) and in particular in the Executive Committees (EC). Efforts for alternatives in development in an additional 'gender and equity' programme, which was added after the mid-term review, and the collapse of the community participation and the gender programme are briefly sketched in Section 9, which is followed by some concluding remarks in Section 10.

2. Theory and Concepts: 'Irrigation Truly is a Man's World'

To position gender in irrigation studies I want to refer to the recent impressive PhD thesis of Margreet Zwarteveen, 'Wedlock or Deadlock? Feminists' Attempts to Engage Irrigation Engineers' (2006). Her research is a milestone in dedicated and concerned irrigation feminist research. She states

> Irrigation truly is a men's world. Rights to water and irrigated land are mostly vested in men, and decision-making about irrigation is likewise dominated by men. Ways of speaking and thinking about irrigation can also be characterized as masculine in that they render the work and activities of women invisible, and denote the analysis of social and gender relations as irrelevant. The irrigation professional is also masculine: most irrigation professionals are men, and professionalism is associated with masculinity. (291)

The extent of participation—by men or women—in community organizations for resource management depends, according to Meinzen-Dick and Zwarteveen (2001: 73), on two factors: rules for membership, which determine eligibility to participate, and the balance of costs and benefits derived from involvement, which influence individuals' decisions to participate.

NO LAND AND WATER RIGHTS FOR WOMEN

Rules for membership in WUGs are problematic as patriarchy and male dominance are well-known causes for the absence of land and water rights for women. The concept of 'water user' as the 'one who owns the land' is deeply ingrained in Indian culture. There is no concept of 'water user' as the 'one who does the work' and is actually the user of the water. Women, in particular landless women, who do the transplanting, weeding and harvesting work are not perceived as 'water users' and therefore not perceived as eligible for membership in WUAs.

The law and practice is that the holder of the land, who therefore is considered as the 'water user', legally controls the water rights. Men inherit land, and if land is acquired by buying, 'the head of the household', the male, automatically becomes the owner of the land. Formal land titles are adjudicated in his name. Although in theory women have legal rights to inherit and own land, the reality is different (Sharma 1980; Agarwal 1994; Rao 2005; Rahman and Van Schendel 1997). The existing patrilocal post-marriage residence pattern cuts women off from house, land and water rights. But, imported Western gender ideologies and perceptions on irrigation as a male domain are also very decisive. Even in matrilocal Laos where the majority of women inherit the house and land, it was oberved that mainly men were members of the newly formed Water Users' Organizations (Schenk-Sandbergen and Choulamany-Kamphoui 1995b; Schenk-Sandbergen 1998). It was, however, the women and girls who provided the financial means for the strengthening of the irrigation schemes and maintenance by weaving till late into the night beautiful skirts which were sold in the market. In the traditional water management groups in Laos the participation of women was equal with men. The new public domain, created by donor-driven institutional reforms in water management transfer, has decreased the formal participation and decision-making role of Lao women in irrigation, although their informal role to influence the decision-making process was substantial (ibid., 1995b: 85).

The cost-benefit factor of participation in water management organizations is different for women compared to men. Women are much more under time pressure because of their heavy, time-consuming household tasks and economic workload. Meetings are often convened at times and places which are impossible for women to attend without loss of status, food and income. Moreover, poor women are socialized to not sit with or speak in front of men and if they do speak, their needs are not listened to. The dynamics and changes in perceptions of cost-benefits to women in various project phases of the TRPP will be outlined in this chapter.

CLASS AND GENDER DIFFERENCES IN 'COMMUNITIES'

The role of 'communities' in natural resource management is a popular concept which, according to an FAO research, is used in more than fifty countries to protect forests in a better way (Agrawal and Gibson 2001: 1). The conviction that 'communities' are better managers of tanks than the state bureaucracies or the Public Works Departments is strong. According to Shah (2003), these perceptions are not based on careful inquiry about the internal power dynamics in the community resulting in inequitable distribution of the resource. It is reported that despite the fact that tank WUAs are promoted as non-political institutions, 'elite capture' and political involvement dominate their functioning (Reddy and Reddy 2005).

The poor and women are often excluded from the 'community', or as 'stakeholders', in the process of transfer of management of water and land resources. There are only a few very interesting documented cases linking poverty and gender with water management reforms, and of higher women's involvement in WUAs and *Pani Panchayats*, but they originate mainly from women's-only organizations (Koppen and Mahmud 1995; Koppen, 1998; SEWA 1997; Schenk-Sandbergen 1995). Reema Nanavaty (2000) rightly emphasizes that the priority should not be to rehabilitate the water resource but the 'need to protect and restore the lives and work of women as water users, managers and owners. If we do this, water as a resource will be protected and restored.'

Gender differentiated access and control of resources analyses are widely used in Gender Assessment Studies, aiming to support empowerment policies and strategies (Rao et al. 1991; Young 1994; Moser 1989). In the participatory Tungabhadra canal irrigation project a Gender Assessment Study was conducted as part of the 'mainstreaming' policy, but the expressed gender needs and interests of the women, even related to the water management and maintenance of the irrigation canals, were ignored as they did not fit into the 'men-streaming' blueprint (Schenk-Sandbergen 2002). Landless women living in camps for twenty years, doing the major share of the agricultural work in irrigation were forgotten in the formulation, design and planning. They were not perceived as 'community' members or stakeholders in the to be revived *warabandis* or WUAs to manage the water. Gender blindness and lack of social awareness are the main reasons why no pro-poor and pro-gender dimensions are part of 'managing-irrigation-together' designs. The 'community' means, in male irrigation thinking, broadly, the landowning male farmers having land in the command area. As pointed out in many studies, 'communities' are not romantic homogeneous groups with common interests and objectives of both women and men (Guijt and Shah 1999).

The detailed social caste/class and gender context is generally hardly known in irrigation reform projects and a thorough analysis on 'who are the stakeholders in the community' to manage the water is rarely made in the formulation phase. Therefore, the rhetoric on equity in distribution of water and benefits is very narrow and relates mostly to the large and small male farmers owning land in the command areas of the irrigation project.

BAD TUBE WELLS, GOOD TANKS?

The interesting study by Anjal Prakash (2005: 15) points to the fact that irrigation ethnography has a long tradition in canal irrigation systems, and these studies were influential in showing irrigation as a politically critical resource in societies characterized by inequitable distribution of power and resources. Prakash states that apart from recent studies, the above assessment has been missing in most of the analyses related to groundwater irrigation. Groundwater extraction by drilling deep tube wells has been widely discussed without much sociological inquiry on the process of groundwater development focusing on the question of who gains and who loses in the course of these developments. According to Prakash, the nature of the relationships between agrarian structure and technological change in the context of agrarian transformation hardly gets precedence in studies. The conclusion of his detailed study shows the 'normal' trend. The unchecked exploitation of groundwater benefited the small minority of upper class farmers (ibid.: 225). As accessibility reduced and the market shrank because of the depletion of groundwater, the upper classes maintained their relative powerful social and economic positions and brought the working classes into a new dependency relationship as sharecroppers which was often worse than the traditional landlord-tenant relationship. The burden is borne by the poor sharecroppers as they subsidize the cost drilling the tube wells by being forced to pay for the water and the land by giving a considerable share of their production to the owner of the land and deep tube well. Moreover, Prakash shows that the women of this new dependent sharecroppers' class bear the burden of all the agricultural work (ibid : 5). He concludes that irrigation strategies and technologies should be devised, in view of the extreme water scarcity situation, to protect the interests of historically marginalized groups. He mentions the restoring of the numerous ponds and tanks in Gujarat that silted up over the years due to neglect as a long-term strategy for recharging shallow aquifers. It is interesting that he considers the rehabilitation of the traditional tank irrigation as a possible solution for the social and ecological problems identified in his study. Tanks are perceived as a 'traditional', 'alternative' and 'appropriate' technology (Shah 2003) to mitigate the social and ecological calamities faced as a result of canal irrigation and, worst of all, the devastating effects of individual deep bore well irrigation (Prakash 2005). Tank irrigation looks more social as a traditional rainwater harvesting technology, more harmless, but experience does not warrant such a hopeful view.

Tank irrigation seems an alternative option as presented in the impressive work of the late Anil Agarwal and Sunita Narain (1997). The authors wrote their book as the growing anti-dam movement in the country was demanding less socially and ecologically destructive systems of water development. They usully raised, the question of the possibility of reviving if these traditional systems on a large scale? The authors warned that the desire to revive them should not be born out of blank admiration for a golden past, stressing that there was an urgent need to analyse the potentials and pitfalls involved in their revival. Rehabilitation of tanks is not an easy task. Siltation and erosion of tank catchments by blind allocation of land are serious economic, technical and political problems. According to Agarwal and Narain, it seems that finally the winds of change have begun to blow. The government, at least on paper, has begun to recognize its responsibility towards traditional water harvesting systems.

In Tamil Nadu, Andhra Pradesh (Sharma 2003) and Karnataka in particular, policy reforms have been developed since the 1990s to rehabilitate tanks with the financial support of international donors (EC, World Bank), and hand them over to local communities as a common property resource. In 1990 Palanisami wrote a small study titled 'Tank Irrigation in South India', and asked, 'what next?' In 2000 he published a book with Easter titled *Tank Irrigation in the 21st Century: What Next?*. The conclusion is that studies have shown that investment in tank management will yield high rates of return, that farmers are capable, in fact eager to participate but are concerned about their legal status (2000: 182). On the 'what next?' question, the sociological analyses of winners and losers in the transfer of management of tanks in a class/caste and gender perspective is missing and should be taken up 'next'. In the following section a modest effort towards this end will be made.

3. History, background and Aims of the Tank Rehabilitation Project Pondicherry

HISTORY

The Pondy project started in 1999 and is still running although technical assistance was closed by the donor (European Commission) in July 2004.[2] The European Commission, the funding agency, has committed an amount of Rs. 28.13 crore for the project, while the Government of Pondicherry has promised to Rs. 4.40 crore. Rs. 2.20 crore will have to be paid by 'community stakeholders'.

Historically, a large part of the land in Pondicherry was irrigated by 84 tanks,[3] which fill up during the monsoon season. These tanks were the backbone of the agriculture of Pondy. Tank irrigation can be traced back two millennia in Tamil Nadu (Meinzen-Dick Suseela 1984: 12), and in Pondicherry stone inscriptions on the walls of the Bahur temple reveal the use of the system since AD 1000. Both construction and renovation of irrigation works were considered to be religiously meritorious acts by the kings and chieftains (ibid.). Gifts of tanks and tank repairs served to legitimize their power position. Remarkably, the daily management and supervision of the tank was under local village control. Village assemblies had special tank committees which were selected annually. Interest term endowments of gold and land, and contributions from all beneficiaries were used to pay for desilting and repairs. The tank committees enforced irrigation rules and arbitrated disputes over water use (ibid.: 13). The French, who ruled Pondicherry for a long time, continued the irrigation management system called the 'Syndicat Agricole'. The former president of the 'Caisse commune' has documents which show that the system was discontinued approximately around 1963, when the Public Works Department (PWD) was authorized to take over the full management of the operation and maintenance of the tanks.

DEEP TUBE WELLS AND NEGLECT OF TANK INFRASTRUCTURE

Presently, only one-third of the 84 tanks are more or less in use, while most of the others are not used for irrigation purposes at all. No traditional water management organizations exist anymore. The main reason for the disuse of tanks is the sinking of innumerable private tube wells (around 7,000) serving both for irrigation of 95 per cent of the 6,600 ha as well as for industrial use. Following the 'Green Revolution', the Government of India heavily promoted the drilling and establishment of bore wells with subsidies for wells and low electricity charges.[4] As a result the use and maintenance of the tank infrastructures declined. The tanks fell into heavy disrepair as a result of weed infestation in the water-spread area, and heavy siltation in the tank bed and supply channels. What is more important is that encroachments cover an average of 20 to 60 per cent of the tank beds, not to mention the encroachments in the *ayacut* (command area) itself. Rich farmers in Vadhanur even drilled deep tube wells in the tanks. Leaking sluice outlets and missing shutters, partly demolished surplus weirs and illegal diversion of water out of the catchment area are the symbols of neglect and non-maintenance.

Because of deep tube well pumping, the level of fresh groundwater has declined to 18 m in 22 years in the north-western part and to 8 m in the south-western part (Technical Proposal 1997: 1). Although there is a law in Pondicherry that no new tube wells can be drilled within 6 km of the coast to avoid seawater intrusion, it is often violated. Seawater intrusion is widely reported in coastal villages, which besides the pumping out of groundwater by bore wells, is also due to overdrawing of water by the new industries that have come up along the coastline since 1985, resulting in non-availability of drinking water and decreasing rice yields.

PROJECT OBJECTIVES AND INSTITUTIONAL SET-UP

In order to counteract the above-mentioned problems the main objective of the project is

> To preserve agricultural incomes from irrigated crop production in Pondicherry by diminishing reliance on increasingly saline underground water resources and promoting a balance in fresh groundwater resources.
> (Technical Proposal 1997: 2)

The strategy of the project is that the rehabilitation of the tanks will be carried out together with the local 'community', and the irrigation tanks and this assets will be handed over to TAs—new water users' institutions formed by the project—which will operate and maintain these tanks after rehabilitation. In order to ensure that the TAs are able and willing to operate and maintain the tanks, they will have to be carefully selected after which they will be involved in the planning and implementation of the rehabilitation works. After the TAs have been formed, the PWD engineers will plan and design the technical works with the participation of the 'community' through the TAs. The TA will be free to select a contractor to implement the work under the supervision of working committees formed by the TA. To make the future operation and maintenance of the tank system financially sustainable, the TA will have to develop and manage tank resources (tree planting and fish rearing) and thus generate their own funds. The message for the farmers is: 'stop using deep tube well water during one season to restore groundwater'.

Although it is a development-cooperation project, no specific regulations are made in Brussel, or activities planned in its formulation to ensure benefits for the poor, in particular landless women. It is assumed that these groups will get, in one way or another, 'indirect' benefits from its implementation. It is, for instance, supposed that landless agricultural labourers will see no decrease in labour opportunities in future as rice yields will not come down because of the use of good tank irrigation water. The perspective of the formulators of the project focuses as usual on the 'irrigation-agricultural-ecological' model.

In the formulation report of the project it is mentioned that, 'as in all European Commission projects, a strong gender component is proposed', and that female COs should be appointed to do the normal community participation work, who then 'will increasingly devote their time to formation of women's groups within the WUAs and Tank Committees, focusing on women's use of water for productive purposes'.

The chief engineer of the PWD who is responsible for implementing the project will ensure the above process.[5] To manage the project a Project Management Unit (PMU) was formed, headed by the project director (Chief/Superintending Engineer, PWD Circle II) advised and guided by the Dutch expatriate project co-ordinator, better known as the team leader, who was residing permanently in Pondicherry.[6]

4. The Approaching Tragedy of the Tank?

After spending some time in the Pondy region one easily learns to recognize the location of a tank. The land- and tank-scape shows an earthen dyke (*bund)* with rows of Palmyra palm trees planted on it. Flora and fauna are abundant around the tank. Many beautiful black and white, big orange, small yellow butterflies, dragonflies and other insects, and rice-birds and eagles can be identified in the area. Frogs and fish make glittering bubbles in the water. In Keelparikalpet tank the white and red water lilies in the very pure water offer a more splendid view than the paintings of Manet. People use the *bund* as a threshing ground. Palm and other trees are marked with blue numbers to show they are government property and auctioned to users. It is a beautiful landscape with a lot of green cover. Sheep can be seen sleeping in the shade of the trees. Black pigs roam in muddy places with stagnant water. There are ruins of old granite stones which were placed as a water meter. The old farmers know that when the water reaches the upper table stone, the tank is half filled, but that rarely has happened since twenty years.

Tanks are under state control, managed by the PWD. The tanks and the surrounding land are in the category of 'common property'. The importance of the tanks as 'common property' which has to be protected and looked after is often symbolized by the temples among the trees at the *bund* with their statues of big red horses and goddesses and god: Iyyannarappan and his two wives, Porkilai and Poorani (twins). They have to protect the tank. It is believed that in the night they ride on horses wielding big swords to protect the common property. The author Mosse writes:

> Tanks are not simply sources of physical inputs (irrigation water). They are also repositories of symbolic resources. Tanks, like village temples, are public institutions expressive of social relations, status, prestige and honour. They are part of the symbolic 'production of locality. (Mosse 1997: 472)

In the project the main focus of the engineers of the PWD is on the future use of the irrigation water in the tank by the farmers (*ayacutdars*) who have land in the command area of the tank (*ayacut*). However, my observations of the tank use, and a study of one of my students of three months (Vuuren 2002) showed that there are many more uses of the tank land and water as, for example, grazing of cows, goats and sheep by poor women, shepherds and children; rearing ducks (duck nomads[7]) and pigs; collection of grass (for fodder and thatching roofs) and firewood by poor women and girls; making mats and baskets from reeds and special species of trees; making pots from the tank soil; making bricks (brick kiln); catching fish; collecting of crabs and snails as food by poor women; catching of rats and snakes by rat hunters; wage labour by landless people working in the fields around the tank; cultivating encroached land; washing clothes (*dhobis*); collecting drinking water for cattle; using the area as an open toilet (by large majority of the population with segregated places for women and men); bathing; collecting medicinal herbs, fruits, Palmyra fruits; toddy tapping; collecting seeds from the Palmyra palms for own use. We learnt that for the poor the tank has strong personal and emotional connotations. Many poor people associate the tank with a 'mother' figure, who cares for them with love. The following field notes testify to this perception:

> One old man carries firewood he fetched from the tank on his head. He sells it for Rs. 5.00: his daily income. He states that 'the tank is like a mother, giving food and money'. He survives already 50 years [*sic*], just because of the tank. And with him the poor people of 18 other villages located around the tank. He also does sometimes [*sic*] wage labour in the tank (if they call him as he is old, thin and weak): weeding and harvesting paddy during two months a year. He is afraid for any change in the tank and its management as it might have a negative impact on his very vulnerable livelihood system.

The above list of uses shows that access and control over the tank area and the tank resources are crucial for the survival of many poor people, mostly landless Dalits living around the tank. Some old landless women, shepherds, and in particular children, spend their whole day in and around the tank to let their goats, cows and sheep graze and to collect grass and cooking fuel. The tank, has more meaning in their life and is more important for them than for the *ayacutdars* who are the favourite stakeholder group and to whom the operation and management of the tank land and water will be transferred. Of great concern is the social impact of the 'transfer-of-management' to the TAs as it might endanger the 'common property' as a survival base for the poor and landless women.

Jodha (1986) has documented the importance of 'common property' resources to the village poor in India. His research shows that the benefits of using the commons were greater for the village poor than the benefits from government programmes targeted for their welfare.

It is also in this perspective that the debate on the 'approaching tragedy of the commons' (Shiva 1988: 83) seems to be relevant for tank rehabilitation programmes. At the moment there is, so to speak a 'free' access for landless women in using and managing the resources of the tank as a common property. However, the 'free' access counts also for the rich and powerful who have encroached on the tank land, sometimes even paying a fee for the encroachment. Commune panchayats[8] try to prevent encroachments on the *bund* by individual persons by planting seedlings of palm trees on it. The brick kiln owner, needing soil from the tank, has a strong interest in keeping encroachers out of the tank. The PWD has tolerated this process for many years. The rich use the tank as a 'gold mine' and appropriate the resources; the poor encroachers use the tank as a 'social safety net', a last resort for their survival. A little imagination is necessary to predict what changes will take place because of the transfer of the management of the tanks to the 'gold miners'. Therefore the effort was to include also the poor and women in the TAs so that they could voice their views and defend their interests at the formal level.[9]

5. The Social Context: The Class/Caste, Gender Character of Tank Rehabilitation and Management

It is important to understand that the surface water in tanks and channels from rainfall and rivers, which is so important for the recharge of the groundwater, is a common resource. It is only after this water goes underground that it emerges as a private good (Meinzen-Dick and Suseela 1984: 69). This fact is crucial for the analysis of access and control over tank water. A common good like rainwater is privatized as soon as it becomes groundwater. It is appropriated by those who can afford the investment of deep bore wells to uplift the ground-water. In social terms it means that, when the objective of the Pondy Project—to increase the recharging capacity of the tank—is realized, the richest and most powerful landowning farmers having bore wells in the tank command area will be the main beneficiaries as they will get double benefits: they will have more groundwater for use in their own fields and they will also have more water to sell to poorer farmers.[10] This is a reality in the Pondy context, as the village communities are not at all a homogeneous group of farmers.

The caste/class situation is very visible in the villages around the tanks. The landowning class, often from the same caste, lives in the main streets in good houses; the landless Dalits live in clusters apart from the upper-class/caste wards, outside the village in colonies or *pets* in small houses and huts with thatched roofs. Even in Pondy which has a reputation of being modern, rich and advanced, the spatial caste/class segregation is broadly the same as in other parts of India.

CLASS CONTEXT IN VILLAGES AROUND TANKS

Generated data on landholding size in the project tank *ayacuts* of all the 84 tanks is shown in Table 9.1.

The polarized class context is also reflected in the findings of our household survey which I could process only in the early years of the project.[11] Community organizers interviewed 4,299 households around 16 tanks which had been taken up for rehabilitation in 2002. The data shows that the number of landless households is alarmingly high in the project area. With the exception of Mannadipet where the percentage is low because of urbanization (28 per cent), at least half, but up to 80 and even 91 per cent, of the villagers are landless. Seasonal migration to the sugar cane fields in Andhra Pradesh, mostly by men, to earn an additional income is common,[12] some have found employment in nearby industries but only a few have a permanent job. Alankuppam tank is an exception, as the majority of the villagers have found jobs in light industries in the Auroville Ashram enclave. In Keelkarikalpet found 78 per cent of the agricultural wage labourers are male. Fom focus group discussions it was clear that the same, or even higher, number of women are also agricultural labourers.

TABLE 9.1: LANDHOLDING SIZE IN PROJECT TANK *AYACUTS* (ha)

Holding size	Holdings in %	Area in %
< 1.0	60	22
1.0–2.0	24	26
> 2.0	16	52
Total	100	100

Source: *Mid-Term Review Mission Draft Report*, May 2002.

Many of these women expressed their desperate need for wage labour and credit facilities from the project.

The percentage of landowning farmers, who will be the main beneficiaries of the tank rehabilitation project, ranges from only 6 per cent to 31 per cent of the population in the villages. Landless groups in the village are dependent on the landowning classes, who are often also prominent political leaders, to get employment, loans and access to water and land.

The above context is the stage from which to start 'community participation' and the formation of TAs in which all stakeholders in the tank are supposed to have equal representation and to manage the tank water together. That there would be conflict, clashes, protests, violence, winners and losers could have been predicted from the beginning.

CASTE CONTEXT IN VILLAGES AROUND TANKS

Caste is an important indicator of land and deep tube well ownership. The main landowning castes in the project area are: Reddiars, Vanniyars or Gounders,[13] and to a certain extent Nadars. Table 9.2 shows that the higher, more powerful the caste the larger is the average landholding per farmer in each caste category in one tank.

In another tank village, where the majority of the villagers are landless and poor, the following caste/land ratio can be given. The majority of the population (68 per cent) in the village is of the SC

TABLE 9.2: AVERAGE LANDHOLDING PER FARMER IN EACH CASTE CATEGORY (KEEZHPARIKKALPET)

Caste	Number of Farmers	Land Extent in Acres	% Landholding by Caste	Average Landholding Per Farmer (Acres)
Vanniyar	31	54.9	51.9	1.77
Reddiar	5	30.5	28.9	6.10
Nadar	5	14.3	13.6	2.86
Scheduled Caste	6	5.9	5.6	1.00
All castes	47	105.6	100.0	2.25

Source: Raghunath, *NGO CERD Field Manual 2003*.

community. They own only about 1.2 per cent of the total land, whereas Vanniyars (19 per cent of the total households) own 34.7 per cent and the Reddiars (5 per cent of the total households) 59.4 per cent of the total land. The ownership of deep tube wells shows the same trend. In one tank the 8 Reddiar families own eight deep tube wells (50 per cent of the total), 30 Vanniyar families own 7 tube wells (44 per cent), 13 Nadar families own one tube well (6 per cent) and 109 SC families own none at all.

GENDER CONTEXT IN VILLAGES AROUND TANKS

Membership of WUAs is mostly restricted to farmers with a land title in the command area. Data of two pilot tanks shows that there are around 12.5 per cent women *patta* holders (mostly widows) who are considered as fully entitled to TA membership.

Reddiar women don't do agricultural work as it would lower the 'prestige' of the family. They feel that the 'men will look down on them' if they have to attend meetings of the TA with a large majority of other caste men. The Vanniyar women have small landholdings and do the weeding, harvesting and transplanting of rice on their own land. Usually they have to buy water from the Reddiars. Vanniyar women have a direct interest in becoming a members of the TA, as it would allow them to use tank water in one season. A few have become members of the EC and, as will be seen in Section 8, they have participated very well in the planning and implementation of the technical works. It was soon obvious that women leaders were scarce and the few identified were already involved in Self-Help Groups (SHG).[14]

Dalit women, in the main, are agricultural labourers in the project area.[15] They are dependent for labour opportunities on the landowning caste in and outside the *ayacut* and on farmers in nearby villages. Women interviewed said that they starve for around six months of the year, as there is no agricultural wage labour. The extremely low daily wage rate of Rs. 17[16] for Dalit women shows the need for employment against a fair wage for these women. As shown earlier, they used the tank almost daily for grazing goats, fetching firewood and as their open toilet. With the tank water and land in disuse they had full access to these tank resources. In discussions with them of the possible consequences of the tank rehabilitation, the argument that there might be more agricultural work with better irrigation in future did not appeal to them. They said that the landowners would bring migrant labourers from other places at are even lower rate. The women became very emotional when the plans for the tank rehabilitation were touched upon. The crucial point was that in several tanks many landless women (and men) had occupied small plots of land (30, 40, 50 cents . . . etc.) for many years to cultivate some rice for three to four months in the year. This allows them to save for the months when they have no work and face serious survival problems. The women 'encroachers' very worried about this negative impact of the tank rehabilitation. They were afraid that they would be evicted and lose access to their small plots of land in the tank area. Being landless, the access to some handkerchief size pieces of land was of extreme importance to them. It was a question of a food-safety-net, status, dignity and identity. They felt threatened that their small plot would be taken away when the earth moving work started in the tank. They were the allies of the rich farmers who had encroached or the tank and installed deep tube wells in the tank, as they sold water to the women and allowed them to cultivate rice in the tank. A new institution such as the TA would regulate the use of the tank, and they fear they would lose their 'customary right' to have a small plot of land to grow food.

What these women expressed was clearly the 'approaching tragedy of the commons': the fear that they would be evicted from the tank by bulldozers and police. And that is exactly what happened, although in many tanks the people vacated 'voluntarily'. In many focus group discussions in villages, poor women expressed that they would vacate the encroachments and cooperate enthusiastically with the project but as compensation they expect employment and income from the project in the implementation of the technical works. They want wage labour to feed their children. Secondly, they want fishponds and latrines. Thirdly they expect the project to support them in forming and giving seed money to self-help credit groups in order to develop some income-generating activity. Whether the project could provide any of these urgent requirement is discussed in the next section.

6. Community Participation: Including Women and the Poor

In view of the above social context the main concept of the community participation approach in the Pondy Project was that all stakeholder[17] groups in the villages around the tank should be mobilized and involved in the project, that all should become members of the TA with the intention that its members participate in the planning, design-making, implementation and development of tank resources, operation, and maintenance and management of the tanks. It was also envisaged that the TAs would act as a catalyst to initiate general development programmes in the villages. This process was successful in the beginning years of the project in almost all of the villages. In particular landless women groups (SHGs) came forward with the help of youth clubs which facilitated the process of membership recruitment, and joined the governing bodies of TAs with enthusiasm.

The first step in involving the poor and landless was to encourage both husband and wife of each household to become members of the global body of the TA and to pay the membership fee of a minimum Rs. 5. With gender-awareness training and division of labour games it was explained to the community organizers, engineers and villagers the important role women play in agriculture, and their use of and interest in the tank. Efforts were made to convince them that women also should become members of the TA and representatives in the EC as well as office-bearer.

In previous tank rehabilitation projects this 'all-stakeholder' approach was not followed.[18] Under British colonial rule in Tamil Nadu, the French in Pondicherry, and the tank improvement projects, the focus was exclusively on the mobilization and organization of the farmers holding land in the *ayacut* of the tank (Maloney and Raju 1994: 4, personal communication with resource persons). As the *ayacutdars* are supposed to be the only tank users, organization of this kind of a WUAs is not as complicated as the Pondy approach to mobilize and organize all the existing tank user groups in the villages around the tank. The latter approach requires much more time, knowledge, dedicated NGO staff, high quality and honest TA members and leaders with a feeling for social justice and women's issues. A key point of the 'all-stakeholder' approach in Pondy was that it challenged caste/class, landownership, political, religious and gender relations as it perserved to give a voice and rights to the poor and the landless women for whom the tank is often their only means of survival. It was hoped that representation would create a communication channel through which they could protest against activities of the project which might have a negative impact on their group. The next subsection will show how far this intention could be realized in view of ECs with an overwhelming majority of landowning representatives, and the PWD as implementing authority.

As the ECs could not be too large (11 to 20 members) for the study the categories of stakeholder groups had to be reduced, and as the rich, powerful farmers were the main contributors in the costs of the rehabilitation (approx. 15 per cent), operation and maintenance, the following proportional representation in the EC was decided: *ayacutdars* (60 per cent), non-*ayacutdar* farmers (10 per cent), other sections including the landless women (30 per cent). Women as a category should have a representation of at least three members in the ECs (*ayacut*, non-*ayacut* and landless category).

SMALL REVOLUTIONS

The formation of the TAs and ECs were small 'revolutions' in itself. The fact that during the formation of the ECs the various caste and class groups, women and men of all status groups could meet and sit, talk and discuss together in the otherwise highly polarized and politically faction-ridden villages of Pondy was a major achievement of the NGOs, and in particular of the community organizers.[19] This is unique and has never happened before, as the villagers are not familiar with the forming of a democratic body. In contradiction to other states in India, election of village panchayat was unknown in Pondy which makes it very difficult to create an acceptable leadership. This achievement should be valued all the more for the many hindrances that had to be overcome: political factions, hostility between villages, hierarchical behaviour, dominance of rich farmers, gender blindness, etc.

The data of 44 tanks in 2003 showed that of the members of the governing body, 58 per cent were men and 42 per cent women, which is a great achievement from a gender 'mainstreaming' point of view. The highest membership rates in the general bodies in 2003 were provided by the landless (40 per cent), followed by the *ayacutdars* (24 per cent), non-*ayacutdar* farmers (12 per cent) and other professional categories (24 per cent).[20]

In the villages small TA offices have been inaugurated and equipped to start the work. Moreover, in some TAs the president belongs to the small farmer without bore wells. However, it cannot be denied that the majority of the office-bearers of the TAs belong to the rich and landowning classes and castes and all are men, with the single exception of a woman office-bearer in Keezhur tank.

7. Negative Impact on Gender and Poverty

Let us now have a look at the project phases after the TAs were formed and the 'community planning' was over. It was in the implementation phase of the physical works, and when the tank resources should be developed, that poor women started to realize that they would be very negatively impacted by the project and their high expectations of employment and income would not be met. The three main outcomes of the project of that proved disastrous for them were:

1. Eviction of poor encroachers without any compensation.
2. Little manual labour could be generated for the landless, particularly for women doing physical work.
3. Little labour could be generated in tank resource development such as tree planting and fish farming.

Eviction of Poor Encroachers Without Compensation

To start rehabilitation work the mandate was to evict all encroachers in the water spread, *ayacuts*, on the *bunds* and in the feeder canals, in short, everywhere; and to prevent at all costs their return after the work was over. Encroachment was considered illegal and eviction was carried out with the help of bulldozers and the police, but, as said earlier, encroachers also left 'voluntarily'. Compensation did not exist as, according to the implementing authorities, it would mean rewarding people for illegal acts and would encourage future encroachment.

A clear integrated policy of the PMU and PWD to evict eneroachers did not exist. This created many problems for the NGOs and COs as they were forced to play the role of the police. From 'friends' of the people they became an 'enemy' of poor which had a detrimental effect on their community participation role to involve the poor in the 'managing-irrigation-together' concept.

The following case in one of the pilot tanks illustrates the problems faced by a few rich and many poor households after their eviction.

In Vadhanur tank there are a few very powerful farmers with *patta* land who have installed bore wells in the tank. They earn a fortune by selling irrigation water to 254 poor families who have encroached on small plots of land in the tank for planting rice home consumption. When the owners of the bore well came to know of the TRPP, they quickly established their own Water Users Society (7 members) to show their power. They did not want to cooperate, as the project is a threat to them, and they know that in order to rehabilitate the tank they will have to be evicted out of it. Many landless people depend on these bore well owners for water, and for wage labour in the tank. Therefore, the majority did not come for meetings and did not want to cooperate with the TRPP. After the eviction of the 254 poor encroachers and bore well owners, this last group convinced their 'clients' to take revenge. The sabotage and opposition by these bore well owners resulted in serious threat to, and assault on the CO, the burning of the sugar cane fields of one of the office-bearers of the TA, and a three-days looting spree of fish with sticks and bare hands by the poor landless men, women and children. The fish was raised by the TA as income generation for the operation and maintenance of the tank. During the implementation of the technical works, permanent police patrols were posted in and around the tank.

The total number of poor encroachers in the tanks is not known. In some villages evicted landless women were very angry and during our visits we were surrounded by large crowds of desperate poor women, begging for some employment in the project. Sixty poor women who had worked in a tank for thirty years were evicted. They lost 150 kg of rice (two bags) with a value of Rs. 1,000, which was a fortune for them.

Two widows, one with small children and whose husband had died recently while trying to rescue two children from the river, said that their paddy cultivation on a small plot of land in the tank was their only means of survival. It was felt that there should be something termed as a 'compassion' encroaching that would be tacitly allowed by the community in a case of a real family calamity. However, such policy, to mitigate the damage, was lacking in the project. In one tank there were thirteen poor encroachers. The authorities had given them the land years ago as a reward in the Family Planning Operation project. They were not even aware that their cultivation in the tank is illegal.

The rehabilitation of the tanks created immense survival problems for hundreds of poor households and created immense tension and unpopularity for the COs after the TAs were formed. Many poor where disadvantaged by the project. What happened to the promise that some income and employment would be provided at a later stage?

LITTLE EMPLOYMENT FOR POOR WOMEN DURING IMPLEMENTATION OF THE TECHNICAL WORK

Some of the work has to be done for tank rehabilitation, as water hyacinth (*Eichornia*) removal, bush clearance, desilting of supply channels, sluice and surplus weir repair and strengthening and sectioning of the dykes, can be done by manual labour. Meetings between the chief engineer and sub-divisional offices in all Circles, COs and with office-bearers of the TAs were organized to discuss the plans, ideas and scope for manual labour. However, very little labour was created for landless men and even less for women.

One of the main reasons was that cost estimates did not take into account the no scope to deploy deployment of wage labourers from landless families in the village but only for the use of machines. In fact machines were cheaper than manual work. It is a shortcomings in the project design is that no quotas are fixed by the donor for how much of the total amount of the costs of the tank rehabilitation is to be spent on providing manual labour to the members of poor landless households (men and women) in the villages of the tank. It should be made compulsory for engineers to make provision for deployment of manual labour in their cost estimates, which should be controlled by the TAs and Project Management Units (PMU).[21]

A futher complication is that the landowning communities in the village are against paying good wages to manual labourers fearing the rates for agricultural labour would go up. They would rather opt for the use of machines and this attitude is encouraged by the fact that the rates given to the TA are adequate only for machine operations. Though in some villages there was an inadequate labour force due to seasonal migration, in other villages, poor Dalit and Vanniyar women fought the right to desilt the village pond.

Nevertheless, there were exceptions depending on the social awareness of the office-bearers, the efforts of the NGOs to insist on manual labour, and the self-confidence of the landless women representatives in the ECs to demand and to defend their interests. For instance,

Mrs T., a landless EC woman member, insisted on manual work for *bund* strengthening. Eighty per cent of the households are landless in her village. Two hunred twenty men worked for nine days. Why only the men? The answer is that the work was too heavy for women as thorny bushes had to be removed. The NGO was very proud as the shape of the *bund* and quality of the work were much superior by manual work than with machines. The removal of water hyacinth was carried out by men and women in one tank and was an enormous success. The planting of trees was also mainly done by men as the soil of the *bund* was slippery and the work heavy. Poor women have contributed a lot to the formation of TAs, but the benefits for the women in terms of employment, income or other practical activities are far below expectation.

DEVELOPMENT OF TANK RESOURCES: TREES AND FISH

The TAs should pursue financial sustainability as after the 'transfer of management' they will have to finance the annual maintenance of the tank and its structures once the rehabilitation is over. The TAs have also to mobilize their own resources to pay their water distributors. The TAs have theoretically the following resources to become sustainable: (1) interest from the corpus fund; (2) income from tank usufruct like fish culture and tree auctions but also boating and tourism; (3) sale of tank silt; (4) water cess collected from command farmers; and (5) other contributions.

It is expected that the main source of income will have to come from the tank usufruct as developing tree plantations on tank land and raising fish in the water of the tanks. But in practice, this expectation is very problematic. Concerning usufruct of tank resources (trees and fishing), the existing situation is that the commune panchayat auctions fish and trees for a nominal amount to village leaders.[22] Who can re-auction the resources for a higher amount. The proceeds accrued are mainly used for the operation and maintenance of temples in the villages. The people consider this as a gift from the tank to the whole community. A major hindrance was the fear of the traditional religious elite (temple trust) that they would lose their customary usufruct rights to maintain temples and to finance religious celebrations as the TAs also claimed part of the usufruct for the maintenance of the tanks. So the usufruct proceeds have to be shared by temple maintenance and tank maintenance, and endless meetings were conducted to avoid conflicts.

A hot gender issue in the resource development of the tank is the auctioning of the Palmyra palm trees on the tank *bund*. These trees belong to the commune panchayat as they grow on government land. The re-auctioning of these trees is a very profitable business as they are used for toddy tapping, and the toddy is often sold in small toddy shops located at the edge of the tank *bund*. Alcoholism is rampant in the area and causes increased poverty, heavier workloads for poor women and domestic violence. In many meetings poor women related that it was unacceptable that the TAs should become sustainable at the cost of poor women. This is a very relevant complaint urgent because it appears that the men have planted new Palmyra saplings in the tanks as to increase the toddy output, while the women want to plant Tamarind and Neem trees for food and medicinal use.

In Bahoor Sitheri tank, the auctioning of toddy tapping has been stopped at the tank *bund* because of the gender awareness of the president of the TA and a woman representative in the EC. The palm trees were usually auctioned for Rs. 30,000 to a political leader and moneylender who made much profit from the toddy business. The TA blocked the auctioning. The toddy mafia assaulted the president and the police took no action. But the women of the village came out to protect their president. After the abolishment of the toddy trade the palm trees are directly auctioned to the poor toddy tappers. They can collect the fruits and palm leaves to sell. The abolishment of the toddy business means a considerable loss of money for the TA but they and the Dalit women are happy. It was observed that the incidence of alcoholism has reduced. When the toddy is not sold at their doorstep, the men 'automatically' drink less.

The project director of the TRPP agreed that a notification should be sent to all presidents of TAs to follow the Bahoor model and to abolish the toddy business. But economic profit is more important than empowerment of poor landless women and the notification was never sent.

Building up the new fish and tree resources around the tank was a major activity in the project although the budget available for subsidy was very meagre. There were tree planting ceremonies and conditions for the survival of the saplings looked fine; but many of the saplings did not survive for many reasons: no water, no care, lack of interest by the men appointed, etc. However, in a few tanks tree plantations were more successful due to the dedication of landless women caretakers who look after the saplings for a very meagre salary and the motivation they get from the supervising NGO.

In another tank, the CO had taken much effort to form a tree-planting committee of landless women. Numerous meetings were conducted to determine the species and locations suitable for tree planting. A map was drawn with a tree-planting plan. In the middle of this process the PMU authorities gave the task of tree planting to the Forest Department, which in turn gave employment to its own male labourers. Digging the pits and even guarding the trees is done by the Forest Department staff. The community participation was thus undermined and, as it be seen, it also restricted the use of the tank by poor women and children. Moreover, this happened in a tank from which more than 250 poor families were evicted and who, as revenge, looted the fish-ponds of the TA. Field notes of the study reveal the following:

> We re-visit the tank and see a huge horrible fence of barbed wire along a substantial area in the water spread of the tank. We speak with three girls (16, 17, 15 years) and a boy (9). The girls dropped out of school after 8th standard. They now have to fetch the grass for the cows from the tank and carry the heavy headload to the house. Earlier, before the tree plantation by the Forest Department, the cows could graze in this part of the tank. Now this is forbidden. They [say] that they are now more afraid of snakes, as the trees and bushes [obstruct] the open clear [view] they had before. The Forest Department promised that the trees [would] grow two years, and that after that time the cattle [could] graze free again in the tank. The girls foresee that the control [of the cattle] will be less as the cows can hide behind the bushes. For the same reasons they will also feel more insecure as 'somebody' can hide behind the trees.

The Forest Department is also involved in other tanks and is forming so-called Village Forest Committees. A notification has been issued in which guidelines for the implementation of Joint Forest Management in Pondicherry are stipulated. All this shows that with the resource development of the TAs, the use by the poor women of the 'common good' has become more restricted and the participatory intention of the project has diminished. Worse, employment was even given to male outsiders while local poor women's groups were trained by the NGOs in nurseries and planting trees.

In 2004 the Government of Pondicherry transferred the usufruct fishing right to some TAs, but only for one year, which is of course too short a time to develop a sustainable fish resource. In several tanks fingerlings were released and the yields were diverse.

It is hoped that the benefits from other resources of the tanks will not be taken away or commercialized at the cost of the poor and weaker sections. It is stipulated in the by-laws of the TAs that the 'usufruct rights of poor people should be maintained according to "customary" rights when they do not endanger the functioning of the tank'. Till date it is uncertain whether the poor will have profit in the future from the development of the resources. It should be kept in mind that the benefits of the development of tank resources will go in the first place into the purses of the TAs to enable them to finance the operation and maintenance of the tanks in the future. The question is, will the tank resources be able to yield a surplus, and will the TAs be willing to invest that in productive activities for the weaker sections in the village?

8. Representation of Women in Tank Associations

The representation of women in 6 ECs of the TAs ranged from 13 to 33 per cent. On average it was one-sixth of the total. The only exception was a tank which was under the supervision of a woman nodal officer, where five out of eleven executive members were women (four landless). In the poorest tank, of the seventeen members four were landless women (no farm women). Fifty-four office-bearers were women, almost all in the position of vice-president or joint secretary.

Although the all-India target for women's representation in government and decision-making bodies is 33 per cent, the number of women members in the ECs of the TAs was only half of that. This is a logical outcome of the proportional allocation of representatives of the stakeholder groups in the EC. However, it is possible to include in the ECs fewer male farmers and more farm-women.

ROLE AND PERCEPTIONS OF WOMEN EXECUTIVE COMMITTEE MEMBERS

First Several workshops and empowerment training camps were organized for women EC members. At first many of the women were afraid to sit in the meetings together with all the men. They said, 'as women we cannot freely speak up and have freedom of movement'.

The situation has improved since. The efforts of the women COs has been vital in overcoming this cultural gender constraint. They were role models, moving around in the villages and conducting meetings with farmers.[23] It was interesting to note that several women EC members were widows. Some married women got the full support of their husbands to become EC members. One EC member said that a farmer had told her he would resign from the EC if a woman was appointed. Women EC members were constrained from coming forward not only by the men but also by the women of 'opposite' parties who undermined their and their families reputation by spreading gossip about them, that they were 'loose' women interested only in other men. During the training the poor women complained: 'Today's, again we lose one day's wage labour, sitting here and talking, but we don't get compensation from the project.'[24]

No woman was appointed treasurer, although the male decision makers in the PMU were strongly advised to do so as it is generally accepted that women will do the job seriously and honestly. Moreover it is socially acceptable for women to be accountants, and women in SHGs have experience in accountancy.

Many women EC representatives are also leaders of SHGs which are basically saving and credit groups. Women's SHGs have been very important for the TRPP for the following reasons:[25]

1. The COs used SHGs meetings as a platform to inform about and discuss with the women the aims and activities of the project.
2. Candidates from the SHGs were nominated and elected as women representatives for the ECs.[26]
3. SHGs have assisted as volunteer groups of the COs in collecting membership contributions for the TAs.
4. SHGs women helped to organize meetings.
5. SHG women provided meals and food during the implementation of the work.
6. Through the SHG women tree-planting in the tanks was initiated.
7. The establishing, or reviving of SHGs by the three NGOs showed to the village women that the project cared about their problems, and that might enhance the social profile of the village.

However, SHGs were considered as women's organizations 'outside' the project by the implementing authorities. Reviving and initiation of groups was done by the NGOs in their 'own' time with their own small staff on a very meagre budget.

9. ALTERNATIVES: THE GENDER AND EQUITY PROGRAMME AND GENDER SPECIALISTS

In many tanks, it appeared after the implementation phase of the physical works that poor Dalit women and SHGs were no longer interested in becoming members of the TAs and did not want to renew their membership for the next year or to pay the fee. Many of them had lost their small plots of land in the tanks and others did not get the employment they had expected. They turned their backs on the TAs and the project, and it was clear that much of the build-up enthusiasm and their involvement in the community participation had seeped away.

To create space for empowerment we pushed to appoint a full-time gender specialist and to give her a budget to start small income-generating activities and empowerment training on all fronts. This was successful. *The Mid-Term Review* in May 2002 says under the heading 'Equity':

> The Project is primarily designed to assist the richest members of rural society, the farmers owning land located on some of the best soils in the Region, in the tank *ayacuts*. Within the *ayacut* there are both large scale and small-scale farmers, and the Project is designed to ensure that all farmers, within the *ayacut* have an equitable share of water. For those living outside the *ayacut*, there is little Project activity which is guaranteed to provide any significant benefit, apart from limited increases in employment opportunities, and possibly, increased activities. (p. 55)

It was recommended that a Gender and Equity Specialist be appointed under Technical Assistance Programme to promote the full participation of women and to improve the quality of life of the below poverty line (Rs. 2,000 per month per household) population in the tank villages. From June 2003 onwards, an additional gender programme was initiated. The appointed gender specialist had excellent NGO experience and knew the TRPP and the Pondicherry government set-up very well.

With a small budget all kinds of gender programmes were taken up in the fields of training and gender entrepreneurial experiments. One of the most successful components was the leasing of land to Dalit women and the use of the System of Rice Intensification Cultivation Methodology to get higher yields. For six SHGs a 50 per cent subsidy was sanctioned to buy power tillers, which could be rented out to farmers, and in this way the group could earn money. Also commercial vermi-compost production was taken up to achieve supplementary income for rural households and to encourage eco-friendly farming and avoid soil degradation. Other activities were fodder cultivation, goat rearing, vegetable/flowers/medicinal plants cultivation and soap, cleaning and washing powder production. The concept of a 'tank shop' was developed and women got an opportunity to sell their products in the tank shop while in the meantime information on the aims of the tank rehabilitation project was disseminated. Fish cultivation in ponds by women SHGs, in which they got the usufruct rights from the commune panchayat, was successful. Other activities were closely related with the TRPP and numerous meetings were organized for gender sensitizing of engineers, exposure trips, showing rainwater harvesting models, etc.

In July 2004, the donor European Commission 'suddenly' closed the Technical Assistance Programme of the project, and EC assistance ended in December 2004. The main reason for this was that the Government of Pondicherry had not taken the required action to increase the electricity rate is step-by-step to limit unrestricted deep tube well pumping to prevent depletion of the groundwater. This was one of the preconditions mentioned in the official agreement between the EC and the Government of Pondicherry at the start of the project. For political reasons the Government of Pondicherry made little effort to increase the tariff. One effort had led to immediate hunger strikes, protest demonstrations and road blockages by angry farmers.

The gender specialist was dismissed in July 2005 and the Gender and Equity Programme was transferred to the male government sociologist. No gender empowerment and poverty alleviation activities and achievements are recorded from that time onwards. Community participation has been reduced to a minimum and the NGOs and COs concentrate mainly on the technical engineering work. The Pondicherry government extended the project for another three years and has decided to finance it during these years. Of the 84 tanks planned for rehabilitation, the work on 61 was completed in July 2004, and the work on the remaining 21 tanks is in progress. It is reported by the NGOs that farmers use the water in some tanks for one season. In other tanks the water is not used for irrigation but to recharge the groundwater. Does this mean that the tube well owners are dominant and do not allow the poorer farmers to use the water as that means less income for them from the sale of water?

10. Conclusion

In the previous sections it has been shown that the poor and landless Dalit women were initially enthusiastic members and participating stakeholders in the TAs, but the costs were too high and their benefits almost zero, and so they withdrew. Many lost their customary user rights over small plots of land in the tank, access to tank resources became even more limited, and little manual labour and income was generated during implementation of the technical work and from tank resource development.

Tank rehabilitation and 'transfer of management' of tanks might have some positive effects on the recharge of the groundwater and the ecological environment, although that still is to be proven, but it has no effect on the reduction of poverty and gender inequality. Even worse, the 'transfer of management' of 'common property' excludes in the rehabilitation process in particular the poor and landless women, and as a consequence re-enforces unequal caste/class and gender relations. As documented earlier, in deep tube well and canal irrigation, the large farmers are the winners and the landless women (and men) the losers. The large farmers have double benefits from the tank project, while the poor and landless women have to pay a high price for facilitating the 'managing-irrigation-together' policy even before the 'real' water management can start.

The lessons to be learnt are that there should be a clear awareness, understanding and commitment on the part of the donor and implementing agency to take 'managing-irrigation-together' projects to the most disadvantaged. The focus needs to shift to how participatory irrigation can provide the poor and landless women with sustainable alternatives to tank use and wider livelihood security by recognizing them as equally capable and responsible members of the community. Low women's participation in irrigation development and institutional reforms relates to their lack of resources in terms of land and water ownership. 'Transfer of management' does not address this crucial point.

Gender 'mainstreaming' in practice is not realistic, impossible and undesirable, in particular in an outspoken caste-class polarized and patriarchal context. Specific income-generating and empowerment activities, in particular for poor, landless women, should be identified, planned and designed in 'common property' projects with budget and staff. The worldwide call by water forums and international water conferences to involve women in water management by 'mainstreaming' gender, is easily made and sounds fine, but is largely an illusion in current male-dominated practice. A solid women's only project would be much more useful in improving the condition of poor women.

As long as knowing and understanding the detailed caste/class and gender context is not made a priority in irrigation policies and strategies, 'transfer of management' and Participatory Irrigation Management will never become a real participatory process which includes the whole community. And 'mainstreaming' women will remain 'men-streaming' without a bit of empowerment or improvement in the living conditions.

NOTES

1. The strategy of mainstreaming, is according to the UN report of 2002 (Gender Mainstreaming), 'the process of assessing the implications for women and men of any planned action, including legislation, policies or programmes, in all areas and at all levels. It is a strategy for making women's as well as men's concerns and experiences an integral dimension of the design, implementation, monitoring and evaluations of policies and programmes in all political, economic and societal spheres so that women and men benefit equally and inequality is not perpetuated. The ultimate goal is to achieve gender equality.'
2. The main reason for the closing is very interesting and is explained in Section 9.
3. For an overview of tanks of south India see the excellent publication of Vaidyanathan (2001).
4. Tube well owners are charged a flat rate of Rs. 75/HP/year plus Rs. 200 per year service charge for electricity. Thus, for a total annual power cost of around Rs. 1,000, they are free to pump 24 hours a day. On average, one tube well serves around 2.25 ha, and pumps 45,000 cum/year.
5. There is no Department of Water Resources in Pondicherry as in neighbouring states.
6. ARCADIS, Euroconsult is the employer of the project coordinator.
7. Duck nomads are people having a fixed tank route every year. They release their flock in a tank for some weeks. After all the food resources are finished they move to another tank and release the flock there. In this way they survive. Any earthwork in the tank will impact them very much. They are a 'mobile' stakeholder group.

8. The commune panchayat is the main administrative unit in Pondicherry.
9. The effort was made by the NGOs, their COs and partly the consultants of the social wing in the PMU.
10. In general, farmers were motivated to use tank water for irrigation as it is perceived as more beneficial than the 'dead' tube well water.
11. There were already agronomical and hydrological surveys in the TRPP, so the household survey was not considered important as a database to analyse the social transformation process. The household survey was conducted and used by the COs as a means to get to know the people and to search for good representatives of the various stakeholder groups.
12. Women told that they join the seasonal migration of the men when there are no small children in the household. Women with grown-up children stay behind in the villages.
13. See, for the origin and status position of the castes in Tamil Nadu, the excellent work by Mencher (1978).
14. There are hundreds of SHGs in Pondicherry (see Section 8).
15. One woman told that the tacit custom of weeding implies that they can take the weeds with them as fodder for the cattle. She has no cattle but gives it to neighbours. In return she can take the cowdung of their animals for cooking fuel.
16. Rs. 17 was the rate in 1999 but in November 2001, Rs. 20 is consistently mentioned as the rate for wage labour from 7.00 in the morning till 13.00 hrs in the afternoon. In 2004 the rate was still Rs. 20.
17. Stakeholders are people, groups or institutions who are likely to be affected by the proposed tank rehabilitation (either negatively or positively) or those which can affect the outcome of the intervention.
18. Under British Colonial Rule in the Madras Presidency the Tank Restoration Scheme was begun in 1883. The direct cause was the famines from 1866 onwards (Meinzen-Dick and Suseela 1984: 17). Tank improvement projects in Tamil Nadu have been sponsored by the state government and the World Bank and the European Economic Community since the 1980s (ibid.: 5).
19. In pilot tanks more than 80 meetings with the community were necessary to form the TA.
20. I wrote 11 reports as the sociologist/gender specialist on 11 missions. This data is from Technical Report no. 31, 9th mission.
21. A quota of a minimum of 30 per cent is considered a reasonable.
22. It is not clear whether all tank resources are auctioned and what rewards are sluiced back to the commune panchayat and the PWD as the custodians of the tank.
23. It was difficult to appoint women COs. At the peak of the project there were 37 COs, 13 of whom were women and 24 men.
24. In the Field School, participants get Rs. 30 per day as attendance fee.

25. See, for a detailed background and history of SHGs, Schenk-Sandbergen, Technical Report no. 19, Report on the Sociologist/Gender Specialist's fifth mission, December 2000.
26. In some tanks where no SHGs existed it was difficult to find a woman leader ready to come forward as EC member.

REFERENCES

Agarwal, Anil and Sunita Narain (eds.) (1997), *Dying Wisdom: Rise, and Fall and Potential of India's Traditional Water Harvesting Systems*, State of India's Environment, A Citizens' Report 4, New Delhi: Centre for Science and Environment.

Agarwal, Arun and Clark C. Gibson (eds.) (2001), *Communities and the Environment, Gender and State in Community-based Conservation*, London: Rutgers University Press.

Agarwal, Bina (1994), *A Field of One's Own: Gender and Land Rights in South Asia*, Cambridge South Asian Studies 58, New Delhi: Cambridge University Press.

Anandhi, S. (2002), 'Interlocking Patriarchies and Women in Governance: A Case Study of Panchayati Raj Institutions in Tamil Nadu' in Karin Kapadia (ed.), *The Violence of Development: The Politics of Identity, Gender and Social Inequalities in India*, London: Zed Books.

Ballabh, Vishwa (2005), 'Emerging Water Crisis and Political Economy of Irrigation Reforms in India', in Ganesh P. Shivakoti et al. (eds.), *Asian Irrigation in Transition, Responding to Challenges*, New Delhi: Sage, pp. 154–77.

Gender Mainstreaming, An Overview (2002), New York: United Nations.

Guijt, Irene and Meera Kaul Shah (1999 rpt.), *The Myth of Community, Gender Issues in Participatory Development*, London: Intermediate Technology Publications.

Gulati, Ashok, Ruth Meinzen-Dick and K.V. Raju (2005), *Institutional Reforms in Indian Irrigation,* International Food Policy Research Institute, New Delhi: Sage.

Gupta, Deepak and L.P. Srivastava (1999), *Status of Participatory Irrigation Management in India: A Documentary Critique,* Institute of Social Sciences, ISS Manuscript Report 13, New Delhi.

Jodha, N.S. (1986), 'Common Property Resources and Rural Poor in Dry Regions of India, *Economic and Political Weekly,* XXI, 27 July 1986.

Kelkar, Govind (2005), 'Development Effectiveness through Gender Mainstreaming, Gender Equality and Poverty Reduction in South Asia', *Economic and Political Weekly,* 29 October 2005, pp. 4690–9.

Koppen van, Barbara (1998), 'More Jobs per Drop: Targeting Irrigation to Poor Women and Men', PhD thesis, The Netherlands Royal Tropical Institute, Amsterdam.

Koppen van, Barbara, and Simeen Mahmud (1995), *Women and Waterpumps in Bangladesh: The Impact of Participation in Irrigation Groups on Women's Status*, Department of Irrigation and Soil and Water Conservation, Wageningen Agricultural University, Bangladesh Institute of Deveopment Studies, Dhaka.

Maloney, Clarence and K.V. Raju (1994), *Managing Irrigation Together: Practice and Policy in India*, New Delhi: Sage.

Meinzen-Dick, Ruth and Suseela (1984), *Local Management of Tank Irrigation in South India: Organization and Operation*, Cornell University, Studies in Irrigation, no. 3, Ithaca: Cornell University.

Meinzen-Dick, Ruth and Margreet Zwarteveen (1998), 'Gender Participation in Water Management: Issues and Illustrations from Water User Associations in South Asia', in Douglas Merrey and Shirish Baviskar (eds.), *Gender Analysis and Reform of Irrigation Management: Concepts, Cases and Gaps in Knowledge,* Proceedings of the Workshop on Gender and Water, 15–19 September 1997, Habarana, Colombo: International Water Management Institute.

——— (2001), 'Gender Dimensions of Community Resource Management: The Case of Water Users' Associations in South Asia', in Arun Agrawal and Clark C. Gibson (eds.), *Communities and the Environment: Ethnicity, Gender and the State in Community-Based Conservation,* New Brunswick, and London: Rutgers University Press, pp. 63–88.

Mencher, P. Joan (1978), *Agriculture and Social Structure in Tamil Nadu: Past Origins, Present Transformations and Future Prospects,* New Delhi: Allied.

Mid-Term Review Mission Draft Report (2002), 'Tank Rehabilitation Project, Pondicherry', Commission of the European Communities, W.S. Atkins Consultants.

Mollinga, Peter P. (2000), 'The Inevitability of Reform: Towards Alternative Approaches for Canal Irrigation Development in India', in Rakesh Hooja and L.K. Joshi (eds.), *Participatory Irrigation Management: Paradigm for the 21st Century* (2 vols.), Jaipur: Rawat, pp. 67–97.

Moser, Caroline (1989), Gender Planning in the Third World: Meeting Practical and Strategic Gender Needs, *World Development.*

Mosse, David (1997), 'The Symbolic Making of a Common Property Resource: History, Ecology and Locality in a Tank-irrigated Landscape in South India', in *Development and Change* 28: 467–504.

Nanavaty, Reema (2000), 'Protecting and Restoring: Not the Resources but Resource Users, Managers and Owners: Women Professionals in Water Sector', in *Water and Nature: Women's Work is Central,* SEWA

Papers presented at the Second World Water Forum, 17–22 March, The Hague, The Netherlands.

Palanisami, K. (1990), 'Tank Irrigation in South India: What Next?' ODI-IIMI. Irrigation Management Network Paper 90/2e, Colombo.

——— and K.W. Easter (2000), *Tank Irrigation in the 21st Century: What Next?*, New Delhi: Discovery Publishing House.

Prakash, Anjal (2005), *The Dark Zone, Groundwater Irrigation, Politics and Social Power in North Gujarat*. Wageningen University Water Resources Series, New Delhi: Orient Longman.

Raghunath, T.P., S. Pushpalatha and T. Srikant (2003), *Field Manual on Community Organisation for Tank Rehabilitation Project Pondicherry*, Pondicherry: Centre for Ecology and Rural Development.

Rahman, Mahbubar and Willem van Schendel (1997), 'Gender and the Inheritance of Land, Living Law in Bangladesh', in Jan Breman, Peter Kloos and Ashwani Saith (eds.), *The Village in Asia Revisited*, New Delhi: Oxford University Press, pp. 237–76.

Rao, Aruna, Mary B. Anderson and Catherine A. Overholt (eds.) (1991), *Gender Analysis in Development Planning: A Case Book*, West Hartford: Kumarian Press.

Rao, Aruna and David Kelleher (2005), 'Is There Life after Gender Mainstreaming?' in *Gender and Development*, 13(2).

Rao, Nitya (2005), 'Women's Rights to Land and Assets: Experience of Mainstreaming Gender in Development Projects', *Economic and Political Weekly*, 29 October, pp. 4701–8.

Reddy, Ratna V. and P. Prudhvikar Reddy (2005), 'How Participatory is Participatory Irrigation Management? Water Users' Associations in Andhra Pradesh', *Economic and Political Weekly* XL(53): 5587–95.

Technical Proposal (1997), 'Pondicherry Tank Rehabilitation Project, India', European Commission, Antea, Arcadis, Pradan.

Sarin, Madhu (1998), 'Community Forest Management: Whose Participation . . . ?', in Irene Guijt and Meera Kaul Shah, *The Myth of Community: Gender Issues in Participatory Development*, London: Intermediate Technology Publications, pp. 121–30.

Schenk-Sandbergen, Loes (1986), *People, Trees and Forest in India*, Annex 2. Report of the Mission of the Government of the Netherlands on the Identification of the Scope for Forestry Development Corporation in India, Den Haag.

——— (ed.) (1995). *Women and Seasonal Labour Migration*, Indo-Dutch Studies on Development Alternatives, New Delhi: Sage.

——— (1998). *Gender, Culture and Land Rights in Rural Laos*. Gender and Development Program, School of Environment Resources and Development, Asian Institute of Technology, Gender Studies, Monograph 7, Bangkok.

——— (2002), Why Gender 'main-streaming' Means 'men-streaming' and Informal 'women-streaming' in Practice: A Case Study of the Tungabhadra Irrigation Pilot Project', IDPAD (research report).

——— (2004), 'Some Gender Dimensions in Managing Water Scarcity', in A. Vaidyanathan and H.M. Oudshoorn (eds.), *Managing Water Scarcity: Experiences and Prospects,* New Delhi: IDPAD/Manohar.

Schenk-Sandbergen, Loes and Outhaki Choulamany-Khamphoui (1995b), *Women in Rice Fields and Offices: Irrigation in Laos, Gender Specific Case Studies in Four Villages*, Heiloo: Empowerment.

Schenk-Sandbergen, Loes and Niren Choudhury (2003), *From Heroines to Beneficiaries: From Beneficiaries to Heroines? The Impact of a Small-scale Irrigation Project on Gender in West-Bengal, Terai, India*, New Delhi: IDPAD/Manohar.

Sengupta, Nirmal (1991), *Managing Common Property, Irrigation in India and the Philippines.* Indo-Dutch Studies on Development Alternatives-6, New Delhi: Sage.

SEWA (Self Employed Women's Association) (1997), *Managing Water for the People by the People.* A Participatory Assessment on SEWA's Experiences with Rural Water Resource Management in Gujarat, Ahmedabad.

Shah, Esha (2003), *Social Designs: Tank Irrigation Technology and Agrarian Transformation in Karnataka, South India*, Wageningen University, Water Resources Series. New Delhi: Orient Longman.

Sharma, Ursala (1980), *Women, Work and Property in Northwest India*, London: Tavistock Publishers.

Sharma, Abhishek (2003), *Rethinking Tanks: Opportunities for Revitalizing Irrigation Tanks: Empirical Findings from Ananthapur District, Andhra Pradesh, India*, Working Paper 62, Colombo: International Water Management Institute.

Shiva, Vandana (1988), *Staying Alive: Women, Ecology and Survival in India*, New Delhi: Kali for Women.

Shivakoti, Ganesh et al. (eds.) (2005), *Asian Irrigation in Transition: Responding to Challenges*, IWMI, New Delhi: Sage.

Singh, Andrea and Neera Burra (eds.), *Women and Wasteland Development in India*, New Delhi: Sage.

Tank Rehabilitation Project Pondicherry (n.d.), Terms of Reference.

Vaidyanathan, A. (ed.) (2001), *Tanks of South India*, New Delhi: Centre for Science and Environment.

Vuuren van, Sonja (2002), 'Bron van Leven', een onderzoek naar het gebruik van land en water rondom een collectieve watertank in de context van overlevingsstrategieen van landloze vrouwen in Pondicherry, Zuid India: Source of Life, research on the use of water and land around a collective watertank in the context of survival strategies of landless women in Pondicherry, South India. Master thesis, Anthropology, University of Amsterdam.

Viegas, Philip and Geeta Menon (1993), 'Bringing Government and People Together: Forest Protection Committees of West Bengal—Role and Participation of Women', in Andrea M. Singh and Neera Burra (eds.), *Women and Wasteland Development in India*, ILO, Delhi: Sage, pp. 171–210.

Young, Kate (1994 rpt.), *Planning Development with Women: Making a World of Difference*, Development Studies, London: Macmillan.

Zwarteveen, Margreet Z. (2006), 'Wedlock or Deadlock? Feminists' Attempts to Engage Irrigation Engineers', PhD thesis, Wageningen, Wageningen Agricultural University.

THEME 6

DISPLACEMENT, CONFLICT AND CRISES: THE FLIPSIDE OF GLOBALIZATION

CHAPTER 10

Caste and Religion in a Transnational Context: The Patidars of Central Gujarat

MARIO RUTTEN

I have known the family of Ashokbhai Patel ever since my first visit to India in 1983.[1] In 1986 I spent one year in Ashok's home village Vepargam in central Gujarat. At that time, Ashok had already moved out of Vepargam. After his marriage in 1984 he had migrated to the city. He became the owner of a small grocery shop with an apartment on the first floor, in which he lived with his wife and three children.

Ashok's parents are still living in the original family home in the centre of Vepargam, with Ashok's younger brother and his family. Owning 8 ha of irrigated farmland, the family belongs to the economic elite of the village. Throughout the years, I have accompanied Ashok's father and younger brother while they made their rounds of the fields. As true gentlemen farmers, they supervise and direct the activities performed by their agricultural labourers, while eschewing any manual work themselves.

Ashok's family is definitely among the wealthier families of Vepargam and it is also part of the social elite of the village. The family belongs to the dominant Patidar caste, an upwardly mobile, middle-ranking peasant caste which can be found in several regions of Gujarat, but is concentrated principally in central Gujarat. One noteworthy feature of this community is their longstanding tradition of specific marriage regulations. From as early as the late-nineteenth century, the Patidars or the Patels of central Gujarat have organized themselves into marriage circles in which daughters are married only to other Patidars families within a distinct group of villages. As long as everyone continued to live in their home village, information on the specific background and status of possible marriage candidates could easily be obtained. Presently, however, there are more Patidars living outside their native villages than in their home villages. This phenomenon has led to the establishment of Patidar organizations in the cities on the basis of their village of origin or their specific marriage circle. An important objective of these organizations is to provide information which will facilitate the search for a suitable spouse and will enable families to establish links with other members of their community.

Since 1993, Ashok has held the position of secretary of the Vepargam Patidar Organization in the city where he as lived since his marriage. This organization was established in 1985. Even though Ashok moved away from Vepargam at the age of twenty-six, he still keeps in close contact with his native village. Regular phone calls to his father and brother keep him informed about the lives of his family members and friends in the village. Whenever there are requests from Vepargam for Ashok's support, financial or otherwise, he is always prepared to host a special board meeting of the Vepargam Patidar Organization at his own home.

This was also the case one evening in July 1999, when I happened to be visiting him. To my surprise, Girish Patel was present at the meeting, together with four other board members of the organization. Girish is the headmaster of the secondary school in Vepargam. Over the years I had met him regularly in the village but I had never seen him in Ashok's home. In fact, his presence proved to be the reason for the meeting that evening. As it happened, he had come from Vepargam especially to collect money for the construction of a Swaminarayan temple in the village. A few months before it had been decided by a committee of Swaminarayan followers in Vepargam that Girish, as headmaster of the school, would collect the money needed from Patels living outside Vepargam. That evening's meeting at Ashok's home was his first stop on his long quest to amass the money and to make the final preparations for the collection that would start two days later.

When I visited Vepargam three years later, in 2002, I was finally able to admire the temple which had been built. While visiting Ashok's family, his father proudly showed me a two-hour video recording of the opening ceremony that had taken place in 2000. As one of the guests of honour, Ashok had come down to Vepargam to attend the ceremony. With the help of other representatives of the Swaminarayan sect, whom he had previously met up with in his home town, Ashok had made a point of ensuring that several key regional political figures from the governing Hindu fundamentalist Bharatiya Janata Party (BJP) would also be present at the ceremony. It had been decided that Ashok's brother would stand in the forthcoming state elections, and Ashok would support him financially. The Hindu–Muslim violence that had broken out in Gujarat following the attack on a train in Godhra on 27 February 2002 had reinforced Ashok's pride in the fact that it was partly through the efforts of his organization the construction of the temple in his home village had been made possible. 'As Hindus, we have become a minority in our own country. It is therefore important to rise up for the rights of our people, even if we live outside our village,' Ashok noted. 'A new temple in the village shows that we Patels will not be pushed aside', he added.

Anthropological studies on social change in Asia regularly report this kind of descriptive account of villagers who collect funds for the construction of a temple. Consequently it is by no means exceptional that this involves people who have moved from their home village to the city, but still maintain close ties with their place of origin. These men and women organize get-togethers with other caste members in their new place of residence, and a substantial number of them regularly return to their home village. Conversely, those who have stayed behind in the village occasionally pay a visit to their family and caste members in the city.

The most conspicuous point about the board meeting of the Vepargam Patidar Organization, however, was the fact that it did not take place in India at all, but in London. Ashok has lived in Britain now for more than twenty years. After his marriage to a daughter of a Patidar family, which belongs to the same marriage circle as Vepargam, Ashok moved to London to join his wife in 1984. It was here that I met him again for the first time in fifteen years.

This introductory case study of Ashok Patel shows the importance of a comparative perspective in the study of Gujarat. It is the closeness of people like Ashok Patel in London to their family and caste members in central Gujarat which gives the impression that today one lives in a world which resembles a village community. The explosive increase in migration movements, in flows of goods and in financial operations have created the image of a 'global village' which encompasses the whole earth. Such developments in the fields of transport and communication, as television and the Internet, have added to an image in which large portions of the world population seem to have been brought closer together than ever before.

Much of the discussion in the literature and media has focused on the nature and social impact of this recent acceleration in the globalization process. The bulk of these studies operate from the assumption that globalization is coterminous with Westernization, a process marked by a spread of influences from the Western part of the world to what have become known as non-Western societies in Africa, Latin America, and Asia. In keeping with the development theories of the 1950s and 1960s, these authors emphasize that Asian developments are to be viewed as treading in the footsteps of the modernization process that formed the basis of the 'advanced' European societies, only at a slower tempo (see e.g. Landes 1998). They point out the tendency of homogenization being the dominant trend within the process of globalization. The oil stain-like spread of the three big Ms, namely, McDonalds, Microsoft, and MTV, over the globe is seen as illustrations of a future society in which local cultures will be threatened and will quickly disappear.[2] It is usually acknowledged that this process does not take place everywhere in the same manner at the same time and has even been delayed in several parts of the world. The final outcome of the globalization process, however, is not questioned; the world presumably taking shape is a global village on the Western model. Following this line of reasoning, the rise in regional movements which emphasize cultural uniqueness is seen as a sign of fighting a rearguard action. Attempts made to strengthen local identities in non-Western societies are thought to gain, at the most, a temporary delay in this process of globalization. There is no escaping the fact that this view equates globalization with Westernization, in which four-fifths of humanity has no role to play other than to react, often supervise defensively, to developments initiated from outside their own society.

The growing presence of immigrants from Asia in Europe has given rise to the notion that globalization is more than just a process of Westernization; it also entails what can be called an Easternization. In the first instance, the emphasis was placed on the contribution of immigrants to the cultural diversity of Europe, preponderantly in terms of introducing new types of food, fashion and music. Although limited to outward appearances, the underlying connotation of the Asian contribution to Western culture was a positive one. Slowly but surely this positive view has been discarded and substituted by a more negative attitude towards the process of Easternization. The recent influx of migrants from Asia, and the conceivable influences they may bring along with them, has led many to regard this process as a threat to European culture. Migrants are said to be largely responsible for the import of traditions into 'modern' European society. Earlier, these traditions were seen as no more than a passing phase, mostly related to an incomplete process of the integration of the first generation of migrants into European society. Lately, the conviction seems to have taken root that these influences have a more permanent character which emanates from the social linkages maintained with their country of origin in Asia by the migrants in Europe.

This chapter discusses these social linkages between Patidar migrants in London and their family members in central Gujarat. It will endeavour to show how the Westernization of Asia and Easternization of Europe are two interconnected aspects of globalization. The changing role of caste and religion in central Gujarat cannot be considered simply a local defensive reaction to global developments from the West. These changes in Gujarat can only be understood from a global perspective. Gujarat is not merely a region where globalization has local effects; instead, developments in Gujarat are an essential component of the globalization process.

Family Linkages

A study on Patidar or Patel migrants in London and their family members in the villages in Gujarat, conducted in cooperation with an Indian colleague, reveals the existence of extensive mutual transnational contacts.[3] Members of the Patidar community in London have a long history of national and international migration. Many Patidars immigrated from Gujarat to East Africa in the early part of the twentieth century and from there to Britain in the 1960s and 1970s. The findings of the research indicate that the members of this community maintain frequent long-distance family linkages with their home region in India, which has resulted in a two-way flow of people, capital and ideas. Marriage arrangements, kinship networks, frequent visits, property, remittances and religious affiliations ensure that many of the Patidar immigrants in London maintain close links with the villages in Gujarat.

One of the indicators of the social links between the Patidar immigrants in Britain and their relatives in the villages in Gujarat are the various types of intense contacts that exist between the members of both groups. Phone calls are an important way of keeping in touch. In accordance with the costs of this type of communication, telephone calls from India to Britain are usually very brief and often made only in emergency situations or for very specific purposes. Patidars in Britain, on the other hand, make phone calls to their families in the village more frequently; some even phone from Britain almost every week for a few minutes. During these calls information is exchanged about the well-being of relatives on both sides.

Navinbhai Bhupendrabhai Patel is forty years old. He lives with his wife and their son in London where they run a grocery shop. Navinbhai was born and brought up in one of the selected villages in Gujarat and married a girl who was a British citizen born in East Africa.

Navinbhai's father, his mother and his younger brother, Yogesh, and his family are still living in their ancestral house in the village. Almost every year, Navinbhai pays a brief ten- to fifteen-day visit to his family. Usually he comes alone, leaving his wife behind in London to take care of their shop. Between his visits Navinbhai keeps in regular contact with his relatives at home. At least once a week Navinbhai makes a brief phone call to his father and his brother Yogesh. These calls are made at a fixed time on a particular day of the week. Navinbhai especially uses telephone cards with a limited amount on them which allows him to talk for a short while. During these brief conversations, the brothers exchange information about the health of their relatives on both sides, about the educational progress of their children and their business undertakings. 'Although our telephone conversations are very brief indeed, it gives us an opportunity to keep in touch regularly and to create the feeling that Navinbhai and his family are not so far away,' Yogesh said after Navinbhai had made his weekly call.

Another important mode of contact between the households in Gujarat and their family members in Britain are the visits which relatives from Britain make to their respective home villages. More than 90 per cent of the 313 households selected in the 6 villages were visited by their relatives in Britain between 1993 and 1998. In total, 768 relatives visited India, which comes to an average of 2.7 relatives per household, of which a substantial number have visited India more than once during this five-year period. Most of these visits were of relatively long duration (59 per cent between one and three months).

In recent years, when many of the older immigrants have retired from an active working life, a pattern of a movement back home to India from Britain during winter has emerged. There are quite a number of the older generation of Patidar immigrants in Britain who could be called 'international commuters'. These are Patidars from Britain who go to India every winter for a period of from about one to five months. In most cases, they live in their own apartment or bungalow in Gujarat on the outskirts of their home village or in one of the nearby towns. Some of them may actually be said to have returned to India as they spend more time in their country of origin than in Britain. Although most of these people did return with the intention of spending their old age in India, a few of them came back because they no longer wanted to live with their family in Britain. The choice is not always an easy one. Having returned to their village of origin, some of them realize that they no longer feel at home there.

Shamalbhai is seventy-two years old and since 1994 he has again lived in the village in which he was born in 1925. At the age of twenty-seven, in 1953, after he had already married, Shamalbhai left his native village. He was invited to come to Tanzania by his father's eldest brother's son whose family had been living there since the 1930s.

In 1956, Shamalbhai came back to his village to collect his wife and their three children. The highly unstable political situation prevailing around 1963 in East Africa prompted, Shamalbhai and his wife to take their children back to Charotar and leave them with Shamalbhai's close relatives in his native village where they could attend the local schools. Although his wife stayed with their children for some months, she again joined her husband in Tanzania in 1964. Together they lived and worked there until 1973, with only one visit to their children in Charotar in 1969.

After their visit in 1973, his wife remarried behind in the village while Shamalbhai returned to Tanzania in 1974. From there he applied for and was granted permission to enter Britain in 1979. Within one year of his arrival in London, Shamalbhai called his wife and their three children to join him in Britain. Shamalbhai, his wife and their children were able to find only unskilled work during their early years in Britain. 'I could only get a job in a factory,' Shamalbhai informed us. 'In Tanzania I had a big shop with assistants and drove around in a Jaguar car, but I had to leave almost all my property behind when I migrated to the UK and had to start again from scratch.' Shamalbahai continued,

I was not really happy in London. It was hard work for very low pay at which my wife and I had to slog away at in those factories, but we did it for our children. By migrating to the UK we wanted to give them a better future, because they would not have had good opportunities in India, with a relatively low education and without much property in the village. After my retirement in 1990, however, my wife and I started to visit India very regularly. In fact, we often used to spend several months a year in India. In 1994, we even returned and took up permanent residence again in my native village, because after my father's brother's daughter had left for the USA, there was no one left in the village to take care of my old father. We then built a new house on the outskirts of the village and since then we live here the whole year round and only occasionally pay a visit to the UK.

Although in the first instance Shamalbhai returned to the village only because of his father, he visibly enjoys being part of village life. Every day he makes his rounds through it and on various evenings he can be found in the village square chatting to old friends. There is a downside: he occupies only a marginal position in his home village:

Although I was born and brought up here, even four years after I have returned permanently, I still do not feel that I am really part of village society. We participate in various activities, but somehow we have difficulty in really mixing with our relatives in the village and have to force ourselves to attend their gatherings. But to be honest, we used to have the same feeling when we were living in the UK, because I arrived there at the age of fifty-five and only worked there for about ten years.

After Shamalbhai had left the room for a short while, his wife also began to say what she thought.

Yes, we also did not feel at home in London, but at least we had our children and grandchildren nearby. I don't like it here at all and hardly leave our house. My whole life I have been able to live in and adjust to different countries. I have lived in Charotar, in Tanzania and in London, but now that we are old, I sometimes feel that we no longer feel at home anywhere and therefore had better keep to ourselves inside our own house.

As is to be expected, there are fewer visits to Britain by Indian relatives compared to the number of visits from Patidar immigrants to India. However, members of more than 20 per cent of the households selected paid a visit to Britain between 1993 and 1998. In total, 128 members journeyed to Britain in this five-year period, which comes to an average of 1.6 relatives per household. This clearly indicates that there are a substantial number of household members from the villages who have visited Britain. These visits are often of a longer duration (78 per cent between one and six months; 14 per cent more than six months).

Although the selection of the households in the six villages in Gujarat was made on the basis of the presence of relatives in Britain, it turns out that 85 per cent of the selected case families have relatives abroad, not only in Britain but also in other countries. This comes to an average of 9.4 per household. With the rigorous immigration restrictions imposed, emigration to Britain decreased rapidly around the late 1970s and early 1980s. Since then, the USA and Canada have become the most popular destinations for Patidar immigrants (Jain 1993; Helweg 1987 and 1990). This is confirmed by the findings from our study. Almost 75 per cent of the relatives of the selected families in central Gujarat live in the USA, while almost 16 per cent live in East Africa.

One of the consequences of this widespread migration pattern of the Patidar community is that today a category of people who can be described as 'world citizens' has been created. They are usually older people who, although they have a residence in one country, often travel between the UK, India, the USA and East Africa throughout the year, staying in each country for a period of a few months. These people sometimes meet each other in different countries where they exchange information about relatives. There are even some cases of transnational holidays in which Patidar relatives from different parts of the world come together to spend their vacation travelling to several countries, as the case presented below demonstrates.

Shantubhai is about seventy-years old and a British passport-holder. After the death of his wife in London in 1987, Shantubhai moved back to his native village in central Gujarat. It was there that we met him for the first time. It was about 6 o'clock in the evening and Shantubhai was just on his way to the Swaminarayan temple at the entrance of the village. After he had paid his respects to the deity, Shantubhai went to the room at the back where he spends at least two evenings a week talking with other Patels from the village. To his surprise, it turned out that Gurubhai, an old friend of his, was also present. Gurubhai lives in the USA but Shantubhai and he have known each other for forty years, since the time both were living in East Africa. Both went to the UK in the early 1970s. In the 1980s, two of Gurubhai's daughters married Patels from the USA and settled there. It was through them that Gurubhai and his wife were later able to emigrate to the USA from the UK.

Over the years, Gurubhai and Shantubhai have been meeting each other in different places. In the past, they used to meet regularly in London at Shantubhai's place of residence when Gurubhai was visiting his two sons and their families. Once they also bumped into each other in New Jersey when Shantubhai was visiting one of his brothers there. More recently, they have met every few years in Shantubhai's home village, which is also Gurubhai's wife's birthplace.

The families of both Gurubhai and Shantubhai have spread over many parts of the globe, following of their early migration to East Africa. Today, two of Shantubhai's four brothers are in the UK, while two of his sisters and their descendants reside in the USA. Moreover, one son of Shantubhai's third brother lives with his family in Tanzania. In fact, before Shantubhai's return to India, only one of his four brothers used to live in their native village, occupying the ancestral house and looking after the small piece of agricultural land belonging to the family. 'Although our family is spread over so many countries, we are still a closely knit family,' Shantubhai remarked. 'Every few years, we organize a tour somewhere in the world for which most members of our extended family come together from different parts of the world. Three years ago, we rented a coach and made a tour which took us to different European countries. In all, there were about thirty of us relatives, both young and old. If all goes well, we are planning to organize a similar family tour to East Asia next year, in which we would like to include Hong Kong, Singapore, and Bangkok. We are already talking to a travel agent about arranging such a tour and we expect that at least twenty of our relatives from the USA, UK and Africa will participate.'

Gujarat in London

As a result of these patterns of migration, the Patels constitute one of the largest groups among the Gujarati Hindus in Britain. Not surprisingly 'Patel' rivals 'Singh' as one of the most famous Indian surnames abroad. According to a conservative estimate of the membership of associations of all the marriage circles in Britain, there were about 30,000 Patels from central Gujarat living in Britain in the early 1990s, of whom 90 per cent resided in London (Lyon and West 1995: 407).

A characteristic feature of the Patel community which we studied in London is that they remain attached to Indian culture and in their social relations to their Gujarati background. Most of the older generation have retained their Patidar identity by organizing themselves on the basis of their village of origin and marriage circle (*gol*). These village-based associations and organizations of village-circles in Britain bring out directories giving details of all the Patidar family members concerned. These directories are mostly used to help to arrange marriages. For this purpose, the associations also organize marriage-*melas*, in which young boys and girls publicly introduce themselves and try to find suitable life partners. The village associations and marriage-circle associations of Patidars in Britain also organize meetings to celebrate Nav Ratri, Diwali and other important Indian festivals, and hold functions like dinner-and-dances at which they eat, drink and dance to the tunes of Hindi songs till late into the night and early hours of the morning at weekends. Moreover, many Patels participate in religious activities. Although most of the active members in these associations belong to the older generations of Patidar immigrants, many organizations also have youth committees in which youngsters are involved and encouraged to organize and participate in various activities.

To a large extent, the various organizations of Patels in Britain continue to follow the pattern of social differentiation between the various marriage circles, although some changes are clearly visible. This, for example, is evident in the case of the Barham Park Veterans Club, of which a number of first generation Patels from one marriage circle have become members over the past few years.

The Barham Park Veterans Club was established in 1947 as a social club for British veterans of the Second World War. The club is located on the edge of a park in Wembley and consists of two buildings with a kitchen, a snooker table, a card room, and a space to play darts. At present there are about one hundred members. Of them, forty are white British men of whom twenty-two are ex-servicemen, the category for which the club was originally established. The remaining sixty members are all of Gujarati origin, almost all of them members of the Patidar community.

Until 1990, the Barham Park Veterans Club did not have a single member of Indian origin. At that time there was a serious danger that the club would be closed as its membership had declined drastically over the previous few years. Most of the war veterans were over seventy years of age. Many of those who were still alive were suffering from health problems and therefore were unable to visit the club regularly. The board of the club then decided to open its membership to outsiders. Within a few years the number of Gujarati members very quickly increased to about sixty in 1999.

Almost all the Indian members of the Barham Park Veterans Club are Patels from the same marriage circle in central Gujarat. All of these Patels have lived in East Africa, especially in Kenya and Uganda. Many of them know each other from their time in East Africa, sometimes even from their childhood years in their home village in India. Although some of them have started to play snooker and darts and join the native British in their competitions, they are clearly an exception. Most of the time the Patels tend to frequent the card room which is in a separate building. There they play Indian card games and exchange views, or simply sit together to talk among themselves in Gujarati. Once in a while they organize a dinner in the club to which their wives are also invited. Although these dinners are open to all members of the club, it turns out that only Gujarati members attend these meetings.

During our stay in London, two wealthy Patels from one of the lower marriage circles became members of the Barham Park Veterans Club. In fact, they were the first Patels from another marriage circle to join. This incident met with disapproval from a section of the Patels. They were of the opinion that the club should be open only to Patels from their marriage circle or for high caste Hindus. They felt that the admission of other Patels would lower the standing of their club. In private, they would point out that the two new members had 'bought' their membership by promising the club substantial donations. Others believed that in Britain they could and should not follow the same divisions as they were used to in Kenya and India. To mark their membership to the club, the two new members hosted a lavish welcome dinner for the other Patel members. However, during our stay in London we never saw them again during the afternoon gatherings at the club, nor did they participate in any of the other social activities.

On the whole, village life in Gujarat still has a profound effect on the first generation of Patidar immigrants. During their formative years, they lived in the village where they attended school and spent their childhood. Importantly, many of them grew up during the patriotic period of the national independence movement which made them even more conscious of being proud of their Indian culture and heritage. The social bonds with their home village and with other Patidar immigrants from the same marriage circle, first in East Africa and later in Britain, have cemented those ties with their village of origin even more firmly. Therefore, the social identity of the first generation of Patidar immigrants is deeply embedded in village life, and the ties with their place of origin and with the members of their marriage circle in Gujarat are still quite powerful.

This caste and ethnic-specific nature of transnational linkages and feelings of solidarity between immigrants abroad and their family members in India is also visible in the field of religion. Among the Patidar immigrants in London, the Swaminarayan Temple is a clear case in point. This temple, established in 1995, illustrates the prominent presence of Hinduism in the UK. Besides the many religious and social gatherings, the Swaminarayan Department in London has its own primary and secondary schools and organizes Gujarati-language lessons. Several Patidar families have proudly taken me to the marble temple in London, where, with the help of modern media technology, efforts are being made to try to promote Hinduism amongst the second and third generation Gujarati immigrants. The original Swaminarayan sect, founded in Gujarat at the beginning of the nineteenth century, has become a global movement with a continuing flow of sect leaders from India visiting diaspora groups in the UK and other countries where the Gujarati diaspora has settled.[4]

In general, it is the world Hindu organization—the Vishwa Hindu Parishad (VHP)—that is in charge of the spread of Hindu ideals from India to the rest of the world. In recent years, this Hindu front organization, established in India in 1964, has set-up local branches in countries with a substantial population of people of Indian origin. It is from these local branches that the VHP tries to promote the Hindutva doctrine. The British branch of the organization, established in 1972, regularly organizes lecture tours, busies itself with religious education in government schools and publishes illustrated magazines, brochures and study books. Through its organizational and personal links with the BJP in India, the VHP endeavours to reinforce nationalist feelings among Indian immigrants and tries to gain support for its Hindutva policy. The Gujarati media in the UK, for example, seems to be playing an ever-increasing role in silencing any possible criticism by the Indian diaspora of the aggression and violence towards religious minorities in India.[5]

These examples of transnational linkages between Patidar immigrants in London and their caste members in Gujarat show how globalization has been indubitably responsible for the increase in Western influences in Asia, but conversely of Asian influences in Europe. Although recently there has been an increasing interest in this oriental side of globalization, there is a preponderant tendency to view it in terms of the import of traditional norms and values from Asia, which are threatening modern European society. Our view of Asia seems therefore to have changed from seeing it as a region where globalization has been taking place at a slower pace than in the West, to a region in the world from which the process of globalization in itself is being threatened.

The Complexity of Transnational Linkages

The foregoing brief account indicates that members of the Patidar community in London maintain frequent long-distance family linkages with their home region in India. Regular visits and frequent contacts keep many of the Patidar immigrants in London closely linked to their villages in Gujarat and the reverse is equally true. The example of Ashok Patel at the beginning of this chapter shows that these transnational linkages between Asia and Europe have several faces. Globalization undeniably causes an increase in the process of Westernization; the growth in the process of Easternization, however, cannot be overlooked. Moreover, these contacts also result in a strengthening of what is usually termed as 'traditional ties' in Asia. The growing importance of caste organizations among the Patidars of Gujarat has been, to a significant degree, determined by the impetus they have received from the members of the same community in the UK and the USA. In their attempts to create their own place in an alien society, the Patidar immigrants make extensive use of traditional ties, resorting to modern means of organization. During the 1970s and 1980s, a significant number of Patidar organizations were set up in the UK and America on the basis of sub-caste marriage circles and villages of origin. This new emphasis on old allegiances found its way back to the home front in Gujarat, where it has breathed new life into the dormant caste organizations of the Patidars. In recent years, under the impulses emanating from sister organizations in the UK and America, several Patidar organizations in Gujarat have become active again or have even been set up for the first time.

This prompts the question whether it might sometimes be more appropriate to speak of parent organizations in the diaspora and of sister institutions in the home region.

In many instances, the visits of the Patidar immigrants to India and of their Indian relatives to Britain are related to the marriages of their family members either in Britain or in India—mostly to a marriage partner from the other country. During the visits of the Patidar immigrants to India, activities related to religion are also very common. During the last twenty-five years, the popularity of the Swaminarayan sect has increased among the Patels in Britain (Pocock 1976). Although many Patels in central Gujarat have been followers of the Swaminarayan sect for a long time, the shift to the Akshar Pursottam 'branch' is a more recent phenomenon and one which is clearly related to the Patel community in Britain. During their visits to India, many relatives make tours of several temples in India, donate substantial amounts to local temples and participate in rituals and gatherings.

The popularity and powerful position of the Swaminarayan sect in Gujarat is also a fairly recent phenomenon, determined to a large extent by the influence of the Gujarati community in the UK and in America. The construction of a large number of Swaminarayan temples in the villages in Gujarat over the past few decades has been financed largely by Gujarati immigrants. Because of its influence in the Gujarati diaspora—first in East Africa, later in the UK and America—the Akshara Purushottam branch of the reformist movement of Swaminarayan centred in Gujarat has gained in strength allowing it to play an important social role and build-up political influence. The 1992 construction of the Akshardham temple complex in the capital of Gujarat, Gandhinagar, financed mainly by its members in the diaspora, illustrates the power and wealth recently acquired by this sect.[6] It is no coincidence that Muslim extremists selected this highly prestigious complex to launch a terrorist attack in 2002 as a reaction to the anti-Muslim pogrom in Gujarat in February and March of that year.

These examples of transnational religious linkages between Patidar immigrants in London and their family members in Gujarat, described earlier, illustrate that the process of globalization is more than Westernization: globalization also entails the spread of influences from Asia to other parts of the world. Although there has recently been more interest in this process of Easternization (see, e.g. Hobson

2004), it is still viewed mainly in terms of strengthening traditional norms and values, which are posing a threat to 'modern' European society. The increasing importance of religion and caste in Gujarat shows, however, that these developments cannot be considered merely a local defensive reaction to global developments coming from the West. The process of adjustment and adaptation as a minority from Asia in a Western society strengthens the existence of transnational linkages and reinforces global identities, which in turn leads to social and cultural changes in the immigrants' country of origin (see also Ballard 1994; Ong 1999).

NOTES

1. All names in the case studies presented in this paper are pseudonyms, an attempt to preserve some measure of anonymity.
2. See, e.g. George Ritzer's publications concerning the 'MacDonaldization of Society' (1993, 1997).
3. Mario Rutten and Pravin J. Patel 2004. This research was funded by the Indo-Dutch Programme on Alternatives in Developments (IDPAD), with additional support from the Amsterdam School for Social Science Research (ASSR) of the University of Amsterdam. The study was based on fieldwork conducted in 1998 among members of the Patidar community in rural central Gujarat and among their relatives in London in 1999. Members of the Patidar community are also known by their common surname Patel. In order to study the linkages between the Patidars or Patels of India and Britain, we collected information through a survey from 313 households in six villages in central Gujarat which have relatives in Britain, out of which 157 were selected for in-depth case studies. This was followed by a survey among 159 Patidar households in Greater London, of which 80 were selected for in-depth case studies. Members of the Patidar households in Greater London originated from the six villages in central Gujarat and many of them were direct relatives of the families studied in India. Most of the quantitative information presented in this chapter refers to the survey conducted in the villages in India on the 313 Patidar households with relatives in Britain.
4. Raymond B. Williams (1984: 185–93); and Rachel Dwyer (1994: 186–90). For an overview of the Hindu diaspora and Hinduism in Britain (and Trinidad), see S. Vertovec (2000).
5. Parita Mukta (2000). See Arvind Rajagopal (1997) for an analysis of the relations between transnational networks and Hindu nationalism in the American context.

6. See, amongst others, Williams (1984), Dwyer (1994) and Mukta (2000). The moral and financial support that Patidar immigrants give to their caste members in Gujarat in an attempt to strengthen religion and to build-up a Hindu nation is an illustration of what Ben Anderson termed 'Long-Distance Nationalism' (1992).

REFERENCES

Anderson, Benedict R. O'G (1992), *Long-Distance Nationalism: World Capitalism and the Rise of Identity Politics*, Amsterdam: University of Amsterdam, Centre for Asian Studies.

Ballard, Roger (ed.) (1994), *Desh Pardesh: The South Asian Presence in Britain*, London: Hurst & Company.

Dwyer, Rachel (1994), 'Caste, Religion and Sect in Gujarat: Followers of Vallabhacharya and Swaminarayan', in Roger Ballard (ed.), *Desh Pardesh: The South Asian Presence in Britain*. London: Hurst & Company, pp. 165–90.

Helweg, A.W. (1987), 'Why Leave India for America? A Case Study Approach to Understanding Migrant Behaviour', *International Migration*, XXV, pp. 165–78.

——— (1990), 'Sikh Identity in England: Its Changing Nature', in J.T. O'Connell et al. (eds), *Sikh History and Religion in the Twentieth Century*, Delhi: Manohar, pp. 356–75.

Hobson, John M. (2004), *The Eastern Origins of Western Civilisation*, Cambridge: Cambridge University Press.

Jain, Ravindra K. (1993), *Indian Communities Abroad: Themes and Literature*, Delhi: Manohar.

Landes, David (1998), *The Wealth and Poverty of Nations: Why Some are so Rich and Some so Poor*, New York: W.W. Norton.

Lyon, M.H. and B.J.M. West (1995), 'London Patels: Caste and Commerce', *New Community*, 21(3) 399–419.

Mukta, Parita (2000), 'The Public Face of Hindu Nationalism', *Ethnic and Racial Studies*, 23(3): 442–66.

Ong, Aihwa (1999), *Flexible Citizenship: The Cultural Logics of Transnationality*, Durham: Duke University Press.

Pocock, D.F. (1976), 'Preservation of the Religious Life: Hindu Immigrants in England', *Contributions to Indian Sociology*, 10(2): 341–65.

Rajagopal, Arvind (1997), 'Transnational Networks and Hindu Nationalism', *Bulletin of Concerned Asian Studies*, 29(3): 45–58.

Ritzer, George (1997), *The MacDonaldization Thesis: Explorations and Extensions*, London: Sage.

——— (1993), *The MacDonaldization of Society an Investigation into the*

Changing Character of Contemporary Social Life, Thousand Oaks: Pine Forge Press (revd. edn. 2000).

Rutten, Mario, and Pravin J. Patel (2004), 'Family Linkages between India and Britain: Views from Gujarat and London', in Srilata Ravi, Mario Rutten and Beng-Lan Goh (eds), *Asia in Europe, Europe in Asia*, Singapore/Leiden: Institute of Southeast Asian Studies/International Institute for Asian Studies, pp. 242–66.

Vertovec, S. (2000), *The Hindu Diaspora: Comparative Patterns*, New York: Routledge.

Williams, Raymond B. (1984), *A New Face of Hinduism: The Swaminarayan Religion*, Cambridge: Cambridge University Press.

CHAPTER 11

Diversion of Land and Displacement in India: Review of Evidence and Issues

AMITA SHAH AND ANIMESH KUMAR

1. Introduction

One of the important and yet less attended downsides of India's major stride towards economic development has been the diversion of land and displacement of a large number of human population from the socio-cultural milieu as well as the natural resources critical for their survival. While there is no systematic assessment of the magnitude and the complexities of displacement faced by people in different situations, a rough estimate suggests that nearly twenty million persons may have been displaced due to various projects of planned development since the 1950s (Fernandes 1994). Apart from the sheer magnitude, the phenomenon has highlighted glaring discrepancies in the way development has been perceived and, at the same time, how the rescue (compensatory) mechanism has actually worked. As a result, there has been a shift of resources from the poorer to the richer sections of the society. It is therefore imperative to evolve a framework which not only seeks to recognize the stakes of the displaced, but also ensures a mechanism to make them reap a fair share of the benefits in the processes of development.

The legal structure governing land alienation and compensation in India represents a fairly complex cobweb of policies which until now had taken a more conservative (and also conservationist) approach to the diversion of land from forest and agriculture to other uses. In practice, however, the policies have been much more liberal without the corresponding transparency in terms of sharing of information about the rationale for diversion of land and the terms at which the diversion took place, including compensatory mechanisms. The process of diversion of land from the forest or agricultural sector thus has been mainly an outcome of a congruence of various vested interests—the state, the private sector (often multinational corporations) and the local elites. Globalization has fostered these processes further by liberalizing the land-use policies.

There is no denying the fact that land, with a more or less given quantum of supply, is the basic and critical factor of production for almost all kinds of economic activities as well as human settlement (Shah et al. 2005). It is therefore essential that its allocation across different economic activities and uses is based on sound theoretical premises, combined with the ground realities of multiple objectives—some of which often go beyond the narrowly defined goals of economic growth *per se*. Entitlement to livelihood and access to factors of production, especially land, is one such important objective that needs to be incorporated while allocating land across different uses and users in a predominantly agrarian economy such as India. The allocation mechanism has to not only address the needs of economic activities or sectors (including housing) but also look into the specific needs of various ecosystems, regions, and communities.

One of the most important problems facing land-use policy in India is asymmetry in the sectoral composition of the gross domestic product (GDP) and employment, or people's dependence on land-based activities for deriving basic livelihood. Although the primary sector accounts for about 24 per cent of the GDP, it provides employment (though partial) to nearly 60 per cent of the people and occupies nearly 64 per cent of the total geographical area (including forest). On the other hand, the secondary and tertiary sectors account for 76 per cent of the GDP and use nearly 7–8 per cent of the geographical area in the country.

Given the heavy dependence on the primary sector for employment and livelihood, the policies, till recently, had been fairly conservative with respect to diversion of land from agriculture or forest to other uses such as development of infrastructure (including irrigation), industry and mining, and urbanization. While this is fairly valid, given the agrarian nature of the Indian society and economy, this well-intended approach is facing severe pressure due to increasing demand from the rapidly growing economic sectors like industry, mining and infrastructure, besides the substantially large increase in population—both factors giving rise to increased urbanization.

The conservationist, hence conservative, policies pursued so far are prohibitive rather than proactive in terms of evolving a rationale for allocating land for the rapidly growing sectors, other than the primary sector, which contribute more than three-fourth of India's GDP. But this does not mean absence of diversion to other uses. In fact, the conservative policies have given rise to processes and mechanisms which have proved counterproductive to the very cause of conservation; for, in the absence of a well-laid-out policy for land allocation, decisions are often taken under duress due to lobbying and political pressure. This prepares a fertile ground for ad hocism and corruption. At the same time, those who get displaced in the process gain little by way of compensation as the procedure does not allow adequate space for building counter pressure, public debate, and properly negotiated outcomes. The result is a 'loss-loss' situation where neither the least damaging solution for allocating land for alternative uses is obtained nor appropriate compensation for the displaced is ensured.

Land allocation has been one of the most contested policy issues. It has triggered many controversies, especially when developmental projects for irrigation, mining and other infrastructure like ports, etc., involved large-scale acquisition of land and/or displacement of people. The latest controversy is over Special Economic Zones (SEZ). In fact, urbanization is the most important use for which land is being diverted (Sharma 2003). The controversy about diversion of land for urban-industrial uses is a pointer to the fact that the issue is not so much about diverting the requisite amount of land for a sector or economic activity, which is important not only for economic growth but also for reducing population pressure in the primary sector. Rather, objections raised are mainly on account of the vested interests that develop over diverting more agriculturally fertile land, invariably without appropriate mechanisms for compensation to the farmers; and also on the rationale for providing fiscal concessions.

The existing, literature, therefore, suffers from the absence of a larger picture pertaining to the magnitude, impact and implications of land diversion owing to different types of development-induced displacement in different parts of the country. The present chapter is an attempt to bridge this gap by reviewing the existing understanding on the various issues related to land-use, diversion from primary sector and displacement in India. The main objectives of the chapter are to examine (a) the extent and magnitude of diversion of land from forest/agriculture through acquisition as well as conversion induced by land market in the urban fringe; (b) the recent reforms in land policies; and (c) the implications for evolving a framework for allocation and use of land with clearly stated mechanisms for sharing of benefits from the development projects with the displaced and the poor.

Section 2 presents a brief account of land diversion and displacement owing to different types of developmental projects and major issues pertaining to each of them. Section 3 discusses the phenomenon of the rapidly growing land market and examines the impact on households in the periphery. A tentative outline for a framework for land policy which simultaneously addresses the issue of use, development (or regeneration and management), and allocation of land across different sectors has been given in Section 4. Finally, Section 5 provides summary of the major observations in this chapter.

2. Land-use and Land Allocation in a Changing Economy: Some Evidence

STATE REGULATIONS AND MARKET FAILURE

Land-use and land markets have been subject to a large number of regulations across countries—developed and developing. The basic rationale underlying state regulations is the non-renewable nature of land, which is the basic factor of production. Land, besides being critical for ensuring sustained economic growth, under different categories of capability and uses, performs specific ecological functions. Each of the various uses, especially in primary sector activities such as crop cultivation, pasture development, plantation, livestock rearing, inland fishery and mangrove cultivation in the coastal areas, has a specific contribution towards sustaining diversity and thereby the ecological balance. Moreover, land and its use or management is also important for facilitating drainage and therefore, governing groundwater regimes or catchments (GOI 2006). This, in turn, has special significance for managing natural resources on a watershed basis. Minerals beneath the surface land also have special implications in so far as they are both exhaustible and non-renewable.

Finally, land, as noted earlier, plays a significant role in shaping the socio-cultural milieu in predominantly agrarian economies.

Although rooted in economic value as an ultimate economic security source, land becomes a symbol of social status and a means of deriving political power.

It is in this context that various economies have tried to evolve a strategy for land-use and its allocation over different sectors. The most important thread underlying the policy approaches across various economies is the recognition of market failure for allocating land across different economic activities, especially the shift away from the primary sector, where the intrinsic value of land as a natural resource is still retained. Obviously, marginal productivity measured in terms of monetary value is not the appropriate indicator for determining the diversion of land from primary to other sectors in the economy. For the demand-supply dynamics, at any given point of time or even in the context of forward trading and speculative transactions, may not completely capture the future as well as the existing value of land and the forest, water and minerals embodied therein. This leaves land markets within mainly urban and peri-urban areas where land is already diverted from primary sector activities and is subject to growth which, at least in theory, is possible to stipulate. Economic theory, especially in the neoclassical tradition, thus is most applicable to land markets in urban and peri-urban areas. For the rest, perspectives emanating from various disciplines or analytical frameworks such as environmental and ecological economics, political economy and development with equity and a human face may have to be combined. Unfortunately, a holistic perspective like this is yet to emerge for simultaneously addressing the critical issue of land-use, allocation and management.

The issue of a land-use and allocation policy, however, consists of a number of divergent scenarios:

1. Diversion of land across different uses within primary sectors, i.e. from pastures, forests and permanent fallow (or wasteland) to cropland and sometimes vice versa, and from any other earlier uses to waterbodies and vice versa.
2. Diversion from the primary sector, i.e. from cropland, pastures, forest to industry, mining and infrastructure including irrigation.
3. Diversion from the primary sector to urban development—this is a special variant of category 2 above. It, however, needs to be treated as a separate category because its location as well as pace is deemed to be limited and subject to fairly approximate stipulations as compared to other two categories.

LAND-USE AND LAND DIVERSION IN INDIA: ESTIMATES AND ISSUES

Increasing demand from some of the rapidly growing sectors (like industry, services and infrastructure) and mounting demographic pressure in the country have led to the conversion of land from the primary sector (i.e. agriculture, pasture, forest) to alternate uses. The proportion of area under non-agricultural use more than doubled between 1950 and 2001, from 3.29 per cent to 7.86 per cent (Table 11.1). Besides this, more than 6 per cent of the area is still in the category of 'barren and unculturable land'. Over time, the area under the two categories of land-use has declined from 16.7 per cent to 14.1 per cent.

An important feature of the changing land-use pattern in India is that only a part of the increase in non-agricultural land seems to have come from the category of barren and unculturable land. As, the evidence suggests, that a large part of the land diverted for irrigation, mining, infrastructure, and urban-industrial use in peri-urban areas has come from forest, pastures and cultivable land. Initially the diversion from primary sector uses was compensated for by a net increase in land under cultivation, a large part of which may have come from culturable wasteland, besides the settlement of forest land for agriculture. Unfortunately this kind of expansion does not seem to be possible anymore. The result therefore is a net decline in cultivated land as observed recently (Reddy 2006).

Unfortunately there is no systematic estimate of the extent of land

TABLE 11.1: CHANGES IN LAND-USE PATTERN IN INDIA

	1950–1	1975–6	2001–2
Forests	14.24	21.92	22.58
Area under Non-Agricultural Uses	3.29	6.13	7.86
Barren and Unculturable Land	13.42	7.09	6.27
Permanent Pastures and Grazing Lands	2.35	4.14	3.48
Land Under Misc. Trees and Groves	6.97	1.19	1.11
Culturable Wasteland	8.07	5.83	4.37
Fallow Lands	9.89	7.16	8.15
Net Area Sown	41.77	46.55	46.19

Source: Ministry of Agriculture, Govt. of India.
Note: Figures as percentage share of total reported area.

diversion for different uses. The land-use data also fails to capture the real picture owing to limitations in the system of land records and illegal (*benami*) transactions, especially in the peri-urban areas. Nevertheless, a recent attempt to gauge the magnitude of land being diverted in the urban periphery of Hyderabad came up with an estimate of 90,000 hectares [ibid.]. Extrapolating this for, say, ten to twelve cities with an average size of Hyderabad gives a figure of nearly one million hectares. This is less than 1 per cent of the total geographical area in the country.

The problem, as noted earlier, is not merely about the magnitude of land being diverted; the issue is, which land, at what cost, and with what kind of compensation package? In the case of peri-urban areas, the land is most likely to be under cultivation at the time of diversion. The following is a brief account of the extent of displacement under major types of developmental projects and the issues related to each of them. This will help in placing in context the recent controversy on diversion of land for urban-industrial uses.

DISPLACEMENT AND ISSUES IN RESETTLEMENT & REHABILITATION (R&R): A BRIEF REVIEW

It has been estimated that over a five-decade period (between 1951–90) more than 20 million people have been displaced by various projects (Table 11.2). Of these, more than 75 per cent of the displacement was caused by irrigation/multipurpose dams, followed by mining activities (12 per cent) and industries (5.9 per cent). The type of land and the process of obtaining it, which varies across different categories of projects, have been depicted in Appendix 11.1.

Another important observation from Table 11.2 is that only 25 per cent of the displaced have been resettled owing to a complex mix of factors—weak policy, inadequate funds as well as administrative set-up, and, above all, low political commitment in the wake of an almost total lack of agency to take up the issue on behalf of the displaced.

Irrigation

Big dams have a peculiar feature of representing one of the most successful experiences in India's economic development, and at the same time being a major culprit of displacement and uneven develop-

TABLE 11.2: EASTIMATE OF DISPLACED PERSONS (DPs) BY TYPE OF PROJECT (1951–90)

	Total DPs (in lakhs)	Percentage of Total DPs	Resettled DPs (%)	Share of Tribals in DPs (%)
Dam	164.0	77.0	25.0	38.5
Mines	25.5	12.0	24.7	52.2
Industries	12.5	5.9	30.0	25.0
Wildlife	6.0	2.8	20.8	75.0
Others	5.0	2.3	30.0	25.0
Total	213.0	100	25.0	40.9

Source: Fernandes, 1994.

ment in the country. The big irrigation projects have contributed significantly towards enhancing India's capacity to produce food grains and thereby provide employment as well as food security (besides flood moderation and drought mitigation), hydropower generation and groundwater recharge (Baijal and Singh 2000). But the flip side of this development is fairly large, especially when one looks at complex ecological issues based on their long-term environmental impact (Bandyopadhyay et al. 2002).

Displacement caused by large irrigation projects is considered to be the most contentious simply because of the fact that they encompass extensive tracts of land. Most of the displaced populations are the inhabitants of the upper reaches. Due to poor quality of land there they generally live in poverty. The construction of dams necessitates their displacement, which only adds to their miserable condition. As the quality of land is generally not good, it doesn't fetch high prices and if land is provided, it is even more uncultivable. The net result of the entire process is that the poor are made to suffer while the farmers in the lower reaches reap all the benefits. Thus, the equity issue remains unattended.

An important aspect of the (R&R) policy in irrigation is the provision of land in the command area. In fact, this should be the acid test for assessing the benefit-cost ratio of an irrigation project. The experience over a long period of time, however, suggests that this is not feasible—politically as well as administratively. Alternatively, the norm of 'land for land' has been accepted as part of the R&R policy. The Sardar Sarovar Project (SSP) on the Narmada River in

Gujarat is exemplary evidence on how the norm could be followed in actual practice (Palit 2004; Iyengar 1997). But the experience elsewhere has been quite disappointing as indicated by whatever limited efforts have gone in managing the R&R package for the oustees in the counterpart of the Narmada project in Madhya Pradesh.

Apparently the main issue is about not finding adequate land for the resettlement of a large number of oustees, not to mention the quality of land and the inadequacy of the requisite support for cultivating the land efficiently in a new environment. The evidences therefore suggest that despite being provided with land the poor quality of it has resulted in negative impacts on the livelihood of the oustees (Sah 2003; Whitehead 1999). Since the process of R&R is still on, it may be premature to make any final comment on the outcome.

While the process is extremely complex, it is critical to recognize that even a moderately successful R&R is contingent upon the process of negotiation and handholding by civil society organizations [or Community Based Organization (CBO)]. The limited success in the case of the SSP is largely attributable to the strong support of an Non-Governmental Organization (NGO) (namely, Arch Vahini) in Gujarat which oversaw the entire process as an officially appointed agency. There is lot to learn from this experience. But the larger issue of effective negotiation still remains unattended. The negotiations should imply effective dialogue between those with land in submergence (losers) *vs.* those in the command (gainers) areas. The state and the CBOs should facilitate negotiations within the overall frame of R&R. Such processes, however, seems quite unfeasible in a young democracy such as India's; the engineering as well as water centric approach to irrigation projects makes it even more difficult.

At this juncture the story of big dams in India seems to be on a rapid deceleration, mainly because of the widespread protests (Khagram 2005). Nevertheless, the unfinished agenda of the R&R in the case of the completed irrigation project needs to be attended to on a priority basis rather than accepting it as a fait accompli. The process, as also evident from the experience of the SSP, has to be long term rather than a one-off resettlement and should be based on possible processes of negotiations as noted earlier.

The costs—human as well as ecological—borne by the society, therefore, need to be seen in the light of the alternative approaches for managing irrigation and power. Attempts have been made to reconcile the large verses the small dam debate by having a middle way in the form of a reduction in the height of the SSP dam while at the same time maintaining the quantum of supply of water to Gujarat (Paranjape and Joy 2006). This is proposed to be done by harnessing local water resources and not relying solely on 'behind-the-dam' storage. Such an arrangement makes a remarkable reduction in the submergence area—and therefore displacement—although with a slight reduction in power generation. Essentially the need is to evolve alternative models which could provide better outcomes in terms of displacement and environmental damages.

Mining

Mining activities represent a situation of somewhat limited options as compared to several other developmental projects like irrigation, industry and infrastructure, given the fact that minerals or mineral-based industries such as coal, cement, and basic metals constitute some of the core sectors have a significantly large multiplier effect throughout the economy. At the same time, location of mining sites is determined by its availability, given the state of the technology. In most cases, the mining sites are found to be having a strong spatial correlation with rich forest/vegetative cover. The challenge, unlike that in the case of irrigation or industry and infrastructural projects, is that of reducing the demand and at the same time undertaking the requisite reclamation measures.

Mining has severe negative impacts on the land quality and directly contributes to environmental degradation and pollution and ultimately affects the tribal population adversely. The situation becomes further complicated when mining of radioactive minerals is involved. Decades of indiscriminate mining has left many villages highly polluted, rendering the lives of the inhabitants miserable due to widespread pollution levels and its ill effects on health and agriculture (Panda 2006).

The long-term effects of mining are more severe than the immediate ones. For instance, a few decades of indiscriminate mining destroys all available agricultural lands. Mining as a major economic activity in a particular area also hinders the growth of other industries. Water resources get exhausted or contaminated with time. Therefore, once the mines are completely exhausted, local populations are left with no livelihood options which further deteriorates their condition (Mahadevia 1999).

Till the proclamation of the Coal Bearing Areas (Acquisition and

Development) Act (CBAA) of 1957, all lands for mining were acquired by the government on the basis of the Land Acquisition Act (LAA), 1894 (Adhikary and Ghosh 2005). However, the CBAA does not even require that landowners be informed personally before acquisition and the information is only published in the gazettee. Thus, the villagers earn about the acquisition too late to raise objections within the specified time limit; sometimes they get the information after the legal period (George, 2004).

The policy followed by Coal India Limited (CIL) for resettlement has been quite popular among the affected population for the simple reason that CIL offered jobs to the displaced population (Adhikary and Ghosh 2005). Thus, the affected population got a share in the benefits of the project and CIL in its turn could use this lure of jobs as a 'bargaining chip' to acquire land for mining. However, with increasing downsizing this is no longer being offered as an option (Herbert and Lohiri-Dutt 2004).

The challenge, therefore, is to work progressively on demand management. While technological advancement is an important feature for reducing the requirement of various minerals, it is essential that these resources not be exploited for export since the multiplier effects, then, would not take place within the domestic economy. The bottomline therefore is to minimize the scale of this activity to a level which can support the economy with a desirable sectoral composition. Wherever necessary, mineral-based activities may take place by ensuring least cost to the environment and adequate measures for R&R. Ensuring appropriate reclamation of the mined area is equally important. Again, a multi-stakeholder agency assumes a critical role in this context.

Industrialization

While industrial growth is more or less synonymous with economic growth, the pattern of industrialization adopted in the Indian planning has been resource-intensive and spatially extensive, having the capacity to absorb additional workforce. The pattern poses two important challenges: First, it extracts substantial amounts of resources, including mineral for energy and land and water for setting up industrial units and the associated urban centres. On the other hand, the sector, with its limited job opportunities, leaves a large army of an underemployed workforce to fend for itself in various activities in the primary and tertiary sectors. Development of some of the basic industries during the early phase of planning had led to large-scale conversions of land, including forest land, for setting up mega-units, mainly in the public sector. But the mega-projects such as steel, cement and oil and natural gas-based plants remained more or less islands of modern growth without generating a significant impact, especially in terms of employment, in the peripheral economy.

Another issue pertaining to job creation is that (i) either the jobs available are of semi-manual type hence not acceptable to the family members of erstwhile landowning households; or (ii) the job is offered to only one member of the household without the provision of it being transferred to the next generation. This raises a question of a long-term partnership in the profits of the industrial unit, built on land which could have been a perennial source of income for the household.

The asymmetry between growth in GDP and employment has continued over a period of time. By 2001, the industrial sector contributed 27 per cent of the GDP (Joshi 2004); its contribution to employment was less than 17 per cent (Datt 2002). While there is no denying that industrialization holds the key to sectoral transformation, essential for reducing pressure on natural resources, limited job creation has jeopardized the expected outcomes. Given this scenario, diversion of land (and forests, minerals and water) may raise special concerns (Reddy 1994).

The twin issues are,

(i) how to make industrial growth more employment-generating so as to absorb communities in the peripheral areas whose livelihood base gets eroded due to islands of industrial growth in the hinterlands; and
(ii) how to minimize the negative impact of industrial growth on natural resources, viz., land, air, water.

The recent spurt in the debate on the creation of SEZs reflects the special relevance of the issues raised above. Given the fact that the country has already set-up a number of free trade zones (FTZ), it is not clear whether SEZs would serve any special purpose in terms of attracting new units and boost exports (Chandrashekhar 2006).

Pending this enquiry, the real issue that has sparked off the controversy is of the leeway given to the industrial units in SEZs with respect to allocation of land, labour regulations and environmental impact assessment. What is worse is that the states are competing among themselves to attract investments by providing fiscal and other concessions, leading to a situation of a 'race to the bottom' within the domestic economy.

The Board of Approvals (BoA)[1] has already (as of October 2006) granted formal and in-principle approvals to 237 and 166 SEZs respectively. As many as 225 proposals are also waiting with the BoA, many of which have already got or are in the process of getting approval (TNN 2006). If one looks at the magnitude of the land being diverted, it does not appear to be very large (Table 11.3). The issue, however, is that the project has led to the state supporting conversion of agricultural land by private operators who eventually may use it for real estate development rather than for promoting industrial growth and exports.

There are some noticeable differences between the formally approved and in-principle approved SEZs. For instance, the average size of SEZs for which approvals have already been granted is less than 150 ha while for the in-principle approved set it is more than 800 ha. More remarkably, there are only eight SEZs in the first set which have an area exceeding 1,000 ha, half of these being in Gujarat. The number for such SEZs in the latter exceeds the former by 50. Out of these 14 are in Maharashtra. Incidentally, a small state like Haryana has as many as 11 such SEZs in the offing, of which six have an area of more than 3,000 ha with the one being planned by Reliance Haryana SEZ having an area of 10,000 ha.

Besides weak justification for providing tax concessions, another important issue that has received attention from various quarters is that of the free hand given to the land-operators and the nexus with centres of political/bureaucratic power. The issue has come up sharply in the light of the International Monetary Fund (IMF), questioning the validity of setting up large numbers of relatively smaller SEZs in contrast to China where the strategy is to promote a few large SEZs (Aiyer 2006). This reinforces the observation about a 'race to the bottom', where the states, in connivance with land operators, seem to have gone on a land acquiring spree in a fast track mode.

It has been alleged that SEZs have translated into a free hand for abusing labour as well as environmental laws, and that they have provided many with land-grabbing opportunities (Fernandes 2006). The early signals clearly suggest that the entire process of land acquisition, development and transfer to individual industrialists involves huge profits. Strangely, the state also becomes appropriator

TABLE 11.3: TOTAL FORMAL AND IN-PRINCIPLE APPROVALS GRANTED BY THE BOARD OF APPROVALS AFTER IMPLEMENTATION OF SEZ RULES (UPDATED TILL OCTOBER 2006)

(Total land in hectares)

	Formal Approvals		In-principle Approvals		Total	
	No.	Total Land	No.	Total Land	No.	Total Land
Andhra Pradesh	45	9,460.8	9	3,768.4	54	13,229.2
Chhattisgarh	–	–	2	2,029.0	2	2,029.0
Chandigarh	2	87.5	–	–	2	87.5
Dadra & Nagar Haveli	–	–	1	80.0	1	80.0
Delhi	1	6.0	1	11.0	2	17.0
Goa	4	291.0	–	–	4	291.0
Gujarat	18	10,398.3	12	8,193.0	30	18,591.3
Haryana	19	818.4	27	43,002.0	46	43,820.4
Himachal	–	–	3	5,030.0	3	5,030.0
Jharkhand	1	36.0	–	–	1	36.0
Karnataka	29	1,672.3	17	4,721.0	46	6,393.3
Kerala	10	569.7	2	414.0	12	983.7
Madhya Pradesh	4	71.3	6	9,309.3	10	9,380.6
Maharashtra*	48	8,377.3	27	22,378.1	75	30,755.4
Orissa	5	745.6	7	4,060.3	12	4,805.9
Pondicherry	1	346.0	–	–	1	346.0
Punjab	4	252.0	7	1,571.0	11	1,823.0
Rajasthan	3	89.2	8	12,251.3	11	12,340.5
Tamil Nadu	25	1,300.6	12	5,078.0	37	6,378.6
Uttarakhand	3	468.2	1	14.0	4	482.2
Uttar Pradesh	8	133.8	10	5,954.3	18	6,088.1
West Bengal	7	170.3	14	11,827.2	21	11,997.5
Total	237	35,294.3	166	139,691.9	403	174,986.2

Source: Department of Commerce, Ministry of Commerce & Industry.
Note: *Areas of two formally approved SEZs not known.

of profit while the primary owner is completely left out of this nexus between the state and the private operators! According to C.P. Chandrashekhar (2006), this is tantamount to 'primary forms of accumulation' by the state which monopoly on allocation of land. This in turn has generated serious protest by farmers, especially when large tracts of agriculturally rich land are being diverted for SEZ under the pretext of 'public interest' (Ghosh 2006).

It is becoming increasingly clear that the issue is not so much about the total magnitude of land (say, less than 0.2 million ha till now) being allocated to an important sector like industry. Rather, it is of the indiscriminate use of monopoly power by the state, which in turn becomes party to accumulation of profit by patronizing land operators. The loss of environmental good, labour welfare and, above all, source of livelihood to the rural communities stands by and large, unjustified. This is particularly so when the farmers, having lost the land, are neither adequately compensated nor made partner in the chain of value addition on a long-term basis.

Coming back to the issue of land conversion, whereas most industrial development lands were acquired on the basis of LAA, the National Thermal Power Corporation (NTPC) follows its own R&R policy. The company adopted such a policy because the projects were often delayed in the absence of rehabilitation resulting in a negative reputation and refusal of loans (Adhikary and Ghosh 2005). The unique point of the policy is that it includes all project-affected persons (PAPs) including landowners and landless. They may opt for land for land (subject to availability) or a house. The policy also provides for self-employment in dairy, poultry, handicrafts, opening own shops, awarding small contracts, etc. (NTPC 1993). A similar pattern is also observed in the number of corporate houses setting up rural development wings. While these are initiatives in a positive direction, the efforts for rural development have, by and large, remained as add-ons to the spatial planning for industrial zones.

Apparently these are some of the positive initiatives if supported by adequate safeguards against environmental damage on the one hand and compensatory regeneration accompanied by people's partnership in the process of wasteland development on the other. At present, both seem to be critically missing.

In this context, the experience from the Project Linkage Approach (PLA) initiated in Gujarat as part of backward area development during the early 1980s may provide some useful insights. The approach was adopted at the time of setting up a large industrial estate in Ankleshwar (Bharuch district in Gujarat), as part of the policy for shifting industries to backward areas. According to the approach, the development of important linkages with the backward villages in the hinterland was integral to the setting up of the industrial area. Four types of linkages were envisaged: transport, training for skill formation, promotion of entrepreneurship, and provision of rural amenities. It was envisaged that these linkages would help the local youth to access employment opportunities and also improve the quality of life of the rural communities that had lost land and were also facing problems of pollution. While the initiative met with only partial success, it may still offer useful lessons (Shah 2001). The approach is unique in the sense that it was part of the developmental policies rather than a voluntary gesture by individual corporate houses, as noted earlier.

Forest: Environment Loss

Development-induced displacement has resulted in two major fallouts: environmental damage and loss of livelihood of the people. This is despite the detailed provisions for compensation under the LAA, 1894 and the R&R policy of 2003.

What differentiates forestry land conversion is the fact that the stakeholders have a wide ranging geographical entity—any loss due to a change in access to forest makes the loser a stakeholder and the person may be having a local, regional, national or even global presence (IEG, 2006). For long, this crucial ecological factor has remained largely ignored. Most of the developmental activities in the forested lands directly affect the tribal population who are the indigenous inhabitants. The tribals form more than two-thirds of the total population displaced due to activities in forests (Table 11.2).

The displacement of tribals from forested areas has always met with stiff resistance from them (Sarangi 1999; Asher and Kothari 2005). This is consequent upon the fact that forests are the primary means of livelihood for these tribals and restrictions imposed on their use leaves them deprived. At the same time, the fact remains that the creation of protected areas and sanctuaries is necessary for conservation of biodiversity. This has necessitated a search for new paradigms of conservation, which are inclusive of people's livelihood requirements. Recently the Indian Board of Wildlife has accepted in principle that there would be no forced displacement from protected areas (Rangarajan 2001). Eco-development projects also accept the principle of voluntary resettlement as part of protected area management. The problem, however, is that people trapped in the protected areas are neither covered by the regular developmental activities nor do they receive adequate compensation for lost opportunities while cooperating in the conservation measures.

In order to resolve the issue of compensation, an expert committee to work out the net present value (NPV) was constituted as mandated by the Supreme Court of India (IEG 2006). The report submitted by the expert committee held that forests were non-tradable. Hence it recommended that NPV calculation should not be based on assumptions of the alternative use of the same land, like urban housing, mining, building up a dam, roads, etc. Instead, the value should be based on the estimated loss due to such activities to be reckoned as an 'opportunity cost' of forest tracts.

NPV estimates vary over space and largely depend on the quality and density of the forest land. For instance, in the states of Madhya Pradesh and Chhattisgarh, the NPV is being recovered at the rate of Rs. 5.80 lakh per ha to Rs. 9.20 lakh per ha. Similarly, in Himachal Pradesh, the value varies from Rs. 1.57 lakh per ha for timber plantations to Rs. 8.57 lakh per ha for dense natural forests (IEG 2006).

The committee recommends a detailed procedure of NPV calculation with significant emphasis on biodiversity, forest cover and density. Importantly, the committee also recommends that NPV can be fully exempted only if the diversion also provides the same kinds of services as forests at the same location (e.g., carbon sequestration, retention of soil moisture, protection of biodiversity, etc.); in all other cases, private or public, no exemption from NPV is allowed. Thus, instead of a blanket claim on exemptions, NPV has been made highly conditional. For instance, while activities like construction of highways, any type of industry (including SEZs), mining and quarrying, etc., do not come under exemption, the relocation of villages, drinking water pipelines, etc., have been given full exemption. Similarly, major irrigation and hydel projects have been recommended for 30 per cent exemption whereas minor irrigation schemes have been given full exemption.

Another issue that deserves mention is in the context of state governments which work on the premise of encashing the special resource base they have at the opportune time. Missing the moment would imply a big opportunity lost. Hence, they have become highly proactive in getting outside investors to provide the financial resources that are extremely scarce. This problem could be resolved if the state governments were to apply the centre for funds as compensation for conservation of natural resources like minerals and forests in their respective states. There have been some moves in this direction where some of the forest-rich states have pleaded for additional resources from the central government as a 'disability fund'. Such options could possibly relieve the states from a distress sale of their natural resources. It would be possible to rationalize excessive exploitation of mineral resources to serve the interests of outside economies, if the federal finance system were to incorporate a mechanism to value conservation and pay for its compensation to financially poor states. Exploring an approach such as this may call for a more holistic framework drawing upon various developmental perspectives, as noted in Section 1.

Given this backdrop, the next section discusses the issue of land conversion in urban periphery, which has certain important differences *vis-à-vis* the issue of land acquisition and displacement discussed in this section.

3. Conversion of Agricultural Land in Peri-Urban Areas: Insights from Existing Literature

There are four important features which distinguish conversion of land in urban fringe areas from the issues of land acquisition and displacement discussed in the previous section:

1. Development of the urban fringe is the single most important factor causing diversion of land.
2. The land is generally sold by the owners rather than being acquired; hence there is the presence of a land market (though imperfect) in the urban fringe. This would imply that displacement 'voluntary' rather than forced.
3. The land in the urban fringe is generally more fertile as compared to wasteland available in areas further away from urban centres.
4. There is a fairly well-developed theoretical literature on land markets and perspectives on peri-urban development.

GROWING URBANIZATION: PUSH AND PULL FACTORS

India has experienced significant growth in its urban population since Independence. Till 1941, the proportion of the urban population was more or less stable at the level of or around 10 per cent. A substantial growth, however, has been experienced post-1980s when the proportion of urban population increased from 23 per cent to the present level of 28 per cent (Table 11.4). It is expected that urbanization will cross 35 per cent by the end of 2025 (Dyson and Visaria 2004).

Another important feature pertaining to the pattern of urbanization is the class composition. It is observed that as large as 68.6 per cent of the urban population lives in class I cities (i.e. having a population exceeding 0.1 million). This has special implications for expansion of the urban sprawl in the periphery of nearby urban centres in the country.

Urbanization in India, as widely recognized, is a result of both push and pull factors. The latter is often found to be the reality given the pace and composition of employment growth in the primary sector. There are also problems on the demand side since growth in the industrial sector has more or less come to a halt. This is what is being termed as 'urbanization moving ahead of industrialization' (Hoselitz 1957: 44) in many developing countries, including India.

But urban centres are bound to experience significant growth—first due to the sheer increase in population and secondly, due to the continued push from the rural economy. The recent evidence from the 59th round of the NSSO, that a substantially large proportion (40 per cent) of the farming households does not perceive agriculture as the desired option, highlights this phenomenon. An important implication of this has been a more activated land market where many more farmers may want to sell off at least a part of their land in order to make an entry into the urban economy for exploring alternative occupations for the subsequent generations.

As noted earlier, there is no systematic estimate of the total land covered by the peri-urban area. A rough estimation puts the number as one million hectares. This once again is not too high a number compared to the proportion of the population that inhabits it and contributes to the GDP. The problem is that of imperfections in the land market, hence the need for regulations, as discussed below.

TABLE 11.4: URBAN POPULATION BY CLASS OF TOWNS

Class	No. of Towns			Urban Population Distribution (%)		
	1981	1991	2001	1981	1991	2001
I (100000 & Above)	226 (5.7)	300 (8.1)	394 (9.0)	52.6	64.9	68.6
II (50000–99999)	325 (8.2)	345 (9.3)	404 (9.2)	14.0	11.0	9.72
III (20000–49999)	883 (22.4)	947 (25.6)	1,163 (26.6)	17.1	13.3	12.3
IV (10000–19999)	1,247 (31.6)	1,167 (31.6)	1,346 (30.7)	11.2	7.9	6.8
V (5000–9999)	920 (23.3)	740 (23.3)	879 (20.1)	4.4	2.6	2.3
VI (Less than 5000)	348 (8.8)	197 (8.8)	192 (4.4)	0.7	0.3	0.2
Total	3,949 (100)	3,696 (100)	4,378 (100)	100.0	100.0	100.0
Share of Urban Population in Total Population				23.34	25.71	27.80

Source: Census of India, 1981, 1991 and 2001.

THEORETICAL PERSPECTIVES: MARKET IMPERFECTION

There has been a fairly rich and growing literature on the theme of conversion of agricultural land in urban and peri-urban areas. It is neither the scope nor within the objective of this chapter, to review the entire literature. The limited objective here is to understand the main features of theoretical applications and empirical findings from studies which have gone into examining the cost and benefit of land conversion.

The vast literature on urban economics provides the basic rationale for urbanization and examines factors which determine the pace and pattern of urban growth in the midst of vast, and at times, stagnant rural economies, especially in developing countries like India. Productivity differentials and the growing population as well as under-employment in rural economies are the two basic forces 'pulling', and 'pushing', the population out of the rural areas. Agglomeration economies, locational economies and economies of scale and scope are the other major factors that operate on the pull side. Growing disparities in public investment in agriculture and allied activities (*vis-à-vis* other sectors) on the one hand, and basic amenities (in rural *vis-à-vis* urban areas) on the other give further impetus to the push factors.

The literature while reinstating the inevitability of urban growth and shift of the labour force away from the primary sector, has paid little attention to the implications of this kind of spatial as well as sectoral shift for the 'determinants of the processes of land allocation between rural and urban areas or, equivalently, between agriculture and non-agriculture' (Bhadra and Brando 1993: 2). The urban economics literature usually treats the role of the rural sector as residual, and most analyses employ the partial equilibrium model in isolation of the agricultural economy.

The above construct is fairly inadequate and unrealistic, where both the growth of the non-agriculture sector and the demand for urban land are situated in a complex mix of push and pull factors where 'equilibrium' may be arrived at by simultaneously changing (or correcting) the operating environment in both the agriculture and non-agriculture sectors and the rural and urban economies. This is essential because of the fact that the two are intrinsically linked to each other, especially in a large agrarian economy such as India's. Besides these there are imperfections that operate in the land markets, as noted earlier. The major imperfections that operate on the demand (pull) and supply (push) sides for urban land are presented in Box 11.1.

Box 11.1: Imperfections in Demand for and Supply of Agricultural Land

Demand Side	Supply Side
Land having scarcity value, hence subject to speculations	The present low level of viability of farming is due to suboptimal levels of technology and natural resource development; this may not reflect the actual potential of the land/sector
Being an important source of social-political power, becomes tool for political corruption/ favours	Does not take into account environmental externalities and future/existence value of land
Asymmetry between lobbying by industry and agriculture sectors; in fact the agricultural lobby representing rich/large farmers may implicitly push for a more liberal policy for conversion of land (lack of level playing field)	Imbalance between public investment for enhancing productivity of land in vast tracts of dryland regions, leading to distress selling of land
Monopsonistic market structure	Absence of institutional arrangements for overcoming low viability of small landholdings
Lack of adequate planning and cumbersome policies regulating land use, leading to non-transparency and corruption	Distress selling of land in the vicinity where land has been acquired for non-agricultural uses

Like most developing economies, India is also characterized by the phenomenon of over-urbanization, mainly due to the 'push' factors driving large numbers of in-migrants to the urban centres. This raises the question of whether the low level of industrialization (and employment growth therein) will ever reach a high enough scale to lift a large proportion of the population to income levels which would initiate the process of de-concentration of urban centres (Vinning et al. 1986). This implies that urbanization, given the population dynamics and sectoral imbalance in terms of output and employment growth, is a reality to reckon with.

An important alternative to land conversion is intensification of land-use, a method followed by some land-scarce countries like Japan and Singapore (UN 1973). However, in a country like India, with a highly skewed land–man ratio, conversion of agricultural lands in the vicinity of urban uses is resorted to.[2]

Recognizing the close interface between the agriculture and non-agriculture sectors and between rural and urban economies, some of the relatively recent strands of thought in urban economics have laid increasing emphasis on Peri-urban Environment or *Rurban* Development (Allen 2003). *Prima facie*, the new perspective is built on the rural–urban continuum and seeks to retain, to the extent possible, *rurality* while planning for urban development and natural resource-use and/or strengthen the coexistence of rural–urban features within and in the periphery of urban areas. Environmental planning and management of peri-urban areas therefore, should draw from three distinct fields, viz., rural, regional and urban planning. This is so because ecological, economic and social functions performed by the peri-urban area affects both urban as well as rural areas. In this situation the debate over 'compact' *versus* 'expanded' cities assumes special significance (Richardson et al. 2000). Whereas the former seeks to minimize diversion of agricultural land, the latter may open up new avenues for agriculture and related services to cater to the urban demand by retaining the basic elements of natural resource management and rural economies. The second approach may require a broad-based development of infrastructure as well as the provision of basic amenities. Both have strengths and weaknesses. What is therefore needed is a comprehensive analysis of cost-benefit under alternative scenarios of growth in rural economies and patterns of urbanization. Such analyses, till recently, have been more or less missing.

In the absence of comprehensive cost-benefit analyses under different scenarios, it would be useful to review some of the empirical studies on the impact of land conversion on the peripheral urban economy.

IMPACT OF LAND CONVERSION IN URBAN PERIPHERY: SELECT EVIDENCE

Land conversion surrounding urban centres presents a typical scenario, different from that in most other conversions; say, in the forest areas or remote rural areas. What makes land conversion in the rural-urban fringe[3] different is that most urban centres have evolved originally because of the natural endowments of the area (Barrow 1991).[4] Thus the fringe lands are generally more fertile and have been put to agricultural use. With increasing population pressure such lands are also bound to feel the pressure (Burton and Matson 1996). The situation is further complicated by an aggregation of uses by a variety of stakeholders. Even the farmers living in the area might find non-agricultural income sources to be more profitable and may resort to land speculations (Renaud 1979).

A number of studies have highlighted the problem created by the loss of agricultural land to accommodate the growing needs of various developmental projects as well as urbanization. While most of the studies, especially on industrial and other developmental projects, have focused on assessing the cost-benefit of the proposed projects in a larger economy-wide or societal context, efforts have seldom, been made to understand how the people who have lost their land have eventually been co-opted into the new economic order and how many of them have remained victims of the 'development' (Sharma 2003). This is mainly due to the fact that (a) adjustment or co-option to the new economic order is a long-drawn process; very few studies have gone into examining the process over a period of, say, 15 to 20 years; and (b) although urbanization-induced loss of agricultural land is relatively larger, it remains unnoticed as much of the land is sold 'voluntarily' under the 'rights to chose' use of the land by the owners.

Evidence from Calcutta

There is, however, a small but growing literature examining the impact of urbanization, especially diversion of agricultural land, on the rural economy and communities. Using a dual economy model in the context of the Calcutta Metropolitan District in India, Dipasis Bhadra (1991) observed that conversion of rural land into urban uses might lead to improvement of the aggregate welfare for the regional economy.

This observation however, is subject to limitations as the welfare impact is shaped by the characteristics of urban economies. The statistical results, as in the case of many developing countries, appear to support the hypothesis of over-urbanization (Tolley and Thomas 1987). This, in turn, may reinstate the case of broad basing the farm economy, which may give a further boost to non-farm activities both in rural as well as in small/medium towns (Mellor 2006).

Unruly Development in Delhi

The pressure of increasing urban space has been felt most severely in Delhi, particularly in the last two decades. The rapid expansion of urban boundaries to the bordering villages has caused widespread changes in the land-use and livelihood patterns in these villages. In a detailed analysis of a rural-turned-urban block in northern Delhi by J.V. Bentinck (2000), the impact of urbanization on the intertwined aspects of land-use and occupation has been largely found to be positive.

Urbanization of these villages has brought them physically and socially closer to the metropolitan city and much of the benefits accrued can be explained by an increase in the opportunities to commute to the city regularly. This has encouraged the village dwellers to opt for formal and informal work in the service sector in the city. But the real boom in the economy in the fringe areas has been brought about by a surge in the rent and tenancy business. Most of the factories and enterprises set-up in these areas belong to the city dwellers; hence the owners—the erstwhile large farmers—realize good amounts on the rented land. Very few villagers have gone in for industrial activity themselves, probably for lack of experience and training, and have instead preferred to enter government service or the transport business. However, this does not mean that only the large farmers have benefited. Marginal farmers, the landless and migrant labourers have all entered the service sector, joining white-collar or blue-collar jobs depending on their educational level. Of these, a few of the economically better villagers have opened small commercial units while the migrant class prefers to work in the newly created small manufacturing units in the village itself.

Another notable aspect of urbanization in the fringe areas of Delhi concerns agricultural activity. Many of the farmers have continued with their agricultural practice, of course with increasingly intensive cultivation and changes in the cropping pattern. Thus floriculture and horticulture, fuelled by a huge market in the city, have replaced staple crops. Many of the villagers have even gone in for high-value perishable crops with some opting to market the produce themselves with a view to reaping higher benefits. Similarly, dairy farming has also signified gains to the farmers. Urbanization has also had some adjunct benefits for agricultural activities, as, for instance, easier access to fields through better roads, flood prevention, and so on. Thus the net effect of urbanization on agriculture in the fringe villages is also found to be positive.

All these factors have been compounded by an obvious increase in urban infrastructural facilities and amenities in these villages. The electricity and water supply, and more importantly health services have greatly improved, bringing increased awareness about health and hygiene.

Thus, it can be largely inferred that urbanization of the fringe villages has had a positive impact on the socio-cultural-economic lives of the original dwellers, across all classes. The obverse side of the story is mainly about ecological concerns. Increased industrial activities have resulted in a sharp increase in various types of pollution. This in turn has had a very bad effect on the health of the poor labourers who generally live in slums close to the factories. Several incidences of asthma and tuberculosis have been found since the establishment of industrial units.

Secondly, a rapid population increase in these villages has resulted in increased congestion. The richer erstwhile landowners have moved out from the villages to settle in the city or elsewhere. However, the poorer small landowners, who have rented out a portion of their living space, face extreme congestion problems. Slum dwellers have their own set of obvious problems.

Most infrastructure-related problems are consequent upon a very rapid urbanization. The provision of facilities by the civic bodies has not been able to keep pace, resulting in narrow lanes and sewerage problems. In several places the existing infrastructure has been found to be extremely incapable of sustaining the burgeoning population.

The reconciliation of economic progress with the protection of environmentally sensitive situations seems to be an arduous task.

What makes the situation in Delhi typical is that the efforts to make the progress ecologically sensitive have had negative externalities on the economic front. With the Supreme Court ordering the relocation of all industrial units from residential localities, the workers in these factories have had to face the brunt. The small manufacturing units were largely dependent on the cheap labour available in the nearby slums and congested corners of the urbanized villages. With relocation these labourers have no other option but to regularly commute long distances, which puts a dent in their already crunched economic condition.

However, overall, it can be safely inferred from the study that the net benefits of the urbanization in the Delhi fringe have been positive. What is missing, however, in this account of the positive impact of urbanization in peri-urban areas is the process through which 'co-option' or integration took place; the terms on which benefits of the land market were shared; and last but not the least, who got left out of the benefits package and why.

There are no clear answers to these questions. What is also important is the generalization of these results when it comes to cities relatively smaller than Delhi and Calcutta. The following observations from Ahmedabad and Baroda in Gujarat may help in understanding these issues.

Ahmedabad and Baroda: Limited Benefits

According to a study by CEPT (1997) for Ahmedabad city, land transactions till the early 1990s were limited in terms of magnitude and spread. The urban sprawl of Ahmedabad city was within 20 km.[5] However, some of the villages had lost up to 60 per cent of their land for non-agriculture uses. Examining the impact of land conversion in the urban periphery of Ahmedabad and Baroda city, Shah (2000) observed that as much as 40 per cent of the land sold by the farmers for industrial uses was irrigated. Only 14 per cent of the sample households (having sold the land) reported having purchased another piece of land. Whereas the reasons for selling the land varied from low viability of farming to lack of interest among the future generation in farming as a profession, in most cases the land was sold to intermediaries who would eventually sell the land to actual users, including land developers. As a result, a substantial part of the land had remained unutilized for a fairly long time. Besides this, industrial growth had created negative externalities in terms of air and water pollution.

Against this background, the employment benefit was quite limited. The study reveals that one-third of the sample households had used a major part of the sale proceeds in productive investment and another 10 per cent indicated investing the money in fixed deposits. The remaining 50 per cent had used the money for social functions or for improving the housing condition. Given the fact that members of the farming households were reluctant to accept blue- or grey-collar jobs in the unorganized industrial sector, many of them had started to question the pace of land conversion in the area.

There has been no concerted effort to address the issue; neither is there any holistic land development agency except for a few metropolitan urban development authorities. The task of urban land development is left to different government departments on an ad hoc basis (UN, op. cit.). The municipal corporations is limited to providing urban facilities, while the district-level self-governing bodies (like *zila parishads*) are too ill-equipped for the task. Consequently, there is no formal master plan for the development of the peri-urban areas. Hence zoning of land-use is also absent, which results in scattered and haphazard development in the fringe area. An important problem in this context is that once the adjacent land is converted, it is difficult to manage farming operations in the vicinity. In fact, this is one of the important mechanisms used by the industry/land developers to get agricultural land, as has been observed in a number of cases.

The reality as seen from the foregoing evidence is thus mixed. There are certainly some gainers among the landowning community and also among the landless, who may obtain alternative occupations in the expanding urban economy, as shown by Bhadra (1991). But it is quite likely that a substantially large proportion of the erstwhile rural households will lose *vis-à-vis* their earlier situation.

The problem in this set of analyses is that of the absence of a counter-narrative. It is difficult to visualize, especially over a longer period of the adjustment process, a scenario that would have obtained in the absence of the development. This is particularly relevant in the light of the fact that agriculture in large tracts of the country is already facing a crisis owing to inappropriate and inadequate policy support. Also, environmental damage is yet to be assessed.

While this may reinstate the rationale for following a more

conservative and restrictive approach, as has been the case till recently, the policies need to respond to the growing compulsions of and/or aspirations for urbanization. Failure to do so would lead to widespread corruption, thereby making the cure worse than the disease itself. Obviously lifting all regulations is not the answer. Rather, what is needed is to explore various alternatives for both rural and urban development with built-in environmental costs. The trick thus lies in working out options and making informed choices rather than succumb to pressure from various quarters—urban planners, agricultural stagnation and the powerful.

What is essential therefore is to explore alternative scenarios where the agriculture sector and the people engaged thereof are to get a better deal in terms of policy support. In this case what appears to be the farmers' choice, to get rid of the land and farming as an occupation, may also undergo changes. Urbanization may then have to face a situation where a large number of farmers make informed choices rather than under the pressure of limited choices. This, in turn, may force the planners to work very systematically and judiciously towards managing urban sprawl and the peri-urban environment (Dhar 1998).

4. From Market to State Failure: Is There a Way Out?

The brief account of land diversion and displacement till now suggests that the state monopoly derived by using the rationale of 'market failure' for the determining allocation of land has, in fact, resulted in the 'state's failure'. This is reflected in terms of the ad hoc and excessive acquisition of land for various industrial (including SEZs), mining and infrastructural projects; an extremely weak compensation mechanism and follow-up thereof; and a haphazard urban sprawl. In most cases the state is seen to facilitate the appropriation of profit by the private developers. How to retreat from this growing syndrome of the dual burden of the failure of market as well as the state? Obviously neither stricter restrictions nor ad hoc liberalization could pave the way for a rational allocation of land across sectors. For the former, as noted earlier, illegal conversion or uncalled-for alienation creeps in, whereas the latter leads to loss of natural capital, both at the societal as well as the individual level.

TOWARDS A HOLISTIC APPROACH

The need of the hour is to reflect on past experiences of policy formulation as well as implementation and move forward towards a more rational and yet pragmatic approach, drawing upon four major strands of developmental perspectives:

- Sectoral Growth, inclusive of food growth self-sufficiency and employment security
- Land-use and Environmental Sustainability
- Management of Peri-urban Areas
- Compensatory Mechanisms

Ideally, allocation of land should be determined by the pace and composition of growth in the production sectors and the associated urbanization, subject to the land capability classification. This would imply acknowledgement by the LAA that land in capability classifications V–VII may be preferred while diverting land for developmental projects and other requirements. At the aggregate level, India has more than 19 million ha of non-cultivable wasteland which constitutes 5 per cent of the total reporting area. Ideally, this land should be diverted for various developmental projects.

The problem, however, is that the location of developmental projects is often governed by exogenous factors, different from land capability classification. For instance, projects related to mining, irrigation and infrastructure such as parts, have limited flexibility in terms of choosing the location. Industrial projects may have a somewhat better flexibility, but the location is significantly influenced by agglomeration economies surrounding an already industrialized urban centre or corridor. Together these leave little scope for shifting the locations of a number of developmental projects (including urban sprawl).

Therefore, the possible options are:

(i) scaling down the proposed size of the project (in the case of irrigation projects);
(ii) exploring technological avenues to find substitute material (in the case of mining activities);
(iii) identifying areas for industrial/clustering or corridor and thereby having spatially concentrated growth with planned development of hinterlands (in the case of industrial estates and linkage approach for rural development);

(iv) improving the social infrastructure, communications and basic amenities in rural areas;

(v) enhancing the productivity of land and water and thereby incomes from agriculture to mitigate distress outmigration from rapidly improving living conditions in rural areas;

(vi) developing wasteland and degraded land by means of compensatory investment and establishing claims of the displaced on these regenerated lands (as in the case of compensatory afforestation); and

(vii) systematically planning and managing peri-urban areas, with rural households having a specific share in the appreciated value of land converted from agriculture. This could be based on the estimated future price of land (say, eight times the present price) plus a proportionate share in the difference between the present price of agriculture and urban land to be paid in terms of land.

Of course, there cannot be a generalized solution across situations wherein huge differences are found in terms of natural resource endowment, types of land diversion, level and composition of economic growth and implications for poverty and rural livelihoods. A common pursuit underlying most such cases, particularly of late, is an increased pro-activeness with respect to attracting investment for infrastructure and industrial growth.

However, many of these states are already at a higher level of industrial development and the challenge before them is to sustain the momentum, whereas for the economically backward but natural resource-rich states the dilemma is to go for large-scale industrialization, while at the same time conserving precious natural resources. Obviously this raises conflicts and complex policy choices

COMPENSATORY MECHANISMS: PROBLEMS AND WAY FORWARD

Although there are clear norms and procedures for compensation under the LAA, the actual practice is far below the provisions made in the policy.[6] It is not the intention here to get into the details of the critical gaps in the process of acquiring land and mechanisms for ensuring compensation, as these aspects have been adequately discussed in recent debates (Asif 1999). Nevertheless, some of the important features of the new policy initiative for paying compensation for conversion of forest land and the draft R&R policy being prepared by the Government of India have been highlighted in this section.

The compensatory mechanisms, as noted earlier, are marked by a significant gap between the norms laid down in the policy and actual practice. This needs to be bridged by evolving alternative institutional mechanisms which are transparent and consultative. The actual implementation needs to ensure that a few components are non-negotiable (Box 11.2).

Box 11.2: Yardsticks for Land Conversions and Rehabilitations

1. Conversion/Acquisition of Land for Urban Growth	Drawing strict boundary for urban sprawl. Ensuring fair deal in terms of present price and future appreciation
2. Industrial Cluster/ Estate	Employment in industrial units, promotion of enterprise development, and rural development through linkage approach in addition to fair deal in terms of price
3. Irrigation Project	Land for land (preferably in command area) along with adequate support for land and water resource development at the rate of 50 per cent of the cost of developing irrigation per hectare
4. Infrastructural Projects like	Regeneration of coastal ecology in the same region along with employment and fair land prices
5. Mining Project	Reclamation of mined land; compensatory regeneration of wasteland preferably in the same region along with fair land prices

Setting appropriate norms of compensation, however, is only a first step. To ensure that the norms are actually put in practice is the real challenge. Policy by itself is not adequate unless it is supported by statutory enactment. While the LAA already has several of the above features, the critical question is, who will ensure effective implementation, especially under the scenario of 'state failure'?

The following aspects assume special significance in this context:

- multi-stakeholder agency to inform, negotiate and oversee the processes of land acquisition and compensation;
- assured financial provision for supporting resettlement and rehabilitation of the PAPs;
- transparency and scope for negotiations within stipulated sphere;
- monitoring over a longer period of time; and
- ensuring avenues for productive investment of the one-time cash compensation received by farmers selling land/PAPs.

The draft R&R policy proposes a special institutional mechanism for taking care of these aspects. But it is essential that such an agency be outside the state's domain.

The bottomline, however, is that if the project cannot pay for the cost of compensation and/or the state is unwilling to accept checks and balance through the agency of the people, especially the project-affected people, it may lead to a primitive form of capital accumulation as noted by Chandrashekhar (2006). In this case, the society may have to be prepared to give up the expected benefits from developmental projects which exclude people who lose their basic source of livelihood.

5. Conclusion

The foregoing analysis presented an overview of the diversion of land from the primary sector to various other uses, and the issues emerging thereof, and the way towards a holistic approach for land-use, sectoral allocation and compensatory mechanisms. Based mainly on secondary evidence from existing studies, the review tried to provide a larger (rather than segmented) picture of land diversion and its implications. This is our view essential for making a connection between the three aspects noted above. The analysis is based on the premise that the issue is not so much of the quantum of land being diverted; rather, the real issue is that of evolving a framework within which more balanced decisions regarding land use, allocation and compensation are taken simultaneously.

The analysis reiterated that the issue is not so much about the total magnitude of land, rather the issue is that of indiscriminate use of monopoly power by the state, which in turn becomes party to accumulation of profit by patronizing land operators. This stands highly unjustified as the 'unholy alliance' leads to loss of environment good, labour welfare and most importantly source of livelihoods of the rural communities. The vulnerability of such populations further increases as the stakeholders—the farmers—are neither adequately compensated nor made partners in the chain of value additions on a long-term basis.

Framework for allocating forest land and compensating for the loss has been a long pending issue especially, when large tracts of forest land are already converted for agriculture as part of the settlement process. Of late, the issue has been taken up at the instance of the Supreme Court to ensure payment of compensation by assessing Net Present Value (NPV). It is of course, accepted that NPV calculation should not be based on the assumption of alternative uses of the same lands. Rather, the NPV should be arrived at by estimating loss due to activities, such as urban housing, mining, dams, roads, etc., and this should be reckoned as the opportunity cost of forest lands.

The critical issue however, is to ensure that the compensation received for loss of forests, is being canalized for regeneration of forest and relocation of people who have been displaced. It is essential to reinstate the primary stakes of forests and forest dwellers in the process of compensation. But who would ensure this? This is a critical issue that need further deliberations.

This suggests a need for exploring alternative developmental scenarios where agriculture sector and people engaged thereof are to get a better deal in terms of policy support. In this case what appears as farmers' choice to get rid of the land and farming as occupation may also undergo changes. Urbanization may then have to face a situation where large number of farmers are making informed choices rather than operate under distress of limited choices. This in turn, may force the planners to go very systematically and judiciously for managing urban sprawl and peri-urban environment.

Obviously neither stricter restrictions nor, ad hoc liberalization could pave the way for a rational allocation of land across sectors, inasmuch as for the former, as we noted earlier, illegal conversion or uncalled for alienation starts operating, while the latter leads to loss of natural capital both at societal as well as individual level.

The need therefore is to reflect on the past experiences of policy formulation as well as implementation, and move forward towards a more rational and yet pragmatic approach drawing upon four major strands of developmental perspectives. This implies moving away from the current approach of segmented policies for agriculture and rural development; conservation and management of natural resources; and industrial-urban growth.

It was noted that the recent policy discourse, especially for R&R, has moved progressively towards minimizing involuntary displacement and strengthening the compensatory mechanisms. Similarly, improvements have been suggested in the price norms for acquiring land for various developmental projects. The real issue, however, is of the almost complete absence of 'agency' which could ensure compliance with the laudable objectives upheld in the policies. The need therefore is to work towards a multi-stakeholder institution for ensuring effective implementation of the policies—both at the stage of deciding on land allocation and subsequently at the stage of processing of R&R.

It would be apt to end referring to Ramaswamy's (Iyer 2006) remark.

> Displacement (where unavoidable) must take place with free, prior, informed consent of the people concerned. . . . The people in the area must be participants in decision-making, and must accept the rationale of the displacement.

An essential addition to this basic principle is, people (and regions) affected by developmental projects must be made legitimate partners (receive compensatory regeneration) on a long-term basis.

NOTES

1. The BoA has been constituted by the Department of Commerce, Ministry of Commerce and Industry under the chairmanship of the Addl. Secy, Department of Commerce (vide No. 14/1/2001-EPZ), empowered to consider proposals under the EOU/SEZ scheme that fall outside the automatic approval procedure.

2. Two notable models of urban land development found in India have been followed in some of the most urbanized states. For instance, Delhi follows the principle of public land ownership and leasing, while Gujarat and Maharashtra follow land pooling and redistribution. Both measures essentially entail compulsory acquisition of land and its development before releasing. While the Delhi model is easier as it involves cash compensation and then release (and thus earning huge profits), the latter model involves minimal cash compensation and displacement as it simply redistributes the land proportionately back to the owners (UN 1973).
3. The term rural-urban fringe was first used by Wehrwein (1942) and has been defined as 'an area of mixed rural and urban populations and land uses, which begins at the point where agricultural land uses appear near the city and extends up to the point where villages have distinct urban land uses or where some persons, at least, from the village community commute to the city daily for work or other purposes' (Ramachandran 1989: 297).
4. Empirical studies have shown that land sold for housing purposes in the fringe areas fetch maximum prices to the farmers and a number of good quality lands are also sold off (Mani and Pandey 2000).
5. The estimates represent significant underreporting because (a) farmers sell the land to another farmer (also *benami* transactions) who uses his/her right to choose its use including for non-agriculture purposes; NA-permission becomes merely a matter of formality in such cases, and (b) NA permission, if not accorded within three months of the application, is deemed to have been granted. Both these lead to actual conversion without necessarily being recorded as NA-land on the official records.
6. At present the procedures laid down in the LAA stipulate estimation of the market value of the land, compensation for standing crops, damages sustained on account of severing with other land, damages to movable or immovable property and expenditures on change of residence or business due to acquisition. Apart from that an interest at the rate of 12 per cent is also paid on account of diminution of the profits of the land between the time of the publication of the declaration and the time of the collector's taking possession of the land. In addition, a sum of 30 per cent on such market value is also awarded, considering the compulsory nature of the acquisition.

REFERNECES

Adhikary, Twisha and Achyuta Krishna Ghosh (2005), *Resettlement and Rehabilitation Strategy for Displacement Caused due to Mining*, Postale: National Seminar on Policies, Statutes & Legislation in Mines.

Aiyar, Swaminathan S. Anklesaria (2006), 'Tehsils as Special Economic Zones', *Indian Express*, 7 May.

Allen, Adriana (2003), 'Environmental Planning and Management of the Peri-Urban Interface: Perspectives on an Emerging Field', *Environment & Urbanization* 15(1): 135–48.

Asher, Manshi and Ashish Kothari (2005), 'The Reality of Resettlement in Orissa', *Down to Earth*, vol. 14, no. 6, 15 August, pp. 40–1.

Asif, Mohammad (1999), 'Land Acquisition Act: Need for an Alternative Paradigm', *Economic and Political Weekly*, vol. 34(25), pp. 1564–6.

Baijal, Pradip and P.K. Singh (2000), 'Large Dams: Can We Do Without Them?', *Economic and Political Weekly*, vol. 35(19), pp. 1659–66.

Bandyopadhyay, J.B. Mallik, M. Mandal and S. Perveen (2002), 'Dams and Development: Report on a Policy Dialogue', *Economic and Political Weekly*, vol. 37(40), pp. 4108–12.

Barrow, C.J. (1991), *Land Degradation, Development and Breakdown of Terrestrial Environments*, Cambridge: Cambridge University Press.

Bentinck, J.V. (2000), 'Unruly Urbanisation on Delhi's Fringe: Changing Patterns of Land-use and Livelihood', Proefschrift, Rijsuniversiteit Groningen, 26 June.

Bhadra, Dipasis and Antonio Salazar P. Brando (1993), 'Urbanization, Agricultural Development and Land Allocation'. World Bank Discussion Paper 201, Washington, D.C.: World Bank.

Bhadra, Dipasis (1991), 'Optimal Land-Use in a Dual Economy: A General Equilibrium Analysis with an Application', paper presented at the Annual Meetings of the Midwest Economics Association, St. Louis, Missouri.

Burton, Tony and Lilli Matson (1996), 'Urban Footprints: Making Best Use of Urban Land and Resources—A Rural Perspective', in Mike Jenks, E. Burton and K. Williams (eds.), *The Compact City: A Sustainable Urban Farm?* London: Oxford & Spon Press.

Centre for Environmental Planning & Technology (CEPT) (1997), 'Gujarat Urban Profile', unpublished report, submitted to National Institute of Urban Affairs, New Delhi.

Chandrasekhar, C.P. (2006), 'Primitive Accumulation', *Frontline*, vol. 23, no. 20, 7–20 October, pp. 24–6.

Datt, Ruddar (2002), 'Economic Liberalisation and its Implications for Employment in India, in Ashok Mathur and P.S. Raikhy (eds.), *Economic Liberalisation and its Implications for Employment in India*. New Delhi: Deep & Deep.

Dhar, T. N. (1998), 'Sustainable Urban Development and Land Use Planning', in Bimal Kumar (ed.), *Urbanisation and Land Use Conflict at Urban Fringes*, New Delhi: A.P.H. Publishing Corporation, pp. 223–50.

Dyson, Tim and Pravin Visaria (2004), in 'Migration and Urbanization: Retrospect and Prospect', in Tim Dyson, R. Cassen and Leela Visaria (eds.), *Twenty-First Century India: Population, Economy, Human Development, and the Environment*, New Delhi: Oxford University Press, pp. 108–9.

Fernandes, Vivian (2006), 'Centre Readies Land Policy for SEZs', CNN-IBN (ibnlive.com).

Fernandes, Walter (1994), 'An Activist Process around the Draft National Rehabilitation Policy', *Social Action*, vol. 45, July–September, pp. 277–98.

George, Ajitha Susan (2004), 'Laws Related to Mining in Jharkhand', *Economic and Political Weekly*, vol. 40, no. 41, pp. 4455–8.

Ghosh, Suman (2006), 'Don't Be Cruel', *The Times of India*, 3 October.

GOI (2006), 'From Hariyali to Neeranchal: Report of the Technical Committee on Watershed Programmes in India', New Delhi: Department of Land Resources.

Herbert, Tony, Kuntala Lahiri-Dutt (2004), 'Coal Sector Loans and Displacement of Indigenous Populations: Lessons from Jharkhand', *Economic and Political Weekly*, vol. 39, no. 23, pp. 2403–9.

Hoselitz, B.F. (1957), 'Urbanization and Economic Growth in Asia', *Economic Development and Cultural Change*, vol. 6, no. 1, pp. 42–54.

IEG (2006), 'Report of the Expert Committee on Net Present Value', Delhi: Institute of Economic Growth (Mandated by the Supreme Court of India).

Iyengar, Sudarshan (1997), 'Resettlement and Rehabilitation in Sardar Sarovar Project: A Review of Policy Reforms and Implementation', Working Paper No. 84, Ahmedabad: Gujarat Institute of Development Research.

Joshi, Seema (2004), 'Tertiary Sector Driven Growth in India: Impact on Employment and Poverty', *Economic and Political Weekly*, vol. 39, no. 37, pp. 4175–8.

Khagram, Sanjeev (2005), *Dams and Development: Transnational Struggles for Water and Power*, New Delhi: Oxford University Press.

Mahadevia, Darshini (1999), *Economic Growth and Environmental Degradation: Case of Gujarat*. New Delhi: Research Foundation for Science, Technology and Ecology.

Mani, Gyanendra and V.K. Pandey (2000), 'Study on Land Transfer and Demand Supply Relations in Land Market in Western Uttar Pradesh', *Indian Journal of Agricultural Economics*, vol. 55, no. 1, pp. 1–13.

Mellor, John W. (2006), 'Pro-Poor Growth—The Relation between Agricultural Growth and Poverty Reduction', in R. Radhakrishna et al. (eds.), *India in a Globalising World: Some Aspects of Macroeconomy, Agriculture and Poverty*, New Delhi: Academic Foundation, pp. 233–75.

NTPC (1993), *Resettlement & Rehabilitation Policy*, New Delhi: National Thermal Power Corporation.

Patit, Chittaroopa (2004), 'Short-changing the Displaced: National Rehabilitation Policy', *Economic and Political Weekly*, vol. 39, no. 27, pp. 2961–3.

Panda, Ranjan (2006), 'Orissa villagers say relocate us, we want to leave right away', *Down to Earth*, vol. 14, no. 20.

Paranjape, Suhas and K.J. Joy (2006), 'Alternative Restructuring of the Sardar Sarovar: Breaking the Deadlock', *Economic & Political Weekly*, vol. 41, no. 7, pp. 601–2.

Ramachandran, R. (1989), *Urbanisation and Urban Systems in India*, Delhi: Oxford University Press.

Rangarajan, M. (2001), *India's Wildlife History: An Introduction*, Delhi: Permanent Black & Ranthambore Foundation.

Reddy, V. Ratna (2006), 'Land Alienation from Agriculture: Use and Misuse of Land for Non-Agricultural Practices', unpublished report, Hyderabad: Center for Economic and Social Studies.

Reddy, I.U.B. (1994), *Industrial Development and Problems of the Uprooted*, Jaipur: Rawat.

Renaud, Bertrand (1979), 'National Urbanization Policies in Developing Countries', World Bank Staff Working Paper No. 347, Urban & Regional Economics Division, Washington, D.C.: Development Economics Department.

Richardson, H.W., C.H. Christine Bae and M.H. Baxamusa (2000), 'Compact Cities in Developing Countries: Assessment and Implications', in Mike Jenks and Rod Burgess (eds.), *Compact Cities: Sustainable Urban Forms for Developing Countries*. London: Spon Press.

Sah, D.C. (2003), *Involuntary Migration: Evidence from Sardar Sarovar Project*, Jaipur: MPISSR and Rawat.

Sarangi, Debaranjan (1999), 'Orissa: Struggles against Sanctuaries', *Economic and Political Weekly*, vol. 34, no. 12, pp. 667–8.

Shah, Amita (2000), 'Conversion of Agricultural Land in Gujarat: Evidence and Issues', unpublished report, Ahmedabad: Gujarat Institute of Development Research.

——— (2001), 'Linking Industrial Growth with Rural Economy: A Case Study of Ankleshwar Industrial Estate in Gujarat', Working Paper No. 125, Ahmedabad: Gujarat Institute of Development Research.

Shah, Amita, Vijay Kakshmi Pandey and Rajalakshmi Kamath (2005), *Sustaining Human Development in Indian States. The Role of Land*, Mumbai: Indira Gandhi Institute of Development Research.

Sharma, R.N. (2003), 'Involuntary Displacement: A Few Encounters', *Economic and Political Weekly*, vol. 38, no. 9, pp. 907–12.

TNN (2006), 'Board to Look at 225 SEZ Proposals over 20 Days', *Times News Network*, 20 September.

Tolley, G.S. and V. Thomas (1987), 'An Overview of Urban Growth: Problems, Policies and Evaluation', in G.S. Tolley and V. Thomas (eds.),

The Economics of Urbanization and Urban Policies in Developing Countries, World Bank Symposium, Washington, D.C.: World Bank.

United Nations (UN) (1993), *Urban Land Use Policies and Land Use Control Measures*, vol. 2 of *Asia and the Far East*, New York: Department of Economics and Social Affairs.

Vining, D.R., T.R. Plaut and K. Bieri (1986), 'Population Redistribution Towards Core Areas of Less Developed Countries 1950–80', *International Regional Science Review*, vol. 10, no. 1, pp. 1–45.

Wehrwein, E.G. (1942), 'The Rural-Urban Fringe', *Economic Geography*, vol. 18, pp. 217–28.

Whitehead, Judith (1999), 'Statistical Concoctions and Everyday Lives: Queries from Gujarat Resettlement Sites', *Economic & Political Weekly*, vol. 34, no. 28, pp. 1940–7.

APPENDIX 11.1: TYPOLOGY OF LANDDIVERSION AND MEDIATING AGENCY

Type of Land	Purpose for Division	End User of Land Instrument	Mediating Agency and Policy
1. Forest	Mining	Private or Public Sector	State-through land acquisition
2. Forest	Protected Area	State	State-through Indian Wild Life Conservation Act
3. Forest and Pvt. Land (of Tribals) in Forest Area	Mining, Industry, Irrigation, Infrastructure	Private or Public Sector	State-through acquisition
4. Agriculture Land	-do-	-do-	State-through acquisition and purchase of land under NA-policy
5. Pastures under Public Ownership	-do-	-do-	State-through land acquisition
6. Land in Urban Periphery (Public or private)	For Urban Growth	-do-	Mainly through purchase by land developers under NA-policy
7. Land for SEZ (public and private ownership)	Industrial Growth Centres	Mainly Private Sector	State-through acquisition and purchase of land

N. NAINAN is currently preparing her Ph.D. thesis on the politics of participation in land markets in Mumbai at the University of Amsterdam.

A. VENKAT RAMAN is Reader (Associate Professor) at the Faculty of Management Studies (FMS), University of Delhi, and teaches courses in the area of Human Resource Management and Health Services Management.

MARIO RUTTEN is Professor of Comparative Sociology of Asia at the Department of Sociology and Anthropology, University of Amsterdam.

JYOTHIS SATHYAPALAN is an Associate Fellow at the Centre for Economic and Social Studies, Hyderabad.

LOES SCHENK-SANDBERGEN is a retired Associate Professor of the University of Amsterdam, Department of Sociology and Anthropology.

SUNANDA SEN formerly a Professor at Jawaharlal Nehru University, New Delhi is currently an Honorary Professor at Jamia Millia Islamia, New Delhi.

AMITH SHAH is a Professor at Gujarat Institute of Development Research, an ICSSR-supported organization at Ahmedabad.

ALAKH N. SHARMA is Director, Institute for Human Development, New Delhi.

CAROL UPADHYA is a Social Anthropologist and is currently a Fellow at the National Institute of Advanced Studies, Bangalore.

Contributors

K.S. BABU is a Faculty Member at the Centre for Economic and Social Studies (CESS) in Hyderabad.

I.S.A. BAUD is Professor of International Development Studies at the Dept. of Geography, Planning and International Development Studies at the University of Amsterdam.

JAMES WARNER BJÖRKMAN is Professor of Public Policy and Administration, Institute of Social Studies, Leiden Univesity.

BYASDEB DASGUPTA is Reader at Department of Economics, University of Kalyani, West Bengal.

S. MAHENDRA DEV is currently Chairman, Commission for Agricultural Costs and Prices, Ministry of Agriculture, Government of India.

ABEY GEORGE, works as Asst. Professor, Kerala Institute of Local Administration (KILA), Mulamkunnathukavu P.O. Thrissur, Kerala.

DEREK JOHNSON is an Assistant Professor in the Department of Anthropology at the University of Manitoba and a research associate at the Centre for Maritime Research (MARE) at the University of Amsterdam.

JYOTHI KRISHNAN is a Research Scholar with the School of Environmental Sciences, Wageningen University, the Netherlands.

ANIMESH KUMAR is currently the Asst. VAM/M&E Officer in the Vulnerability Analysis and Mapping/Monitoring and Evaluation Unit of the United Nations World Food Programme, Country Office-India at New Delhi.

SHIPRA MAITRA is currently Professor of Urban Management in Amity School of Urban Management, Amity University, UP.